Politics and Developm[ent]

Published by one of the world's leading publishers on African issues, 'Politics and Development in Contemporary Africa' seeks to provide accessible but in-depth analysis of key contemporary issues affecting countries within the continent. Featuring a wealth of empirical material and case study detail, and focusing on a diverse range of subject matter – from conflict to gender, development to the environment – the series is a platform for scholars to present original and often provocative arguments. Selected titles in the series are published in association with the International African Institute.

Already published

Mobility between Africa, Asia and Latin America: Economic Networks and Cultural Interactions, edited by Ute Röschenthaler and Alessandro Jedlowski

Agricultural Development in Rwanda: Authoritarianism, Markets and Spaces of Governance, Chris Huggins

Liberia's Female Veterans: War, Roles and Reintegration, Leena Vastapuu and Emmi Nieminen

Food Aid in Sudan: A History of Power, Politics and Profit, Susanne Jaspars

Kakuma Refugee Camp: Humanitarian Urbanism in Kenya's Accidental City, Bram J. Jansen

Development Planning in South Africa: Provincial Policy and State Power in the Eastern Cape, John Reynolds

Forthcoming titles

AIDS in the Shadow of Biomedicine, Isak Niehaus

Negotiating Public Services in the Congo: State, Society and Governance, edited by Kristof Titeca and Tom De Herdt

Economic Diversification in Nigeria: Fractious Politics and the Paradox of Prosperity, Zainab Usman

About the editors

Jörg Wiegratz is Lecturer in Political Economy of Global Development at the School of Politics and International Studies, University of Leeds.

Giuliano Martiniello is Assistant Professor of Rural Community Development in the Faculty of Agriculture and Food Sciences at the American University of Beirut.

Elisa Greco is a Research Associate at the Sustainability Research Institute, School of Earth and Environment, University of Leeds.

Uganda

The Dynamics of Neoliberal Transformation

Edited by Jörg Wiegratz, Giuliano Martiniello and Elisa Greco

Published with the support of

ZED

Uganda: The Dynamics of Neoliberal Transformation
was first published in 2018 by Zed Books Ltd, The Foundry,
17 Oval Way, London SE11 5RR, UK.

www.zedbooks.net

Typeset in Plantin by Swales & Willis Ltd, Exeter, Devon
Index by Nataliya Mykhalchenko
Cover design by Steve Marsden
Cover photo © Emmanuel Owaraga

Printed and bound by CPI Group (UK) Ltd, Croydon, CR0 4YY

MIX
Paper from
responsible sources
FSC
www.fsc.org   FSC® C013604

ISBN 978-1-78699-109-6 hb
ISBN 978-1-78699-108-9 pb
ISBN 978-1-78699-110-2 pdf
ISBN 978-1-78699-111-9 epub
ISBN 978-1-78699-112-6 mobi

Contents

Illustrations

Figures

Tables

About the contributors

Godfrey B. Asiimwe is an Associate Professor and Head, Department of Development Studies, Makerere University.

Ronald R. Atkinson is a Senior Research Associate at the Rule of Law Collaborative and the Walker Institute of International and Area Studies, University of South Carolina.

Barbara Bompani is Reader in Africa and International Development, Centre of African Studies, the University of Edinburgh and Research Associate at the African Centre for Migration and Society, the University of the Witwatersrand, Johannesburg.

Adam Branch is University Lecturer in African Politics and the Director of the Cambridge Centre of African Studies at the University of Cambridge.

Anneeth Kaur Hundle is an Assistant Professor of Anthropology at the University of California, Irvine.

Ben Jones is a Senior Lecturer in the School of International Development at the University of East Anglia.

Jon Harald Sande Lie is a Senior Research Fellow at the Norwegian Institute of International Affairs.

Kristen Lyons is an Associate Professor in the School of Social Science at the University of Queensland, Australia, and a Senior Research Fellow with the Oakland Institute (US).

Rose Nakayi is a Senior Lecturer of Law at the School of Law, Makerere University.

Adrian Nel is a Senior Lecturer in the Discipline of Geography in the School of Agriculture, Earth and Environmental Science, at the University of Kwazulu-Natal.

Malin J. Nystrand is a Post-Doc Researcher and Lecturer at the School of Global Studies, University of Gothenburg.

David G. Pier is an Associate Professor in the Department of African, African American, and Diaspora Studies at the University of North Carolina, Chapel Hill.

Joshua B. Rubongoya is Professor in the Department of Public Affairs at Roanoke College in Salem, Virginia.

Laura Smith is a PhD candidate at the Sustainability Research Institute, School of Earth and Environment, University of Leeds.

Sarah N. Ssali is an Associate Professor and Dean, School of Women and Gender Studies, College of Humanities and Social Sciences, Makerere University.

Gordon Tamm has a background in social science research and academic teaching and is an advisor and analyst in the field of international development cooperation.

Kristof Titeca is an Assistant Professor at the Institute of Development Policy and Management at the University of Antwerp.

James Van Alstine is Associate Professor in Environmental Policy and Co-Director of the Sustainability Research Institute at the School of Earth and Environment, University of Leeds.

Julia Vorhölter is a Lecturer and Post-Doc Researcher at the Institute of Social and Cultural Anthropology, Göttingen University.

Karin Wedig is German Society for International Cooperation (GIZ) Chief Economist for Africa (formerly Assistant Professor, University of Denver).

Japhy Wilson is Lecturer in International Political Economy at the University of Manchester.

Adrian Yen is a PhD candidate in Anthropology at the University of California, Davis.

Acknowledgements

The dearth of critical collections on the 'New Uganda' as a neoliberal capitalist society struck us during a dinner at the Indian restaurant Khana Kazana in Kampala, in July 2015, where the idea of this book was first conceived, and its rationale deliberated, using small papers that a startled, patient waiter supplied from his notebook. In that period, all of us were undertaking research in Uganda; Giuliano was a Research Fellow at the Makerere Institute for Social Research (MISR) and Elisa was a MISR Visiting Teaching Fellow. At the end of the long journey that has given form to that embryonic idea, the book is seeing the light. For this, we wish to deeply thank all the persons and institutions without which this work would not have been possible. We thank all the authors and their continued engagement with this project, which has been truly collaborative and collective. Special thanks to all the people in Uganda who in different spaces and situations have over the years shared their time, knowledge and views with us. We also thank all students and faculties at Makerere University, and the Economic Policy Research Centre (EPRC) with whom we have interacted over the years. All of you have supported the making of this collection.

As editors, we would furthermore like to thank the *Review of African Political Economy* (RoAPE) for supporting this project since the very beginning. We particularly appreciated the continuous engagement of the members of RoAPE's Editorial Working Group, who offered comments and revisions at different stages of the work. RoAPE generously subsidised part of the publication with the intent of supporting radical analysis of neoliberalism in Africa. A particular thank you goes to Alex Beresford, Adam Branch, Ray Bush, Peter Dwyer, Ben Jones, Kristen Lyons, Norah Owaraga and David G. Pier for offering very helpful comments on the introduction and conclusions of the book. We furthermore thank all colleagues and staff at our respective institutions – the University of Leeds and the American University of Beirut – for their professional and collegial support during the three years of gestation of this work, including the granting of some sabbatical leave. We thank Nataliya Mykhalchenko for proofreading the pre-submission manuscript and producing the index, and Alice Mills for her proofreading work earlier in the process. Thanks to Ken Barlow at Zed Books and Zed's editorial work, the manuscript has substantially benefitted from comments and revisions offered by Ken and three anonymous reviewers. We would finally like to thank our families, friends and colleagues for the sustained support and encouragement offered throughout this project.

Introduction: interpreting change in neoliberal uganda

Jörg Wiegratz, Giuliano Martiniello and Elisa Greco

> Who controls the past controls the future: who controls the
> present controls the past. (*1984*, George Orwell)

Those who want to better understand the dynamics of contemporary Uganda face a bifurcated scenario: two different narratives persist at global and local levels that seem, taken together, hard to reconcile. One is of a Uganda emerging from years-long civil war in the late 1980s, and then within a few years becoming an international success story. This 'Uganda as a success' narrative praises the post-1986 policy reforms which have stimulated economic growth, with sustained GDP growth and foreign direct investment (FDI) attraction matched by steady progress in poverty reduction and gender empowerment. Central to this narrative is the leadership of a president who is a progressive moderniser, acting with the interest of the nation at heart. In short, Uganda has never been better. Such accounts parade 'impressive', 'successful' and 'admirable' achievements in social, political and economic spheres. Very powerful actors promote this narrative, year in, year out: from the World Bank (WB), International Monetary Fund (IMF) and various international and bilateral donors of the country, to influential international and domestic scholars and analysts, and the Ugandan government and establishment. The same actors have produced a plethora of official statistics and econometric studies that supposedly provide evidence of this stated steady progress. A prime example of this celebratory narrative about the new Uganda as an astonishing exemplar of reform success is the Kampala speech of the IMF Managing Director, Christine Lagarde, in January 2017, 'Becoming the Champion: Uganda's Development Challenge', which states:

> This gathering provides an opportunity to congratulate Uganda
> for its impressive economic achievements and to speak about the
> possibilities of the future. I do not normally begin my speeches
> with statistics, but today will be an exception. That is because the
> numbers tell us a great deal: Uganda has experienced a *threefold
> increase* in per capita GDP over the past generation. And you have

reduced extreme poverty to one-third of the population. This
made Uganda one of the countries that has more than achieved
the United Nations Millennium Development Goal of halving
poverty by 2015. This is an African success story. (Lagarde 2017,
emphasis in original).

Couched in orthodox neoliberal language, the 'Uganda as a
success' narrative pushed by the IMF is consistent with its 'Africa
rising' narrative of economic optimism (IMF 2014), which mirrors
the enthusiastic rhetoric of the African Renaissance narrative led by
former South African President Thabo Mbeki in the early 2000s.
Accelerated economic development spurred a renewed optimism
among economists who predicted a luminous twenty-first century
for African economies (Severino and Ray 2011, Economist 2011,
Perry 2012). The argument is that China's and India's demands
for African raw materials, following the extraction-centric export-
oriented route that raised GDP levels in the 2000s, represents the
best option for Africa to grow wealthy (Bond 2014a).

Lagarde made her visit just months after the highly controversial
2016 political elections that were accompanied by repression against
sections of the opposition and critics of the government, as well as
accusations of substantial and outright vote rigging. The outcomes
of the 2016 elections further deepened the government's legitimacy
crisis. This leads us to discuss the second narrative about Uganda,
which captures the extent of this crisis, characterised by the prevalence of a patrimonial mode of rule supported by the president's ruling
group. This formation uses state power to advance private economic
interests and functions through a far-reaching business and political
network, which includes the president's extended family to political allegiances and foreign investors. To denounce the self-seeking
attitude prevalent in the ruling party, the National Resistance Movement (NRM), Ugandan street politics have mockingly renamed it
the 'National Robbery Movement'. The state has come to be associated with increasing political repression, a decline in public services
and generalised economic insecurity. Public debates refer to 'mafias',
a 'mafia state', a 'vampire state' (e.g. Tacca 2016), a country occupied, controlled and exploited by a tiny 'clique' of powerful domestic
actors and their foreign allies. Uganda has experienced recurring
food shortages and chronic indebtedness, and a social crisis characterised by increased inequality, widespread violence and increased
criminality. This second narrative of 'Uganda in crisis' is articulated
by the 'people on the street', sections of the political opposition,

the media, non-governmental organisation (NGOs), the religious community and a range of critical national commentators. One can listen to it on TV news and debates, in churches and mosques and read about it via media articles and social media platforms.

The lived experiences of the majority of Ugandans who toil in the fields and factories and work in the informal economy – Fanon's 'wretched of the Earth' – provide evidence of the ongoing social crisis. Ugandan society is characterised by high levels of suicide (especially among the youth), poverty-driven deaths, preventable illnesses and generalised destitution (see e.g. Daily Monitor 2010, 2011, 2014, 2016, 2017a, 2017c). The 'Uganda in crisis' narrative has been explicitly adopted by the main opposition party, the Forum for Democratic Change (FDC) in its speeches and manifestos. It is also the dominant narrative of online activist groups – for example, 'Free Uganda' and 'Ugandans at heart' – and is common in academic research and NGO reports about state violence and repression, corruption and land disputes (Branch and Mampilly 2015, Martiniello 2015b, Wiegratz 2016).

This book intervenes in this crucial debate about what constitutes the 'New Uganda' (Wiegratz 2016). How do we make sense of a country that has undeniably been transformed 'beyond recognition' in the last three decades? In short: by whom, why, how and to what effect was Uganda transformed?

Social sciences scholarship on Uganda has to date not sufficiently analysed the contradictions generated by this all-encompassing process of change triggered by neoliberal reforms in the country. In particular, until the early 2010s a substantial share of scholarly research, often linked to donor money, has kept a celebratory tone about the country's overall development path. Scholarly analyses have been paying disproportionate attention to the problems and challenges of liberal transition and development in an underdeveloped, post-conflict African country. Scholarship has focused on 'politics' and 'development' in a narrow sense of governance, poverty reduction (Hickey 2005, 2013) and political power dynamics including political settlements (Tripp 2010, JEAS 2016 special issue), political emergencies, party and electoral politics (Kiiza *et al.* 2008, Perrot *et al.* 2014), patronage politics (Mwenda and Tangri 2005), conflict management, humanitarian assistance, or peace-making (Opongo 2013, Khisa 2015).

These foci of attention have been partly brought about by the particularly tormented political history of a country which looked like an 'unsteady state' (Saul 1976) for the best part of the 1970s and

1980s. In rapid succession, Uganda experienced several coups d'état (Obote I, Idi Amin, Obote II, Museveni's Bush War), internecine political successions, external interventions and internal conflicts with rebel military formations in the northern regions (from the late 1980s to mid-2000s). Given the protracted instability of state power in post-colonial Uganda, it is understandable that scholarly research has focused on political processes on one hand, and on President Yoweri Kaguta Museveni as the emblematic figure behind the thirty years of monopoly power maintained by the NRM since 1986, on the other. This extended period of relative political stability and continuity at the helm of the state, which allowed Uganda to be turned into a 'donors' darling', a 'success story' and reform model for international development agencies (e.g. WB 2010) are also the focus of this academic debate.

Arguably, the celebratory tone of academic and consultancy accounts provided support to the granting of billions of US dollars of aid to the country, from which academics and consultants in turn also benefited. These accounts and the associated statistical country-based data sets produced by development economists are part and parcel of an underlying politics of numbers which sees African states and donors at the forefront of the struggle to control and shape data production about development or lack thereof (Jerven 2013, 2015).[1] These incursions in development scholarship have often contributed to narrowly defined research, leading to equally narrow interpretations on the causes of under-development in Uganda. The narrow focus of research had political implications. Eschewing the analysis of structural causes of the Ugandan crisis means foreclosing the possibility of redressing it. The focus on governance has an enormous analytical appeal within academia and it contributed to shaping donors' interventions in Uganda (Jones 2009), progressively acquiring a hegemonic position in scholarly debates. This hegemonic focus takes its theoretical tools from 'pure' United States-based political science scholarship, borrowing methods from positivist and empiricist traditions. It produced an informative debate on the politics of the NRM government, its reproduction, exercise of power and regime maintenance. A key concern of this literature is how the government's strategies concerning regime survival interact with and affect dynamics of nation and state building (Rubongoya 2007, Kiiza et al. 2008), political order (Hickey 2013), democratisation (Tripp 2010, Sjögren 2013) and economic development (Golooba-Mutebi and Hickey 2013).

There is a lot to learn from these accounts and their respective data sets. However, a good part of this literature has substantial gaps and fails to discuss some key features of the new Uganda. The first gap is the impact of global capitalism and global political economy on Uganda. This requires a study of the dynamics of Western and Eastern imperialism and their political, economic and cultural dimensions. The second under-researched area concerns the processes of societal transformation, including class formation, consolidation, struggle and compromise (and related core aspects such as dispossession, exploitation etc.), and the ways in which they shape, for instance, political power and market structures. A third overlooked area is the interaction of local and national power structures and dynamics with international political economic patterns.

The analysis of inherently conflictual and contradictory processes of capitalist transformation – and related imperialist interventions – has been left out of the picture. The analytical categories of capitalism and class barely feature in the last thirty years of scholarship on Uganda. Also wanting, especially in terms of data, is the analysis of major aspects of the 'ruling coalition', specifically with regard to state–capital relations, the fusion of economic and political interests and power and the business activities of top state officials. The role of Ugandan tycoons in the process of capital accumulation is missed out. A significant part of this literature, overridden by normative preoccupations, has eschewed a critical approach to the study of the political economy of the state and of class, and the dynamics of capital accumulation. The analysis of inter-linkages between the 'political' and 'economic' in capitalism has been silenced (Wood 1981), not just in the academic debates, but also in policy-making discourses, resulting in a narrative that fictitiously separates the state and the market. This reiterates a long tradition within bourgeois social sciences which compartmentalised knowledge by consolidating the idea of an original division of social sciences in the triumvirate of capitalist institutions: the market (economics), the state (politics) and civil society (sociology).

This book is an attempt to point to the gaps generated by this analytical imbalance of three decades of scholarship. In no ways do we claim that this attempt is exhaustive, nor is it systematic. We hope though that it will provoke response and encourage our generation of scholars to focus on how internal and external forces interplay in Uganda, to better understand the dynamics of endogenous and exogenous factors by starting from an analysis of how the country's position within global capitalist economic structures of power and the international division of labour impact the country's development and inhibit or facilitate its abilities to increase the material wellbeing of broad sections of the population, constituted by the subaltern classes.

This collection points to the failure of dominant mainstream economic theories in giving a historical account of economic facts, their inability to explain the social content of economic relations and practices, and therefore to interpret the forces and conflicts at work in the economic process (Aglietta 1999, Bond 2004). Shaped by development economists, these severely a-historical, abstract and flawed accounts have consolidated their positions as cross-field 'expert' narratives (Mitchell 2002). The WB has become the gate-keeper in key societal debates, imposing its narrative – or 'Bank Speak' – as the natural horizon of possible analysis, debates and poli-cies (Bayliss *et al.* 2011, Moretti and Pestre 2015). In Uganda's case, key WB publications about the country's economy (World Bank Uganda Economic Update) have an unrivalled analytical weight in official discourse. The shortcomings of political economy analysis on Uganda descend from the relationship between economics and the other social sciences and the influence of the WB on knowledge production (Harrison 2004, Mamdani 2007, 2011).

Neoliberal Uganda: explanans and explanandum

The present collection aims at reopening the debate on capitalist political economy in Uganda, after decades marked by a lack of critical scholarship on the topic. The intention is to revive the rich analytical tradition informed by neo-Marxist and dependencia paradigms in the study of transformation of East African political economies and social formations, especially in the colonial and post-colonial era (Brett 1972, Cliffe 1976, 1977, Mamdani 1976, 1987, Tosh 1978, Nabudere 1981). We argue that there is an urgent need of scholarly research detailing the multifaceted neoliberal reordering of African countries towards market societies – and how these market societies actually operate. This book contributes to addressing these major gaps in African studies and debates, through a multidiscipli-nary perspective on three decades of transformation of the economic, political, social, ecological and cultural structures of Uganda, as a major exemplar of neoliberal capitalism in Africa.

The common denominator of the book is *neoliberalisation*, under-stood as a process of systematic and substantial transformation of Ugandan state, economy and culture towards a 'market society', i.e. a society characterised by marketisation of social relations, a general empowerment and hegemony of capital (especially of large private corporations), and the corresponding restructuring of people's subjectivities, relationships and everyday practices so as to make all realms of society operate market-like (Dean 2002, Harrison 2005, 2010). As a market society, Uganda shares key characteristics with other exemplars of market society across the globe, such as economic growth, lowered inflation, FDI, reduced official poverty, and liberal discourse prevalence, alongside significant levels of wealth concentration, poverty, economic inequality, insecurity and precarity, social injustice, un(der)employment, public sector crumbling, commercialised politics, militarised state, dispossession, marginalisation and impoverishment of sections of the population, societal crises and – in the face of people's discontent and resistance – state repression (Wiegratz 2016: 72). The deluge of literature on neoliberalism (Springer *et al.* 2016a) that led some to be nauseated by the term and sceptical of its analytical relevance (Dunn 2016) seems to have left Uganda out of the spectrum. Uganda is one of the most neoliberalised African countries yet there is only a very limited scholarly debate on the operations of neoliberalism, against the context of an otherwise 'over-studied' country. This years-long silence is a consequence of the entrenched power of mainstream scholarship which, given its connections with development donors, turns a blind eye towards neoliberalism as a frame of analysis. As a consequence, we observe two trends. First, there is a lack of an analysis of what parallels the Ugandan case has with other neoliberal cases across the globe. Partly as a consequence of this, the second trend is a disproportionate analytical attention to the role of Uganda's President Museveni and his agency as the *explanans* of the key characteristics of post-1986 developments in the country. Here we are arguing that Museveni is not an explanans but rather an explanandum, which calls for a detailed analysis of national and transnational class alliances and global and local neoliberal forces and processes.

While the emergence and consolidation of neoliberalism since the 1980s in the capitalist heartland and periphery have been widely researched (e.g. Williams and Young 1994, Harrison 2004, 2005, Robison 2006, Harvey 2007), there are relatively few extensive studies and comprehensive debates that explicitly explore different aspects of neoliberalism in specific African countries other than South Africa (e.g. Bond 2014b, James 2014, Ferguson 2015). The usage of the term neoliberalism as an analytical category in political economy literature has become more contested in the last decade (arguably as a result of the alleged exhaustion of the neoliberal project and the claims of the beginning of a post-neoliberal era). However, we maintain that it is necessary to explore the ways in which neoliberalism institutionalised itself and now operates in different social and political milieux. Uganda is a good example of that, as are Kenya and Tanzania. Yet, analysing neoliberalism often runs the risk of using 'neoliberalism' as 'some sort of totalising rhetorical signifier or trope' (Springer *et al.* 2016b: 11) – in other words, seeing everything as 'neoliberal'. While many elements of our time period of concern can be read as neoliberal, some others may not be neoliberal per se – although the boundaries are often blurred by the unrelenting capacity of neoliberalism to manipulate, co-opt and eventually render systemic and 'mainstream' the movements and ideologies which revolt against it (Harvey 2005). As anywhere else, in Uganda neoliberal and non-neoliberal or pre-neoliberal elements interact and mix – i.e. any neoliberalised social formation being partly a product of historical processes prior to the neoliberal era (Wiegratz 2016). An analytical focus on neoliberal transformation allows us to distinguish the impact that policies, reforms, programmes, agendas, discourses and practices that we analyse as 'neoliberal' (Harrison 2010) have had on various realms and issues in Ugandan polity, economy, society and culture.

Restructuring Uganda

The task at hand is to analyse how neoliberal capitalism has restructured Uganda and to detail the dynamics of its neoliberal transformation. The collection strives to offer a historically grounded and dialectical analysis of neoliberalism as a 'project', through the different processes it generates. These processes bring about particular changes, tensions, conflicts and contradictions that are partly general to capitalism. The study of neoliberal Uganda is thus also the study of contemporary capitalism in the country, articulated in its neoliberal variant. Against the depoliticised narratives of international development provided by various international development agencies, donors and scholars, which stress the positive virtues of capitalist market and society, this collection offers a set of interpretations which, while emerging from different disciplinary backgrounds, share a politically and economically grounded analysis of the neoliberal-capitalist restructuring of Ugandan society, its socio-ecological implications and the responses from below.

Through neoliberal policies, discourses and practices, contemporary capitalism has restructured Uganda by extending the realm of commodification, commercialisation and marketisation deeper into Ugandan society. This restructuring has consolidated a capitalist social order and social domination. In this sense, neoliberalism is about a renewed dominance of capital over other classes and the expectation and demand of capital to rule society as a whole. Neoliberal societies can then be categorised 'simply' as societies affected by this set of marketisation policies and related discourses, agendas and programmes that are advanced by state and capital and its 'civil society' allies (Whyte and Wiegratz 2016: 229, Wiegratz 2016). Neoliberalism is also constituted by three interconnected domains: its rhetoric and ideological tools, its scholarship and its policies (Fine 2010).

Such heuristic endeavour is furthermore significant, as in Uganda social struggles have rampantly (re)emerged in response to the commodifying, exploitative, extractive and dispossessing logic of neoliberal social engineering. Especially in the last decade, worsening socio-economic conditions and state authoritarianism (Anderson and Fisher 2016) have been met by popular protests in both urban and rural contexts. Protests included street demonstrations and food riots in major cities in 2011, coinciding with skyrocketing global food prices (Martiniello 2015a: 514). The Walk to Work campaign, launched by opposition leaders and Action for Change activists, contested rising poverty and a generalised increase in the costs of living, including transport, fuel, food and social services. This put basic needs squarely on the political agenda and represented the biggest challenge to the political authority of the NRM regime since the end of the war (Branch and Mampilly 2015). Rural protests are marked by recurring social struggles over land, including women-naked protests, and have seen small-scale rural producers pitted against the state and large agri-business companies (Martiniello 2015b). Struggles against dispossession have involved forestry commercial companies, conservation schemes and protected areas (Cavanagh and Benjaminsen 2015, Westoby and Lyons 2016); pastoralists populations and oil companies (Muhereza 2015); and estate speculators, brokers and municipalities, and urban and peri-urban impoverished communities.

This edited collection cannot fill all the gaps, yet it hopes to advance critical and radical scholarship on post-1986 Uganda. While contributors come from different theoretical perspectives, they all share an intellectual dissatisfaction with a significant part of the recent scholarship on Uganda and their ontological and epistemological underpinnings. Since the late 1970s, neoliberal restructuring of academia involved a recasting of the aims, objectives and instruments of academic institutions and the associated modes of enquiry. The 'neoliberal university' is less about the advancement of analytical understanding and circulation of ideas, transmitted as a 'gift' of one epistemic community to another and to society as a whole (Halvorsen 2017). Instead, it is more like a centre of 'applied expertise and vocational training ... [that is subordinated] to a society's economic strategy' (Collini 2016: 33); thereby risking the devaluation of its time-honoured task of training for democratic and critical citizenship, encouraging critical thinking and defending academic freedom (Mittelman 2013: 7). This restructuring has created de-politicised and sanitised research, instead of more radical social enquiries that for instance challenge the ways in which power is exercised and inequality (and more broadly social order) is maintained (Bush forthcoming). In synthesis, the neoliberal university is a major site in the 'struggle between knowledge for its own sake and commodified learning' (Heller 2016).

Given this perception of the state of affairs concerning Uganda scholarship and debate, the book does not offer insights on 'development' or 'democracy' or the failings of post-1986 policies. The analytical aim is avoiding yet another prescriptive analysis telling the government what it should do better in the future to achieve its stated policy objectives of becoming a prosperous, stable, peaceful middle-income country with reduced poverty. Besides the obvious risk of starting from neo-colonial assumptions – to which the 'good governance' agenda is particularly prone – this type of analysis usually points at how markets can be made to work 'better' for Uganda. The collection instead offers an analytical interpretation of the existing social, economic and political dynamics by prioritising 'why' questions. The hope is to revive a political economy analysis of processes of change and (under)development: that is the political underpinnings of economic structures, relationships, practices and discourses, including the overall configuration of power relations in public policy formulations, which is intimately related to historical processes of institutional evolution, economic accumulation, class formation and the social struggles which accompany these processes. The book also provides an analysis of the economic underpinning of matters of state, society and culture, including the links between power, interests, policy and practice.

Given the multifaceted character of neoliberalism, the collection calls upon a wide range of disciplines – political science, political economy, political ecology, geography, anthropology, gender studies, history, law, development studies, development economics, religion studies – with the aim of providing a multidisciplinary understanding of these processes of capitalist restructuring and change. This collective effort is necessary to pool not just the evidence but also the analytical skills needed to advance our understanding of contemporary Uganda, decades after the post-1986 landmark collections *Changing Uganda* and *Developing Uganda* (Hansen and Twaddle 1991, 1998).

This is in no way an exhaustive collection. After decades of substantial scholarly gaps in the field of critical political economy in Uganda, producing a systematic political-economic analysis of the country's changes and processes would require more comprehensive data collection and more sustained interventions about theoretical aspects of the analysis. Nonetheless we hope this collection will make a useful contribution, provoke some meaningful debate and help re-open a field that has been purposefully neglected and marginalised in neoliberal academia, both in Uganda and elsewhere. In this respect, it builds upon a scarce literature that focuses mainly and explicitly on aspects of neoliberal processes and changes in the country (e.g. Mamdani 2007, Branch 2011, Lie 2015, Boyd 2015, Pier 2015, Wiegratz 2016).

Embedding neoliberalism in Uganda

We now turn to the questions of embedding neoliberalism in Uganda and its periodisation, acknowledging the contradictory outcomes of the neoliberal project.

First decade: taking the neoliberal pathway (1986–1996)

When it rose to power after a guerrilla war against the Obote II government, the NRM – under the leadership of President Museveni – promised to bring improvements and 'fundamental change' on various fronts. The new government envisioned a shift to a pro-people, broad-based, humane, accountable and moral government and state, and a transformation of the economy from a peasant economy to a modern, diversified, independent, self-sufficient industrial economy that would bring about a middle-class based society (Mamdani 1995, Asiimwe 2002, Rubongoya 2007). However, handling a country that just emerged from protracted conflict, the government suffered from contested legitimacy and a thin power base; with widespread opposition threatening the political stability of the new powers in the state house.

In hindsight, the first decade of Museveni's rule, which led to the approval of a new Constitution (1995), saw the gradual, steady move from the rhetoric of radical left-leaning politics towards a neoliberal reform agenda. During this decade, within a political setting of regime continuity, policies shifted from the initial radical stances emerging from the post-war conjuncture (Museveni 2000, 2007) to the implementation of Structural Adjustment Programmes (SAPs) in the late 1980s, and then liberalisations, privatisations, 'de-regulation' and public sector reform in the 1990s (Hansen and Twaddle 1998, Ddumba-Ssentamu 2002).

The timing reflected wider neoliberal interventions on the African continent, pushed by the international financial institutions (IFIs) (Campbell and Loxley 1989, Onimode 1989, Mkandawire and Olukoshi 1995). The restructuring of Uganda started through structural adjustments, accompanied by continuous financial and technical assistance and persistent reform pressure and incentive from the country's various multilateral and bilateral donors that remained a key characteristic for the next thirty years (Wiegratz 2010, 2016, Lie 2015). The 1987 Economic Recovery Programme (ERP), for instance, involved amongst others the IMF, the WB, the African Development Bank, the Paris Club members (Ddumba-Ssentamu 2002); the IFIs, the EU, the UK and the US remained major donors by 2017. Relative stability in the country after the NRM came to power combined with rapid (post-war) economic growth gave Museveni considerable domestic and foreign support, silencing the fact that the regime had put persistent constraints on democratisation (Tripp 2000, 2010).

Second decade: Uganda as showcase of post-Washington consensus (PWC) (1996–2006)

From the mid-1990s to mid-2000s – the decade between the new Constitution and Museveni's third term in 2006 – the country became a star performer of liberal economic reforms, and, in the view of the WB and others, a 'development model' to be followed elsewhere in Africa and beyond (Kuteesa *et al.* 2009, WB 2010). The country was at the forefront of global experiments in development reform, such as the 1997 Poverty Eradication Action Plan (PEAP), the WB Poverty Reduction Strategy Papers (PRSPs) and the IFIs' original Heavily Indebted Poor Countries (HIPC) initiative. Regarding the latter, Uganda was the first beneficiary in 1998 and received additional relief under the enhanced HIPC initiative in

2000, amounting to about two billion US dollars debt relief in total. Uganda was also in the first round of beneficiaries of the Multilateral Debt Relief Initiative later in the mid-2000s onwards (IMF 2013). The success story case – and the official rhetoric of donor support – was mainly built on the country's official figures for economic growth and poverty reduction and to a lesser extent on certain social indicators such as improvements in health and education. This is displayed in exemplary fashion in IMF press statements from 2000 that announced further debt relief to the country:

> While Uganda remains one of the poorest countries in the world, analytic work supported by the World Bank indicates that there was an 18 percent reduction in poverty between 1992/93 and 1996/97 (declining from 56 to 44 percent) owing primarily to strong economic growth. Substantial improvements in various welfare indicators have also been recorded, the most notable in the area of primary education, where the net primary enrollment rate increased from 56 percent in 1995/96 to 94 percent in 1998/99. (IMF 2000a).

On the basis of the figures that the IFIs and the government produced, donors could extend their support to the Ugandan government in its effort to expand the economy, reduce poverty and improve the living conditions of the poor. As we read in an IMF press statement:

> Uganda's eligibility for debt relief under the enhanced HIPC Initiative is a recognition by the international community of the progress made in implementing economic reforms and poverty reduction. It also recognises that Uganda's poverty reduction strategy, as laid out in its PRSP, will contribute to continued economic growth and an improvement in the quality of life of the poor ... The enhanced HIPC debt relief ... will create room for additional public expenditures on poverty reduction. Resources made available by debt relief ... will be ... allocated to key antipoverty programs, spelled out in the PRSP. The PAF has provided a transparent link between donor support, including debt relief, and the government's poverty reduction program. (IMF 2000b)

The statement below also indicates what donors wanted, besides 'helping the poor': a commitment to neoliberal economic orthodoxy and a deepening of the reforms (i.e. a further embedding and locking-in of neoliberal capitalism):

> Uganda's eligibility for debt relief under the enhanced Initiative recognizes the effectiveness of Uganda's poverty reduction strategy to date, the application of resources from debt relief under the original HIPC framework to its poverty reduction programs, the iterative process involving civil society in the formulation of the poverty reduction strategy, and the authorities' continued commitment to macroeconomic stability ... Support under the enhanced HIPC Initiative is critical for Uganda to advance its poverty reduction programs, while deepening structural reforms and maintaining macroeconomic stability.
> (IMF 2000a)

That said, concomitantly with the neoliberal post-Washington-consensus-shift towards 'good governance' and the importance of de-centralised 'lean' state institutions, Uganda also became a show-case of decentralisation and various public sector and governance reforms generally (Andrews and Bategeka 2013). In this period, IFIs and donors reinforced the NRM's rule for its capacity to ensure a sort of political stability, needed for reform continuity. There was also a noticeable change in Uganda's role in key regional dynamics. The country became a strong ally of the US as a basis for 'peace missions' and a crucial partner in the US-led war on terror (Branch 2011, Fisher 2013, 2014). The dismal record of the government's actions concerning people in northern Uganda during the years of violent political conflict there revealed major characteristics of state action under NRM rule (Finnström 2008, Dolan 2009); something that had profound implications for rural populations and was extended to other parts of the country especially in the third reform decade.

More specifically, the key pillars of the new economic model for neoliberal Uganda included a private sector emphasis. The economic reforms of the 1990s, spearheaded by the country's membership of the World Trade Organisation in 1995, included currency reform, the liberalisation of the foreign exchange markets and the export crops sectors (coffee, cotton), the abolition of marketing boards, the dismantling of cooperatives and the deregulation of consumer and producer prices (Wiegratz 2009, 2010, 2016). New 'business-friendly' laws on investments, taxes and profit expatriation were paralleled by the privatisation of most state-owned businesses and parastatal companies. The economic 'deregulation' also lifted

the protective buffers for weak economic actors such as peasants and workers. New semi-autonomous state institutions such
as the Uganda Investment Authority (UIA), the Uganda Revenue
Authority (URA) and the Privatisation Unit were established to
carry out these reforms, alongside the sectoral counterparts: the
development authorities in sectors such as coffee, cotton, tobacco
and tea. New regulatory bodies oversaw activities in the liberalised
power-generation and distribution, insurance, telecommunication,
and broadcasting sectors. Certification systems replaced export and
import licensing systems and the private sector took on the export
of non-coffee commodities. Tax and tariff systems were simplified,
revenue collection restructured, enterprise subsidy systems thinned
out. The properties expropriated under Amin were returned to the
Asian community. The financial sector liberalisation entailed the
liberalisation of interest rates and capital accounts, while the power
of the Bank of Uganda was strengthened. Some local banks closed,
mostly under controversial circumstances; large foreign banks, such
as Standard Bank and Barclays, started to dominate the sector
(Mamdani 1995, Brett 1998, Hansen and Twaddle 1998, Reinikka
and Collier 2001). The Poverty Eradication Programs (1997/98–
2008/09) and the Plan for Modernisation of Agriculture (2001–2009)
supported enterprise development, agricultural zoning, and large-
scale agriculture (Martiniello 2015a). Under the slogan of 'securing
food security through the market', the plan increased the commercialisation of agriculture through diversification and specialisation
by abolishing the earlier systems of agricultural extension services
and marketing boards, which focused on major export cash crops,
and had reduced price volatility and provided inputs and credits to
farmers (Bategeka *et al.* 2013: 2). The stated objective was to increase
farmers' income-price by reducing taxation and establishing private
marketing agencies. Driven by the ideological objective of fostering
state withdrawal from economic activities, the goal was to create
space for market capitalism with a particular focus on private sector
development.

The economic reform process was generally characterised by an
increased level of economic and social insecurity and high unemployment, which for the majority of the people resulted in economic
and psychological hardship and an increase in corruption and fraud
(Wiegratz 2010, 2016, Tangri and Mwenda 2013).

This decade saw a significant increase in foreign aid, resulting from
both donors' interest in supporting the neoliberal reform process
(Harrison 2004) and Uganda's new geopolitical role as military

guardian and strategic basis in the US war on terror in the region. Increased foreign aid substantially retarded the democratic reforms, which often remained at a mere formal and procedural level, and donors conveniently 'overlooked' significant democratic gaps, like the suppression of freedom of expression and the press, repression of dissidents and the rise in corruption (Tripp 2010). In this decade, two of the key reform outcomes that made Uganda a global 'success story' occurred: rapid economic growth and significant poverty reduction. According to official figures, Uganda's reform-induced growth was poverty reducing:

> Following the end of the armed conflict in 1986, the ruling …
> [NRM] led by President Museveni introduced a number of
> structural reforms and investments, which led to a sustained
> period of high growth and poverty reduction between 1987–2010
> … Real … [GDP] growth averaged 7.3% between 2000 and
> 2010 [up from about 6.3 per cent in the 1990s], placing Uganda
> amongst the fastest growing economies in the world. (WB 2017)

This UNDP 2013 HDR report similarly makes the link between liberal reforms and significant poverty reduction:

> Uganda's high growth during the 1990s was poverty alleviating
> because of income growth in agriculture through large scale
> absorption of labour, especially in the cash crops sector that was
> buoyed by world prices and improvement in agriculture's terms
> of trade. (UNDP 2013: 72, 78)

It is noted, however, that population growth and inequality have affected per capita income growth (at 3 per cent in the 2000s) and poverty outcomes (WB 2017, UNDP 2013). More specifically, the national headcount poverty level for the 2000s was in the 30 per cent range and fluctuated over the years, increasing more recently due to a slow down in growth and agricultural production and trade (Nuwagaba and Muhumuza 2017). Poverty was mainly a rural phenomenon and manifest among farmers especially. Poverty and inequality in some reform years increased in rural areas as well as in specific regions, especially in northern Uganda (Deininger and Okidi 2003, Okidi *et al.* 2007). Furthermore, overall welfare inequality levels increased especially in urban areas. Between 2000 and 2003, the richest 20 per cent experienced a 9 per cent increase in consumption expenditure, while the rest of the population faced a decline. While the distributional pattern of growth in household consumption expenditure for the period 1992–2003 disfavoured the poor, some parts of that period favoured the poorest 20 per cent disproportionably and resulted in above-average growth in consumption expenditures (Kappel *et al.* 2005, Okidi *et al.* 2007). The Gini index increased from 0.37 in 1997 to 0.4 in 2000 and has remained above 0.4 ever since (GoU 2014, Nuwagaba and Muhumuza 2017). The following decade, that we now turn to analyse, has seen a major debate on the veracity and accuracy of the figures on poverty reduction and development successes of this decade.

Third decade: neoliberal maturity – enclosures, extractivism and financialisation (2006–2016)

The key figures cited for the case of success for the overall reform period are the decline in official national poverty levels to 19.7 per cent by 2014 (down from around 56 per cent in the early 1990s and 70 per cent in 1980). Up to the early 2010s, the country was among the top ten growth performers in the world and one of the top six fastest growing economies in Africa, besides being a 'high achiever' in terms of growth and social development indicators (e.g. UNDP 2013, WB 2010). According to the WB, Uganda was the eleventh/fourth fastest growing economy in the world/Africa; if oil and mineral rich countries were removed, Uganda was first in Africa (Mwenda 2016). And there is also the view that 'Uganda has been, and continues to be, a public sector reform leader in Africa' (Pruce 2014: 1, see also Andrews and Bategeka 2013).

Yet, new matters such as inequality have been acknowledged by the reform coalition as a problem. By the end of the 2000s, there was recognition by the WB, for instance, of a 'substantial and growing urban–rural inequality and inequality between regions' (2010: 4). Accordingly, while the urban areas of central and western regions generally benefited from growth, 'wide swaths in rural areas and the north and east were left behind … [P]overty reduction in north and north-eastern regions has only been marginal' (*ibid.*). Inequality levels have worsened in the 2010s; the Gini index stood at 0.43 in 2009 and 0.47 in 2014 (Nuwagaba and Muhumuza 2017). There was growing debate about the phenomenon by 2017; also in government and international development circles. Oxfam dedicated an extensive report to the matter (*ibid.*). Ever more evident was that neoliberal reforms enabled private capital accumulation strategies of state elites, through their control of the state for the advancement of their personal business interests via reform (Tangri and Mwenda 2013, see also Szeftel 2000, Beresford 2015).

By the mid-2010s, Uganda contained the particular mix of economic characteristics that has been found to be common among neoliberalised countries worldwide (Wiegratz 2016): growth accompanied by high wealth concentration, poverty, economic insecurity, un-/under-employment etc. Millions were food insecure; 11.8 per cent of the population could not afford two meals (2014/15). And, almost 2/3 were estimated in the recent Uganda poverty status report to earn less than 2$/day, thus classed by government statistics as 'poor' (19.7 per cent, at up to 1$/day) or 'non-poor insecure' (43.3 per cent, 1–2$/day) (2012/13) (GoU 2014). Other estimates suggested that 88.3 per cent of Ugandans (30.6 million) could live on less than 3$/day (Muhumuza 2016). If we couple this with persistent inflationary pressures (9 per cent over the last five years) the misery of the poor working population expands as the purchasing power of the Ugandan shilling (UGX) has weakened. The latest official poverty figure has increased between 2012/13and 2016/17: from 19.7 to at first 27 per cent; then UBOS revised this figure downward a few months after publication to 21.4 per cent, signalling a contentious politics of numbers which involves a plethora of competing methods of measuring (Daily Monitor 2017b, 2018, Twinoburyo 2018). Further, corruption has remained high in the 2010s. The World Bank estimated that Uganda loses UGX 500 billion (approx. $300 million) annually due to corruption and expressed worries about Uganda's image as a reform model (WB 2010). In recent years more regularly, government received criticism from (and was occasionally penalised by) donors over matters of corruption and human rights.

Partly reflecting the above trends, public debates focused on precarity, extreme poverty, food insecurity, unemployment, inequality, foreign control of the economy, corruption and state violence as well as crime and insecurity. High levels of public debt, external trade deficit and interest rates remained major problems; so was public sector performance (Bukenya and Muhumuza 2017). Economic growth itself declined and averaged 5 per cent in the 2010s (WB 2017). The overall economic slowdown and the accumulation of reform-induced problems across state, economy and society contributed to societal crisis, a decline in government legitimacy and increase in state repression, and people's discontent and resistance as further key feature of the 2010s (Wiegratz 2016, Anderson and Fisher 2016).

The establishment ideology and rhetoric has also partly shifted from 'poverty reduction' to 'shared prosperity' and 'wealth creation'. The aspiration of turning Uganda into a middle-income country which offers 'prosperity for all' and 'inclusive development' (NRM 2016) was first conveyed through the National Development Plan (2010) and was also the core message of the NRM's electoral programme for the 2016 campaign, which sidelines poverty and poverty reduction in favour of a more explicit message on fostering domestic accumulation, coherently with neoliberal visions. Government discourse was rife with reference to economic patriotism, Buy Uganda, local content and populism. As we write, the government seems to be increasingly interventionist in its quest for accelerated modernisation via large energy and transport infrastructure projects – particularly mega dams, hydro-electric projects, roads, railways – agro-business and industrialisation, especially as a result of the increased bilateral cooperation with China. Despite rhetorical shifts, however, the overall ideology remains that of modernisation through economic growth, aiming at the transformation from peasant to modern industrial economy.

In this decade, the government increasingly used the army to run 'civil' programmes, allegedly as a quick fix to longstanding implementation problems and corruption of the public service. In agriculture, the UPDF-led Operation Wealth Creation, headed by Museveni's brother Salim Saleh, was now engaged in the provision of inputs and extension services, thereby crowding out NAADS. Further, many of the most visible actors in mass-media public debates on politics, governance and development were the very organisations that IFIs and Western donors had orchestrated and/or financed, i.e. had initiated, helped to establish and/or supported for years to grow and stabilise: Advocates Coalition for Development and Environment (ACODE), Anti-Corruption Coalition Uganda (ACCU), Uganda Debt Network (UDN), Civil Society Budget Advocacy Group (CSBAG), Private Sector Foundation Uganda (PSFU) and so on.

The financialised trends in the Ugandan economy saw an increase in real estate speculation and a related boom in the building sector, rather than investments in productive activities. The ongoing drive towards neoliberal reinforcement in private property rights through land-titling programmes and the policy support given to land grabs and green grabs testifies to the reinforcement of a pattern of plunder of natural resources and primitive accumulation (Martiniello 2013). Finally, a larger economic presence of Chinese companies in the building and infrastructures sector and developments in the oil sector fuelled the establishment's aspirations around a new growth and development success story. Some development politics analysts are once again impressed and optimistic, citing 'compelling evidence that Uganda has displayed relatively high levels of state capacity and elite commitment to govern oil in the national interest' (Hickey and Izama 2017: 29).

The constant deterioration of the living conditions for a large section of the Ugandan people mentioned above is consistent with a changing political economy which is reorganising Uganda as an (agro) extractive economy. The extractive sector – mining, oil and gas – could potentially emerge as the core of the national economy, with limited or non-existent linkages to other sectors, and plenty of incentives to advance financialisation, real estate speculation and luxury consumption, following the extractive pattern established, for example, in Mozambique (Castel-Branco 2014). There is the possibility that current trends signal the creation of an enclave economy constituted by large-scale plantations, export-oriented monocultures and extractive activities such as oil and mining (Ferguson 2006, Mhone 2001, Olukhoshi 2007). On the basis of this extractive core, Uganda could possibly follow the pattern of extractives-led development, emulating the Latin American patterns of extractive rentier developmental states (Veltmeyer and Petras 2014). In the first case, the creation of an enclave economy would reiterate extractive and dispossessing trends in capitalism while further tying natural resources into international circuits of accumulation where surplus is transferred. This model of extraction has little or no substantive linkages with local economies and impacts both the environment and rural communities negatively.

The narrative structure of the book

In what follows, we expose the narrative structure of the book, which is purposely organised around four thematic sections based upon the previously raised sets of research questions and debates: 'The state, donors and development aid'; 'Economic restructuring and social services'; 'Extractivism and enclosures'; 'Race, culture and commoditisation'.

Part I: The state, donors and development aid

Our first section shows how actors from the international development/aid sector (IFIs etc.) had a major role in advancing market society, by providing substantial financial, ideological, discursive and military resources that kicked off and kept in place neoliberalisation, providing technical 'assistance', insisting on certain policies and programmes (and de-campaigning others), and exerting keep-on-track pressure on government and other actors when needed. Foreign actors, in extraordinary ways, boosted the power of government and domestic ruling classes more broadly and severely altered the power structure and relationships (including inter-class power asymmetries) of the country. In this regard, *Lie* analyses the new global aid architecture that emerged in the mid-1990s, based on 'partnership' among donors and host governments under the unifying banner of 'good governance'. Contrary to the common vulgate that sees neoliberalism as a process that destroys the state, the IFIs transformed its role in the economy with the stated aim of creating an enabling business environment through legislative and institutional reforms. These practices consisted of new and sophisticated forms of control by donors who officially intended to minimise the misuse of funds, while furthering the ideological discourse (and policy direction) of good governance, transparency, accountability, participation, decentralisation and multiparty democracy within the government agenda. Lie argues that the World Bank concealed its influence on the government's policies, through various indirect techniques of governance, while the ideology of 'partnership' contrasted with the actual practices, where direct governance defined the operational limits of the government vis-à-vis the directives of the Bank. The relationship between the Bank and GoU was a constitutive element of the neoliberal project.

The strong ties between the government, IFIs and donors were decisive for the restructuring of Uganda. These ties are further analysed in *Atkinson*'s chapter, which argues that the World Bank's financial assistance was based on an assessment of northern Uganda as a post-conflict scenario. This assessment systematically evaded the acknowledgement of a prolonged armed conflict. The financial support, which began during a period of intense military conflict with rebel movements in the northern regions, rapidly became more obviously 'political' as the Bank silently ceded on the government pressures to use a growing part of development assistance to fund military and security expenses. The restructuring of the economy along neoliberal lines and its integration within global markets required the Bank to turn a blind eye to the atrocities and violence committed by the army against civilian populations.

In the (post-)conflict north, the state heavily relied on international humanitarian and development organisations to indirectly rule over a rebellious population. These organisations used new technologies of power and furthered the depoliticisation of development. *Branch and Yen* argue that the use of internment camps positioned Acholi populations under threats of state militarism and humanitarian and peacebuilding discipline. Developmental reconstruction and peace-building initiatives encompassed a wide range of interventions, from microcredit to community-conflict resolution. All these programmes further expanded the neoliberal logic of making the individual responsible for self-governing him/herself and for reinstating peace and rehabilitation, while erasing from the picture the structural causes of violence in the north, such as the national and interna-tional structures of power and inequality. This chapter documents the latest forms of intervention, such as extensive use of psycho-phar-maceuticals to deal with trauma and provide psychosocial support, in a context of drastic cuts to public health expenses. Psycho-phar-maceuticals, often dumped by transnational corporations (TNCs) in poor countries for profit or for reputation boosting, remain the most abused form of interventions amongst the poor.

Neoliberalisation has undermined democratisation through the imposition from above of a procedural rather than substantial form of democracy. Moreover, by redefining the structures of governance, neoliberalisation fragments society and alienates people's participa-tion, running against genuine participatory democracy (Chomsky 1997). *Rubongoya* analyses the dialectic between 'the legacy' – the set of strong elements typical of social/nationalist movements of the pre-independence and immediate post-colonial period that charac-terise NRM politics – and neoliberalism. Rubongoya argues that this dialectic has produced a 'political settlement' which fostered partic-ular processes of state making and wealth accumulation and brought about the contemporary power structures and the corresponding clientelist political system, characterised by allocations of rents and patronage within the ruling coalition. Powerful foreign actors have been central to the emergence of the ruling coalition and to its persistence, not least because they provided crucial resources to the NRM, including funds for electoral campaigns. Interacting with Uganda's long-standing political culture, neoliberal policies have enabled the NRM to pursue and achieve its core objective: power consolidation and regime maintenance.

Decentralisation has been another central tenet of neoliberal reforms during the post-Washington consensus. In 1986, Uganda was a strongly centralised system of government and administration. In 1987/88, the National Resistance Army (NRA) implemented a radical decentralisation programme, building on the 'resistance councils' – a committee system that emerged from the guerrilla war (Tidemand

1994). The formalisation of local committees at the end of the war was meant to support popular democracy through local councils (LCs), functioning on the basis of direct representation. During the mid-1990s, the councils were reformed. *Titeca* observes that the decreasing electoral support for Museveni between 1996 and 2006 went hand in hand with the decentralisation reforms, which turned the local governments from a radical democracy institution into a tool for patrimonialism, used mainly to mobilise support for the regime. The proliferation of districts – from thirty-three to more than 120 – became a tool in a broader 'repertoire of domination' (Poteete and Ribot 2011) to consolidate support for a government that has been losing popular consensus and has increasingly relied on repression and patrimonialism to stay in power. Myriad small district governments with little to no implementation capacity and financial autonomy did not increase local participation and bottom-up governance, but rather served as an instrument to carry out central government's directives in a more capillary way even in contexts of local discontent. 'Districtisation' thus perpetuates divide and rule politics, and creates very docile local governments with little financial autonomy. The civil service became the largest employer and jobs are allocated through clientelistic relationships. The single quality of most LCs is their unfettered allegiance to the NRM and Museveni (Tripp 2010).

Neoliberal ideology and discourse erased class from narrative and analysis, thus sanitising 'technical' development interventions and glossing over the class character and outcomes of the reforms. A central point in *Wilson*'s chapter on the Millennium Development Villages (MDVs) project is that the erasure of class from ideology is far from a 'technical blip' in the development industry or an implementation failure that can be redressed. It is, on the contrary, a deliberate choice, aimed at smoothing the edges of rather brutal processes of exclusion exacerbated by development projects. Projects such as the MDV have accelerated and exacerbated the class dynamics in the countryside, while portraying a society – often (un)defined as composed by 'communities' – where poverty has environmental, not social, causes. Also, they have in-built biases leading towards elite capture and misuse of funds. The MDV project, under the banner of turning the poor into entrepreneurs, boosted the accumulation process of the pre-existing rural entrepreneurial elite while pushing the poor – who were predominantly the landless – into wage labour for the emerging local capitalist class exacerbating existing inequalities because it subordinated inputs allocation to land ownership. The mystification of turning the poor into self-employed/entrepreneurial actors – fitting with Sachs' 'end of poverty' narrative (2005) – was thus not only reiterating the ideology of the development industry, which stressed the transformative power of international aid; more ambitiously, it created a 'fantasy machine'. Wilson's interpretation of aid as a 'fantasy machine' helps capture why the narrative of development systematically obliterates the inconvenient truths.

Part II: Economic restructuring and social services

The next set of chapters show that neoliberal reforms have hardly resolved core socio-economic problems affecting the majority of the population. *Asiimwe*'s chapter shows that the economic growth miracle was to a significant extent based on the effect of large sums of aid, which sometimes constituted half of the national budget, creating public-expenditure-driven growth. The reforms induced stagnation, decline or minimal growth in key productive sectors, such as agriculture and industry. Small-scale producers and workers – mostly youth and women – were systematically marginalised by the policy reforms. Asiimwe argues that Uganda's growth is not based on a structural transformation of the economy, but rather on a deepening of primitive accumulation occurring through corruption – which is the use of extra-economic force to access and control resources – aid dependence, widespread economic trickery and the dumping of low quality foreign products that crowd out local products. Asiimwe observes that donors' policy preferences systematically produced anti-poor and anti-development effects, as the commodification of health and education left the majority of the population with sub-par access, or denied access altogether.

The privatisation of social welfare services has been promoted aggressively through initiatives that emphasised public–private partnerships on paper, but are part of a wider privatisation strategy. The government reduced public funding, dropped many of its responsibilities and replaced its role with private sector contracting for social provision. Such reform dynamics are investigated in *Nystrand and Tamm*'s chapter. Reforms have entrenched and increased socio-economic and spatial inequalities across classes, among different regions of the country, and across the urban/rural divide. With the increase of private provision and commodification of education and health also came the privatisation of responsibility for social protection to family networks and the over-reliance on informal social and kin support. These processes created a social group that is completely excluded – the extremely, or 'chronic' poor. The downsized, 'decentralised' and resource-starved public sector created a dysfunctional local service provision. Private and donor-funded service providers introduced fees and payments for services and market-based schemes. Social services reflect the new class divisions: private for those who can afford it; and public for the poor, with private, cash-based facilities being preferred across classes. While private provision is sometimes better than the public, it is also evident that many private schools for example have experienced problems with quality, fee levels, transparency and grade inflation. In the health sector, drugs supply provision is dysfunctional and corruption among staff is the norm. The reforms created a situation where only very few are covered via formal social security; and informal, voluntary collectivist schemes for special events – like burials and health emergencies – also operate almost exclusively on a cash basis, thus further excluding the poorer groups.

Health sector restructuring has contributed to the exclusion and marginalisation of wider sections of populations from accessing medical care, widening respective class and geographical divides. This is the broader picture behind the negligence and corruption in the sector, which the media often depicts as the causes of poor service delivery. In her chapter, *Ssali* retraces the history of the neoliberalisation of the sector. Starting from the much-resisted introduction of users' fees in 1999 and their abolition in 2001, she remarks on the overall continuity of the state of disruption and abandonment that the sector experienced after the end of the war. The reforms eroded the state's sense of responsibility in terms of provision towards its citizens. Ssali argues that notwithstanding a reform-related more-than-threefold increase in the per capita public expenditure for health services, delivery has not improved. This is the paradoxical result of donors' funds having been directed towards sectoral programmes – typically for communicable diseases like HIV – rather than preventive healthcare. Also donor funds have been very unevenly distributed across districts. The reforms have undermined state capacity for service delivery. The neglect of preventive healthcare has had a negative effect on the poor and it partly explains the sustained high incidence of preventable diseases and the high mortality rates associated to them. About 97 per cent of healthcare costs are borne by households, which makes these expenses one of the most burdensome for the poor.

Part III: Extractivism and enclosures

Uganda is being transformed into an extractive enclave where much of FDI flows into the extractive industries so as to take out the maximum of high-demand resources, at lowest cost within the shortest period of time. This trend leads to an accelerated commodi-fication of natural resources and land dispossession caused by oil and gas exploration, agribusiness projects and neoliberal environmental conservation initiatives (Martiniello 2015a). The commodification of environmental conservation and the use of market devices has been recognised as a key feature of financialisation and thus of the neoliberal conjuncture. It is in this context that forests are being increasingly commercialised, while the neoliberal forestry discourse, which originated in foreign circuits and was propagated by external actors, expands market mechanisms to the governance of nature and externalises the functions of the state to non-state actors such as NGOs, donors and firms. This is the focus of *Nel*'s chapter, which argues that the state becomes an important promoter of neoliberal forestry governance, by providing incentives through the UIA and URA to plantation companies with financial and technical capaci-ties required to advance large-scale commercial initiatives. The logic of capital accumulation is supported by prioritising the interests of large-scale users such as agri-business and forestry industrialists over those of smallholders and indigenous populations. Market-oriented discourses of price mechanisms and the rise in demand of environmental services expand the value that can be provided by, and extracted from, natural resources by decomposing it into multifarious and segmented markets. In doing so, their conserva-tion becomes increasingly alienated from the public domain and the debate increasingly depoliticised. The outcome of accelerated capitalist restructuring and domination of the forestry sector is mani-fested in the further separation of populations from National Parks and Forests Reserves resources on which many dwellers depend for their livelihoods.

In the field of conservation and forestry, an extractivist vision of development is gaining currency and extending support to 'green economic initiatives' – such as plantation forestry, carbon offset markets and other payments for ecosystem services. These initiatives are based upon the assumption that the market can deliver optimal economic and ecological results, the outcome of which poses enor-mous pressures to convert forestry towards uses related to these initiatives. *Lyons* points to the failure of these initiatives in mitigating atmospheric pollution and climate change and argues that these initiatives are tied to specific patterns in the globalisation of trade and investments, particularly to processes of financialisation, epito-mising neoliberal capitalism. The expansion of the neoliberal green economy and the associated structures of governance contributed to further entrench North/South divides by enabling industrialised countries to preserve astonishingly high levels of carbon emissions on the basis of their offsetting activities in the non-industrialised countries. Lyons also argues that strategies of capital accumulation are underpinned by a combination of both structural (direct) and slow (or soft) violence, giving several examples of these types of violence.

Neoliberalisation is based on an unprecedented expansion of land enclosures, dispossession and displacement. Primitive accumulation happens through the appropriation of land (and the resources impinging on it) by an emerging social class, leaving the majority of people in society landless. As in many rural societies, class formation and class dynamics are an ongoing process (Bernstein 2010, Greco 2015). *Smith and Van Alstine* argue that with the aim of allowing the oil industry to become established in western Uganda, the state re-regulates and ensures the land enclosure needed for oil explorations, which have caused displacement of a significant number of people who lived and worked on the site earmarked for the refinery. Explorations are also accompanied by heightened state-led surveillance, securitisation, militarisation and repression, in order to ensure a 'stable' investment climate. The president's Special Forces are often deployed in oil exploration areas, limiting the freedom of movement and access to natural resources. This negatively affects local people's livelihoods and often results in land dispossession and community fragmentation. In some instances, communal land is transferred to powerful investors and speculators. Affected populations have very little say in the process and compensations for lost land and assets or livelihood restrictions are often delayed and inadequate. Land grabbing related to explorations generates further land conflicts and has been associated with the increase of physical violence.

A similar extractivist tendency can be noted in a different sector – fishery – which is a productive sector of key importance for national food security. *Wedig* analyses the activities of the government to manage fisheries resources in Lake Victoria in the face of declining wild fish stocks and a high dependency on fisheries, both for export earnings and food security. The strategies focus on advancing FDI-led aquaculture development, paying limited attention to the needs of small-scale fishers (SSFs), who may be pushed out of the sector, and fish workers, who will continue to face poor working conditions on fish farms. These strategies are shaped by the global agenda for fisheries management, which international agencies advance through global policy frameworks and associated funding mechanisms aimed at reforming the world's fisheries through private property rights over both fishing grounds and large water areas for cage aquaculture. Proponents of this agenda promise increased export earnings and improved food and nutritional security by arguing that investors, by virtue of their ownership of fisheries resources, will be incentivised to maximise production sustainably. Following this logic, the government seeks to expand fish production by selling exclusive use rights over particularly productive lake areas to corporate investors interested in large-scale aquaculture. The chapter shows that the negative repercussions of a private-property-based approach are likely to be drastic and devastating for mostly poor fishers and fish workers who directly depend on declining wild fish stocks. It advances processes of state-protected primitive accumulation and accumulation by dispossessions, including aquaculture-related water grabbing, and drives the exclusion of SSFs through a system of corporate hegemony that is unlikely to prevent the overexploitation of the lake's ecosystem.

Neoliberalism, and generally the capitalist order, has to a significant extent been locked-in: not just via policy and legal changes such as neoliberal constitutionalism (Gill 1995), but also through specific patterns of economic and political priorities of dominant domestic classes. In Uganda, land has been at the core of socio-political struggles, which intensify as land reforms are implemented through the creation of legal and policy institutions aimed at liberalising land ownership and markets. *Nakayi* argues that similarly to other reforms in East Africa, land tenure reforms instituting individualisation, formalisation and titling are often in strident contradiction with existing social relations of access and use of land on the ground as they neglect the socially embedded character of land. Nakayi argues that though land law reforms contain some degree of social justice in the protection of tenants against arbitrary evictions by landlords, uneven power relations on the ground often bypass these legal measures and prevent their implementation. In the context of weak rural institutions and decentralised land rights, safeguard measures to defend tenant rights have been eroded as the government is increasingly finding itself under pressure from commercial and propertied classes. Yet, though the government is keeping its hands in the regulation of rent and terms of tenancy in order to keep control of the countryside especially for purposes of political consensus, land reforms have been instrumental to the politics of class formation. Land law reforms have also consolidated the notion that markets represent the best mechanism for allocating land to the fittest producers in the countryside, further eroding the security of tenure for poor smallholders and marginalising debates over uneven redistribution of resources.

As various chapters in Part III show, significant sections of the subaltern classes at the sharp end of restructuring were hit by the reforms and marginalised by powerful economic processes and actors. Many major reforms were in significant ways not only anti-poor, but also anti-indigenous and anti-developmental, displaying a strong bias against local productive sectors, small-scale actors and local capacity-building and power.

Neoliberalisation has been marked by escalating social and class conflicts, which shape and in turn are shaped by patterns of capitalist development. Yet people often oppose these exclusionary developments, which are intrinsic to the extractivist project. This resistance has become a key characteristic of the Ugandan polity, and multifarious responses from below have emerged in the countryside, including visible and open forms of resistance and hidden, non-confrontational forms of contestation of state authority which reshaped political agency and practice of subaltern actors. As shown by *Lyons*, who has documented hidden forms of resistance to conservation areas and forestry plantations, these include continuing practising agriculture on land licensed to a company, fence-breaking, moving cultivation and animal grazing onto steep slopes or riparian zones, and burning trees planted by the company within their licence area. Further, as *Smith and Van Alstine* write, civil society's resistance activities in the oil regions have been repressed by the state (also via legal changes concerning 'public order management'), and levels of fear and suspicion of some communities vis-à-vis the state are high (also regarding current and future exclusion from oil benefits). To date, capitalist development in the oil sector has generated upheavals for communities and people and fostered a particularly hierarchical and repressive state–society relationship. Within this context, much of the industry's corporate social responsibility (CSR) activities are a sort of token, charity-type benefit for affected communities, in the name of enhancing the reputation and legitimacy of the project and giving the impression of win–win outcomes and partnerships, thereby containing critique and resistance. They are rarely rolled out in a democratic and people-centred manner, and they don't really alter who wins and loses from oil development. Finally, some local communities organise and articulate their interests by making demands to the state and capital. Oil development has thus also brought about changes regarding political agencies of traditionally marginalised groups.

Part IV: Race, culture and commoditisation

Chapters in this part explore the intersections between class, race and culture, and the ways in which neoliberal transformation contributes to the moulding of the cultural, social and moral norms that shape society. *Hundle*'s analysis of the case of Ugandan Asian returnees is telling in this regard. 'Asians' who started returning to Uganda in the 1980s, constitute to date a demographically very small proportion of the population. Most of them have no Ugandan citizenship and are thus formally excluded from electoral politics, hence relying on patronage networks and personal links with politicians. This transnational elite has double residence abroad, has established substantial businesses and plays a prominent role during electoral campaigns. Hundle distinguishes between 'new money' – relatively new Asian businesses working in association with big TNCs – and 'old money' – family businesses established through family networks across East Africa and the Indian Ocean in colonial times, typically evolved into corporations expanding via partnerships and shareholding organised through extended family and kinship ties. The government promoted the return of 'Asians' via incentives and diplomatic advocacy. Returnee family firms were granted economic citizenship and, from that position, advocated for neoliberal reforms which would provide them with the environment they needed to reconstruct their business. Post reforms, investment by these firms increased across most economic sectors. Ugandan Asians have built an image of themselves as contributors to national development. Further, the process of returning properties to them unleashed a process of concentration of property. The neoliberal project also involved the creation of an ethno-racialised 'foreign investor' urban class and community of South Asians. The group has been represented, ideologically, as a FDI-carrying 'business community'. The political influence of returnee firms is vast not only as FDI carriers, but also as employment generators and for their strong regional networks in East Africa. The FDI policy opens up new possibilities for racial elite class formation.

Not just international capital and transnational actors but also religion plays a crucial role in reproducing the social order of neoliberal Uganda. *Bompani* speaks of a new religiously infected moral economy, a new religiously framed public action and public morality and the moralisation of public debate and the country generally. In the country's new religious market, Pentecostal-charismatic churches (PCCs) have dramatically gained credence as a fairly 'new' religious actor in terms of followers, importance, ambition and influence in a public space previously dominated by the Anglican and the Catholic Church. The reasons for this rise of PCCs in significance and power are closely linked to the neoliberal reforms and their repercussions and the government's related politics. Museveni's reintegration of religion into public affairs, especially since the early 2000s – and his provision of legal and social protection, safety, support and economic opportunities to PCCs as part of that – signalled a return to the post-independence political practice of making particular religious groups an ally of the government and a (pro-state) mediator between state and society. PCCs gained prominence and legitimacy in the 2000s due to the general rise in prominence of non-state actors, especially NGOs and particularly faith-based organisations (FBOs), in international development, and their role in development, relief and public health interventions, for instance in the fight against HIV and the substantial US funding from conservative Christian donors. Strong ties were forged between PCCs and various top state actors, including members of the Museveni family, which enhanced the symbolic power of the government as a benevolent and trust-worthy force. PCCs provided theological legitimation to neoliberal policy objectives, leadership and government, by adding a religious dimension and thus re-moralising the neoliberal project (replacing the highly technical, economics-driven, 'There Is No Alternative' narrative). PCC's role and power is also explained in another way: it gives believers an interpretive frame to understand and manoeuvre their restructured, in-crisis country, respective changes and oppor-tunities, their own life trajectory and social interactions in it, and related social worries and anxieties. The beliefs offered by PCCs offer an imaginary of clarity and hope for a redeemed, moral and flourishing future Pentecostal Uganda. PCCs and NRM share an exclusionary societal vision: the sinful, immoral, non-conforming are to be targeted for discipline, reform and legal action. The parallels to neoliberal reform ideology and discourse loom large: individual commitment and all-encompassing reform whose expected benefits justify present hardships.

The remaining chapters in the section show that reforms and their effects have advanced, especially among the youth, neoliberal moral values and subjectivities, and the commodification of cultural, economic and political life. Cultural and political identities have been turned into commodities to be bought by aid organisations, politicians and external 'sponsors'. Foreign actors promoted various aspects of neoliberal culture, including the 'sell-yourself culture' and the, 'neoliberal self'. Corporates have become powerful cultural actors as sponsors and filled the gap left by the state disinvestment in culture. *Vorhölter's* chapter shows how and why young dancers in northern Uganda become 'identity entrepreneurs'. She observes that these cultural groups have learnt to perceive of themselves and consciously act as entrepreneurs, rather than members of a collective entity (kinship, class). They tend to prioritise short-termism, instrumentalism, flexibility, pragmatism and self-interests and often switch cultural styles and political allegiances depending on situational context and according to calculations of expected benefits. There is an erosion of beliefs in, and commitment to, absolute values and long-term loyalties. The economic strategies employed by these youth must be seen against a backdrop of various processes: the monetarisation of not only economic but also social and political life, the dream of living a 'modern' life including consumerist lifestyle being unattainable to most of the youth, and the global discourses of consumption and individual liberties circulated also via the highly present aid industry. Vorhölter argues that the commodification of cultural life is just one example of a broader process, traceable also in political behaviour, as political allegiances are commodified and politicians and voters alike increasingly make choices based on instrumental rationality rather than a commitment to a political programme, values and ideologies.

The imaginary and aspirations of the youth have been impacted by neoliberal discourses, ideologies and formats of producing private and public life, advanced by foreign actors, including TNCs, NGOs and Western states and their respective interests. The gap between optimistic ideology and the harsh reality of neoliberalism led to frustration, anger and ideological disorientation, as well as a search for ideological clarity. Frustrations about the realities of jobless growth are felt particularly by the youth. Contrarily to what they had been promised, education has hardly been a way out of rural poverty. Young Ugandans were told that if they had a degree they stood a good chance of getting a job in the sense of formal employment, with the security attached to a monthly wage. *Jones'* portrait of the lived reality of educated male youth in a rural district shows a clash between material reality and imaginary. He argues that the material realities of the educated youth revolve around farming, occasional wage work in the rural town and the family obligations and social networks which are not only part of a shared past, but also a manifestation of the narrowing of social space and the disproportionate reliance on social networks for access to social services analysed earlier in this collection. He argues that farming takes up a considerable share of this youth's time, but it is absent from their conversations and leisurely activities in public spaces, which are instead oriented towards the imitation of urban and cosmopolitan lifestyles typical of the wealthy. The imaginary of these young men is made of unfulfilled, frustrated aspirations on salaried employment and the associated urban and Westernised lifestyle.

Finally, *Pier*'s chapter shows how the art sector, grossly under-funded by government, is now influenced by corporate sponsorship of national cultural events that supposedly strengthen national coher-ence and identity, and draw in the cooperation of all sorts of local actors from schools to politicians who tend to praise the sponsor and thus become part of the corporate participatory marketing campaigns. He observes a fusing of commercialism and nation-alism, as campaigns tap into the sense of patriotism and regional pride of participants that get a chance to present their home region and its traditional culture on stage to a national audience under corporate lights and compete both for prize money and recognition. These emotion-tapping campaigns spread their highly commercial atmosphere deep into rural areas, capturing the imaginary of the youth and are thus a significant force in subjectivity formation. Pier notes an appropriation of cultural institutions for corporate profit interests. Further, the not-for-profit arts initiatives conducted by foreign-led NGOs also have a pro-neoliberal effect, in particular in terms of the full embrace of radical forms of individualism, an expressive, rights-bearing self, and cultural and spatial mobility. This is true for the National Theatre in Kampala but also in 'up-country' locations. The National Theatre has become a cosmopolitan space that celebrates global movement and entrepreneurial fluidity, with the artistic energy increasingly projected outward, toward a global cosmopolitan community, rather than inward toward the peoples of the nation in the name of producing a national spirit and binding the diverse and fissiparous Ugandan cultures and interests into some-thing solid and durable.

Note

1   The latest statistics and projec-tions on Uganda continue to illustrate some of the politics characterising the New Uganda. For example, the recent *Global Growth Projections* ranking by the Centre for International Development (CID) at Harvard University placed Uganda as the second fastest growing economy in the period to 2026, only topped by India (7.5 per cent vs. 7.89 per cent growth p.a.). Other statistics and rankings indicate

for example that Uganda will be one of the best performing *wealth markets* in Africa in the next decade (AfrAsia Bank Wealth Report); or that the country is doing relatively well in a ranking on *economic complexity* (position 75 out of 127 countries in 2016, up from position 101 out of 117 in 2006; Harvard University). In contrast with this, alternative data – what can be called counter-figures – are circulated by citizens and observers, for instance on independent media, and on social networks (Twitter, Facebook, etc.). For example, a ranking produced by global economic analysis and forecasting firm FocusEconomics listed Uganda as the third poorest country worldwide (based on GDP per capita calculations at a projected USD 738 in 2018). While the Harvard growth study emphasises a national level macroeconomic indicator, the FocusEconomics study uses a per capita indicator, which shows

the average distribution of GDP divided by the number of people (the latest government figure of this indicator is USD 797 for the FY 2017/18). We do not wish to go into academic debates concerning which indicator is 'better' (i.e. more appropriate to determine the increase or decrease of wellbeing and wealth in a country like Uganda), but, again, note the importance of paying attention to (i) who produces, interprets, disseminates and uses data, and how, and (ii) the power relations, political and economic interests, discourses etc. that characterise Uganda's data politics. A final indicator then: the United Nations Development Programme's *Human Development Index* for Uganda increased by 0.216 (from 0.3 to 0.516) between 1990 and 2017. The country is currently in position 162 – thus in the low human development country grouping (less than 0.550) – in a ranking of 189 countries (2017).

References

Aglietta, M. (1999), *A Theory of Capitalist Regulation: The US Experience* (London: Verso).

Anderson, D. M. and Fisher, J. (2016), 'Authoritarianism and the securitization of development in Uganda', in T. Hagmann and F. Reyntjens (eds) *Aid and Authoritarianism in Africa: Development without Democracy* (London: Zed).

Andrews, M. and Bategeka, L. (2013), 'Overcoming the limits of institutional reform in Uganda', ESID Working Paper No. 27, University of Manchester.

Asiimwe, G. B. (2002), *The Impact of Post-colonial Policy Shifts in Coffee Marketing at the Local Level in Uganda: A Case Study of Mukono*

District, 1962–1998 (Maastricht: Shaker).

Bategeka, L., Kiiza, J. and Kasirye, I. (2013), 'Institutional constraints to agricultural development in Uganda', Economic Policy Research Centre, Kampala.

Bayliss, K., Fine, B. and Van Aeyenberge, E. (eds) (2011), *The Political Economy of Development: The World Bank, Neoliberalism and Development Research* (London: Pluto).

Beresford, A. (2015), 'Power, patronage, and gatekeeper politics in South Africa', *African Affairs*, 114(455), pp. 226–48.

Bernstein, H. (2010) *Class Dynamics of Agrarian Change* (Winnipeg: Fernwood Publishers).

Bond, P. (2004), *Looting Africa* (Pietermaritzburg: University of KwaZulu-Natal Press).

Bond, P. (2014a), 'Africans rising against Africa rising', *Forschungsjournal Soziale Bewegungen*, 3.

Bond, P. (2014b), *Elite Transition: From Apartheid to Neoliberalism in South Africa* (London: Pluto).

Boyd, L. (2015), *Preaching Prevention: Born-Again Christianity and the Moral Politics of AIDS in Uganda* (Athens, OH: Ohio University Press).

Branch, A. (2011), *Displacing Human Rights: War and Intervention in Northern Uganda* (Oxford: Oxford University Press).

Branch, A. and Mampilly, Z. C. (2015), *Africa Uprising: Popular Protest and Political Change* (London: Zed).

Brett, E. A. (1972), *Colonialism and Underdevelopment in East Africa* (London: Oxford University Press).

Brett, E. A. (1998), 'Responding to poverty in Uganda: Structures, policies and prospects', *Journal of International Affairs*, 52(1), pp. 313–37.

Bukenya, B. and Muhumuza, W. (2017), 'The politics of core sector public reform in Uganda: Behind the façade', ESID Working Paper No. 85, University of Manchester.

Bush, R. (forthcoming), 'Researching the countryside: Farmers, farming and social transformation in a time of economic liberalization', in F. Cavatorta and J. Clark (eds) *The Methodological and Ethical Challenges of Conducting Research in the Middle East and North Africa* (Oxford: Oxford University Press).

Campbell, B. and Loxley, J. (1989), *Structural Adjustment in Africa* (New York, NY: St. Martin's Press).

Castel-Branco, C.N. (2014), 'Growth, capital accumulation and economic porosity in Mozambique: Social losses, private gains', *Review of African Political Economy*, 41(1), pp. 26–48.

Cavanagh, C. and Benjaminsen, T. A. (2015), 'Guerrilla agriculture? A biopolitical guide to illicit cultivation within an IUCN Category II protected area', *Journal of Peasant Studies*, 42(3–4), pp. 725–45.

Chomsky, N. (1997), 'Market democracy in a neoliberal order: Doctrines and reality', *Z Magazine*, November.

Cliffe, L. (1976), 'Rural political economy of Africa', in I. Wallerstein and P. C. W. Gutkind (eds) *The Political Economy of Contemporary Africa* (London: Sage), pp. 112–30.

Cliffe, L. (1977), 'Rural class formation in East Africa', *Journal of Peasant Studies*, 4(2), pp. 195–224.

Collini, S. (2016), 'Who are the spongers now?', *London Review of Books*, 38(2), 21 January, pp. 33–37.

Daily Monitor. (2010), 'Man, 75, hangs self after losing money', 25 March.

Daily Monitor. (2011), 'Suicide on the rise in eastern Uganda, say police', 22 July.

Daily Monitor. (2014), 'Woman jumps to death at workers house', 25 December.

Daily Monitor. (2016), 'Six out of your 10 friends have thought of committing suicide', 23 September.

Daily Monitor. (2017a), 'Pregnant mother falls off mango tree, dies', 21 April.

Daily Monitor. (2017b), '3.4 million more Ugandans slip into poverty', 28 September.

Daily Monitor. (2017c), 'Suicide cases on the rise in Masaka', 25 November.

Daily Monitor. (2018), 'Poverty level increases to 21.4 per cent, says UBOS', 18 January.

Ddumba-Ssentamu, J. (2002), 'Economic liberalisation in

Uganda: The recent experience and challenges', in N. B. Musisi and C. P. Dodge (eds) *Transformations in Uganda* (Kampala: MISR), pp. 57–76.

Dean, M. (2002), 'Liberal government and authoritarianism', *Economy and Society*, 31(1), pp. 37–61.

Deininger, K. and Okidi J. (2003), 'Growth and poverty reduction in Uganda 1992–2000: Panel data evidence', *Development Policy Review*, 21(4), pp. 481–509.

Dolan, C. (2009), *Social Torture: The Case of Northern Uganda, 1986–2006* (New York, NY: Berghahn).

Dunn, B. (2016), 'Against neoliberalism as a concept', *Capital & Class*, 41(3).

The Economist, (2011), 'The hopeful continent: Africa rising', *The Economist*, 3 December.

Ferguson, J. (2006), *Global Shadows: Africa in the Neoliberal World Order* (Durham, NC and London: Duke University Press).

Ferguson, J. (2015), *Give a Man a Fish: Reflections on the New Politics of Distribution* (Durham, NC and London: Duke University Press).

Fine, B. (2010), 'Locating financialisation', *Historical Materialism*, 18(2), pp. 97–116.

Finnström, S. (2008), *Living with Bad Surroundings: War, History, and Everyday Moments in Northern Uganda* (Durham, NC: Duke University Press).

Fisher, J. (2013), '"Some more reliable than others": Image management, donor perceptions and the global war on terror in East African diplomacy', *Journal of Modern African Studies*, 51(1), pp. 1–31.

Fisher, J. (2014), 'Uganda's war, Obama's advisers and the nature of "influence" in Western foreign policy-making', *Third World Quarterly*, 35(4), pp. 686–704.

Gill, S. (1995), 'Globalisation, market civilisation, and disciplinary neoliberalism', *Millennium*, 24(3), pp. 399–423.

Golooba-Mutebi, F. and Hickey S. (2013), 'Investigating the links between political settlements and inclusive development in Uganda: Towards a research agenda', ESID Working Paper No. 20, University of Manchester.

Government of Uganda (GoU). (2014), *Poverty Status Report 2014* (Kampala: GOU).

Greco, E. (2015), 'Landlords in the making: Class dynamics of the land grab in Mbarali, Tanzania', *Review of African Political Economy*, 42(144), pp. 225–44.

Halvorsen, T. (2017), 'International co-operation and the democratization of knowledge', in T. Halvorsen and J. Nossum (eds), *North–South Knowledge Networks: Towards Equitable Collaboration between Academics, Donors and Universities* (Cape Town: African Minds), 277–309.

Hansen, H. and Twaddle, M. (eds) (1991), *Changing Uganda* (Kampala: Fountain).

Hansen, H. B. and Twaddle, M. (eds) (1998), *Developing Uganda* (Oxford: James Currey).

Harrison, G. (2004), *World Bank and Africa: The Construction of Governance States* (London: Routledge).

Harrison, G. (2005), 'Economic faith, social project, and a misreading of African society: The travails of neoliberalism in Africa', *Third World Quarterly*, 26(8), pp. 1303–20.

Harrison, G. (2010), *Neoliberal Africa: The Impact of Global Social Engineering* (London: Zed).

Harvey, D. (2005). *Neoliberalism: A Brief History* (Oxford: Oxford University Press).

Harvey, D. (2007), 'Neoliberalism as creative destruction', *The ANNALS of the American Academy of Political and Social Sciences*, 610(21), pp. 22–44.

Heller, H. (2016), *The Capitalist University: The Transformation of*

Higher Education in the United States 1945–2016 (London: Pluto).

Hickey, S. (2005), 'The politics of staying poor: Exploring the political space for poverty reduction in Uganda', *World Development*, 33(6), pp. 995–1009.

Hickey, S. (2013), 'Beyond the poverty agenda? Insights from the new politics of development in Uganda', *World Development*, 43, pp. 194–206.

Hickey, S. and Izama, A. (2017), 'The politics of governing oil in Uganda: Going against the grain?', *African Affairs*, 116(463), pp. 163–85.

IMF. (2000a), 'Press release: HIPC debt relief for Uganda increased to a total of US$2 billion: Additional relief for Uganda's poverty reduction programs', 8 February.

IMF. (2000b), 'Press Release: IMF and World Bank support debt relief for Uganda', 2 May.

IMF. (2013), 'Multilateral debt relief initiative – questions and answers', Available at: www.imf.org/external/np/exr/mdri/eng/index.htm [last updated 5 August 2013].

IMF. (2014), 'Africa Rising – Building the Future'. IMF Conference, May 2014, Maputo, Available at: www.africa-rising.org/ [accessed 10 October 2016].

James, D. (2014), *Money from Nothing: Indebtedness and Aspiration in South Africa* (Palo Alto, CA: Stanford University Press).

Jerven, M. (2013), *Poor Numbers: How We Are Mislead by African Development Statistics* (Ithaca, NY: Cornell University Press).

Jerven, M. (2015), *Why Economists Get It Wrong* (London: Zed).

Jones, B. (2009), *Beyond the State in Rural Uganda* (Edinburgh: Edinburgh University Press).

Journal of Eastern African Studies (JEAS). (2016), Special issue: The NRM regime and the 2016 Ugandan elections, 10(4).

Kappel, R., Lay, J. and Steiner, S. (2005), 'Uganda: No more pro-poor growth?', *Development Policy Review*, 23(1), pp. 27–53.

Khisa, M. (2015), 'Political uncertainty and its impact on social service delivery in Uganda', *Africa Development*, 40(4), pp. 159–88.

Kiiza, J., Makara, S. and Rakner, L. (eds) (2008), *Electoral Democracy in Uganda: Understanding Institutional Processes and Outcomes of the 2006 Multiparty Elections* (Kampala: Fountain).

Kuteesa, F. *et al.* (2009), *Uganda's Economic Reforms: Insider Accounts* (Oxford: Oxford University Press).

Lagarde, C. (2017), 'Becoming the champion: Uganda's development challenge', January 27.

Lie, J. H. S. (2015), *Developmentality: An Ethnography of the World Bank–Uganda Partnership* (New York, NY: Berghahn).

Mamdani, M. (1976), *Politics and Class Formation in Uganda* (New York, NY: Monthly Review Press).

Mamdani, M. (1987), 'Extreme but not exceptional: Towards an analysis of the agrarian question in Uganda', *Journal of Peasant Studies*, 14(2), pp. 191–225.

Mamdani, M. (1995), *And Fire Does Not Always Beget Ash: Critical Reflections on the NRM* (Kampala: Monitor).

Mamdani, M. (2007), *Scholars in the Market Place: The Dilemmas of Neoliberal Market Reform at Makerere University 1989–2005* (Dakar: CODESRIA).

Mamdani, M. (2011), 'The importance of research in a university', MISR Working Paper No. 3, Kampala.

Martiniello, G. (2013), 'Accumulation by dispossession and resistance in Northern Uganda', MISR Working Paper No. 11, Kampala.

Martiniello, G. (2015a), 'Food sovereignty as a praxis? Rethinking the food question in Uganda',

Third World Quarterly, 36(3), pp. 508–25.

Martiniello, G. (2015b), 'Social struggles in Uganda's Acholiland: Understanding responses and resistance to Amuru Sugar Works', *Journal of Peasant Studies*, 42(3–4), pp. 653–69.

Mhone, G. (2001), 'Labour market discrimination and its aftermath in Southern Africa', UNRISD Conference Paper, Geneva, Durban, 3–5 September.

Mitchell, T. (2002), *The Rule of Experts: Egypt, Techno-politics and Modernity* (Berkeley, CA: University of California Press).

Mittelman, J. (2013), 'The global transformation of universities: Racing for the top', Public Lecture, MISR, Kampala, 22 May.

Mkandawire, T. and Olukoshi, A. (eds) (1995), *Between Liberalisation and Oppression: The Politics of Structural Adjustment in Africa* (Dakar: CODESRIA).

Moretti, F. and Pestre, D. (2015), 'The language of World Bank reports', *New Left Review*, 92, pp. 75–99.

Muhereza, F. (2015), 'The December 2010 "Balaalo" evictions from Buliisa district and the challenges of agrarian transformation in Uganda', MISR Working Papers No. 17, Kampala.

Muhumuza, F. (2016), 'How weak is our economy if 30.6m Ugandans live on less than $3 a day?', *Daily Monitor*, 15 March.

Museveni, Y. K. (2000), *What Is Africa's Problem?* (Minneapolis, MN: University of Minnesota Press).

Museveni, Y. K. (2007) [1997], *Sowing the Mustard Seed: The Struggle for Freedom and Democracy in Uganda*. Revised edition (Oxford: Macmillan).

Mwenda, A. (2016), 'Uganda's economic growth dilemma', *The Independent*, 8 July.

Mwenda, A. M. and Tangri, R.

(2005), 'Patronage politics, donor reforms, and regime consolidation in Uganda', *African Affairs*, 104(416), pp. 449–67.

Nabudere, D. W. (1981), *Imperialism and Revolution in Uganda* (Dar es Salaam: Tanzania Publishing House).

National Resistance Movement (NRM). (2016), *NRM Manifesto 2016–2021. Steady Progress: Taking Uganda to Modernity through Job-Creation and Inclusive Development*.

Nuwagaba, A. and Muhumuza, F. (2017), *Who Is Growing? Ending Inequality in Uganda. A Study of the Drivers of Inequality in Uganda* (Kampala: Oxfam).

Okidi, J. A. *et al.* (2007), 'Uganda's experience with operationalizing pro-poor growth, 1992 to 2003', in T. Besley and L. J. Cord (eds) *Delivering on the Promise of Pro-poor Growth: Insights and Lessons from Country Experiences* (New York, NY: Palgrave), pp. 169–98.

Olukhoshi, A. (2007), 'Enclavity', in P. Bond (ed.), *Beyond Enclavity in African Economies: The Enduring Work of Guy Mhone* (Durban: Centre for Civil Society), pp. 7–24.

Onimode, B. (1989), *The IMF, the World Bank and African Debt: The Economic Impact* (vol. 1); *The Social and Political Impact* (vol. 2) (London: Institute for African Alternatives and Zed).

Opongo, E. O. (2013), 'Historical dynamics of the northern Uganda conflict: A longitudinal struggle for nation building', in K. Omeje and T. R. Hepner (eds), *Conflict and Peacebuilding in Africa's Great Lakes Region* (Bloomington, IN: Indiana University Press), pp. 85–105.

Perrot, S., Makara, S. and Lafargue, J. (eds) (2014), *Elections in a Hybrid Regime: Revisiting the 2011 Ugandan Polls* (Kampala: Fountain).

Perry, A. (2012), 'Africa rising', *Time*, 3 December.

Pier, D. G. (2015), *Ugandan Music in the Marketing Era: The Branded Arena* (New York, NY: Palgrave).

Poteete, A.R. and Ribot, J.C. (2011), 'Repertoires of domination: Decentralization as process in Botswana and Senegal', *World Development*, 39(3), pp. 439–49.

Pruce, K. (2014), 'Closing the gap between form and function: A new approach to institutional reform in Uganda', ESID Briefing Paper No. 2, University of Manchester.

Reinikka, R. and Collier, P. (eds) (2001), *Uganda's Recovery: The Role of Farms, Firms and Government* (Kampala: Fountain).

Robison, R. (ed.) (2006). *The Neoliberal Revolution: Forging the Market State* (London: Palgrave).

Rubongoya, J. B. (2007), *Regime Hegemony in Museveni's Uganda: Pax Musevenica* (New York, NY: Palgrave).

Sachs, J. (2005), *The End of Poverty: How We Can Make It Happen in Our Lifetime* (London: Penguin).

Saul, J. S. (1976), 'The unsteady state: Uganda, Obote and General Amin', *Review of African Political Economy*, 3(5), pp. 12–38.

Severino, J.-M. and Ray, O. (2011), *Africa's Moment* (Cambridge: Polity).

Sjögren, A. (2013), *Between Militarism and Technocratic Governance: State Formation in Contemporary Uganda* (Kampala: Fountain).

Springer, S., Birch, K. and MacLeavy, J. (eds) (2016a), *The Handbook of Neoliberalism* (London: Routledge).

Springer, S., Birch, K. and MacLeavy, J. (2016b), 'An introduction to neoliberalism', in S. Springer, K. Birch and J. MacLeavy (eds) *The Handbook of Neoliberalism* (London: Routledge).

Szeftel, M. (2000), 'Accumulation and Africa's "catastrophic corruption"', *Review of African Political Economy*, 27(84), pp. 287–306.

Tacca, A. (2016), 'Will Uganda remain a vampire state for another five years?', *Daily Monitor*, 21 February.

Tangri, R., and Mwenda, A. M. (2013), *The Politics of Elite Corruption in Africa: Uganda in Comparative African Perspective* (New York, NY: Routledge).

Tidemand, P. (1994), 'The resistance councils in Uganda: A study of rural politics and popular democracy in Africa'. PhD Thesis, Department of Development Studies, Roskilde University.

Tosh, J. (1978), 'Lango agriculture during the early colonial period: Land and labour in a cash crop economy', *Journal of African History*, 14(3), pp. 473–90.

Tripp, A. M. (2000), *Women and Politics in Uganda* (Oxford: James Currey).

Tripp, A. M. (2010), *Museveni's Uganda: Paradoxes of Power in a Hybrid Regime* (Boulder, CO: Lynne Rienner).

Twinoburyo, E. N. (2018), 'Income, food poverty on the rise: The 2020 target to be missed', *New Vision*, 3 April.

UNDP. (2013), *Human Development Report. The Rise of the South: Human Progress in a Diverse World* (New York, NY: UNDP).

Veltmeyer, H. and Petras, J. (eds) (2014), *The New Extractivism: Post-Neoliberal Development Model or Imperialism of the Twenty-first Century?* (London: Zed).

Westoby, P. and Lyons, K. (2016), '"We would rather die in jail fighting for land, than die of hunger": A case study examining the ambiguous role of corporate-led community development in the bio-green economy', *Community Development Journal*, 51(1), pp. 60–76.

Whyte, D. and Wiegratz, J. (2016), 'The moral economy of neoliberal fraud', in D. Whyte and J. Wiegratz (eds) *Neoliberalism and the Moral*

Economy of Fraud (London: Routledge), pp. 229–52.

Wiegratz, J. (2009), *Uganda's Human Resource Challenge: Training, Business Culture and Economic Development* (Kampala: Fountain).

Wiegratz, J. (2010), 'Fake capitalism? The dynamics of neoliberal moral restructuring and pseudo-development: The case of Uganda', *Review of African Political Economy*, 37(124), pp. 123–37.

Wiegratz, J. (2016), *Neoliberal Moral Economy: Capitalism, Socio-cultural Change and Fraud in Uganda* (London: Rowman & Littlefield).

Williams, D. and Young, T. (1994), 'Governance, the World Bank and liberal theory', *Political Studies*, 42(1), pp. 84–100.

Wood, E. M. (1981), 'The separation of the economic and the political in capitalism', *New Left Review*, 1(127), pp. 67–95.

World Bank. (2010), *Country Assistance Strategy for the Republic of Uganda for the Period FY 2011–2015* (Washington, DC: World Bank).

World Bank. (2017), 'Uganda – Overview', Available at: www.worldbank.org/en/country/uganda/overview [accessed 10 April 2017].

Part I

The state, donors and development aid

I
Donor-driven state formation: friction in the World Bank–Uganda partnership

Jon Harald Sande Lie

Introduction[1]

The formation of neoliberal Uganda has been highly influenced by external development actors, their changing policy priorities and new modalities for delivering aid. Since the turn of the millennium, following the World Bank's 1997 Development Report *The State in a Changing World*, the Bank's emphasis changed from 'getting the market right' through state deregulation to 'getting the state right' (Moore 1999) by promoting good governance policies addressing the client state's internal affairs (Doornbos 2003). This policy shift coincided with changes at the structural level of aid, evolving into what has been labelled the new aid architecture (Mosse 2005, Lie 2015b): instead of the donor imposing its policies on passive aid recipients, the partner government was now to take an active part in formulating and implementing its own development strategy while the donor withdrew to a role as funder and controller of the government's initiatives. This partnership modality entailed consigning power from donor to recipient, turning passive clients into active agents, granting governments greater freedoms and responsibilities in their partnership with the World Bank and other bilateral donors.

In Uganda, the new aid architecture got its particular and contextual rendering. In the formation of the World Bank–Uganda partnership in the mid-2000s, which is the scope of this chapter, the Bank struggled to reconcile conveying greater freedoms and responsibilities to the Government of Uganda while simultaneously ensuring the government would commit to the Bank's prioritised good governance policies. To overcome this challenge, the World Bank started to employ new, tacit and indirect governance mechanisms through which the Bank aimed to make its own policies those of the recipient. These mechanisms were premised on the Bank's ability to frame the partnership formation and the conditions under which the Ugandan government could exercise the freedom it had been granted to devise its own development strategy. The mechanisms employed are reminiscent of Foucault's notion of governmentality as the 'conduct of conduct' (1991). I refer to this indirect power as 'developmentality' (Lie 2015a, 2015b, see the coda section below) in order to disengage and broaden Foucault's focus on state power (de Carvalho 2016), and to address the particularities, intentions and effects of the new aid architecture. Developmentality evolved in the nexus of freedom and control, participation and conditionality, as the Bank employed new public management structures to be able to 'govern at a distance' (Rose and Miller 1992: 181). These neoliberal governance structures enabled the Bank to pay heed to the new aid architecture's rhetoric of national ownership while retaining influence over the government's own policies. Central here is the use and framing of national ownership, where ownership, according to a donor informant, 'exists when they do as we want them to do, but they do so voluntarily' (cited in Randel et al. 2002: 8). As the Ugandan government gradually adopted the Bank's policies and procedures, it was increasingly put under external supervision – and instead of acting on behalf of and being accountable to its citizens, the government has increasingly become accountable to its external donors and the Bank in particular.

The practices and effects of the new aid architecture have been instrumental in the formation of neoliberal Uganda. First, this chapter outlines some brief historical background, including the main girding tenets of the new aid architecture as manifested in the Poverty Reduction Strategy Paper (PRSP), being the new disbursement tactic of the Bank to which Uganda soon became a pilot country. The second part explores how Uganda's existing development strategy was adopted as the country's PRSP but gradually came to bear the imprint of the Bank's template. The third part demonstrates the practical partnership encounter between the Bank and its Ugandan counterpart. These two parts together shows the working of developmentality, which is returned to in the final coda section.

A donor darling meets the new aid architecture

Uganda was until 2005 celebrated as a donor darling, a success story and a showcase for Western-led development efforts (Cargil 2004, Dijkstra and van Donge 2001, Harrison 2001, Kuteesa et al. 2010). There are at least three important reasons for this. First, the Ugandan government has, since Museveni assumed power in 1986, been quite successful in promoting poverty reduction, economic growth and social and political stability, while also crafting a new Constitution that, at least partly, reinstalled democratic rule. As emphasised in this book's introduction, this brought about much needed political stability and continuity at the helm of the state, being important prerequisites for both state formation but also the state's international relations. Second, and interrelated, Museveni won donors' praise for his ideological affinity with Western development discourses and for adopting donors' structural adjustment programmes demanding reforms to cut government spending, liberalise the economy and privatise state enterprises – all the while he talked about African self-reliance and independence from donordriven reforms. Third, the extolment of Uganda was also driven by factors external to Uganda: the geopolitical momentum and rationale of the international development apparatus was lost with the end of the Cold War, pressuring donors to demonstrate results to maintain moral and economic support at home. Combined, these factors led to a massive increase of foreign aid and actors to Uganda from the mid-1990s by donors wanting to be part of and contribute to the success story.

When the World Bank in 1999 rolled out its new partnership model and disbursement tactic centred around a nationally produced Poverty Reduction Strategy Paper (PRSP), Uganda was chosen as one among five pilot countries. The government's existing Poverty Eradication Action Plan (PEAP) was soon to be transformed into the country's PRSP. This – being an expression of the new aid architecture's focus on partnership, participation and ownership – thus marked a radical shift from donors' previous hands-on engagement with a plethora of small projects, to the support of the government's own strategy in the form of direct budget support. In the 2000–2005 period 48–53 per cent of the Ugandan national budget was provided for by external development assistance, thus giving external actors significant influence and leverage over Ugandan state formation and the government's own policies and processes (Mwenda 2010, Rubongoya 2007).

In 2005 Uganda's partnership relation with the international development donor community was critically challenged, effectively reconstructing the donor image of Uganda as a show case and donor darling. Since 1986 Uganda enjoyed largely cordial relations with the international donor community. These relations derailed during the political transition of 2005 when Museveni announced that he would alter the Constitution to lift the two-term limitation on the presidency, allowing him to run for a third term in office. The World Bank has a particular apolitical mandate, restraining it from involvement in its counterparts' domestic political affairs. Simultaneously, and perhaps paradoxically, it also stresses the good governance agenda, through which it seeks to shape client governments according to a particular standard. Museveni's bid to alter the Constitution, allowing him to participate in the 2006 election, triggered a harsh response among donors, including the World Bank, epitomising how external actors in the name of development seek to influence their counterpart's state formation processes despite Uganda's partnership relations with international aid agencies that are founded on the principles of national self-determination and domestic ownership to the externally funded development strategy. The 2005 events amplified and made visible how external actors are involved in internal political processes. The conditions for this are, however, the result of the general World Bank–Uganda partnership formation since 1999, where processes enhancing the Ugandan government's self-determination and freedom have been accompanied with mechanisms and procedures through which the Bank seeks to make its policies those of its Ugandan counterpart. This indirect governance – or developmentality (Lie 2015a, 2015b) – is both enabled by and undermining the new aid architecture.

The new aid architecture refers to certain general changes at the structural and policy level of international aid (Mosse 2005, Lie 2015a) that also came to influence Uganda's relationship with foreign donors. First, the new aid architecture involves donors' withdrawal from running their own project to route their funding through aid receiving partners in support of their policies and procedures, turning erstwhile passive clients into active agents. Second, it involved greater attention to policy and public sector reforms rather than conventional investment projects, as illustrated by the emphasis given to good governance policies. Third, it meant going beyond the conventional economic growth paradigm to a wider attention to poverty reduction. Fourth, it entails a move from *ex post* to *ex ante* conditionality, meaning that aid is disbursed only after policies and processes have been sufficiently implemented: aid is not assisting implementation but rather serves as an incentive mechanism in rewarding good performance (Sending and Lie 2015). The new aid architecture thus epitomises what has been called the transition from first- to second-generation reform (Harrison 2004) – akin to what Atkinson in this volume refers to as the first and second phase of neoliberal Uganda – where the ethos is that 'process' is as important as 'policy', and where the aid relation involves constructing 'an appropriate system of government to allow governance states to absorb and operationalise funds and technical assistance' (Harrison 2004: 21).

The PRSP model represents the World Bank's operationalisation of the new aid architecture. Incepted in 1999, it aimed to alter asymmetrical aid relations through changes at both the structural and policy levels of aid. It departs from the Washington consensus era of structural adjustment where the Bank's imposed privatisation and liberalisation policies not only bypassed the state in the planning process but also aimed to dismantle state structures. The PRSP reinstates the role of the state, focusing on the state as both a means and an objective for international development, as illustrated by the dominant discourses of partnership and good governance respectively (Abrahamsen 2004). Bank-driven state formation is challenging not only because of the Bank's apolitical mandate restricting its involvement in a client's domestic political affairs. It is also challenging because the state formation policies of good governance are nominally, as per the PRSP model, supposed to be devised, implemented and 'owned' by the government subject to these policies and reforms. Hence, the difficult task facing Bank bureaucrats under the PRSP regime was how to get their Ugandan counterpart to adopt the prioritised good governance policies without jeopardising the partnership relation and local ownership.

Rolling out the PRSP in Uganda: the formation of PEAP

The Ugandan PRSP was locally dubbed the Poverty Eradication Action Plan (PEAP), which has its particular historical trajectory (Mugambe 2010) (from 2010, the PEAP was renamed the National Development Plan (NDP); NDP I covered the period 2010/11–2014/15, and NDP II, 2015/16–2019/20). The way the World Bank rolled out its PRSP model in Uganda and the way the Ugandan PEAP has changed since it was first adopted as the basis for the Bank's support inform us about how the Government of Uganda poverty reduction strategy's policies and structure have gradually come to resemble those of the Bank.

The Ugandan PEAP was introduced in 1997, two years prior to the inception of the PRSP system. The first PEAP (1997–1999) was largely detached from the Bank's realm and indeed a sovereign product of the Government of Uganda. The second PEAP (2000–2004) served as Uganda's first PRSP, marking its entry point into the new aid architecture. By the time the third PEAP (2004/5–2008/9) was adopted, the Bank's PRSP model had been fully engrained into it in both structure and policy.

The first PEAP established the government's policy framework for poverty eradication until 2017, far exceeding the PRSP's midterm outlook. It presumably drew on a consultative process initiated by President Museveni in 1995, when he mobilised members of parliament, government ministers and donors and took them to the Luwero triangle north of Kampala (Museveni 1997) to show them the poor state of roads, schools, dispensaries, infrastructure and the extent of poverty in the region. From this process, the government largely managed to align donors to the idea of a national poverty strategy, as formulated in the 1997 PEAP. In 1999, the government formulated a new development plan, *Vision 2025*, with an overview of long-term goals and aspirations, epitomised as 'prosperous people, harmonious nation and beautiful country' (MFPED 1999). While this provided the vision, the PEAP established the operational policy framework for poverty reduction in a two-decade perspective. To most donors and government representatives, the historical trajectory of PEAP and in particular its precedence to the Bank's PRSP model have somewhat different meanings. To the donors it signals strong national ownership, commitment and leadership of the PEAP with regard to both its creation and implementation. The PEAP is praised as 'homebrewed' and a sovereign product of a government showing willingness to reform. Among government officials, the same historical trajectory is read as it was Uganda and not the Bank that came up with the idea of a comprehensive national strategy.

The PRSP framework was launched in January 1999. Already in December 1999 the government started revising its existing PEAP planned to last until 2017, allegedly because it recognised that 'the poor had not been sufficiently consulted' (Isooba and Ssewakiryanga 2005). The Bank's need for a PRSP pilot country should, however, not be disregarded as a motive. The revision process went unprecedentedly fast: a draft version was presented in March 2000 and already in May the Bank and IMF approved a *summary* of the revised PEAP as the Ugandan PRSP. The tedious and rigid Bank procedures were bypassed because there was a shared understanding between the government and the Bank that Uganda should be a pilot country with effect already from 1999. While a driving factor for the Bank was that it needed willing pilot countries – preferably showcase countries already demonstrating willingness to comply with

Bank policies – the Ugandan government needed funding for its development strategy. The government was also lured by two tasty carrots. First, that funding under the PRSP regime would come as budget support. Second, that being a PRSP country meant inclusion in the much-coveted debt relief programme (the Heavily Indebted Poor Countries/HIPC initiative, started in 1996, made cancelling of previous debt conditional on having a PRSP accepted by the Bank), increasing to an aggregate level of approximately US\$ 2 billion 'as soon as Uganda has finalized a poverty reduction strategy paper ... which has been broadly endorsed by the Boards of the World Bank and IMF' (IMF 2000).

While the first PEAP was fast-tracked in the Bank system into a PRSP, the revision of PEAP II was much more extensive and characteristic of the traditional Bank–client interface. Although the second PEAP was to run throughout 2004, the revision process started already in November 2002. First came the formulation of a Poverty Status Report, now installed as a biannual event undertaken by the Ministry of Finance, Planning and Economic Development (MoFPED), as the body responsible for overseeing and implementing the PEAP, to present evidence on progress towards the targets spelled out in the PEAP. This revision included contributions from NGOs because of the Bank's demand for increased civil society participation. Second, driven by the rationale of both maintaining control over the revision process and creating a node for internal (domestic actors) and external (with donors) PEAP communication, the MoFPED established a PEAP secretariat to ensure it was on top of the process.

The revision process started in mid-July 2003 with a 'stakeholders' workshop' where a new design for further decentralised consultation emerged. The Bank referred to its PRSP model, requiring planning and consultations to extend beyond the government to include district and local government, the private sector and civil society organisations. These consultations were divided into fourteen sectoral working groups, reflecting the sectors spelled out in the Bank's PRSP template. All these requirements were skipped in the first PEAP revision process due to the need to fast-track the process, but given ample attention in the second revision process. In this process the Ugandan PEAP is increasingly inscribed into the Bank's realm in process, form and content despite the ownership rhetoric. The government's poverty reduction strategy is gradually detached from the government's sovereign domain with significant imprints from both external actors but also domestic, non-state actors.

The many required consultations made the PEAP revision more extensive, comprehensive and challenging, thus impeding the process. Although the PEAP secretariat outlined a strict timeframe for preparing PEAP III by the end of 2003, it took a year from the launch of the revision process and one and a half years after consultation before the third PEAP was finalised (see Ssewakiryanga 2004). The government restrained the involvement of civil society organisations (CSOs). These organisations thus turned to the Bank, referring the PRSP idea of inclusive and participatory processes, whereupon the Bank would demand the government to include the CSOs – thus demonstrating how the politics of participation is externally driven (Isooba 2005: 44. Brock 2004) and how the Bank acts as a guardian of procedural matters (Lie 2015b).

The processes from PEAP I to PEAP III have brought to the fore a strategy that increasingly bears the Bank's stamp in terms of procedure, structure, result and jargon – thus underpinning the notion of developmentality and how the Bank increasingly has made its own discourses those of the Ugandan government. The first PEAP outlined various general prioritised programme areas (primary health, rural feeder roads, primary education, provision of safe water and the modernisation of agriculture). By the second PEAP, when it also became accepted as the PRSP, these were renamed 'pillars', in line with the common Bank parlance and its PRSP setup. Pillars represent broad goals for national poverty reduction, of which PEAP II contains four (creating an enabling environment for sustainable economic growth and transformation; promoting security and good governance; directly increasing the ability of the poor to raise their income; directly improving the quality of life of the poor). PEAP III renamed and expanded the number of pillars to five (economic management; production, competitiveness and incomes; security, conflict resolution and disaster management; good governance; human development). These renamed pillars now appear in a language that is closer to that of the Bank and its internal organisation of different, thematically focused knowledge networks: 'directly improving the quality of life of the poor' is now 'human development'; 'creating an enabling environment for sustainable growth and transformation' is now simply 'economic management'. Note also that none of these themes were explicit in the first PEAP, devised by the government before the Bank weighed in. In the second version the topics appeared, and in the third PEAP the Bank's labels and standards are in place.

On the policy level, the most important change relates to *good governance*, referring to the government's process of decision making and the process by which decisions are implemented or not. Good governance is thereby a qualitative measure of the governance environment referring to certain characteristics like participation, government transparency and accountability, political decentralisation and multiparty democracy (Doornbos 2003). Donors' good governance agenda thus concerns the internal workings and practices of the recipient state, and as such in Uganda also involves the overall PEAP process. Good governance became increasingly prominent in Uganda's PEAP parallel to the Bank's growing involvement in the process. While totally absent in the first PEAP and lumped together with 'security' in the second, good governance was singled out as an independent pillar in the third PEAP. There might be various reasons for this. Although the Bank's governance agenda dates back to the mid-1990s it was not until about 2000 that it started to gain momentum and become a significant part of the Bank's lending portfolio, as part and parcel of the PRSP model. As the Bank moved into budget support and the Government of Uganda was granted greater freedoms and responsibilities over the policy-making and implementation process, it became cardinal to the Bank that Uganda had a governance system capable of, and able and willing to manage these tasks in a satisfactory manner. The good governance agenda made it possible for the Bank to deal with the state apparatus' internal procedures of checks-and-balance systems, to maintain some control and minimise misuse of the budget support provided. The temporal change of the PEAP to a mid-term outlook of three to five years in accordance with the PRSP template – in addition to annual benchmarking practices where the Bank assesses the government's performance according to stipulated 'prior actions' (see below) – enabled the Bank to monitor the government's performance and alter its policies on a frequent basis.

The more productive side of the good governance agenda entails state building measures – to build capacities enabling the state to develop itself. This is, however, not without limitation as the measures taken need to abide with the precepts outlined by the Bank's notion of good governance. There are thus both restraining and productive features inherent to the good governance agenda. These evolved parallel to the PRSP model, illustrating how the state has become both a means and an objective for development: the greater the role of the Ugandan government in the overall PRSP process, the more emphasis the Bank puts on internal procedures and the state's ability to conduct these tasks.

The formal order of the PRSP-model is one emphasising national partnership and ownership, to enhance commitment in order to improve aid effectiveness. Yet, as the PEAP I–III trajectory above demonstrates, the PEAP has increasingly come to bear the Bank's imprint on both the policy and structure of the Ugandan poverty reduction strategy. This process demonstrates the more eventual history at the discursive level of how the government gradually has adopted – and thus become responsible for – the Bank's policies and procedures. The next section turns to the practical encounter between the Bank and its Ugandan counterpart, demonstrating the notion of developmentality in practice, being akin to the neoliberal logic of responsibilisation described in this book's chapter by Branch and Yen.

Indirect governance through 'prior actions'

Discrepancies between the formal order and practice of partnership became tangible during my fieldwork in 2005 and 2006; in 2005/6 I did multi-sited ethnographic fieldwork, spending two months in Washington DC within the World Bank's headquarters and ten months (over two periods) in Uganda, spending long periods within the Office of the Prime Minister (OPM), which is the ministry responsible for managing the government's relations with external donor institutions (Lie 2015b). My informants' partnership renderings were compartmentalised as either donor conditionality or national ownership. Both Bank and government representatives insisted on the government's ownership of the Ugandan PEAP, referring to it as 'a good home-brew'. On the other side, government staff also claimed being pushed by the Bank, which was confirmed by Bank-staff who argued for 'gap filling' when the government staff lacked the knowledge, capacity or will to comply with the Bank's established discourses. There is thus a disjuncture between the formal order of partnership and its practical formation. The order and practice of partnership should, however, not be seen as compartmentalised entities as the informal practices that undermine the formal order of participation and ownership are put in place by the PRSP order itself.

One such governance practice draws on the notion of 'prior actions', which are benchmarks or 'soft conditions' that the Ugandan government needs to fulfil before the Bank disburses any funds. This system is part of the PRSP-model, and the prior actions are derived from the government's PEAP. This mechanism enables the Bank to retain a sense of control over what it finances despite its counterpart being responsible for the overall policy making. The system is, however, somewhat more intricate. While the Ugandan government produces its 'own' PRSP, the Bank responds with a country assistance strategy highlighting those of the government's policies it is willing to support. These strategies are, however, only pertinent to the policy level. The financial side of the partnership agreement comes with the Poverty Reduction Support Credit (PRSC), which is solely formulated by the Bank and grants the receiving government the resources to implement those parts of the PRSP the Bank wishes to support: as the PRSC translates into budget support it allows the government to control and prioritise over funds and spending. For the Bank, the PRSC provides an arena to engage in direct policy dialogue with the government when negotiating the progress and achievement of the prior actions. This dialogue occurs four times a year, each representing different stages – identification, pre-appraisal, appraisal and negotiations – of the Bank's annual PRSC process, or mission. The prior actions are redressed and assessed at each stage, and all measures need to be completed before the loan and credit agreements can be signed. The prior actions involve continuous monitoring and evaluation of the government's progress and implementation of its 'own' development strategy. This constitutes a mechanism enabling the Bank to monitor its client's progress and respond to any mismanagement or deviations on a regular basis. Hence, the government's development strategy is under constant surveillance by the Bank, and failure to fulfil these prior actions can result in everything from nothing to aid cuts, discontinuation of budget support or termination of the whole partnership. The Bank does not see prior actions as imposed conditions since they draw on the PRSP and have been defined and agreed upon by the Bank and government together in an early stage of the mission. The Bank sees prior actions as policy measures the country agrees to take before the Bank approves and disburses a loan. Government staff, however, sees them as regular conditions both due to the limited influence they hold over defining them, but also for the practices and effects the prior actions entail.

The Ugandan political transition in 2005/6 made the Bank–government partnership and the discussions over prior actions take a critical turn, thus wrecking the established picture of Uganda and its President Museveni as a donor darling and an African success story. The construction of Uganda as a donor darling happened notwithstanding critical governance concerns prior to 2005, as the Bank's dependence on Uganda as an example of success to legitimise continued aid spending meant turning a blind eye to malpractices in the state apparatus (Harrison 2001). The grave governance issues mounting from 2005, however, compelled the donor community to respond.

The political transition involved three elements, all contentious to the Bank and its apolitical mandate preventing it from interfering in its counterpart's domestic politics. First, that President Museveni altered the constitution, allegedly by bribing several members of parliament, to lift the presidential term limits and allow him to run for a third term in office. Second, that he insisted on holding a costly referendum to reinstall a multiparty political system, albeit no one had voiced any opposition to this transition. Third, was the process leading up to the general and presidential election in early 2006, when the main opposition candidate was harassed by the police and dragged to court several times over what later appeared to be false allegations of treason and rape, thus blocking the opposition's political campaign. In response to this mismanaged political transition, most bilateral donors cut or withheld development aid and notably budget support: in April Britain withheld £5 million in direct budget support due to preliminary concerns about the political transition. Later, Ireland reduced its aid by €3 million and Norway cut $4 million, being one-third of its budget support. The Netherlands reduced its aid by €6 million in November, and in December Sweden made an $8.3 million cut while Britain made an additional £15 million reduction – all with explicit political reasoning. Initially, the Bank did nothing but restate its apolitical mandate restricting involvement in Ugandan domestic politics.

This soon changed when prominent Bank member states and senior staff in DC weighed in indicating that the Ugandan budget support programme might not pass the Bank's board if the main opposition candidate was behind bars, fearing allegations of turning a blind eye to political concerns while giving money to corrupt leaders. Talking about good governance while financing a bad government would not look good to the Bank. Hence, while the board discussion of the credit scheme was postponed until the turmoil was settled, the country team was also told by executive directors at the headquarters level 'to send a message' since the political situation was not conducive to the Bank's polities nor did it provide for any sound policy environment to yield good results. Thus in playing the good governance card, the Bank returned to the prior actions as a means to respond.

The prior actions agreed upon by the Bank and the government now came under renewed scrutiny. At an earlier stage of the mission, three out of eleven prior actions were identified as being either 'at risk' or 'off track', while they need to be considered as 'completed' to pass and release funds. Prior actions are assessed by Bank-staff and represent highly subjective measures of selected PRSP-policies where the Bank would like to see 'improvement', 'progress' or 'satisfactory implementation'. The prior action considered to be off track relates to the PRSP's good governance objective and the role of the Inspectorate of Government. The two anticipated prior actions deemed to be 'at risk' both concerned economic management, i.e. excessive public administration costs and poor alignment of ministries' agricultural reforms. The government, however, did not endorse these assessments, saying they are exaggerated and based on old data, thus requesting the Bank to look into the matter again. The Bank agreed while restating the need to be convinced and observe satisfactory progress in meeting the prior actions. In a meeting between the parties two weeks later, after revisiting the assessments, the Bank representatives claimed to have identified serious governance concerns, too slow progress, lack of commitment and a government performing poorly vis-à-vis its own policies. However, about a month later and when finalising the loan portfolio an updated assessment of the prior actions was provided. To the government's delight, all prior actions were now marked as 'completed', including those previously deemed as 'at risk' or 'off track' – with one exception: the prior action on 'budget execution' was downgraded from 'on track' to 'partially met' because the public administration expenditures exceeded budget. This did not surprise those in the government given their extra expenses with the recent census emplaced on them by the Bank and the preparations for the referendum and general election. The Bank, however, saw this only as bad financial management and that the government lacked the ability to monitor and control its own budget.

This was perhaps a minor thing, but when the loan agreement finally was brought before the Bank's board – delayed nearly five months – 'the directors approved a ten percent reduction of the PRSC amount to US$135 million to reflect their concern about expenditure overruns in the public administration budget' (Daily Monitor 2006). This meant cutting US$15 million, which came as a surprise to most of the actors involved. The government was shocked by this harsh response, forcing it to reduce many of the planned activities spelled out in the PRSP already approved by the Bank. Needless to say, it soon became common knowledge that the Bank cut aid over political and not economic mismanagement. But the prior actions enabled the Bank to be political while at the same time couching its cut as due to technical concerns. The prior actions enabled the Bank to respond although formally having withdrawn from direct operational engagement and having handed over responsibility of the overall development process to its counterpart. The prior actions demonstrate how the Bank still is present and relevant to its counterpart's decision making, but now in a more subtle and tacit manner – all the while it can uphold its partnership model and reassert its commitment to its girding tenets of ownership and participation.

Coda: developmentality in the World Bank–Uganda partnership

Uganda has entered a new form of donor-driven state formation after the introduction of the PRSP-model. The Government of Uganda has formally been granted greater freedoms and responsibilities for externally funded development initiatives – but this freedom has its limitations. The partnership discourse has been accompanied by various indirect governance techniques through which the World Bank seeks to make its policies those of the government, as illustrated by the historical trajectory of the Ugandan PEAP. The partnership discourse builds on an idea about the self-caring, self-entrepreneurial state. But when the state lacks the capacity or will to fulfil the freedoms and responsibilities granted by the partnership discourse, the donor seeks to retain control through new means. As the case above shows, this implies new forms of indirect, neoliberal governance. The effect is the Ugandan government has been put under external supervision, and instead of acting on behalf of and being accountable to its citizens, the state becomes accountable first and foremost to its donors.

The World Bank–Uganda partnership reveals practices that are both instigated by and undermine the girding ideas of the PRSP model. These ambiguities demonstrate the interlocking of conditionality and participatory approaches, and that the practices of the new aid architecture purporting to greater involvement and freedom also entail mechanisms of indirect control and tacit governance. This form of governance, or developmentality, is contingent on the Bank making its policies those of the recipient – as illustrated by the PEAP formation and the prior actions. Through the liberal concepts of participation, partnership and ownership, the Ugandan government has become accountable to the Bank for implementing its 'own' policies outlined in the PEAP. The client government's nominal ownership of and responsibility for the processes and objectives of these provide the contingency for the Bank to respond based on its own assessment of the government's progress. Since the prior actions are derived from the PRSP, the government is seen to own them and, consequently, failure to attain them is a responsibility exclusively to be borne by the government itself. Developmentality involves the process of responsibilisation in which the receiving end is made responsible for the policies and their implementation regardless of the Bank's involvement, influence or imposition. The process of responsibilisation is found in the nexus between conditionality and participation and points to developmentality working as a means of indirect rule. While the Bank conveys to its Ugandan counterpart greater freedoms, it also retains control by orchestrating the 'conduct of conduct' through other means and instruments, thus juggling the formal order and informal practices of the participation and conditionality concepts.

Developmentality points to mechanisms where the Bank involves itself in Ugandan domestic politics and state formation, nominally being the sovereign responsibility of the client state as proposed by the PRSP model itself. This does not mean that the Bank is hegemonic or that the Ugandan government has fallen prey to the donor community. The fact that the Ugandan government went through with the mismanaged political transition despite being threatened by aid cuts demonstrates a sense of resistance to the Bank, dominant donor discourses and the power of developmentality.

Note

1 This chapter was written as part of the research project 'Developmentality and the Anthropology of Partnership', funded by the Research Council of Norway (project no. 262524).

References

Abrahamsen, R. (2004), 'The power of partnerships in global governance', *Third World Quarterly*, 25(8), pp. 1453–67.

Brock, K. (2004), 'Ugandan civil society in the policy process: Challenging orthodox narratives', in K. Brock, R. McGee and J. Gaventa (eds), *Unpacking Policy: Knowledge, Actors and Spaces in Poverty Reduction in Uganda and Nigeria* (Kampala: Fountain), pp. 94–112.

Cargill, T. (2004), 'Uganda: Still the donors' darling', *World Today*, 60(2), pp. 26–27.

Daily Monitor. (2006), 'World bank gives Shs240b for poverty', 20 January.

de Carvalho, B. (2016), 'The making of the political subject: Subjects and territory in the formation of the state', *Theory and Society*, 45(1), pp. 57–88.

Dijkstra, G. and van Donge, J. K. (2001), 'What does the "Show Case" show? Evidence of and lessons from adjustment in Uganda', *World Development*, 29(5), pp. 841–63.

Doornbos, M. (2003), '"Good governance": The metamorphosis of a policy metaphor', *Journal of International Affairs*, 57(1), pp. 3–17.

Foucault, M. (1991), 'Governmentality', in G. Burchell, C. Gordon and P. Miller (eds), *The Foucault Effect: Studies in Governmentality* (Chicago, IL: University of Chicago Press), pp. 87–104.

Harrison, G. (2001), 'Post-conditionality politics and administrative reform: Reflections on the cases of Uganda and Tanzania', *Development and Change*, 32(4), pp. 657–79.

Harrison, G. (2004), *The World Bank and Africa* (London: Routledge).

IMF. (2000), Press Release: HIPC debt relief for Uganda increased to US$ 2 billion: additional relief for Uganda's poverty reduction programs, 8 February, Available at: www.imf.org/en/News/Articles/2015/09/14/01/49/pr0006 [accessed 9 January 2018].

Isooba, M. (2005), 'Civil society participation in Uganda's PRS process: Opportunities and dilemmas', in A. Hughes, and N. Atampugre (eds), *Civil Society and Poverty Reduction*. Participatory Learning and Action No. 51. International Institute for Environment and Development, pp. 43–46.

Isooba, M. and Ssewakiryanga, R. (2005), 'Setting the scene: The Ugandan Poverty Eradication Action Plan', in A. Hughes, and N. Atampugre (eds), *Civil society and Poverty Reduction*. Participatory Learning and Action No. 51, International Institute for Environment and Development, pp. 39–42.

Kuteesa, F., Tumusiime-Mutebile, E., Whitworth, A. and Williamson, T. (eds) (2010), *Uganda's Economic Recovery: Insider Accounts* (Oxford: Oxford University Press).

Lie, J. H. S. (2015a), 'Developmentality: Indirect governance in the World Bank–Uganda partnership', *Third World Quarterly*, 36(4), pp. 723–40.

Lie, J. H. S. (2015b), *Developmentality: An Ethnography of the World Bank–Uganda Partnership* (New York, NY: Berghahn).

MFPED. (1999), *Vision 2025: A Strategic Framework for National Development* (Kampala: Ministry of Finance, Planning and Economic Development).

Moore, D. (1999), '"Sail on, o ship of state": Neo-liberalism, globalisation and the governance of Africa', *Journal of Peasant Studies*, 27(1), pp. 61–96.

Mosse, D. (2005), *Cultivating Development: An Ethnography of Aid Policy and Practice* (London: Pluto).

Mugambe, K. (2010), 'The Poverty Eradication Action Plan', in F. Kuteesa *et al.* (eds), *Uganda's Economic Reforms: Insider Accounts* (Oxford: Oxford University Press), pp. 157–71.

Museveni, Y. K. (1997), *Sowing the Mustard Seed: The Struggle for Freedom and Democracy in Uganda* (London: Macmillan).

Mwenda, A. (2010), 'Uganda's politics of foreign aid and violent conflict: The political uses of the LRA rebellion', in T. Allen, and K. Vlassenroot (eds), *The Lord's Resistance Army: Myth and Reality* (London: Zed), pp. 45–58.

Randel, J., *et al.* (2002), *The Reality of Aid, 2002: An Independent Review of Poverty Reduction and International Development Assistance* (Manila: IBON).

Rose, N. and Miller, P. (1992), 'Political power beyond the state: Problematics of government', *British Journal of Sociology*, 43(2), pp. 173–205.

Rubongoya, J. B. (2007), *Regime Hegemony in Museveni's Uganda* (New York, NY: Palgrave Macmillan).

Sending, O. J. and Lie, J. H. S. (2015), 'The limits of global authority: World Bank benchmarks in Ethiopia and Malawi', *Review of International Studies*, 41(5),

Ssewakiryanga, R. (2004), 'The corporatist state, the parallel state and prospects for representative and accountable policy in Uganda', in K. Brock, R. McGee and J. Gaventa (eds), *Unpacking Policy: Knowledge, Actors and Spaces in Poverty Reduction in Uganda and Nigeria* (Kampala: Fountain), pp. 74–93.

World Bank. (1997), *The State in a Changing World*. World Development Report 1997 (Oxford: Oxford University Press).

2
Our friends at the bank? The adverse effects of neoliberalism in Acholi

Ronald R. Atkinson

Neoliberalism in Museveni's Uganda is now thirty years old (1987–2017), divided by this volume's editors into three decade-long periods. The first two of these coincide closely with the twenty-year long northern Uganda war that ravaged the Acholi sub-region. This chapter begins with overviews of these two periods, during which numerous World Bank (WB)-funded neoliberal programmes were introduced in war-affected Acholi, especially during the second. These included the 1992 Northern Uganda Recovery Plan (NURP I); the country-wide 1997 Poverty Eradication Action Plan (PEAP), revised in 2000 and 2004; and 1999's NURP II, with a Northern Uganda Social Action Plan (NUSAF) component added in 2002. Commencing these programmes during the war presented the WB with a dilemma. It did not want to be seen involved in a conflict area, and thus 'consistently either termed northern Uganda a post-conflict situation or simply ignored the presence of continuing armed conflict'. This sleight-of-hand had serious harmful effects in Acholi, as budgetary and programmatic support from the Bank and other donors contributed, directly or indirectly, to funding the Ugandan military, enabling it to conduct and even expand a war that the WB essentially disregarded. In consequence, Bank projects in Acholi enabled 'the construction of a security state and the prolongation of war and violence' (Branch 2011: 123–24; see also Collier and Pradhan 1998).

The third section focuses on a crucial confluence of personalities, policies and politics marking the transition between the first and second decades of neoliberalism in Uganda. This confluence is captured in an award-winning documentary titled *Our Friends at the Bank* (1997), filmed over fourteen months in 1995–1996, containing remarkable footage of meetings both within and between the Government of Uganda (GoU), the Bank and other donors. Among the many revealing aspects of these meetings is the extent to which an assertive and wily Ugandan president was able to shape the agenda and successfully promote his priorities. While not discounting wider structural and power dynamics, or the effects of particular neoliberal programmes that included the Acholi sub-region, this chapter argues that the film provides a window into some of the most important dynamics underlying the neoliberal project in Uganda, including both direct and indirect support enabling Museveni, his government and his army to carry out decades of war in northern Uganda in the manner it did, with its attendant adverse effects on the Acholi people.

The fourth section discusses the troubled third decade of Museveni's neoliberal Uganda, positing continuing negative effects for Acholi despite the end of active conflict, including threats to Acholi customary land and an initiative by the collective Acholi leadership in response to those threats. The final section provides a brief conclusion.

Neoliberalism and Acholi, 1987–1996

When Yoweri Museveni was sworn in as Uganda's president in January 1986, the country's economy was devastated following a decade-and-a-half of mismanagement and conflict, beginning with Idi Amin's regime and continuing through the five-year war that brought Museveni to power. As had been true throughout the 'bush war', Museveni's stance towards neoliberal policies and programmes when he assumed office 'was frankly hostile'. This was partly a product of his (then) long-time leftist political ideology, but seems also due to his antipathy to the former Ugandan president who had been his main adversary during the war, Milton Obote, who was one of the very earliest of sub-Saharan African leaders to adopt these packages (Hansen and Twaddle 1991: 2, 16–17, 1998: 2–3, 6–8).

But the anti-neoliberal economic programme enacted over the first two years of Museveni's National Resistance Movement (NRM) government – including barter deals with communist countries and freezing, even attempting to raise, the exchange rate of the Uganda shilling – proved utter failures. Thus, by 1997/98, write Hansen and Twaddle: 'Effectively, there were then only two realistic economic options open to Uganda at government level; accepting the advice offered by the International Monetary Fund, the World Bank, and the Paris Club quickly, or accepting it less quickly'. Museveni chose the former, even though the relationship he was entering into was highly unequal. Indeed, argue Hansen and Twaddle: 'It was doubtless partly the inequality of this relationship which prompted Museveni to change position – from being the most severe critic of the World Bank and the IMF in the early and mid-1980s to becoming one of their most eloquent supporters ten years later'. 'But', they continue:

> there was probably also another reason. Pressures by the more advanced capitalist countries for political changes as well as for economic reforms in the Third World multiplied in the years immediately following the end of the Cold War. Politically, Museveni was unwilling to yield to the demands by any outsiders for multi-party democracy to be re-established quickly in Uganda. (1998: 7)

Thus it seems that even when his – and his government's – position was at its weakest, Museveni was manoeuvring, and perhaps even manipulating his much stronger 'partners': acceding, or appearing to accede, to unpalatable economic prescriptions while fending off political pressures more threatening to his core agenda.

But if Museveni's pivot to accept neoliberal economic policies was initially grudging, the former Marxist soon proved an especially adept and zealous convert, implementing a textbook neoliberal package of macroeconomic stabilisation, internal structural adjustment, and other programmes designed to further the neoliberal agenda. The resulting annual GDP growth over the next decade, along with an activist response to the HIV/AIDS crisis and an increased presence of women in legislature and government, helped make Uganda the most influential development model of the 1990s, while also making Uganda's president a favourite of the Western, especially US, elite and media – all of which brought international legitimacy, financial support and rare influence and agency with respect to influential donors, including the WB (Introduction; Harvard Business School 1998, Tripp 2000: 181–85, Mallaby 2004: 13, Kinsman 2010, Fisher 2011, 2013a, 2013b, Reid 2017: 275–78, Epstein 2017; see Reno 2002 for a critique of the growth data validity).

From the beginning, this overwhelmingly positive Western response masked or minimised many shortcomings of both the lauded Ugandan economy (notably growing inequality and regional disparities, rising external debt and out-of-control corruption) and other harmful aspects of Museveni's rule, including pervasive under-mining of democratic governance and rule of law. In many respects, Museveni benefitted by comparison with the violent and dysfunc-tional leadership of his predecessors, particularly Idi Amin. Indeed, in his new history of modern Uganda, Reid argues that the outside world's typical, 'faintly racist', image of Amin as 'a violent buffoon, a murderous joke, an African stereotype' cast 'a long shadow … there would be no NRM, no Museveni, perhaps even no neoliberal economics, without him' (2017: 64–66). This was essentially grading Museveni on a very lenient curve, much to his advantage.

Meanwhile, conflict in northern Uganda was mostly minimised or disregarded by the international community, which largely accepted a simplistic 'official discourse' of the war promulgated by the GoU, as one of 'good' (the GoU and its allies) vs. 'evil' (the insurgents, especially the Lord's Resistance Army or LRA). This was despite widespread, often blatant human rights violations not only by the rebels but the GoU and its army (Amnesty International 1992). Indeed, the latter – including looting, beating, raping and killing – initially sparked the insurgency in mid-1986. And while fighting waxed and waned over the next decade, civilians faced violence and displacement from both sides (Behrend 1999, Finnström 2008, Dolan 2009, Allen and Vlassenroot 2010, Atkinson 2010, Branch 2011, Lamwaka 2016, Epstein 2017).

And even when the GoU made military gains, they rarely achieved a secure hold over the Acholi countryside, effectively precluding substantive implementation of neoliberal projects in the sub-region, including NURP I (1992–1997), 'an emergency operation aimed at restoring economic and social infrastructure as well as reviving economic activities'. Budgeted initially at $600 million and targeting fourteen districts (only two within Acholi, the epicentre of conflict), less than $94 million was disbursed by the programme's end (Dolan 2009: 45). Moreover, lack of coordination, long implementation delays and corruption also contributed to NURP I's virtual irrelevance in Acholi (Kreimer *et al.* 2000: 55–72).

Neoliberalism and Acholi, 1996–2005

The transition between the first and second phases of neoliberal Uganda was a time of change for neoliberalism's Washington establishment. First laid out by James Wolfensohn when he became WB president in June 1995, new prominence was to be placed on poverty reduction, education, the environment and health (discussed further in the following section). A few years later, an emphasis on donor–recipient 'partnership' based on the latter's 'good governance' and involving their 'participation' and 'ownership' was accompanied by a shift from donors' projects-approach to direct budget support to the government and its own strategies. Uganda was chosen as one of five pilot countries to institute the new approach, which entailed incorporating Uganda's 1997 Poverty Eradication Action Plan (PEAP) into a WB 'partnership model and disbursement tactic' template, generating a Ugandan-based 1999 Poverty Reduction Strategy Paper (PRSP) (Brock *et al.* 2002, Brock *et al.* 2004, IMF 2005, Lie 2015, this volume).

Under the new model, Uganda did record an overall reduction in poverty, although inequality increased, especially rural/urban and regional inequality, with northern Uganda in general and Acholi in particular most negatively affected. And Uganda's performance on 'good governance', supposedly at the core of the new approach, remained at formal and procedural level. Still, Uganda was widely proclaimed as a 'showcase' of the new neoliberal approach, accompanied by continued support for Museveni's rule, including a heightened alliance with the US in the name of political stability, domestically and regionally (Introduction this volume).

The Bank struggled to reconcile the GoU's new-gained freedoms and responsibilities under PSRP, writes Lie in this volume, while also obtaining GoU commitment to the Bank's good governance approach. This proved a difficult task. While acceding to Bank expectations or pressures on many issues (such as revising broad government strategies or programmes such as PEAP), in instances where strong GoU or especially Museveni priorities were involved (see next section), it was the Bank and other donors who often caved.

Meanwhile, following adoption of a new 1995 constitution (Moehler 2008), Uganda held its first elections since Museveni took power in 1996. With political parties banned, but the National Resistance Movement (NRM) affiliation allowed on the pretext that it was a 'movement' only, Museveni won the presidency with some 75 per cent of the vote. His 10 per cent support in Acholi followed a campaign that was aggressively hostile towards the north in general and Acholi in particular (Finnström 2010: 78–79, Atkinson 2010: 292–94, Mwenda 2010: 54, Muhumuza 1997; see also Human Rights Watch (1999) on the NRM's democratic and human rights abuses surrounding the 1996 elections; Epstein (2017: 144–47) on electoral abuses in the 2001 presidential election; Prunier (2009) on GoU's involvement in neighbouring Zaire/Congo, including direct military intervention). A few years earlier, in 1994, Museveni scuttled a promising peace initiative, after which six interrelated developments reshaped both the remainder of the war and the relationship between Acholi and Uganda's central government and its neoliberal project:

1   The conflict became increasingly entangled in
    international politics, especially with neighbouring Sudan,
    where the GoU supported southern Sudanese rebels
    while the Government of Sudan provided sanctuary
    and support to the LRA. This geopolitical configuration
    brought the military and strategic interests of Uganda
    and the US into close alignment, especially following the
    September 2001 terrorist attacks on the US by al-Qaeda,
    which had links with the Sudanese government.

2   Both rebel and government fighting and abuse against
    civilians intensified, with the ensuing decade marked by
    some of the war's most intense violence following a flawed
    operation in 2002 against the LRA in southern Sudan
    called Operation Iron Fist.

3   The Ugandan government initiated a policy of forced
    encampment in the Western half of Acholi in 1996,
    extended to most of the rest of the sub-region in 2002.
    This dislocated some 90 per cent of the Acholi popula-
    tion, a million people or more, into squalid, minimally
    protected and minimally serviced camps, leaving them
    vulnerable and impoverished.

4   The limited services that were provided to camps came
    primarily not from the state, but from international
    donors and local and international NGOs, leading even-
    tually to a virtual NGO flood into Acholi during the last
    years of the war and early post-conflict period.

5   The camps also led to a perverse form of 'displaced
    development' promoted by the Bank and other donors,
    including NURP II and NUSAF. This 'development'
    helped entrench the camps, depoliticise the war, enable
    state withdrawal from service provision and effectively
    blame the ills of camp life *not* on the war or the state,
    but on a lack of social cohesion and social capital among
    the camps' population – all while promoting imported,
    palliative projects supposedly to build social cohesion
    and capital (Branch and Yen this volume, Branch 2011,
    Gulooba-Mutebi and Hickey 2009).

6   By displacing the vast majority of Acholi off their land,
    forced encampment meant that most Acholi land was
    then 'empty'. This did not go unnoticed by powerful
    individuals and groups, who as early as the later 1990s
    initiated projects to utilise such 'available' land for

large-scale commercial farming and other forms of
'development'. Neither did it go unnoticed by Acholi,
many of whom feared (however accurately) that forced
encampment was a plan to grab Acholi land (Adoko and
Levine 2004, Atkinson 2008).

Our Friends at the Bank?

Our Friends at the Bank is a valuable historical document, one most
readers of this chapter are unlikely to have seen. It focuses on four
contested issues dominating relations between Uganda and the Bank
during the mid-to-late 1990s. The first three of these were core GoU
(and Museveni) priorities: (i) funding infrastructure vs social investments, (ii) defence spending and (iii) debt relief. Crucially, all were
resolved in Museveni's favour. The fourth issue, concerning Bank
and IMF pressure to sell off the state-owned Uganda Commercial
Bank (UCB), did produce fierce debate in the Finance and Treasury
Ministries, as well as among Uganda's political and economic
elite more generally. But it did not pit the Bank and IMF against
Museveni. Indeed, after being shown documents indicating UCB
corruption and bad debts, Museveni is shown promptly saying:
'Let's privatise it', he says. 'No problem' (minutes 67–78). In any
case, for Acholi and northern Uganda, the effects of the productive Bank–government relationship were highly adverse, because the
increased aid, though most technically non-military, freed up monies
for the army.

The film opens with James Wolfensohn's first day as Bank President (1 June 1995), when he laid out – without abandoning Bank
macroeconomic staples – new emphases: poverty reduction, education, the environment and health (see also Mallaby 2004). Later
that year, reflecting these new approaches, Bank Vice-President for
Africa, Kim Jaycox is shown in a Washington meeting with Ugandan
officials, promoting spending on primary education; the Ugandans
counter with arguments for the immediate and direct economic
benefits of focusing on roads, a long-standing Ugandan priority
included in NURP I. Not long after, in November 1995, Wolfensohn, Museveni and a small group of others meet in New York.
Museveni and Wolfensohn spar over the issues that dominated the
Washington meeting. Eventually, Museveni, lounging in a soft-cush-
ioned chair, refers to his 'previous job of fighting', then cites Mao
Tse-tung's dictum that striking out in different directions is 'bad

fighting'. Thrusting his right arm straight ahead, he says it is better to 'concentrate your blow in one area'. For Museveni, this meant roads, not education.

Wolfensohn responds:

> Obviously we agree that roads are essential for development. The question of whether it's the only thing you do, or whether it's the first thing you do, or ... [leaves sentence dangling]. And it's clear now, I think, as a matter of priority that we should take a look at it, so ... [again, breaks off]. But my guess is you will get your way, which I think you are used to doing.

Laughter ripples through the room. Wolfensohn, smiling, adds quietly: 'You will have a lot of undereducated people using the roads'. Museveni replies: 'No problem. Once they have got incomes ...' (Chappell 1997: minutes 8–12). Later that month, Jim Adams – WB's East African Director, who was in the New York meeting and actually supported Museveni's position – met with Museveni in Uganda and informed him that Wolfensohn would be 'delighted' to finance a road construction programme (Mallaby 2004: 223).

The film's second topic, defence spending, is introduced with a brief montage of Museveni's successful presidential campaign in May 1996, before cutting to scenes of the Ugandan army while a voiceover intones that rebel challenges in the north mean that 'the cost of equipping and maintaining troops continually increases'. The film next (minutes 12–34) documents numerous, often querulous, meetings focused on donor concerns about Uganda's military spending. Ugandan officials, including Museveni, push back, and ultimately prevail.

In the first meeting shown, in Kampala, Brian Falconer, WB British representative in Uganda, emphasises to Ugandan officials that donors in general are concerned about the military budget, while also 'obviously aware of problems, especially in the north'. However, he continues, he has argued with the Defence and other ministries that the Bank and other donors need budgetary details and justifications. But none have been forthcoming. Next, Museveni faces a large contingent of donors who question him about the lack of transparency and unaccounted-for growth in military spending. These issues, a donor spokesman states, threaten 'the entire macroeconomic programme and development budget'. Museveni's response argues for flexibility, saying that increased spending was necessary for defeating the 'criminals' – politicians and soldiers from northern

Uganda – who had earlier been bested on the battlefield and then in the election, but were now returning. Donors quickly assure Museveni that they don't 'quibble' about the need for defence-budget flexibility, while asserting that if defence spending keeps 'squeezing' areas of 'true development' this would hurt the country. Museveni essentially dismisses this argument, claiming that Uganda's defence budget is actually 'not much', and it was 'not realistic' to be concerned about it (see Mwenda 2010: 51, for a summary of defence budget numbers, with Uganda's (official) military budget increasing from $42 million in 1992, to $88 million in 1996, $200 million in 2004, and $260 million in 2010). In the next filmed meeting, chaired by an obviously displeased Brian Falconer, donors continue pushing for more information on defence spending. Falconer begins:

> Every time I come to talk I seem to put the same record back on, OK? And I don't get an answer. I'm sort of playing the music to myself ... The level of items in the budget, the quality of the budget, is what is in question. Security is a very large item, OK? And I've acknowledged time and time again it is not what is in the defence budget; it is the ratio or proportion of defence ... that is the problem.

Defence Minister Amama Mbabazi responds by noting that the defence budget's percentage rise is less than it appears, as the total budget has grown. But another donor representative interjects: 'In the course of this discussion, you have told us in fact that the UPDF [Uganda People's Defence Forces] has acquired tanks in the last year. This is the first instance, as far as I know, to that effect, and these tanks were not, I think, forecast in last year's discussion'. Falconer quickly follows: 'So, there is a very genuine concern that the [overall development] programme itself, if it continues in this way and we don't have the dialogue, is not going to be supportable from the donor community'. At this point, the Uganda Finance Minister, Nkanji intervenes. He thanks all present, particularly Mbabazi. Then, looking across the table at the donor representatives, Nkanji says, in a firm but pleasant manner: 'But I want to say that, or to ask the question: "Who are you [gesturing]?" ... You are our friends. Mr Falconer, I say so ... But Uganda takes, in the last analysis, its own decisions'. Later, in the midst of several donor meetings, the Bank's Brian Falconer and Jim Adams are invited to Museveni's ranch in south-western Uganda. Almost immediately after greetings, President Museveni begins:

What are the donors saying? Are they saying that the Europeans were wrong to fight Hitler? And that as long as they were fighting Hitler they should not get resources? ... So what are they saying now? What are the donors saying? That it is bad to fight Idi Amin [a 'fight' that ended seventeen years earlier]? That we should have left Amin in charge of the whole country? What are they saying exactly?

Adams responds by suggesting that the first task is to make clear the magnitude of the threat, why a certain level of military expenditures are needed, and then presenting this to (re)assure donors. Museveni interjects:

Donors surely understand about constitutional government and law and order. How can there be development without constitutional government and law and order? But the insurgents are against constitutional government. So defending the constitution, surely any parliament would understand this.

May I tell you just a little bit of information? There are thirty mass graves in Luwero. And each of these mass graves contains more than 2,000 skulls. So that is a figure of just about 70,000 skulls in just Luwero area alone. These were murdered extra-judicially. These are the groups we are fighting now. The ones who were killing people in the whole country are the ones now who are killing people in one corner of our country. And you are saying we should not spend money to wipe these people out? If you are saying there are more efficient ways of doing, OK, we can look at those. That's a good argument that I can listen to. But to say that that is an illegitimate expenditure, it is a wrong expenditure, it is squandering resources, it is really not correct.

Returning to Kampala, Adams says to Falconer that if Uganda asks for an extra $10 million this year, to be used efficiently and effectively, then OK. Falconer assents, but adds that the issue is not going to go away. In the end, however, it does, with the Bank eventually agreeing to Uganda's budget, increased defence spending included. The documentary segues into the issue of debt by noting that just two weeks after becoming Bank President, Wolfensohn made a multi-nation journey to sub-Saharan Africa (Mallaby 2004: 84–115). Showing his arrival in Uganda, a voice-over intones that

Wolfensohn 'has come in person to give important news ... the Bank is studying a plan to reduce the burden of debt, and Uganda, with its impressive record of growth, could benefit'.

Next, Wolfensohn is filmed travelling to the president's ranch where he addresses a large group of Ugandan officials. He acknowledges 'that some structural adjustment programmes are incorrect'. But, he adds, it is a 'simplistic notion that all structural adjustment is wrong', seemingly a warning that this neoliberal staple could not be ignored as part of debt relief (minutes 35–39). Later, Wolfensohn and other Bank officials are shown meeting in Kampala with Finance Minister Nkanji, Treasury Secretary Emmanuel Tumusiime-Mutebile and others, where both Uganda's rising foreign debt (about $3 billion) and debt service (about $200 million) are discussed. Nkanji asks if the latter might be rescheduled/reduced. Wolfensohn responds, without specifics, that he 'will deal with it' (minutes 40–42); note, Mallaby (2004: 219–31) lauds Tumusiime-Mutebile's brilliance and organisational skills, as did Jim Adams, contributing greatly to their close working relationship.

The next year, in the autumn of 1996, the Bank and IMF publically unveil its debt relief programme for select nations that had demonstrated strong economic growth utilising the neoliberal model yet still had continuing poverty and unsustainable international debt: the 'Highly Indebted Poor Country (HIPC)' initiative. To get to that point, Wolfensohn had successfully overcome long-standing opposition to the idea of debt forgiveness by most officials at the Bank, the IMF and the US Treasury and Federal Reserve (see Daseking and Powell (2000) and Evans (1999) for papers on debt relief by IMF insiders following the HIPC launch, and Woods (2006: 141–78) for an examination of the debate over debt relief and its essential failure as an effective policy tool, particularly in Africa).

As the initiative was being debated and crafted, including the complex economic metrics that would largely determine a country's eligibility, the film shows numerous debates concerning Uganda's eligibility, both within the Bank and between Bank staff and others, including Ugandan officials and the IMF. Overall, wide-spread opposition to Uganda's inclusion is made clear, including two usually decisive voices on African issues within the Bank: Kim Jaycox and Jim Adams. But these debates, as noted, came long after Wolfensohn had broached the idea of debt relief with Uganda, and then said that he would 'deal' with it. In one revealing scene, Adams, alone with Jaycox in the latter's office, reveals that Uganda is not on the IMF's list of eligible candidates, but is on the Bank's. Jaycox responds:

You can't have this, [Uganda's] 7 per cent growth and be crying
about forty-year money! Ten year grace, three-quarter of 1 per cent
interest ...! If you can't pay it [Uganda's debt obligations] then,
what the hell are we talking about? ... If you can't afford that, what
can you afford? Nothing. ...Why can't they afford more debt, more
imports, if they get a growth of exports like that?

As Jaycox escorts Adams in a friendly manner to the door, Adams
agrees: 'Of course they can. So this isn't a big issue. OK?' Adams is
then shown reinforcing IMF opposition to Uganda's eligibility for
debt relief in a heated, larger meeting attended by Nawal Kamel,
Wolfensohn's appointed economist to head the team defining the
debt initiative's terms. Kamel demurs, stating that if 'the numbers
show [Uganda's] debts beyond sustainable, [she] will offer dollar-for-
dollar debt relief in that amount'. Still later, in another contentious
large group meeting, Adams and IMF officials again emphasise their
opposition to Uganda's inclusion in the HIPC, arguing that Uganda
doesn't need debt relief (minutes 42–47, 64–67).

The last scenes of the film, from October 1996, show a beaming
Dr Kamel reporting to colleagues that the annual Bank meeting,
centred on debt, 'went very well', before cutting to Wolfensohn's
public announcement outlining the debt-relief programme. 'All-in-
all', he concludes, 'I think we've had a wonderful morning. I think
it's very good news for the poor of the world. And all of us at the
Bank look forward to working constructively with the individual
cases with which we will deal, almost immediately' (minutes 78–81).

A voice-over coda to the film notes that the IMF subsequently
requested, and received, delays in implementing the programme.
Thus, those selected for the initiative were not announced for months.
On 12 March 1997, the *New York Times* reported that Uganda 'will
be the first'. Eventually Uganda's HIPC debt forgiveness was about
$350 million, just over 10 per cent of its then-international debts and
almost twice the amount that Finance Minister Nkanji had earlier
asked Wolfensohn about possibly forgiving (HBS 1998: 14).

Our Friends at the Bank vividly highlights personalities and politics
crucial to the Uganda–Bank relationship from the mid-to-late 1990s
forward, helping to overshadow shortcomings in the neoliberal agenda
itself and the inefficiency, incompetence and corruption of its implementation in Uganda. Meanwhile, Museveni, his government and his
army obtained the resources – and cover – to pursue the northern
Uganda war with minimal international scrutiny or criticism. The
consequences for the people of Acholi were devastating.

Neoliberalism and Acholi, 2006–2017

As neoliberal Uganda transitioned from its second to third decade, irregularities and violence surrounding Uganda's 2006 elections undermined Uganda's status as 'donor darlings', with episodic aid suspensions or cuts and greater donor scrutiny and intrusion into Uganda's budget and use of aid monies (Lie this volume). These negative responses, however, tended to be relatively brief and followed by resumptions, even increases, in financial and political support for both Uganda and its president, especially from the US, as Uganda aligned itself even more closely with the US 'war on terror'. Indeed, as a chapter title in Epstein (2017: 154) posits, Museveni discovered 'a new treasure trove' of US money and political support by committing the largest contingent of African Union forces fighting al-Shabaab in Somalia.

In post-war northern Uganda, the primary neoliberal programme targeting the region was the Peace, Recovery and Development Plan (PRDP) (2007–2012), extended as PRDP-II (2012–2015). Focused on infrastructure and funded at hundreds of millions of dollars, PRDP was marked by inefficiencies (the first dispersal of funds occurred two years late), massive corruption (most egregiously in the Office of the Prime Minister, where the programme was housed), dubious projects, lack of oversight and politically motivated geographical expansion far beyond war-affected areas, diluting effects where they were most needed (Marino 2008, Ogwang 2015). In Acholi, evidence of substantive or durable impacts from PRDP is minimal, while the pervasive corruption and political manipulation of Museveni's neoliberal Uganda, combined with what seems continued GoU intentional marginalisation of the sub-region, continue to adversely affect – and infect – post-conflict Acholi.

This was despite increased Acholi electoral support for Museveni and the NRM, which rose from about 10 per cent in 2006 to around 40 per cent in 2011 and 2016 – still well below the 60 per cent plus totals for Museveni and NRM overall (GoU 2016; Epstein 2017 challenges these figures). Two underlying dynamics seem especially important in Acholi's shift. The first derives from a favourite Museveni tactic: strategically dividing existing districts to fragment opposition and create new patronage networks, including additional electoral opportunities for local NRM candidates (Mwenda 2007, Green 2010). In Acholi, the number of districts rose from three in 2006 to seven in 2011 (with an eighth added after the 2016 elections). Second was a widespread notion that after overwhelmingly opposing the NRM for twenty years and reaping no developmental or political gains, many Acholi in 2011 and 2016 made a calculated gamble to provide electoral support to Museveni and other local NRM politicians – a gamble with thus far no discernible positive results.

At the same time, neoliberal-influenced pressure – including from the GoU and Museveni personally – to privatise land holding in Acholi increased, in the name of opening such land to commercialisation, investors and other forms of 'development'. This has contributed to land disputes, advantaged numerous wealthy and powerful individuals and groups, and threatened the security of Acholi customary, clan-based – *not* individuated – land, access to which comprises the major asset available to most rural Acholi in the aftermath of war and displacement (Atkinson 2008, Atkinson and Owor 2013, Hopwood and Atkinson 2013, Martiniello 2015). Note that during this period a WB document (2009) took an opposing position, identifying as one of three major policy actions in Acholi that 'government must suspend issue of land titles in rural Acholi until IDP return is completed and sensitisation on land rights has taken place'.

Without minimising either the current dismal trajectory of neoliberal Uganda or threats to Acholi land, this section concludes by noting a 2016–2017 project initiated by an assembly of political, community and cultural leaders from across Acholi intended to address these threats. The (donor-funded) project investigated and documented details of Acholi customary land as currently perceived and practised, in order to provide an evidentiary base to advocate for policies to secure and protect that land. A total of 141 clan-based land holding groups were studied, located in more than one-third of the sixty-three rural sub-counties across Acholi. And while variations existed across the sample, overall results indicate that, in less than a decade after leaving camps, most Acholi have resettled customary clan-based land that has been largely reconstituted, organised and managed along lines that embody principles and practices that are both long-established and broadly accepted (Atkinson *et al.* 2018; see also Bymugisha 2013 which argues that securing and protecting such collectively held land is the first of ten key elements important for improving land administration in Sub-Saharan Africa).

Conclusion

In conclusion, Uganda's three decades of neoliberalism have had overwhelmingly perverse effects on Acholi. This has been due in part to negative or skewed impacts accompanying much of neoliberalism's imported ideology, architecture and specific programmes, as well as the ways these have been manipulated, mismanaged and abused by those in power in Uganda – all of which have been explored in various ways by the editors and other contributors to this volume. But these generally negative effects on Acholi have been filtered through the crucial dynamic of the sub-region being wracked by war during twenty of neoliberalism's thirty years in Uganda. This chapter argues that the perverse effects of neoliberalism in Acholi were due less to any particular neoliberal programme than to the failure of the international neoliberal establishment to sufficiently acknowledge the war and its largely uncritical and unexamined embrace of the Ugandan president as he pursued that war – all depicted in compelling fashion in *Our Friends at the Bank*. Finally and more broadly, the film also provides a window into an ongoing conundrum of neoliberalism in Uganda. As expressed by Hansen and Twaddle, writing in the same mid-1990s time period as the documentary: 'There is therefore a serious gap between the donors' demands for increased social expenditure and reduction of poverty in Uganda and the government's ability to meet these additional demands'. But, Hansen and Twaddle then ask:

> To what extent are these demands principally the demands of donors rather than Ugandans? It is difficult to answer this question straightforwardly for several reasons. One reason is that ... the government's financial policies and donors' demands have become so closely intertwined that it is difficult for those not party to government–donor discussions to decide which are the more important. (1998: 10)

The nature and range of the meetings depicted in *Our Friends at the Bank* provide unique insights that help answer this important question, not just for Acholi but Uganda more generally. It shows how Museveni essentially manoeuvred and manipulated to avoid, or limit, meeting such donor demands. The current poor quality of Uganda's health and education provision, and continuing rise in inequality, suggest that he is continuing to do so.

References

Adoko, J. and Levine, S. (2004), 'Land matters in displacement: The importance of land rights in Acholiland and what threatens them', Civil Society Organisations for Peace in Northern Uganda (CSOPNU) and Land and Equity Movement in Uganda (LEMU), Kampala.

Allen, T. and Vlassenroot, K. (eds) (2010), *The Lord's Resistance Army: Myth and Reality* (London: Zed).

Amnesty International. (1992), 'Uganda: The failure to safeguard human rights', London.

Atkinson, R. (2008), 'Land issues in Acholi in the transition from war to peace', *The Examiner,* Human Rights Focus, 4, pp. 3–9, 17–25.

Atkinson, R. (2010), 'Afterword: A perspective on the last thirty years', in R. Atkinson, *The Roots of Ethnicity: The Origins of the Acholi of Uganda* (Kampala: Fountain), pp. 275–35.

Atkinson, R., Latigo, J, Ahirirwe, S. and Alobo, S. (2018), 'Instituting the protection of rights to customary land ownership in Acholiland: A research project of the Joint Acholi Sub-Region Leaders' Forum (JASLF) and Trócaire', Field research report', Kampala, April.

Atkinson, R. and Owor, A. (2013), '"Land grabbing": The Ugandan government, Madhvani, and others versus the community of Lakang, Amuru District', *Journal of Peace and Strategic Studies,* 1(1), pp. 50–63.

Behrend, H. (1999), *Alice Lakwena and the Holy Spirits: War in Northern Uganda, 1985–92* (Oxford: James Currey).

Branch, A. (2011), *Displacing Human Rights: War and Intervention in Northern Uganda* (Oxford: Oxford University Press).

Branch, A. and Yen, A. (2018), 'Neoliberal discipline and violence in northern Uganda', in J. Wiegratz, G. Martiniello and E. Greco (eds), *Neoliberal Uganda* (London: Zed).

Brock, K., McGee, R. and Gaventa, J. (eds) (2004), *Unpacking Policy: Knowledge, Actors and Spaces in Poverty Reduction in Uganda and Nigeria* (Kampala: Fountain).

Brock, K., McGee, R. and Ssewakiryanga, R. (eds) (2002), 'Poverty knowledge and policy processes: A case study of Ugandan National Poverty Reduction Strategy', Research Report No. 53, Institute of Development Studies.

Byamugisha, F. (2013), 'Improving land governance in sub-Saharan Africa: A ten point program to scale up land policy reforms and investments', World Bank, Washington, DC.

Chappell, P. (1997), *Our Friends at the Bank,* First Run/Icarus Films.

Collier, P. and Pradhan, S. (1998), 'Economic aspects of the transition from civil war', in H. Hansen and M. Twaddle (eds), *Developing Uganda* (Kampala: Fountain), pp. 19–37.

Daseking, C. and Powell, R. (2000), 'From Toronto Terms to the HIPC Initiative: A brief history of debt relief for low-income countries', *International Economic Policy Review,* 2, pp. 39–58.

Dolan, C. (2009), *Social Torture: The Case of Northern Uganda, 1986–2006* (New York, NY: Berghahn).

Epstein, H. (2017), *Another Fine Mess: America, Uganda, and the War on Terror* (New York, NY: Columbia Global Reports).

Evans, H. (1999), 'Debt relief for the poorest countries: Why did it take so long?', *Development Policy Review,* 17(3), pp. 267–79.

Finnström, S. (2008), *Living with Bad Surroundings: War, History, and Everyday Moments in Northern Uganda* (Durham, NC: Duke University Press).

Finnström, S. (2010), 'An African hell of colonial imagination?: The Lord's Resistance Army in Uganda, another story?', in T. Allen and K. Vlassenroot (eds), *The Lord's Resistance Army: Myth and Reality* (London: Zed), pp. 74–89.

Fisher, J. (2011), 'International perceptions and African agency: Uganda and its donors 1986–2010'. DPhil Thesis, University of Oxford.

Fisher, J. (2013a), '"Some more reliable than others": Image management, donor perceptions and the global war on terror in East African diplomacy', *Journal of Modern African Studies*, 51(1), pp. 1–31.

Fisher, J. (2013b), 'The limits – and limiters – of external influence: Donors, the Ugandan Electoral Commission and the 2011 elections', *Journal of Eastern African Studies*, 7(3), pp. 471–91.

Golooba-Mutebi, F. and Hickey, S. (2009), 'Governing chronic poverty under inclusive liberalism: The case of the Northern Uganda Social Action Fund', Chronic Poverty Research Centre Working Paper No. 150, University of Manchester.

Government of Uganda, Electoral Commission. (2016), '2016 General election results'.

Green, E. (2010), 'Patronage, district creation, and reform in Uganda', *Studies in Comparative International Development*, 45(1), pp. 83–103.

Hansen, H. and Twaddle, M. (eds) (1991), *Changing Uganda* (Kampala: Fountain).

Hansen, H. and Twaddle, M. (eds) (1998), *Developing Uganda* (Kampala: Fountain).

Harvard Business School (HBS). (1998), 'Uganda and the Washington Consensus', Case Study 9-798-047 (revised 7 October 2002).

Hopwood, J. and Atkinson, R. (2013), 'Land conflict monitoring and mapping tool for the Acholi subregion: Final report', Kampala: Human Rights Focus and UN Peacebuilding Programme.

Human Rights Watch. (1999), 'Hostile to democracy: The movement system and political repression in Uganda', 1 October.

International Monetary Fund (IMF). (2005), 'Uganda: Poverty Reduction Strategy Paper', IMF country report No. 05/307, Washington, DC.

Kinsman, J. (2010), *AIDS Policy in Uganda: Evidence, Ideology, and the Making of an African Success Story* (London: Palgrave Macmillan).

Kreimer, A. *et al.* (2000), *Uganda: Post-conflict reconstruction*. OED evaluation country case study series; post-conflict reconstruction (Washington, DC: World Bank).

Lamwaka, C. (2016), *The Raging Storm: A Reporter's Inside Account of the Northern Uganda War 1986–2005*, ed. R. Atkinson (Kampala: Fountain).

Lie, J. (2015), 'Developmentality: Indirect governance in the World Bank–Uganda partnership', *Third World Quarterly*, 36(4), pp. 723–40.

Mallaby, S. (2004), *The World's Banker: A Story of Failed States, Financial Crises, and the Wealth and Poverty of Nations* (New York, NY: Penguin).

Marino, J. (2008), 'Is the PRDP politics as usual?: Update on the implementation of Uganda's Peace, Recovery and Development Plan', Beyond Juba Project, Kampala.

Martiniello, G. (2015), 'Social struggles in Uganda's Acholiland: Understanding responses and resistance to Amuru Sugar Works', *Journal of Peasant Studies*, 42(3–4), pp. 653–69.

Moehler, D. (2008), *Distrusting Democrats: Outcomes of Participatory Constitution Making* (Ann Arbor, MI: University of Michigan Press).

Muhumuza, W. (1997), 'Money and power in Uganda's 1996 elections', *African Journal of Political Science*, 2(1), pp. 168–79.

Mwenda, A. (2007), 'Personalizing power in Uganda', *Journal of Democracy*, 13(3), pp. 23–37.

Mwenda, A. (2010), 'Uganda's

politics of foreign aid and violent conflict: The political uses of the LRA rebellion', in T. Allen and K. Vlassenroot (eds), *The Lord's Resistance Army: Myth and Reality* (London: Zed), pp. 45–58.

Ogwang, T. (2015), 'Rethinking peace, post-conflict reconstruction and development interventions in northern Uganda: Opportunities and challenges', *Advances in Social Sciences Research Journal*, 2(10), pp. 157–73.

Prunier, G. (2009), *Africa's World War: Congo, the Rwandan Genocide, and the Making of a Continental Catastrophe* (Oxford: Oxford University Press).

Reid, R. (2017), *A History of Modern Uganda* (New York, NY: Cambridge University Press).

Reno, W. (2002), 'Uganda's politics of war and debt relief', *Review of International Political Economy*, 9(3), pp. 415–35.

Tripp, A. (2000), *Women and Politics in Uganda* (Madison, WI: University of Wisconsin Press).

Woods, N. (2006), *The Globalizers: The IMF, the World Bank, and Their Borrowers* (Ithaca, NY: Cornell University Press).

World Bank. (2009), 'Uganda – post-conflict land policy and administration options: The case of northern Uganda'.

3
Neoliberal discipline and violence in northern Uganda

Adam Branch and Adrian Yen

War and neoliberalism in Uganda

In the early 2000s, Uganda was characterised by a deep divide. In the south, reconstruction, development and democratic transition were the order of the day, and the National Resistance Movement (NRM) government enjoyed massive donor support for its economic structural adjustment policies and its apparent commitment to efficient technocratic planning and the tenets of good governance and decentralisation. The 'bush war' that had brought Museveni and the National Resistance Army (NRA) to power in 1986 was a receding memory, and the security that the president had established in the south, in contrast to the widespread state violence suffered under the Obote II and Amin regimes, ensured him significant popular support. Driving north, however, upon crossing the Nile's booming rapids at the heavily guarded Karuma bridge, one entered a different world. Travel on the ramshackle roads was possible only by day, and then often by military convoy, always ready for a rebel ambush. People no longer lived in their homesteads but huddled instead in wretched internment camps, where the government had forced them as part of its counterinsurgency. The land sat empty and overgrown, while people survived on a minimal ration of World Food Programme donations. The state presence was largely restricted to its military and security apparatus: foreign aid organisations and NGOs ran almost the entire infrastructure of relief aid and rudimentary service provision in the camps into which, by 2003, the entire population of Acholi region had been displaced by the Ugandan military (Finnström 2008, Dolan 2009, Branch 2011).

The co-existence of these two apparently radically divergent realities within the same, small country and under the same government demands explanation. One interpretation turns to ethnic politics: the southern-based NRM government was carrying out a programme of repression and revenge against the north, which had held power from independence until the NRM victory. Another explanation looks to political strategy: the NRM used the war in the north as a justification to militarise internally and secure external military funding, to maintain a large sector of its budget out of donor control, and to consolidate its rule by maintaining a state of fear in the south over the possibility of northern rebels coming to power (Mwenda 2010).

Our research approach in the years we have spent living and working in northern Uganda has been to start with the concrete reality in the affected communities and then to move up to higher analytical and wider spatial registers from that foundation. To this end, in order to understand the forms of political power that were being exercised in the northern warzone, we began in the archipelago of internment camps that riddled the Acholi countryside and that had been formed and maintained through a regime of extreme state violence against the rural Acholi population. At that local scale in the camps, it became clear that people in their daily lives were facing an overpowering alliance between the violence of the Ugandan state and the discipline and regulation of international humanitarian and development organisations, whom the state relied upon to control the population. We explored this complementary, transnational arrangement of power deployed upon the population as well as how the camps' displaced inhabitants were surviving materially and trying to make meaningful lives for themselves in the face of destitution and violence. Thus, the form of power revealed in northern Uganda made apparent the close ties that can emerge in a conflict zone between the neoliberal discipline of humanitarianism and peacebuilding and state militarism, as well as the gaps and inadequacies in what is sometimes rendered as a totalising form of power.

After this introductory section, the next section focuses on how the discipline and regulation exercised by international organisations during the war conformed to and promoted a neoliberal social logic. This neoliberal social logic involves the extension of the market model of individual consumers, each responsible for governing her or himself, to all domains of society. People are treated as rational, welfare-maximising individuals, in which welfare is to be achieved through individual decisions to utilise available resources, and the state is absolved of responsibility. The chapter thus explores one dimension of what the introduction describes as *neoliberalisation*, the systematic advance of Ugandan society towards a 'market society' which involves restricting subjectivities and practices (Dean 2009 [1999], Harrison 2010).

This chapter demonstrates how this logic is illustrated by developmental peacebuilding interventions. Attention to this neoliberal social logic allows us to explore the continuity between the discipline and regulation that were present during the war years and the forms of power that have been operative as part of reconstruction and rehabilitation since the open fighting ended in 2007 and people were allowed to leave the camps. In the third section we focus on one specific form of intervention in the post-war period – the use of psycho-pharmaceuticals to deal with trauma and provide psychosocial support – and show how those war-time logics have continued up to the present, in particular by promoting the self-governing of individuals, this time mediated at the neurochemical level by powerful drugs. While we do not deny that hundreds or even perhaps thousands of afflicted individuals have found relief through these interventions, we want to focus on the ways in which the use of psycho-pharmaceuticals fails to address the structural problems underlying the reproduction of individual and collective suffering, reinforcing the neoliberal order of peacebuilding.

State violence has also continued in the post-war period. Whereas during the war, violence was largely an effort to control the population, in recent years violence has become the cutting edge for state-led projects of grabbing resources from the north, in particular land, in a form of accumulation by dispossession. The massive violence and devastation – social, economic, environmental – of the war left the population particularly vulnerable to the incursions of neoliberal capitalism, and so today's dispossession is built upon a legacy of state violence stretching back thirty years and continuing into the present.

Neoliberalism under internment

Background to displacement

Civil war was an enduring aspect of life for Uganda's Acholi population for over twenty years. Rebel groups, some with significant popular support, operated in the Acholi subregion of northern Uganda ever since Museveni, at the head of the NRA, seized power from a principally Acholi government in 1986. The Lord's Resistance Army (LRA), headed by the infamous Joseph Kony, emerged as the most potent rebel force in the early 1990s, at a point when the support enjoyed by other rebel organisations among the Acholi peasantry had dissipated, a casualty of the rebels' military failures and the government's brutal counterinsurgency.

In that atmosphere, the LRA interpreted their reduced popular support to indicate that the Acholi had come to support the government, and the rebels turned their violence upon suspected government collaborators and supporters. The LRA became infamous for massacres, maiming and the forced recruitment of thousands of Acholi, many of them children. The Ugandan government's counter-insurgency was also brutal, as the NRA and its successor, the Uganda People's Defense Force (UPDF), focused their violence on destroying suspected rebel support among civilians. The most devastating period began in 1996, when the government instituted its policy of forced displacement and drove hundreds of thousands of Acholi peasants out of their villages into camps through a campaign of violence.

The forced displacement of several hundred thousand civilians into ad hoc camps in a matter of a week created a massive humanitarian crisis (Branch 2011). The displaced population began abandoning the camps and protesting their horrific conditions; it was at this point that international aid agencies responded and began their first major operation in northern Uganda in the months following. The same qualities that made the camps attractive to the Ugandan government – a concentrated, easily surveilled and controlled population – made them particularly attractive to aid agencies, as did Uganda's status as a favourite of Western donors (*ibid.*).

In the following years, forced displacement expanded to encompass the entire rural Acholi population – one million people – and the presence of relief agencies expanded in step, effectively quelling popular dissent – but always dependent upon the threat of state violence in the background. By 2007, running the camps was costing donors US$200 million per year as over 100 international agencies came to provide an entire rudimentary civil administration in the camps. This culminated in the mid-2000s, when the aid agencies launched a 'camp management' strategy, parcelling out Acholi-land sub-county by sub-county between themselves in the name of rendering the camps more sustainable – and, in effect, more easily surveilled and controlled. From the beginning, therefore, the aid agencies faced the challenge of controlling the displaced civilian population for the state and for their own operations, which they did by constructing a regime of disciplinary peacebuilding, conforming to a neoliberal social logic. The result, we argue, was to promote individual self-regulation among the displaced, effectively obscuring the state violence upholding displacement and diverting people from political action that potentially could have remedied their condition.

Peacebuilding's logic

Although the delivery of humanitarian aid comprised the most spectacular form of intervention in northern Uganda, starting in the early 2000s peacebuilding became a central part of the landscape as well. Peacebuilding is a concept that can encompass a wide range of interventions during and after conflicts, including development, education, microcredit, community-conflict resolution, human rights promotion, psychotherapy, civil-society promotion, transitional justice and traditional reconciliation. Peacebuilding has increasingly espoused a 'rights-based approach', which in practice has emphasised participation, empowerment and capacity-building in the name of efficacy and sustainability (Barnett *et al.* 2007, Fox 2001). This turn, from simply providing aid, to demanding the participation and active involvement of the supposed beneficiaries in peacebuilding activities set the stage for a neoliberal turn in intervention by declaring war-affected populations responsible for bringing peace, justice and rehabilitation (Chandler 2002).

There is a distinct logic behind peacebuilding: violence is seen as leading to social breakdown in forms ranging from a loss of traditional authority, to underdevelopment, a fragile civil society and widespread psychological trauma (Collier *et al.* 2003). This social breakdown is thought to then cause further violence, ostensibly against particularly 'vulnerable' populations, such as women, children, the elderly or the disabled. Intervention is thus directed toward rebuilding social order, where a stable social order is equated with peace and social disorder is expressed as a deficiency in any one of those different social, personal or economic domains (Branch 2011). By presenting peace as re-established through externally compensating for internal deficiencies, peacebuilding thus perniciously internalises the causes and consequences of violence within the war-affected community, presenting violence as stemming from deviation on the part of groups or individuals. In so doing, peacebuilding's logic erases the fact that violence in Acholiland, while certainly having led to grave problems within the displaced community, is not caused by internal breakdown but by national and international structures of violence and inequality, in particular a state policy treating the civilian population as enemies and subjecting them to a brutal counterinsurgency campaign, supported by Western donors and aid agencies.

Thus, because the violent context and its underlying causes remain unchanged, peacebuilding gives its subjects an impossible task as they are made responsible for causing and remedying their own suffering. Peacebuilding thus replicates the logic of economic neoliberalism, which makes people themselves responsible for resolving their poverty, when that poverty is in fact caused by vast economic and political structures far beyond the reach of individuals (Pupavac 2005). Peacebuilding intervention is to build new subjects to function within what is cast as a peaceful, normal, social order as socially, economically, psychologically and culturally healthy beings (Duffield 2001). As autonomous expressions of agency are interpreted as deviance, whether as conflict, psychological trauma, human rights violations, refusal to submit to authority, or as antisocial, anti-cultural and anti-traditional behaviour, individuals' agency is to be steered into peacebuilding's own models of law-abiding individuals, entrepreneurs, civil-society actors, empowered youth and women, or even 'proper' Acholi. People are required to believe that and act as if they had the power to resolve conflict and bring peace, development and recon-struction to their communities. Those conforming to these models are thus required in effect to adjust to living with and accepting a violent social and political order that remains in place, beyond question, even as it may become even more repressive (for an exploration of this logic in participatory development, see Cooke and Kothari 2001).

Peacebuilding as neoliberal discipline thus functions through the agency of the beneficiaries themselves, as participation becomes the key guiding principle. As Mark Duffield puts it, 'People in the South are no longer ordered what to do – they are now expected to do it *willingly* themselves' (Duffield 2007: 34). Participation occurs every time someone attends a community reconciliation workshop, takes out a microcredit loan, provides testimony to an international court, starts a community-based organisation, or takes a Prozac pill. People are disciplined into managing themselves in the midst of extreme deprivation in the name of participating in peacebuilding – they are 'empowered', but only to exercise that power within the channels proffered by peacebuilders (Branch 2011). In northern Uganda, the result was to place widespread deprivation beyond challenge, as the spread of techniques of social self-regulation by NGOs and interna-tional organisations in a context of neoliberal state withdrawal from the responsibility for material welfare (or even survival) insulated from political contestation the structures producing that deprivation and suffering. This system of social self-management in the midst of extreme deprivation is what we identify as a neoliberal social logic, or as some have framed it, neoliberal governmentality (Ferguson and Gupta 2002).

Northern Uganda's experience with peacebuilding also illumi-nates the importance of violence to this neoliberal self-regulation:

intervention there had its path to implementation made smooth
by the extreme physical violence and political repression faced by
the Acholi rural population. The lack of significant local or national
Acholi leadership, the co-optation of potential leaders by the international NGO structures, and the concentration of the increasingly
desperate Acholi peasantry into camps, made northern Uganda a
useful ground for experimentation by international agencies, for
instance in the development of the 'cluster approach' or the International Criminal Court's intervention into the war. But, again, to
frame the causes of the war and civilian suffering as internal to the
population itself was to ignore the violence of the Ugandan state,
the role of donors in supporting that state for its embrace of neoliberal structural adjustment, and the role of humanitarian agencies in
supporting the camps for so many years. It was to displace responsibility for causing and resolving violence to the very people devastated
by that violence, exculpating all but the Acholi themselves. In what
follows, we will examine the promotion of development in the camps
and then psychosocial support in the post-war period, both of which
illustrate the deleterious political consequences of peacebuilding's
neoliberal internalisation of responsibility for war and peace to the
Acholi community.

Displaced development

During the war, the camps were a terrain of expansive development
interventions, many run by the World Bank (WB) (for the broader
context of the World Bank's involvement in Uganda, see the chapter
by Lie in this volume). In its documents, the Bank deployed the
cause-and-consequence formula to argue that northern underdevelopment had helped cause the conflict and that, once conflict had
erupted, violence and underdevelopment had become united into a
vicious circle. The medium for this mutually reinforcing interaction
was social breakdown, often conceived as the lack of 'social capital',
and so the solution to conflict was to rebuild social capital so that
the north could use development funds effectively and emerge out
of conflict. No attention was paid to the role of the government in
sustaining the war or preventing development in the north, nor, of
course, to the role of donors in allowing the government to execute
its policy in the north or to divert massive amounts of funds to the
military campaign (for more on this facet of the WB's relation to the
Ugandan state, see the chapter by Atkinson, this volume).

Instead, the WB's massive Northern Uganda Social Action Fund
(NUSAF) sought to build peace through an effort to 'support

sustainable social, cultural, and economic growth' (OPM 2002: 5). This participatory development strategy conformed to the logic of peacebuilding described above, and served as a depoliticising force, preventing the articulation of, or organisation around, the violence people faced as a result of the war and the camps. This occurred through several routes.

First, the conceit that development could be promoted among a population living in internment camps, and that return home was not the *sine qua non* of development, could serve only to help entrench the camps and occlude the fact that people were living in them because of political violence by the Ugandan government and donor complicity with that violence. It put those larger systems of violence that kept people in the camps out of bounds – development was to be promoted within those impossible limits, whose existence was taken for granted, and if people's material welfare did not improve, it was their own fault. In this way, camps may be thought to represent an extreme, but not exceptional, case of the management of precarious populations by neoliberal social logics elsewhere.

This same neoliberal logic of responsibilisation is seen in a major component of development programming during the war: the provision of microcredit, grants and livelihood support to women, youth, orphans and former rebels. In the case of youth in particular, there was a clear managerial dimension to these programmes: those sectors of the population most likely to join the rebels or otherwise disturb social order were given the opportunity to learn trades – but trades that, at best, might provide a small income and at worst were useless in the context of continued economic breakdown and displacement. Instead, it was the pedagogical function that mattered: teaching people to see their economic deprivation as resolvable through their own initiative. The Bank tailored its distribution of funds not to projects that could realistically lead to economic development or broad-based poverty reduction but rather to initiatives that would offer the promise of money to recalcitrant sectors of the population to keep them from becoming politically disruptive or challenging authority. The neoliberal Ugandan state was further absolved of responsibility for remedying people's harsh conditions, which were instead to be solved through people's own agency.

The situation in the camps represented an extreme form of a broader tendency seen with neoliberal development: the expansion of private organisations – in this case, NGOs – into public social service provision and promoting development through self-help entrepreneurship. As far back as 1989, the WB had argued that 'experience suggests that the management of primary services could be placed with decentralised agencies – local government, local communities, or NGOs' (WB 1989: 84). The withdrawal of the state and the vast expansion of NGOs in a rudimentary service delivery role led Acholi displaced persons to re-orient their demands away from the state and toward the international community through local aid agencies. The politics of material wellbeing and survival was transformed into access to foreign handouts, mediated by NGOs, which had the task of teaching the rural poor that they did not need state assistance but rather should look to themselves.

While claiming to deliver depoliticised development, what actually ended up being depoliticised in this form of 'inclusive neoliberalism', as Golooba-Mutebi and Hickey (2010) term it, are those people who are supposed to participate in interventions and be 'empowered' as a result. For one thing, the idea that the massive structural causes of poverty in the north could be effectively addressed by shifting the agency for transformation to the displaced Acholi peasantry was nonsensical. By blaming poverty on a lack of social cohesion and insufficient entrepreneurialism on the part of the Acholi, the WB economists dismissed the role that the long history of collusion between donors, capitalists, and the Ugandan political elite played in underpinning poverty. Thus, NUSAF, as Golooba-Mutebi and Hickey (2010: 1232) put it 'may actually have exacerbated the tendencies that contributed toward this situation in the first place', by reorienting people away from those responsible for the larger problems and toward blaming themselves.

Depoliticisation also characterised NUSAF's effect on local government, as the Bank went around the Local Council (LC) system in the distribution of funds and the implementation of projects because the LCs had the tendency, according to the Bank, to 'politicize development'. LCs were incorporated into this transnational administration only as surveillance tools and sources of information, and significant power over resources was, instead, given to ad hoc 'community committees' established under the guidance of NUSAF and under the trusteeship of NGOs, creating administrative systems that were unaccountable to the population but accountable to foreign donors. The Bank's strategy thus entrenched an opaque transnational administrative system that tended to co-opt and discipline the most active and engaged members of the community and undermine potentially accountable local government.

Peacebuilding thus misconstrues the cause of conflict and seeks to re-establish peace and order based not on legitimate or democratic social or political forces but on models imported by the peace-builders. In Acholi, these models and their putatively empowering, capacity-building, and participatory interventions gave rise to forms of organisation that did not have the potential to challenge the regime of displacement and structural violence under which people lived. The consequence was that peacebuilding managed the possible eruption of unmanageability among the displaced and thereby indirectly perpetuated the humanitarian crisis and the camps. By trying to impose a reified social order through discipline, these interventions also stifled the emergence of democratic social orders based upon contentious political and social organisation and action, precisely what would have been necessary to challenge the national and transnational structures that sustained the war. Individuals and groups were steered towards identities that could not challenge the forms of violence, repression and inequality that they faced, whether local, national or international. Thus, neoliberal peacebuilding naturalised and placed the violence, domination and inequality in the camps beyond question or contestation. This policy served the interests of the aid agencies, which looked to expand and legitimate their activities out of their own self-interest. Donors were able to maintain the fiction that their aid was going to a Ugandan regime committed to protecting the civilian population from the terrorist LRA. And the Ugandan government was able to maintain high levels of donor funding, which it could channel towards militarisation and towards networks of political patronage in order to maintain its grip on power (Mwenda 2010), while withdrawing further from responsibility to its population, relying on aid agencies to maintain a controlled population. Peacebuilding helped create a self-reproducing system that no one with power had an interest in challenging, and so the civilian devastation continued for years.

Today, years after the end of the war, the transnational promotion of self-management among vulnerable, war-affected populations in the name of peacebuilding takes a newly material form in the large-scale distribution of psycho-pharmaceuticals and the inculcation of practices of self-medication. We consider this regime of neoliberal governance as it has developed in the post-war period in northern Uganda in the following section.

Post-conflict peacebuilding: pharmaceutical governance

Although open fighting ended in northern Uganda almost ten years ago, the legacy of the war continues and sets the context for current forms of post-conflict peacebuilding. For one thing, the north remains far behind the rest of the country in all development indicators, with large inequalities in land access, loss of livelihoods and a growing, highly precarious semi-urban population (Branch 2013, Whyte *et al.* 2014). However, these conditions are not simply the inevitable after-effects of armed conflict; instead, they are being actively reproduced and often intensified by ongoing forms of state violence in the service of the economic interests of state elites and domestic and foreign capitalists. The most notable form this has taken is in land dispossession mediated by state violence, whether for creating 'development' through agro-business – such as in the thousands of acres allotted to sugar cane plantations – or for ranching schemes, for expanding oil extraction, for expanding game reserves, or simply for allocating to state or military elites (Martiniello 2015, Hopwood and Atkinson 2015, Atkinson and Owor 2013). Security roads that had been built into some of the most remote areas during the war are now being used to extract resources, in particular timber. Charcoal burning is another route through which the natural resources of the north are being grabbed, as massive areas of trees are being cut and burned for charcoal to be shipped to the south, both for industry and for urban areas, where nearly 90 per cent of the population depends on charcoal for fuel. State violence is thus not only entrenching economic deprivation and stripping away natural resources, but also precipitating a looming environmental crisis in the north as forests and wetlands disappear, water sources are polluted by mining and oil extraction, and land is concentrated in the hands of elites. All this would not have been possible without the devastation visited upon the Acholi community already by twenty years of war and ten years of forced internment. As Martiniello argues, 'long-term forced internment, dependence on food aid and extreme poverty generated by war created the pre-conditions for systematic land dispossession through both the state and market' (Martiniello 2015: 658).

Today's violent extractive economy, taking the form of neoliberal accumulation by dispossession, is the backdrop against which post-conflict reconstruction and peacebuilding initiatives take place. One of the most notable forms such initiatives are taking today is in the growing distribution of psycho-pharmaceuticals to broad sectors of the population in the name of addressing widespread trauma. This represents perhaps the most invasive, direct form that neoliberal discipline and self-government have taken within peacebuilding, seizing upon the very chemistry of people's brains in the name of helping them deal with the violence and legacy of the war. It also represents a highly expansive form of intervention as the concern to address trauma caused by the war has been given dramatic urgency by a series of epidemiological studies that have proclaimed spectacularly high rates of trauma in northern Uganda (Amone-P'Olak *et al.* 2014). A 2008 report even announced that Acholi had been diagnosed with the highest rate of PTSD *ever encountered*, as scientific expertise and humanitarian crisis are mobilised in order to legitimate the deployment of psycho-pharmaceuticals in northern Uganda (Roberts *et al.* 2008).

The deployment of psycho-pharmaceuticals should be placed in the context not only of the war but also of the sweeping neoliberal reforms that began in Uganda in the late 1980s, when WB and International Monetary Fund (IMF)-funded economic recovery plans demanded massive cuts to social welfare. This set the stage for a comprehensive decentralisation of the country's healthcare system, and so, over the next two decades, the adjustment logic would inform the devolution of the state's coordination of key services to individual districts and NGOs, with rural communities in many cases assuming the principal burdens. Even as reports indicated the harmful consequences of these measures – what later WB programmes would refer to as the 'social costs of adjustment' – the bureaucratic restructuring in Uganda would continue relatively unabated and eventually crystallise around a new National Health Policy in 1999.

The provision of psycho-pharmaceuticals in northern Uganda today, especially at remote rural health centres, is in large part a consequence of this broader neoliberal national structural overhaul as it intersects with the legacy of the war and ongoing violence. Pharmaceutical therapies are prescribed by mental health workers within this decentralised, defunded healthcare system as they increasingly rely upon drugs as the most viable alternative to other, more costly, forms of care such as counselling or talk therapy. Particularly in remote rural areas, where decentralisation's curtailment of human resources and infrastructure has been felt the hardest, and where the provision of qualified staff remains inconsistent, drugs of all sorts are increasingly looked to and promoted as the most efficient and sustainable form of care available. Thus, while the growing availability of psychiatric pharmaceuticals in the north may be relatively recent, the process of devolving healthcare in general by pharmaceutical means in Uganda is not, and follows a trajectory seen throughout the Global South: as national health expenditures decline, and as states are increasingly asked to accommodate an expanding and unrealisable set of 'universal' health standards, drugs are often promoted as the most 'sustainable' form of care for the rural and urban poor. The expansion of pharmaceutical use has also been pushed forward by large pharmaceutical companies who seek to expand markets in the Global South, where older regimes of drugs can be sold or dumped for significant economic profit or even for the reputational boost of providing drugs to the African poor (Day 1997, Samsky 2012, Andallah 2016). African states are often very willing to adopt these new regimes, both since they further remove the burden from state healthcare systems and because states are pressured by activists in the international community to facilitate the distribution of drugs to their population, as access to pharmaceuticals becomes framed as the fulfilment of an inalienable human right to be achieved through either market mechanisms or arrangements with NGOs or drug corporations (Petryna *et al.* 2006).

As with the delivery of relief aid and the promotion of development during the war, the provision of mental healthcare in northern Uganda today takes place through an opaque transnational, public–private structure. For instance, the turn to pharmaceuticals has been steered by World Health Organization (WHO) guidelines, and the implementation enabled by financial support and human resources provided by international institutions and agencies like the WB, the Italian Cooperation, and the UK Department for International Development (DFID), as well as by clinical expertise provided by major Western universities and research institutions. The African Development Bank has played a major role, funding a mental health unit at the government's referral hospital in Gulu, which became the key site from which mental health programmes and services focusing on 'war-related' problems radiated out into the rest of the region.

Through community sensitisations, rural clinics, and outreaches, mostly coordinated through Gulu, with assistance from international organisations, a large swath of the Acholi population has been exposed to psycho-pharmaceuticals as the centrepiece of this expansive regime of intervention. Generic tri-cyclic anti-depressants like imipramine and amitriptyline and anti-psychotic medications like haloperidol and chlorpromazine are most heavily used and, together with a range of sedatives and anti-convulsants prescribed through new diagnostic categories, have become the first order of clinical response for some of the most frequently diagnosed conditions, including anxiety, depression and post-traumatic stress.

The distribution of psycho-pharmaceuticals has also followed trends within neoliberal peacebuilding and sought to become more participatory and sensitive towards 'local culture'. In Uganda, this is seen in a new global mental health initiative called Wayo Nero which, with funding from Grand Challenges Canada, endeavours to expand access to drugs by recruiting and training honorary '*wayos*' and '*neros*' (meaning 'aunties' and 'uncles' in Acholi) to make referrals for basic mental healthcare in areas heavily affected by violence during the war, such as around massacre sites, all in the name of improving access and availability for rural people to pharmaceutical treatments (a model borrowed from HIV counselling programmes in Rakai). Thus, Acholi social networks and cultural idioms are mobilised in order to assist in the expansion and sustainability of psycho-pharmaceutical use.

The widespread deployment of drugs has introduced a new form of responsibilisation for those Acholi using them, rendering the rural poor, largely abandoned by the state, themselves responsible for managing their own deprivation and suffering under the guidance of NGOs (Povinelli 2011). The drugs regimes have reordered the priorities of entire households and shaped a new habitus around self-medicating with powerful pharmaceuticals, refilling prescriptions, drug compliance and attending the counselling and clinical consultations that allow continued access to the medicines. Drugs themselves, and anti-depressants in particular, have thus become a vital part of everyday life for many rural Acholi. Indeed, they have enabled thousands to realise a degree of relief from a litany of afflictions including headaches, nightmares, sleeplessness, body aches and visions. However, in a region struggling to remake itself in the aftermath of the conflict, such a devolvement of care and responsibility by pharmaceutical means, through which people already living at the margins are asked to neuro-chemically manage themselves with little supervision, serves to absolve the state of its most basic obligations and to help perpetuate an order of economic and political marginalisation that was a major cause of the civil war in the first place.

In this way, drugs can play a palliative role for the medicated Acholi population, providing them with a route for 'making do' and achieving an everyday kind of functioning that, according to the proponents of pharmaceutical mental health interventions, has allowed individuals and communities to overcome or at least come to terms with a traumatic past. However, the violence that the Acholi community faces on a daily basis is not just a thing of the past, to be overcome in today's supposedly normal, post-conflict present. Instead, the community continues to be subject to the violence of neoliberal dispossession, and so drugs have the potential to inure individuals – at the biochemical level – to the larger structures of violence determining their lives and the acute social suffering those structures produce (Biehl 2004). People are anesthetised against the political violence that continues to be wielded by the state, violence that is entrenching the very conditions that can lead to the anxieties and symptoms that the drugs purport to address. Pharmaceutical or therapeutic governance (Pupavac 2005) comes to characterise this vicious cycle as neoliberal discipline, with its depoliticising promotion of self-management for intense suffering and its naturalisation of the structures that cause that suffering, is reproduced in today's post-war period through psycho-pharmaceuticals. The neoliberal logics of discipline and state violence that developed during the war have proven resilient in the transition away from open conflict to the present post-conflict period, raising difficult questions for the meaning and possibilities of sustainable peace in today's neoliberal era.

Conclusions

Today it may be a different face of capitalism that is most apparent in Acholi sub-region: a state-driven extractivism that is taking advantage of often desperate poverty, a breakdown of community solidarity and structures of unaccountable and often militarised authority, all legacies of the war (Atkinson and Owor 2013, Lenhart 2013, Sjögren 2014, Martiniello 2015). Rural Acholi find themselves dispossessed of land and resources as the value of the north becomes increasingly defined around its exploitable minerals, oil, wildlife, water and trees. Land is a target for enclosure and value extraction whether through sugarcane, sunflower or pine and eucalyptus plantations, infrastructure, tourism or refugee camps. Meanwhile, the disciplinary social dimensions of neoliberalism remain present but in a new form, largely organised through expanding regimes of climate change adaptation and resilience. Just as during the war and immediately after state violence and neoliberal discipline entered into a collaborative relationship, so today it remains to be seen how exactly a coercive state-driven extractivist development will come to terms with a sustainable, consensual, 'green' development.

References

Amone-P'Olak, K. *et al.* (2014), 'The influence of different types of war experiences on depression and anxiety in a Ugandan cohort of war-affected youth: The WAYS study', *Social Psychiatry and Psychiatric Epidemiology*, 49(11), pp. 1783–92.

Andallah, H. (2016), 'Why big drug firms are seeking new markets in Africa', *The East African*, 30 July.

Atkinson, R. and Owor, A. (2013), 'Land grabbing': The Ugandan government, Madhvani, and others versus the community of Lakang, Amuru District', *Journal of Peace and Security Studies (Gulu University)*, 1.

Barnett, M. *et al.* (2007), 'Peacebuilding: What is in a name?', *Global Governance*, 13(1), pp. 35–58.

Biehl, J. (2004), 'Life of the mind: The interface of psychopharmaceuticals, domestic economies, and social abandonment', *American Ethnologist*, 3(4), pp. 475–96.

Branch, A. (2011), *Displacing Human Rights: War and Intervention in Northern Uganda* (New York, NY: Oxford University Press).

Branch, A. (2013), 'Gulu in war … and peace? The town as camp in northern Uganda', *Urban Studies*, 50(15), pp. 3152–167.

Chandler, D. (2002), *From Kosovo to Kabul: Human Rights and International Intervention* (London: Pluto).

Collier, P. *et al.* (2003), *Breaking the Conflict Trap: Civil War and Development Policy* (Washington, DC: World Bank and Oxford University Press).

Cooke, B. and Kothari, U. (eds) (2001), *Participation: The New Tyranny?* (London: Zed).

Day, M. (1997), 'Dud drugs dumped in crisis zones', *New Scientist*, 11 January.

Dean, M. (2009) [1999], *Governmentality: Power and Rule in Modern Society* (London: Sage).

Dolan, C. (2009), *Social Torture: The Case of Northern Uganda 1986–2006* (Oxford: Berghahn).

Duffield, M. (2001), *Global Governance and the New Wars: The Merging of Development and Security* (London: Zed).

Duffield, M. (2007), *Development,*

Security, and Unending War: Governing the World of Peoples (Cambridge: Polity).

Ferguson, J. and Gupta, A. (2002), 'Spatializing states: Toward an ethnography of neoliberal governmentality', *American Ethnologist*, 29(4), pp. 981–1002.

Finnström, S. (2008), *Living with Bad Surroundings: War, History, and Everyday Moments in Northern Uganda* (Durham, NC: Duke University Press).

Fox, F. (2001), 'New humanitarianism: Does it provide a moral banner for the 21st century?', *Disasters*, 25(4), pp. 275–89.

Golooba-Mutebi, F. and Hickey, S. (2010), 'Governing chronic poverty under inclusive neoliberalism: The case of the Northern Uganda Social Action Fund', *Journal of Development Studies*, 46(7), pp. 1216–39.

Harrison, G. (2010), *Neoliberal Africa: The Impact of Global Social Engineering* (London: Zed Books)

Hopwood, J. and Atkinson, R. (2015), 'Developing a land conflict monitoring and mapping tool for the Acholi sub-region of northern Uganda', JSRP Paper No. 28.

Lenhart, L. (2013), 'Alleged land grabs and governance: Exploring mistrust and trust in northern Uganda. The case of the Apaa land conflict', *Journal of Peace and Strategic Studies*, 1(1), pp. 64–85.

Martiniello, G. (2015), 'Social struggles in Uganda's Acholiland: Understanding responses and resistance to Amuru Sugar Works', *The Journal of Peasant Studies*, 42(3–4), p. 653–69.

Mwenda, A. (2010), 'Uganda's politics of foreign aid and violent conflict: The political uses of the LRA rebellion', in T. Allen and K. Vlassenroot (eds), *The Lord's Resistance Army: Myth and Reality* (London: Zed), pp. 45–58.

Office of the Prime Minister of Uganda (OPM). (2002),

'Community reconciliation and conflict management handbook', Northern Uganda Social Action Fund, 8 April.

Petryna, A., Lakoff, A. and Kleinman, A. (eds), (2006), *Global Pharmaceuticals: Ethics, Markets, Practices* (Durham, NC: Duke University Press).

Povinelli, E. A. (2011), *Economies of Abandonment: Social Belonging and Endurance in Late Liberalism* (Durham, NC: Duke University Press).

Pupavac, V. (2005), 'Human security and the rise of global therapeutic governance', *Conflict, Security and Development*, 5(2), pp. 161–181.

Roberts, B. *et al.* (2008), 'Factors associated with post-traumatic stress disorder and depression amongst internally displaced persons in northern Uganda',

BMC Psychiatry, 8(1).

Samsky, A. (2012), 'Scientific sovereignty: How international drug donation programs reshape health, disease, and the state', *Cultural Anthropology*, 27(2), pp. 310–32.

Sjögren, A. (2014), 'Scrambling for the promised land: Land acquisitions and the politics of representation in post-war Acholi, northern Uganda', *African Identities*, 12(1), pp. 62–75.

Whyte, S. R. *et al.* (2014), 'Urbanisation by subtraction: The afterlife of camps in northern Uganda', *The Journal of Modern African Studies*, 52(4), pp. 597–622.

World Bank. (1989), *Sub-Saharan Africa: From Crisis to Sustainable Growth* (Washington, DC: World Bank).

4·
'Movement legacy' and neoliberalism as political settlement in Uganda's political economy

Joshua B. Rubongoya

Introduction

The onset of multiparty politics in Uganda (2005) has been accompanied by a shift toward the elevation of politics (the state) and the diminution of economics (or the market) – thus, a clear retreat from a classic neoliberal philosophy espousing market primacy. There has been a political instrumentalisation of the market as a strategy for supporting the prerogatives of the regime in post-structural-adjustment Uganda. Economic reforms in the multiparty dispensation have had to pass a litmus test, i.e. do they contribute to the twin outcomes of improving the electoral prospects of the regime and most notably the economic fortunes of its political elites. Moreover, party elite behaviour has taken on a dynamic akin to pre-independence nationalist movements or what Hyden (2011) has called the 'movement legacy'. This chapter focuses on a dialectic between the latter (henceforth referred to as 'legacy') and neoliberalism, in order to explicate how these two have shaped the distribution of power and the allocation of rents and patronage to form a ruling coalition. The latter is understood as the totality of groups and individuals who support the ruling elite (Whitfield *et al.* 2015). The second and related mission aims at explaining how neoliberalism as both policy and rhetoric provided the financial oxygen while legacy political culture offered the normative scaffolding for Uganda's political settlement (PS) most notably in the multiparty era. Thus, neoliberal processes and their impact on Ugandans' experiences form the basis of this analysis *but* they are complemented by legacy political culture, and agency is associated with a dynamic ruling coalition interacting with ordinary citizens. Thus, to better explain Uganda's contemporary economy this theoretical perspective utilises the 'how' and 'what' functions of PS theory while deploying neoliberalism theory to provide answers to the 'why' question. This hybrid paradigm corrects for PS's lack of analytical depth (Moore 1998) by adding a more robust theoretical framework. The conclusion extrapolates the deep-rooted nature of the legacy and the transience of neoliberalism in Uganda. It posits a shift by the National Resistance Movement (NRM) away from neoliberalism to developmental nationalism as the new expression of the movement legacy. The analysis is presented in two related parts: the early 'systemic vulnerability' (1986–1996) phase and the latter 'hegemonic stability' period comprising two segments: 1996–2006 and 2006–2016.

For purposes of clarity, a distinction should be made between the 'movement' – a political system formed by President Museveni's NRM to replace political parties – and legacy or a form of political behaviour inherited from pre-independence nationalist movements. The drivers of the movement system are clear descriptors of the legacy. Hyden (2011) describes the latter as a built-in tendency for collective action to be framed in terms of a battle against a common enemy whether perceived or real. While this dynamic was key to the success of the nationalist movements it has been detrimental to post-colonial governance. For example, in typical legacy fashion, the incumbent NRM party views opposition elites/parties less as opponents worthy of healthy competition and more like 'a common enemy' to be neutralised or co-opted. The resulting concentration of power in the executive directs resource allocation and marketisation processes toward the construction of a hegemonic regime or what I have called a *Pax Musevenica* (Rubongoya 2007). This power structure is marked by proscribed political competition and suppressed regular rotation between incumbents and opposition political elites. The legacy is therefore descriptive of a political culture or a set of underlying norms that appear to have interlocked well with those of neoliberalism to produce a synthesis, i.e. a political settlement. Out of this legacy/neoliberal dialectic have emerged several trends: (a) a deeply embedded political class that has accumulated enormous wealth in an economy that has registered an average GDP growth rate of 5.19 per cent in 2014–2017 (www.tradingeconomics.com: UBOS), (b) not surprisingly, a rapidly growing gap between rich and poor and (c) a sharpening social class consciousness. The roots of the legacy are located in the period preceding independence from British rule.

The historical antecedents of the movement legacy

Political organisation (and behaviour) in Africa continues to be heavily influenced by the legacy of pre-independence social/

nationalist movements. Understanding the character of movements and their relationship to the struggles for independence illuminates party behaviour and politics in Africa. Hyden (2011, 2013) has identified the following six defining characteristics of movements akin to nationalist struggles and characteristics of post-colonial politics. In *orientation* political movements tend to focus around a *cause* as opposed to *issues*; the regime often constitutes the *level* of operation; the main *arena* of operation is often society while the *method* of operation is mobilisation. Membership tends to be diffused and most importantly movements' claims to resources are often unconstrained by rule of law. As will be evident below, the latter characteristic is central to understanding resource allocation patterns and the ubiquitous clientelist networks that interlock with the marketisation strands of neoliberalism to produce a unique political settlement. What were the lines of continuity between pre-independence social movements and post-colonial political organisation?

First, prospects for independence from a hegemonic colonial state compelled Africans to transcend their socio-cultural differences in pursuit of a supreme cause, i.e. self-determination and self-rule. 'Cause' has thus remained a defining attribute of party behaviour. Under the NRM, the 'cause' has fundamentally focused on regime entrenchment and in particular President Museveni's stay at the helm of both party and state. Issue-driven politics has remained tangential to this overarching objective.

Second, the nationalists' biggest requisite need was unity to vanquish the colonial state and not competition. Similarly, the NRM's original imperative was to mobilise one unified and coherent organisation that would trigger a critical mass of resistance against Obote's army. Having assumed power (1986) the NRM deemed competition from opposition parties as 'inconvenient'. Multipartyism (since 2005) has not been followed by inter-party competition. Inside the NRM competition only occurs under controlled conditions and definitely not at the level of party leadership where Museveni cannot be challenged.

Third, mobilisation (and not campaigning) for a worthy cause and against a common enemy was crucial for the success of the nationalist movements. During the NRM bush war there was heavy emphasis on popular mobilisation with Luwero as the epicentre. Because of this legacy, the NRM has remained mobilisational first and campaign-oriented second. NRM mobilisation strategies take place in (civil and non-civil) societal spaces not unlike those of the nationalist movements.

In sum, legacy political dynamics constitute a political culture underpinning Uganda's political economy. The NRM has taken full advantage of donor aid from both bilateral and multilateral purveyors of neoliberalism. These financial flows have been crucial to the NRM political recruitment objectives, chief of which was the construction of a loyal ruling coalition. This class has in turn expanded the reach and influence of the NRM by creating a labyrinth of patron–client networks that have helped the re-composition of Uganda's hegemonic project in which rule of capital is supreme (Saad-Filho and Yalman 2010). This neoliberal/legacy dynamic has continued to shape the distribution of resources and ipso facto of economic and social relations of subordination.

Movement legacy as frame for Uganda's political settlement

Understood as ideology, policy, discourse or class project, neoliberalism is bound to re-arrange not just the logic of the state but more importantly state–society relations. Therefore, to understand the impact of neoliberalism it is crucial to employ PS theory to shed light on the complex societal shifts and political/economic transformations in Uganda's post structural adjustment era. A PS emerges when the distribution of benefits supported by its institutions is consistent with the distribution of power in society *and* the economic and political outcomes of these institutions are sustainable over time (Khan 2010). It is a 'set of institutions and power relations characterizing the social order in a particular country' (*ibid.*). Political settlements analysis directs attention to key elite bargains (and social compromises) that shape the balance or distribution of power among contending social groups and classes (*ibid.*). It derives key conclusions regarding state making, domestic class consolidation and state/party reproduction. Finally, it helps describe why the NRM accepted and implemented structural adjustment policy, the strident neoliberal slant that followed and its decline after 2005.

Not unlike most African states, Uganda's PS is a clientelist one. It is supported by complex networks of patron–client relationships that form the underpinnings to *informal* bargains and institutional arrangements (*ibid.*). Khan (2010) further argues that clientelist political settlements have two dimensions: patron–client allocative rules, and informal adaptations to the ways in which particular formal institutions work in the allocation of benefits and distribution of power. State making and wealth accumulation occur as a result of these *informal* clientelist contestations which find their expression in the more visible *formal* institutions such as the Uganda Investment Authority (UIA), Uganda Revenue Authority (URA), etc. Thus, state making and wealth accumulation have been shaped by the imperatives of neoliberal economic, ideological and policy drivers such as free markets, capitalist social relations, respective subjectivities and the hegemony of capital (Harrison 2005). But state making occurred in the context of a legacy/neoliberal dialectic.

The legacy-neoliberal dialectic in the era of Pax Musevenica

There are two phases of Uganda's post-1986 PS over the thirty years of *Pax Musevenica* – the first one from 1986 to 1996, described herein as the period of 'systemic vulnerability' (Doner *et al.* 2005, Henley 2013). It is a period characterised by liberal politics and structural adjustment, the latter acting as precursor to the neoliberal ideology, policy and rhetoric of the 2010s. The second or 'hegemonic stability' phase has run from 1996 to date. These two decades are Janus-faced. The first, from 1996 to 2006, was the most neoliberal period in Uganda. Ugandans experienced heavy doses of neoliberalism as 'project' by which commodification, commercialisation and marketisation were planted and nurtured through both policy and rhetoric. Neoliberalism not only shaped the social order in Uganda but it also framed the state allocation of resources and the distribution of power between state elites and society.

The legacy (as political culture) would also begin to take more concrete form. The political emerging settlement was itself an expression of a stable ruling coalition made so by the absence of competing political parties. However, this changed in 2005 when movement politics was ended, multiparty politics restored, and the constitution amended to remove the term limits provision. This second face of 'hegemonic stability' was characterised by a more inward-looking NRM steering a more strident state. The market was instrumentalised – it now served the interests of the ever-shifting ruling coalition. The latter began experiencing internal tensions as the NRM purged non-conformists to better equip itself for multiparty competition. The flow of patronage increased, thus fortifying the clientelist political settlement. And as the legacy effect became more pronounced, so did the drift away from policy toward the rhetorical dimensions of neoliberalism. What explains the dynamics of each phase? How does the dialectic of the legacy and neoliberalism frame the PS and with it, Uganda's development prospects?

Systemic vulnerability (1986–1996)

Although their argument is based on observations from South East Asia, Doner *et al.*'s (2005) reference to 'systemic vulnerability' as providing incentives for growth-enhancing governance is apropos for explaining Uganda's political economy during this first decade. As explained below, systemic vulnerability is an outcome of a mix of external threats, resource scarcity and the threat of domestic protests against the regime. Thus in order to consolidate and legitimise NRM power during this period there was a need 'to offer side payments [patronage] to important interests domestically' (*ibid.*). Henley (2013) argues that this combination of factors provides a strong incentive for elites to increase the availability of resources.

Systemic vulnerability in Uganda can be located at four key co-ordinates. First, the NRM government had not secured full control of the entire country as rebel groups opposing it, together with pockets of Obote's retreating military, continued to present resistance and opposition. There was therefore an urgency to elimi-nate resistance and provide security and stability. The campaign to rid the country of armed rebellion would continue well beyond 1996, most notably because of the resilience of Joseph Kony and his Lord's Resistance Army (LRA) (Kayunga 1997). Nonetheless the NRM government's immediate duty was to quell an alphabet soup of rebel groups ranging from the ADF, UDA, PRA, UNRF and UPA to the UFA (see Rubongoya 2007, 2010 for a detailed analysis of these groups). Local Defense Units (LDUs) were set up in all areas under NRM control and the NRA was augmented with new trainees. Most significantly the NRM instituted training schools known as *mchaka mchaka* to train and equip citizens with basic defence skills and incul-cate political values among civilian participants – norms that greatly contributed to its legitimacy and power consolidation project. The narrative at this time was that all citizens should be able to defend themselves against any future abuses by a tyrannical leader. However, this marked the genesis of the military (and related security agencies) as a key and enduring section of the emerging political settlement. In an atmosphere of insecurity, NRM elites rolled out these policies and programmes because of the prevailing softness (vulnerability) in a gestating political system that was sitting atop a tattered economy.

Second, vulnerability was symptomatic of prevailing poor eco-nomic conditions. Production sectors were moribund, the currency

worthless and most institutions of the economy in need of rehabilitation. Museveni's socialist ideals and aspirations were well known
(Kanyogonya in Museveni 2000). However, systemic vulnerability
and a dose of pragmatic thinking help shed light on why an avowed
socialist in Museveni would perform a *volte-face* and embrace
Structural Adjustment Programmes (SAPs) for economic revitalisa-
tion. Uganda was badly in need of aid and loans, and thus Museveni's
government accepted International Monetary Fund/World Bank
SAPs. Privatisation and the sale of most public-owned economic
enterprises was central to this programme. International financial
institutions (IFIs) soon emerged as key drivers of Uganda's developing
political settlement. The SAPs and the 1987 Economic Recovery
Program (ERP) became the precursors of IFI-driven neoliberalism in
Uganda. The marketisation process was complemented with incentives to attract foreign entrepreneurs, most notably Asians expelled
by Amin in 1972. The Asian commercial bourgeoisie (later led by the
Chinese) would become key drivers of the incipient settlement as an
important section of an emerging foreign commercial class. Their
financial campaign contributions became (and remain) critical to the
regime maintenance project. In the agricultural sector government
policy provided incentives (e.g. farming implements and seeds) for
increasing production in areas such as coffee, dairy, fisheries, etc.
By 1996 the economy was on the mend boasting a robust 7 per cent
growth rate over the previous five years. Uganda became the darling
of IFIs and a showcase for neoliberal economic policy success. Thus
the country entered the era of hegemonic stability with the goodwill
of the international financial community which would be strengthened by Uganda's willingness to join the 'war on terror' during which
both multilateral and bilateral aid increased and became securitised
(Rubongoya 2010).

Re-institutionalising politics represented the third co-ordinate.
The rules and norms that would be key to a new political arrange-
ment were vital for legitimising the state and the NRM government.
In typical political movement fashion, the NRM forbid parties from
directly participating in politics, presenting itself instead as a band-
wagon open to all political office aspirants. Kasfir (2000) has argued
that within the limits of this so-called 'movement' democracy, the
1989 local elections were not only free and fair but they helped legitimise the NRM as it began its transition from guerrilla army to civilian
government. As part of the legitimacy project, the NRM formed a
'broad-based' government – political elites from previous regimes
were absorbed. The resulting sense of inclusiveness was politically

appealing, signalling a fresh and improved political dispensation. This would dramatically change in the hegemonic stability period and particularly after 2005 when multipartyism caused a hardening in the political arteries of the NRM forcing it to be exclusive. Nonetheless, for now, revamped civil–military relations provided an improved public image of the NRM.

Finally, in 1995, following country-wide consultations, a new constitution was promulgated thus concluding the civilianisation of the NRM government. However, a cursory look at the Constitution reveals several areas representing seeds of the legacy that would sprout and mature after 1996. For example, 'movement democracy' and its supporting system were legalised in the Constitution, thus dispelling any hope that multiparty political competition would be re-introduced soon. Furthermore, as vulnerability eased several laws were enacted by parliament entrenching the movement system and further proscribing competitive political contestation. Democracy was evolving but social mobilisation remained a key strategy of political organisation which mostly occurred at (civil) societal level.

Clearly, systemic vulnerability promoted a liberal brand of politics – a hallmark of NRM's first ten years – while also providing a progressive dimension to NRM elite behaviour which culminated in the 1996 elections. The state could now legitimately claim the right to command and conduct public affairs (Rubongoya 2007). Moreover the ruling coalition was intact and a consensus built around the Ten Point Programme was still holding. Thus growing legitimacy lowered the cost for ruling coalition coherence. The NRM had therefore constructed enough governance capacity. However, the more concrete forms of the legacy lay hidden deep in the subconscious of the NRM and the typical clientelist identity of the PS would come into sharper focus in the second phase of hegemonic stability.

Hegemonic stability (1996–2006) (I)

As the phase of systemic vulnerability diminished and the regime expanded its authority, legacy political behaviour (supported by free-flowing aid) became a more dominant driver of the elite bargains that ultimately determined the distribution of benefits and the eventual economic and political institutions shaping the NRM's staying power. The NRM legitimacy project dovetailed well with the prevailing neoliberal ideological orientation toward poverty reduction and pro-poor politics. Using classic legacy strategy the NRM government had co-opted key sections of civil society in order to implement the donor-pushed, now seven-year-old, Poverty Eradication Action Plan (PEAP). The Ministry of Planning and Economic Development initiated the Poverty Action Fund (PAF), which ring-fenced finance from debt relief for areas of government expenditure deemed to be pro-poor (Hickey 2013). As a result, expenditure in the areas of education and health increased from 18 per cent to 35 per cent of the budget between 1997 and 2005 (Piron and Norton 2004). The following were accepted and became either policy or policy underpinnings: macroeconomic stability, market competition, rapid export growth, foreign direct investment (FDI), economic 'modernisation', deregulation of consumer and producer prices. This neoliberal marketisation/privatisation thrust was also linked to the ideological rhetoric of 'good governance', i.e. 'government downsizing, decentralisation and devolution of power'. However, the reality was that the no-party system was institutionalised in the 1995 Constitution and when this provision was lifted in 2005 the presidential term limits statute was repealed. The so-called broad-based government ended and the new multiparty dispensation existed only in name. Political space was proscribed: (a) key sections of civil society were co-opted and (b) the NRM now held an overwhelming majority of seats in parliament. Several pieces of legislation were passed that bolstered NRM hegemony: the 2002 anti-terrorism law was so sweeping it also curtailed the capacity of civil society to engage freely in interest articulation (Rubongoya 2010); the 2005 Political Parties and Organizations Act (PPOA) was enacted to control and shape party behaviour/organisation; later the 2013 Public Order and Management Act (POMA) infused state repression in the language of law and order.

Clearly, the NRM was a political movement not a party open to contestation with others and open to competitive co-existence on ideological or programmatic grounds. The proponents of neoliberalism not only provided the life blood of the regime, i.e. funding 50 per cent of recurrent budget expenditure and creating the environment for donor (e.g. World Bank) support but they looked the other way in light of growing NRM autocracy. Hickey (2013) sums up this interface between legacy behaviour and neoliberal benign neglect:

> donors were looking for a success story which could be used
> to justify their new approach, and were willing to overlook
> the government's tendencies in other areas, most notably the
> opposition to multiparty politics, growing levels of corruption
> and military involvement in the Congo.

The donor community therefore became the substructure to the emerging ruling coalition and as such a key element of the political settlement. The ideological hegemony of neoliberal rhetoric touted Uganda as a fast-growth state with significant poverty reduction (18 per cent according to the IMF between 1992/93 and 1996/1997) – one that was deserving of increased financial support. But to reiterate, donor funding also unwittingly found its way to clients of the regime mostly in the form of rents which are the physical manifestation of the endemic corruption in Uganda's political system/settlement. Following the 11 September 2001 terrorist attacks the NRM was quick to join the US in the global 'war on terror'. The ensuing securitisation of aid greatly benefitted the political movement goals of the NRM especially now that aid flowed into the state coffers ostensibly to ensure Uganda's continued military presence in Somalia (Rubongoya 2010).

Hegemonic stability (2006–2016) (II)

Several key political events shaped the second phase of hegemonic stability and, against neoliberal flattering narratives, continued to transform Uganda's political settlement. This period marks two general elections (2011 and 2016) in the so-called multiparty, no-presidential-term-limits dispensation. Second, the intraparty fragmentation intensified in general but the more consequential was that inside the NRM. As a result the cost of maintaining NRM support increased with the 2011 elections estimated to have cost $350 million (Fisher 2014) with some of it coming from supplementary budget requests and the donor-supported Consolidated Fund. In the 2016 elections, costs were even greater owing to further intraparty fragmentation caused by former Prime Minister Amama Mbabazi's candidacy. The Alliance for Campaign Finance Monitoring (ACFIM) estimates the 2016 election to have cost a minimum of $716 million, most of it spent by NRM candidates (quoted in Wilkins 2016). Patronage inflation resulted from the high levels of economic growth (6.3 per cent of GDP in 1990 and an average of 7 per cent per year in the 2000s) of the previous two decades when Uganda had transitioned out of the highly indebted poor country (HIPC) category and consequently incomes (especially for urban dwellers) had risen. Politically this meant that the government needed much more money to buy off a relatively wealthier populace due to intraparty fragmentation.

Increased demand for patronage also intensified corruption established at $300 million annually by the World Bank. This led to decreased financial support from donors followed by a concomitant rise in the domestic versus foreign share of Uganda's budget after 2004/5 (Hickey 2013). This shift has had three significant effects, all of which have re-shaped the organisation of power in Uganda. First, as reliance on Western aid declined, political elites asserted more policy autonomy; the pro-poor, donor-led PEAP programme was replaced with a National Development Plan (NDP) in April 2010. The NDP was underpinned by new rhetoric aimed at the 2011 and 2016 general elections. It involved slogans like: 'structural transformation', 'modernisation' and finally 'middle income status'. Second, independence from donors led to a shift in ideological orientation from laissez faire to a nationalist/populism that reified state over market. In the NDP, for example, under 'roles of the state' is listed the following: 'ensuring that public goods are supplied' and 'reducing inequality'. Under the civil society section it states: 'Government enjoys productive partnerships with civil society ... and together with stakeholders [will] find more sustainable sources of financing the work of the NGOs' (Uganda NDP 2010/11 to 2014/15: 64, 66). This appears to indicate intensified political movement behaviour by the NRM in the coming decade. Third, as neoliberalism has faded in significance, elite incentives now flow from a different source. The ruling coalition has pivoted in the direction of a more nationalistic/populist political economy and will become more strident as newly discovered oil begins to flow. Chinese investments in oil exploration coupled with other forms of bilateral aid from Beijing replaced Western aid, thus injecting China directly into Uganda's political settlement. The rents that will predictably flow from this new economic development will only serve to strengthen the ruling coalition.

Finally, high rates of economic growth characteristic of the hegemonic stability period have not been accompanied by equally impressive levels of development; in some areas poverty and inequality increased most notably in the north (Deninger and Okidi 2003). What Makoba (2011) has called growth without development and equity has caused Museveni to pivot toward a more state-oriented, populist ideology – a shift from poverty reduction to state-led growth. The prospects of success using this productivist paradigm, however, are poor, given that the NRM has shown no commitment to coherent and strategic redistribution. Take for example the Plan for Modernisation of Agriculture (PMA), 2001–2009, which was intended to improve the conditions of the rural poor; instead it enriched the state/ruling class and a key ruling coalition section – the medium and large-scale farmers (Martin-iello 2015). Thus, clientelistic redistribution is framed by intensified intraparty fragmentation and as such stymies popular redistribution. These developments in turn impact the political system by transfer-ring the character of the ruling coalition.

The political settlement in neoliberal perspective

The critical turning point in the political economy of Uganda can be located at the nexus of two key developments in 2005, namely the lifting of the ban on opposition party contestation and repeal of presidential term limits. Renewed opposition party activities had the following important implications: (a) what became the NRM-Organization (NRM-O) party was now forced to accept (at least in principle) what it had always rejected, i.e. inter-party political competition. The no-party system had allowed the NRM to handle and quell dissent in-house, now it had to shift gears and lay out strat-egies that would ensure NRM victories amidst withering opposition party critics; (b) the NRM could now expel intransigent members; however, these elites (e.g. Kizza Besigye and Augustine Ruzindana) then became ardent foes due to their familiarity with the internal workings of the NRM-O machine; (c) the stakes for Museveni's designs to be president for life were now quite high – they culmi-nated in the 2017 NRM campaign to lift the presidential age limit from the constitution.

The innovative ideas and institutional coherence of the systemic vulnerability period were now replaced by the old, tired schemes of immediate post-colonial politics with its legacy trappings of divide and rule, restricted political space, mobilisational and identity poli-tics. The NRM had (in principle) allowed opposition party politics while depressing their activities, marginalising and co-opting their leadership and blocking channels of financial support.

Overall, the ruling coalition now rests on a dynamic and complex network of power centres the first of which comprises agents of state and local government, leaders of churches and mosques, a cadre of lower level, patronage-dependent rural supporters with personal connections to State House, and key political elites/bureaucrats in the Ministry of Finance, Planning and Economic Development (MoFPED), Bank of Uganda (BoU), etc. The second is the myriad security agencies ranging from police, para-military forces and army to intelligence networks and LDUs who help to provide what

Ugandans value the most – stability and peace. Uganda's military extends outside its boundaries as peacekeepers in Somalia and Sudan – the crux of regime legitimacy and indispensability. This element also connects the ruling coalition to US bilateral aid, amidst declining donor support. Nonetheless donor advisory and discursive input continues to shape policy, e.g. the NDP. Together with the technocracy of MoFPED and BoU, donors and bilateral allies have enabled Uganda's macro-economic stability. However, with declining donor support and economic growth the ruling coalition has shifted investment focus away from production sectors to real estate. Uganda's building boom is a consequence of neoliberal strengthening of private property rights and titling all of which underscore a new development characterised by Martiniello (2013) as natural resource and primitive accumulation.

The third crucial component of the ruling coalition and thus settlement comprises foreign investors, particularly the Chinese and their local Ugandan counterparts. These economic groups are well organised, closely aligned with the NRM and politically powerful. They are the life blood of emerging development and the source of badly needed patronage often in the form of campaign finance. Chinese investments in road, rail and energy infrastructure has helped the credibility of Museveni's rhetoric touting middle-income status for Uganda.

Conclusion

Notwithstanding the re-introduction of opposition party politics, the NRM has never disavowed its identity as a political movement. While the political culture of the movement legacy somewhat diminished in the first ten years, the post-2005 era witnessed a clear shift in which the state/regime have gained supremacy over market dominance. Indeed this political instrumentalisation of the market is an offspring of the legacy. As a political movement, the NRM has mounted contentious challenges against opposition elites while mobilising Ugandans around several nationalistic causes such as the urgency of 'fundamental change' 'nation building', 'prosperity and education for all', the 'war on poverty', etc. In governing Uganda, Museveni has framed collective action in terms of a battle against a common enemy. In the period of systemic vulnerability the common enemy was identified as 'backwardness', 'multiparty politics' and 'poverty' but in the last two decades the stigma has been associated with competitive opposition politics. NRMs shared collective action and identity – both key requisites for political movements – began during the bush war and have been sustained through the *mchaka mchaka* and other socialisation strategies. Common and overlapping interests and values of the ruling coalition have formed the basis for mobilisation against opponents. Legacy *modus operandi* is also evident in the frequent disregard for rule of law, which is viewed in instrumentalist terms, i.e. if it contributes to regime survival, otherwise informalism and personalistic relations prevail. Indeed centralisation of power embedded in vast patron–client networks provides evidence of the resilience of movement legacy politics.

The steady and constant flow of patronage and the creation of clientelist networks of support have been key ingredients to NRM survival as a political movement, hence the significance of donor and IFI financing as a dimension of state building through budget support. But equally critical has been the role of neoliberal discursive and ideological rhetoric which has legitimised the state and bolstered regime hegemony. As aid became securitised in the aftermath of 9/11, bilateral support (with fewer strings attached) became easier to funnel into maintenance of the political movement. However as all these sources of support have decreased, Museveni has acquired new sources of funding, most notably from China and in future from oil sales. Not surprisingly a new anti-elitist political strategy is now evidenced by the president's preference for populist modes of service delivery (Hickey 2013). This, coupled with a new rhetoric (cause) of attaining middle-income status by 2017 also marks a shift to a new ideology – developmental nationalism – and a pivot toward an enclave development model. The market has clearly taken a back seat in relation to the state. The prospects for success will depend on whether the political movement that is the NRM has the political will and resolve to implement a coherent programme of social (rather than clientelist) redistribution in an atmosphere of deepening intraparty fragmentation.

References

Deninger, K. and Okidi, J. (2003), 'Growth and poverty reduction in Uganda, 1998–2000: Panel data evidence', *Development Policy Review*, 21(7), pp. 481–509.

Doner, R., Ritchie, B. K. and Slater, D. (2005), 'Systemic vulnerability and the origins of developmental states: Northeast and Southeast Asia in comparative perspective', *International Organization*, 59(2), pp. 327–61.

Fisher, J. (2014), 'The limits – and limiters – of external influence: The role of international donors in Uganda's 2011 election', in S. Perrot, S. Makara, and J. Lafargue (eds), *Elections in a Hybrid Regime: Revisiting the 2011 Ugandan Polls* (Kampala: Fountain).

Harrison, G. (2005), 'Economic faith, social project and a misreading of African society: The travails of neoliberalism in Africa', *Third World Quarterly*, 26(8), pp. 1303–20.

Henley, D. (2013), 'Sources of developmental ambition in Southeast Asia: Political interests and collective assumptions', Developmental Regimes in Africa Working Papers No. 2, London.

Hickey, S. (2013), 'Beyond the poverty agenda? Insights from the new politics of development in Uganda', *World Development*, 43, pp. 194–206.

Hyden, G. (2011), 'The barriers to party systems in Africa: The movement legacy', *Africa Review: Journal of African Studies Association of India*, 3(2), pp. 103–22.

Hyden, G. (2013), *African Politics in Comparative Perspective*. 2nd edition (New York, NY: Cambridge University Press).

Kasfir, N. (2000), '"Movement" democracy, legitimacy and power in Uganda', in J. Mugaju and J. Oloka-Onyango (eds), *No-Party Democracy in Uganda: Myths and Realities* (Kampala: Fountain).

Kayunga, S. (1997), 'The impact of armed opposition on the movement system in Uganda', in J. Mugaju and J. Oloka-Onyango (eds), *No-Party Democracy in Uganda: Myths and Realities* (Kampala: Fountain).

Khan, M. (2010), 'Political settlements and the governance of growth enhancing institutions', SOAS Working Paper, July.

Makoba, J. W. (2011), *Rethinking Development Strategies in Africa:*

The Triple Partnership as an Alternative Approach. The case of Uganda (Bern: Peter Lang).

Martiniello, G. (2013), 'Land dispossession and rural social movements: The 2011 conference in Mali', *Review of African Political Economy*, 40(136), pp. 209–20.

Martiniello, G. (2015), 'Social struggles in Uganda's Acholiland: Understanding responses and resistance to Amuru Sugar Works', *Journal of Peasant Studies*, 42(3–4), pp. 653–69.

Moore, M. (1998), 'Death without taxes: Democracy, state capacity and aid dependence in the Fourth World', in M. Robinson and G. White (eds), *The Democratic Developmental State: Politics and Institutional Design* (Oxford: Oxford University Press), pp. 84–121.

Museveni, Y. K. (2000), *What Is Africa's Problem?* (Minneapolis, MN: University of Minnesota Press).

National Planning Authority. (2010), Uganda National Development Plan (2010/11 to 2014/15), Kampala.

Piron, L. and Norton, A. (2004), 'Politics and the PRSP approach: Uganda case study', Overseas Development Institute Working Paper No. 240, London.

Rubongoya, J. (2007), *Regime Hegemony in Museveni's Uganda: Pax Musevenica* (New York, NY: Macmillan).

Rubongoya, J. (2010), 'The politics of Uganda's anti-terrorism law and its impact on civil society', in J. Howell, and J. Lind (eds), *Civil Society under Strain: Counter Terrorism Policy, Civil Society and Aid Post 9/11* (Sterling, VA: Kumarian Press), pp. 209–26.

Saad-Filho, A. and Yalman, G. L. (2010), 'Introduction', in A. Saad-Filho and G. L. Yalman (eds), *Economic Transitions to Neoliberalism in Middle-Income* (London: Routledge), pp. 1–8.

The Ten-Point Political Programme,
Available at: www.austria-uganda.
at/dokumente/Ten-Point%20
Programme.pdf [accessed 5
November 2016].

Whitfield, L. *et al.* (2015), *The Politics
of African Industrial Policy: A
Comparative Perspective* (New York,
NY: Cambridge University Press).

Wilkins, S. (2016), 'Who pays for
pakalast? The NRM's peripheral
patronage in rural Uganda',
Journal of Eastern African Studies,
10(4), pp. 619–38.

5
More is less? Decentralisation and regime control in neoliberal Uganda

Kristof Titeca

Introduction

When the National Resistance Movement (NRM) captured power and formed a government in January 1986, it found a highly centralised administrative structure started by the 1967 Local Administration Act and maintained by successive regimes (Nsibambi 1998). The NRM quickly went about changing this by introducing what was soon to be branded one of the most ambitious and radical decentralisation policies in sub-Saharan Africa (Asiimwe and Nakanyike 2007), whose 'scale and scope of the transfer of power and responsibilities to the local level' were considered exceptional (Steiner 2006: 5). Equally exceptional was the growth in the number of districts in Uganda: the number of districts increased from 33 in 1986 to 112 districts in 2018, with the growth being particularly strong since 2008.

At the same time, recent years have seen a wide range of measures which have subverted earlier decentralisation measures, and have contributed to recentralisation: the graduated tax – the most important autonomous source of income for local governments – was abolished just before the 2006 elections. Preceding this in September 2005, Chief Administrative Officers were no longer hired by the local government, but by the national government. Moreover, the grip of the Resident District Commissioner – the direct representative of the president at a district level – over local politics strongly increased.

To make sense of these processes this chapter will show how the dynamics of de- and re-centralisation, while apparently contradictory, are different sides of the same coin: both are manifestations of the evolving strategies of the Museveni regime to tighten its grip on power. Second, these strategies fit firmly in the neoliberalisation of Uganda and its political culture. As shown in the introduction, neoliberalism as a project not only materialises itself economically, but is more encompassing, including social, cultural and political formations. This chapter is particularly interested in how neoliberalisation manifests itself in political formations, i.e. the commodification, commercialisation and marketisation of politics. Illustrated earlier in this book, decentralisation was a central part of the neoliberal post-Washington consensus with its emphasis on good governance. In doing so, and as this chapter will show, decentralisation did not enhance participation at the local level, but rather served as a patronage instrument of the national government: devoid of other patronage instruments in a neoliberal context, the national government increasingly turned to decentralisation to appease demands for patronage. In doing so, the number of districts grew significantly, but their power was strongly reduced: their capacity for autonomous decision making had been severely curtailed, as the national government wanted to reduce their independence, which represented a potential threat to power. This argument is developed in the following sections. This chapter begins by explaining the link between neoliberalisation, patronage and decentralisation.

Neoliberalisation, patronage and decentralisation

The introduction of decentralisation and neoliberalism were closely connected. The retreat of the state provided the necessary context for decentralisation to develop; and Structural Adjustment Programmes (SAPs) were the 'political-economic channel for disseminating decentralisation discourse to the Third World' (Schuurman 1997: 154). Economic liberalisation and decentralisation went hand in hand, as the latter reshaped 'economic policymaking from central authority to localities, nongovernmental organizations, and private markets' (Ozcan 2006: 121). It has been argued that in the context of a minimal state, deregulation and privatisation, decentralisation may 'appear as a way for many nation-states to give democracy some substance' (Schuurman 1997: 161). Countering this, it has been argued that in reality decentralisation has the opposite effect of draining the political out of local governments, by sidelining issues such as participation and political or structural change: it has been shown how decentralisation is sometimes primarily interested in promoting economic efficiency rather than political change and it is often underpinned by rational choice visions and narratives of efficiency, rather than ideas of local governments as a seedbed of democratic practice (Mohan and Stokke 2000: 250). The participatory and empowering nature of decentralisation is therefore being questioned: 'while sharing similar rhetorics with grassroots, bottom-up forms of participation, they tend to promote top down models of participation' (Dagnino 2007, cited in Guarneros-Meza and Geddes 2010: 120). More generally, decentralisation is considered to be contributing to the status quo, or even of being reactionary as it furthers fragmentation (Harvey 1989: 277, cited in Schuurman 1997: 165), often allowing political elites to reproduce existing power configurations (Guarneros-Meza and Geddes 2010: 123).

The ways in which decentralisation measures have been introduced in this context have been named 'strategies of subversion' (Resnick 2014: 61) or 'repertoires of domination' (Poteete and Ribot 2011). The former can be defined as 'tactics used by central governments in the fiscal, administrative and political domains' which are 'aimed at reducing the autonomy of local government' (Resnick 2014: 61); while the latter can be described as 'myriad tactics government officials and nonstate actors use to limit meaningful shifts of authority associated with decentralization' (Poteete and Ribot 2011: 440), or the 'routine claim-making actions available to actors as they seek to gain, expand, or defend positions of dominance vis-à-vis particular types of other actors' (*ibid.*). This is an ongoing process, through which hierarchy is reproduced (*ibid.*; while others highlight how powerful actors are 'resisting' decentralisation, Poteete and Ribot use the term 'domination', as resistance is often used to analyse the actions of the poor against domination by the powerful). Repertoires of domination are therefore various strategies that are used to maintain power; as Resnick (2014: 62) points out, different from Poteete and Ribot's repertoires of domination, strategies of subversion are not necessarily aimed at retaining power, but are primarily focused on accountability. This chapter is primarily focused on power, hence we rely on repertoires of domination. These are closely related with the broader political context: decentralisation and the general political climate mirror and reinforce each other.

In the context of neoliberalisation, districts became an important commodity in the political marketplace. This also was the case in Uganda: traditionally, the Museveni regime had used patronage to sustain its power. Structural adjustment and good governance programmes had made it increasingly difficult to use government resources to do so, as these led to the privatisation of large parastatals, a reduction in the size of the civil service and army, and the elimination of the state marketing board monopolies over key primary commodities. These measures dramatically reduced the available rents for patronage (Green 2010). In this context, decentralisation opened new avenues for political patronage. As Mwenda (2007: 31) observed: 'with each new district came a raft of government jobs, each one a patronage opportunity'. In this way, neoliberalism, patronage and decentralisation are closely tied together. Yet, while the number of districts increased, independent and autonomous local governments were seen as a threat to the power of the Museveni regime. The establishment therefore had to find ways of neutralising these threats, which will be described in detail below.

The evolution of decentralisation in Uganda

The roots of Uganda's decentralisation process can be found in the Resistance Councils installed during the rebellion of the NRM. These locally organised councils were installed to provide support to the rebellion, but were also conceived as a way to establish popular democracy. The NRM argued that decentralisation was part of their agenda to establish local democracy and in line with their 'Ten Point Programme' written during the guerrilla war, which was supposed to guide the NRM government while in power (Muhumuza 2008: 64). In this way, the NRM's decentralisation effort was a 'home grown' policy (ibid.: 64) at a time when the international policy environment had become largely in favour of decentralisation reforms.

The 1995 Constitution and the 1997 Local Government Act formally implemented decentralisation and were described as 'among the most detailed and comprehensive legislative frameworks in sub-Sahara Africa' (Steffensen and Trollegaard 2000, cited in Awortwi 2011: 365). These legal measures decentralised a whole range of services (see Awortwi and Helmsing 2015: 303 for a list), core fiscal control functions (Steffensen 2006) and the political process. In other words, when introduced by the NRM decentralisation had the explicit aim to introduce popular democracy, with a whole range of formal measures applied to guarantee this. At the same time, decentralisation played an important role for the national government: it allowed the rebel group turned government (the NRM) to acquire political legitimacy. It also provided the necessary institutional infrastructure in order to 'galvanize political support and reward loyalists' (Muhumuza 2008: 68). This meant that from the beginning, there was a tension between technocratic and political incentives for decentralisation (Francis and James 2003).

The above situation started changing gradually, as political incentives prevailed over technical ones. A primary reason for this was the increasingly competitive political climate in Uganda, as support for President Museveni had been reducing steadily: in the 1996 elections, President Museveni had achieved 76 per cent of the votes; in 2001, 69 per cent; and in 2006, the year multiparty elections had been introduced, 59 per cent of the votes (Titeca 2014). While the 2011 and 2016 presidential elections were convincingly won by President Museveni, the electoral context was increasingly tense and contested. In general, there is a consensus that the popularity of the NRM has long reduced (Perrot *et al.* 2014). Several analysts suggest that this electoral support is not necessarily backed by ideological support for NRM policies or a legitimisation of the regime. Rather, it indicates other factors, such as the NRM's success in making clear to the electorate that it will remain in power by any means and that the opposition is not a credible alternative (*ibid.*: 6, Reuss and Titeca 2017).

This leads to a second point: the regime increasingly relies on repression and patronage in order to sustain its rule. The Museveni regime has become progressively autocratic and repressive, with many academic analysts characterising it as a 'hybrid regime', 'in which elements of democratic practice mask authoritarian and personal rule' (Barkan 2011: 4, Tripp 2010, Perrot *et al.* 2014). Given the declining intrinsic popularity of the Museveni regime, the demand for patronage – particularly in a way that ties clients to the centre – has further intensified. Joel Barkan uses the term 'inflationary patronage', in these circumstances, in which there is the need for 'ever-increasing amounts of money to maintain oneself in power and increasing levels of corruption to provide the required funds' (Barkan 2011: 11).

In this context, particularly the 2005–2006 period was a watershed period: a 2005 referendum on multiparty politics allowed the return to the multiparty system in 2006. In doing so, an increasingly competitive political environment was established. This, in combination with President Museveni's grip on power, had consequences for decentralisation, as districts became an important commodity in the political marketplace. Newly introduced decentralisation measures became a 'repertoire of domination' for the national government: instead of a politically empowering local government, a 'minimal' local government was introduced whose primary purpose was not to increase local participation, but instead reproduce governmental power.

The next sections will analyse a number of major policy interventions in the decentralisation process, illustrating the above dynamics: the efforts to recentralise the power of local government, particularly the recentralisation of the Chief Administrative Officer (CAO);

the abolishment of the graduated tax; followed by an analysis of the multiplication of districts. By looking at these measures, the following repertoires of domination are illustrated: first, decentralisation became an important patronage instrument; second, decentralisation allowed for an important 'divide and rule' policy; and finally, local governments became largely dependent on the central government, making them void of any real power.

Recentralisation and decentralisation: two sides of the same coin

The abolishment of graduated tax and the financing of local governments

The graduated tax was a personal tax collected from all able-bodied adults above eighteen years of age in gainful employment in Uganda. Graduated personal tax has its origins in the colonial era. In a bid to force the local population into the market economy, the colonial government came up with the first tax legislation in 1919 under the Local Authorities' Ordinance (URA 2011). In 1953, graduated personal tax was introduced to finance local governments (*ibid.*). While its collection was costly, it nevertheless was an important source of revenue: earlier studies have shown how 75 per cent of all revenue of the rural local governments came from the graduated tax, and 35 per cent of the taxes of the urban local governments (The Uganda Local Government Finance Commission 2001). Nevertheless, the tax was very unpopular among Ugandan citizens. Just before the 2006 elections, President Museveni abolished the tax. While the move was electorally popular, it had a major effect on the financing of local governments and their financial autonomy. Graduated tax compensations in the subsequent year were largely insufficient, while other local sources of revenue were also scarce. The creation of new local taxes – such as the local services tax or local hotel tax – introduced partly to replace the graduated tax failed to raise the necessary revenue, and were generally not very relevant for rural districts (Manyak and Katono 2010, Awortwi and Helmsing 2015: 304). Moreover, other direct taxes collected from bodabodas or market vendors for example, have been opposed by politicians for electoral gain (Goodfellow and Titeca 2012).

In these circumstances, local government funding comes from the national government, with only 5 per cent of the budget estimated as being locally generated (Manyak and Katono 2010). Importantly,

95.5 per cent of funds to local governments are conditional grants (The Uganda Local Government Finance Commission 2014), which have very strict modalities. Naturally, conditional grants have a major impact on the functioning of the local governments: spending priorities are identified at the national level in a top-down manner, with very little participatory planning (Grossman and Lewis 2014). As Table 5.1 shows, the segment of the national budget reserved for local governments has steadily declined over the years. Whereas in the financial year 2003/4, this used to be 25.47 per cent, it dropped to 15.68 per cent in 2014/15. The number of conditional grants also increased sharply: from 26 in 2003/4 to 50 in 2013/14 (The Uganda Local Government Finance Commission 2014).

Moreover, all elected leaders have to be paid by the national government. In this situation, the accountability of local government actors are primarily directed upwards, towards the national government – a situation that has a negative impact on the accountability relationship between voters and elected leaders (Tumushabe *et al.* 2013: 71; in the words of Tumushabe et al. (2013: 27): 'The associated capture undermines the accountability relationships that should exist between citizens as beneficiaries of public services and elected leaders'). All of this has greatly undermined the financial and fiscal autonomy of the local governments, who are primarily looking upwards to the national level for funding. It has been observed that local governments have been reduced to 'administrative extensions of the central government' and are mainly focusing on implementing programmes of the central government (*ibid.*: 71). Muhumuza (2008: 72–73) goes as far as to argue that due to this revenue structure, decentralisation has become 'a sham' and 'disguised decentralisation' as an institutional structure is nothing but a façade to attract donor funds.

Recentralisation of the Chief Administrative Officer

Recentralisation also happened in other fields. In September 2005, a constitutional amendment was made, in which districts' Chief Administrative Officers (CAOs) were no longer hired and fired at the local level, but rather managed by the central government. Before that, district local governments were hiring and firing all categories of civil servants, including CAOs (Nabaho 2013: 17). Around the same time, district tender boards were abolished and replaced by contract committees consisting of administrative personnel, chaired by the CAO. This also meant that the tender process fell under the authority of the central rather than the local government (Tripp 2010: 119–20,

Table 5.1 – Transfers to local government

	2003/4	2004/5	2005/6	2006/7	2007/8	2008/9	2009/10	2010/11	2011/12	2012/13	2013/14	2014/15
Total transfer to local govts (UGX billions)	741.5	805.5	856.3	982.2	1060.9	1172.3	1338.9	1474.8	1655.7	1855.5	1979.0	2360.2
National budget (UGX billions)	2911.8	3150.8	3852.0	3852.0	4465.0	5464.0	7044.5	7376.5	9630.0	10902.8	12904.0	15054.0
% of direct transfers	25.47	25.56	25.50	25.50	23.76	21.45	19.01	19.99	17.19	17.20	15.34	15.68

Source: The Uganda Local Government Finance Commission (2014).

Manyak and Katono 2010: 8). While there were problems with the exposure of CAOs to local political pressure (Manyak and Katono 2010: 7, Nabaho 2013, Francis and James 2003), this signified reduced local accountability and further fed into a recentralisation drive. As the constitutional review commission report already argued in 2003, 'without local control of the CAO, councils would have limited control over the entire local government performance' (Nabaho 2013: 21). Importantly, the recentralisation of the CAO's role is also related to multiparty competition and the declining popularity of the Museveni regime, because CAOs were frequently accused of being opposition collaborators (Oloka-Onyango 2007, Nabaho 2013, Awortwi 2011). After the 2006 presidential and parliamentary elections, President Museveni 'threatened to appoint only cadres who subscribe to the NRM government philosophy as CAOs' (Awortwi 2011: 368–69). Moreover, in 2009, CAOs were given one-month military and ideological training (*ibid.*: 369). Recentralising CAOs can therefore also be seen as part of the broader electoral strategy of the Museveni regime to retain power.

The creation of districts

The progressive increase in the number of districts in Uganda – from 37 districts to 112 by the end of 2010 – is at its core a political decision and has positively influenced the NRM's election results (Green 2010). During electoral campaigns, new districts were often promised. Once created, the districts were used in various ways, both to reward supporters, but also to improve results in opposition areas. Awortwi and Helmsing (2015: 310) show how the increase in districts is particularly strong in the eastern and northern regions, both of which are clear opposition areas. Between 1997 and 2008, they had an increase of 166 and 200 per cent in new districts respectively; and indeed, the creation of these districts had a positive impact on the election results in them.

The increase in districts was particularly strong from 2005 onwards: between 2005 and 2010, about eight new districts were created every year; and from mid-2008 to 2010 around one district per month (*ibid.*: 302). This primarily happened for the reasons outlined above: the increasingly competitive environment through the introduction of multiparty democracy. At the same time, the opposition was growing more powerful and was becoming an increasing threat for the regime (*ibid.*: 309). Now more than ever, districts were considered useful electoral tools. As a result, districts were particularly promised during election campaigns: while in 2012

President Museveni introduced a moratorium on the creation of new districts (Uganda Radio Network 2015a), this was withdrawn in light of the 2016 elections. Just before the 2016 vote, another twenty-three new districts were approved by parliament (Uganda Radio Network 2015b). During the same period, more subnational units were being created: forty-three new constituencies in the run-up to the elections (Mugerwa 2015). It is often explicitly acknowledged by the Museveni regime how a district is created in return for votes. For example, after a newly created district voted for the opposition, President Museveni argued that he 'has regretted granting Bukomansimbi a district status because its residents voted for Opposition leaders in the 2011 general elections' (Mambule and Ssekweyama 2015). He further stated that this had made him 'regret why I accented [sic] to Bukomansimbi becoming a district. The MP you voted does not know where I live nor do I know where he lives. You made the same mistake when it came to electing the Woman MP' (*ibid.*). Through such statements, the president confirms considering district creation as an electoral strategy and patronage gift, in which new districts are supposed to vote for the ruling party.

The creation of new districts is also a strategy of subversion. As Lewis (2014: 572) argues, the proliferation of administrative units 'diminishes individual units' bargaining leverage with the centre as well as units' joint capacity for acting collectively on behalf of policies that advance the interests of all localities'. This helps to prevent the emergence of any threat to power, both at an individual level – the emergence of a big man – or the collective action of subnational units. Districts' bargaining power is lower than before, and smaller than that of bigger and more established units (*ibid.*: 575). In other words, territorial change is used to fragment territorial units (districts) in which powerful leaders and groups pose a challenge. A case in point is Amuru district, which was created in place of Gulu district in 2007, at a time when Norbert Mao was chairperson of the latter: Mao had announced that he would contest the presidency against Museveni in 2011 (Observer 2008). Splitting Gulu district was therefore an effective manner of curbing Mao's political power. In other words, while the multiplication of districts creates the image of an empowered local level, the opposite occurs: instead of fostering political participation or empowerment, decentralisation is used as a tool by the elites in place to entrench top-down existing political power configurations.

Recentralisation and decentralisation: what's happening?

Through the above measures, decentralisation started playing an increasingly important role as a means of patronage, in order to rally political support. At the same time, the autonomy of local governments was increasingly seen as a threat to the regime. Instead, local-level patronage dynamics became more firmly embedded in national-level patronage dynamics: the creation of districts became a source of developing clientelist relations, controlled by the centre, in which the creation of jobs played an important role. In the words of Tumushabe *et al.* (2013: 28):

> local governments consider central government transfers as a
> form of donation that is dependent, not on the tax contributions
> by their electorate, but rather on the magnanimity of central
> government politicians. It is this clientelistic relationship between
> voters and local elected leaders on the one hand, and local
> governments and national elected leaders on the other that
> undermines the accountability relationships needed to improve
> service delivery and governance.

The greater reliance of local governments on the centre for budgets equally fed into this scheme of increased control and influence by the national government, as this made local governments vulnerable to pressure and patronage from above. Further contributing to this is the fact that the ruling NRM party dominates most of the local government councils: councillors are thus primarily concerned with guaranteeing their place in the party. The appointment of Resident District Commissioners and CAOs, controlled by the centre, also allowed further political control – reinforced by Aili Mari Tripp's argument that the main quality of these people is their political allegiance to the NRM (2010: 117).

Autonomy of local governments

The above measures seriously affected the autonomy of districts. Initially, power was being concentrated at the district level: as argued above, the initial institutional decentralisation structure gave extensive responsibilities to the local governments, particularly at district level. The position of the district chairperson was considered to be a particularly powerful one. The current measures of recentralising are therefore primarily inspired by a fear of the political autonomy of local governments, which were considered to have too much independence (see also JICA 2008, cited in Nabaho 2013). The next sub-sections briefly describe how the increased power of the Resident District Commissioners, and the interventions of the president, further contributed to reducing the power of local governments.

The Resident District Commissioner (RDC)

An important instrument in reducing the autonomy of local governments is the role of the Resident District Commissioners (RDCs). The 1995 Constitution clearly stated that the RDC should remain politically neutral in their activities. Article 203 of the Constitution for example argues that the RDC is a senior civil servant and therefore bound by the civil service rules and regulations, among which is neutrality when conducting public affairs. Nevertheless, RDCs are appointed by the president, and tend to sometimes engage themselves in political affairs. The increasingly competitive political climate after 2006 further increased these tendencies. For example, RDCs became important electoral instruments for the Museveni regime. Several reports on the 2011 elections illustrate how RDCs were actively campaigning for President Museveni and the NRM (European Union Election Observation Mission 2011: 24) and were involved in harassing opposition members (ICG 2012: 26, Barkan 2011: 8). The main role of the RDC is therefore to play the 'eyes and ears of the President' in respective districts (Barkan 2011: 8). Because of the RDCs closeness to the president and the party in power, they have tended to overshadow all other offices at the local government level: RDCs monitor, inspect and supervise central government programmes, such as national and regional roads constructed by the Uganda National Roads Authority (UNRA) or the National Advisory Agricultural District Services (NAADS). In sum, the increased responsibilities of the RDC have further undermined the autonomy and hold on power of local governments.

Presidential intervention

A legislator on the Parliamentary Committee for Presidential Affairs argued how 'the top political leadership finds it easy to use the budgets they control to patronise voters/societies' (Matsiko 2015). In other words, national and local budgets are used by political elites for electoral purposes. This becomes particularly clear through the continuous personal interventions of President Museveni in the affairs of local governments. First, there are the many presidential pledges: when visiting particular localities, a variety of issues are promised to be addressed by the president, such as refurbishment of hospitals, schools, other social installations, electricity, roads, equipment and cars (Imaka 2013). In this context, the president wants to be seen as the person providing development to a district, rather than the local government as such. Presidential gifts are another issue: on visits, President Museveni hands out cash. For example, in the financial year 2014/15, 90 billion Uganda shillings was budgeted for these donations; while in reality this might be higher (Matsiko 2015).

Moreover, local governments are sometimes obliged to pay these pledges through the existing Sectoral Conditional Grants that are sent to them. As the president of the Uganda Local Government Association argued 'Local Governments strongly recommend that the funding to meet the Presidential Pledges should be disseminated outside the Sector Conditional Grants, as additional funding, instead of using the existing inadequate district budgets to be used to meet these pledges' (Ngobi 2014). Naturally, all of this further reduces the autonomy of local governments, making them further dependent on the national government. The increase in conditional grants is part of this strategy, as it enables 'the president to have a stranglehold over Local Government finances so that he can claim credit for any infrastructure and services that the Central Government would direct Local Governments to provide' (Awortwi and Helmsing 2015: 308).

Conclusion

This chapter has shown how decentralisation measures became important repertoires of domination, used to further entrench the power of the ruling party. Whereas local governments were initially introduced as a means to promote popular democracy, they also came to be an important patronage network to establish and maintain the electoral and popular legitimacy of the Museveni regime. Over the years, the latter aim took over prominence: the most important goal of decentralisation was no longer to introduce popular democracy, but instead to be an instrument to entrench the power of the regime. The year 2006 was particularly crucial, with the return to a multiparty system creating an increasingly competitive political environment. This fostered an increasing patronage pressure towards the regime, and districts became an important commodity in this context of inflationary patronage: there was a particularly strong growth in districts from 2005/6 onwards. In doing so, decentralisation became a neoliberal tool promoting top-down decision making, rather than bottom-up participation. By promoting fragmentation and recentralisation, decentralisation became an important tool for the reproduction of power of the national government: on the one hand, decentralisation became an important tool in a general 'divide and rule' policy, taking away power from potentially influential opposition support bases. On the other hand, key local government personnel and financing became largely dependent on the central government. All of this needs to be understood in the neoliberal context of Uganda: in a situation where other means of patronage have become much more difficult to access, not least given the reduced number of civil servants, local governments have largely taken over this patronage role. This has resulted in a situation in which local governments are primarily used as a source of patronage, but have limited local autonomy.

References

Asiimwe, D. and Nakanyike, B. M. (eds) (2007), *Decentralisation and Transformation of Governance in Uganda* (Kampala: Fountain).

Awortwi, N. (2011), 'An unbreakable path? A comparative study of decentralization and local government development trajectories in Ghana and Uganda', *International Review of Administrative Sciences*, 77(2), pp. 347–77.

Awortwi, N. and Helmsing, A. H. J. (2015), 'Behind the façade of bringing services closer to the people: The proclaimed and hidden intentions of the government of Uganda to create many new government districts', *Canadian Journal of African Studies*, 48(2), pp. 297–314.

Barkan, J. D. (2011), *Uganda: Assessing Risks to Stability* (Washington, DC: Center for Strategic and International Studies).

Dagnino, E. (2007), 'Dimensions of citizenship in contemporary Brazil', *Fordham Law Review*, 75(5), pp. 2468–82.

European Union Election Observation Mission. (2011), 'Uganda: Final Report. General Elections 18 February 2011'.

Francis, P. and James, R. (2003), 'Balancing rural poverty reduction and citizen participation: The contradictions of Uganda's decentralization programme', *World Development*, 31(2), pp. 325–37.

Goodfellow, T. and Titeca, K. (2012), 'Presidential intervention and the changing "politics of survival" in Kampala's informal economy', *Cities*, 29(4), pp. 264–70.

Green, E. (2010), 'Patronage, district creation and reform in Uganda', *Studies in Comparative International Development*, 45(1), pp. 83–103.

Grossman, G. and Lewis, J. (2014), 'Administrative unit proliferation', *American Political Science Review*, 108 (1), pp. 196–217.

Guarneros-Meza, V. and Geddes, M. (2010), 'Local governance and participation under neoliberalism: Comparative perspectives', *International Journal of Urban and Regional Research*, 34 (1), pp. 115–29.

Harvey, D. (1989), *The Conditions of Postmodernity* (Oxford: Blackwell).

Imaka, I. (2013), 'Museveni's unfulfilled pledges', *Daily Monitor*, 14 November.

International Crisis Group (ICG). (2012), 'Uganda: No resolution to growing tensions', International Crisis Group, Africa Report No. 186.

Research Group, Institute for International Cooperation, Japan International Cooperation Agency (JICA). (2008), *Decentralised Service Delivery in East Africa: A Comparative Study of Uganda, Tanzania and Kenya* (Tokyo).

Lewis, J. (2014), 'When decentralization leads to recentralization: Subnational state transformation in Uganda', *Regional and Federal Studies*, 24(5), pp. 571–88.

Mambule, A. and Ssekweyama, M. (2015), 'Museveni regrets giving residents district', *Daily Monitor*, 26 February.

Manyak, T. G. and Katono, I. W. A. (2010), 'Decentralization and conflict in Uganda: Governance adrift', *African Studies Quarterly*, 11(4), pp. 1–24.

Matsiko, H. (2015), 'Museveni's cash worries MPs', *The Independent*, 17 May.

Mohan, G. and Stokke, K. (2000), 'Participatory development and empowerment: The dangers of localism', *Third World Quarterly*, 21(2), pp. 247–68.

Mugerwa, Y. (2015), 'House approves 43 new constituencies', *Daily Monitor*, 5 August.

Muhumuza, W. (2008), 'Pitfalls of decentralization reforms in transitional societies: The case of Uganda', *Africa Development*, 33(4), pp. 59–81.

Mwenda, A. (2007), 'Personalizing power in Uganda', *Journal of Democracy*, 18(3), pp. 23–37.

Nabaho, L. (2013), 'Recentralization of local government Chief Administrative Officers appointments in Uganda: Implications for downward accountability', *Commonwealth Journal of Local Governance*, 13(14), pp. 17–29.

Ngobi, F. G. (2014), 'Paper presentation by the President of Uganda Local Government Association (ULGA) at the National Consultative Budget Conference for FY 2014/2015', *UGLA*, 16 January.

Nsibambi, A. (1998), *Decentralization and Civil Society in Uganda: The Quest for Good Governance* (Kampala. Fountain Publishers).

Observer. (2008), 'Mao: I'd make a good president', 5 November.

Oloka-Onyango, J. (2007), *Decentralization without Human Rights: Local Governance and Access to Justice in Post-Movement Uganda* (Kampala: Human Rights and Peace Centre).

Ozcan, G. B. (2006), 'A critical analysis of decentralisation and local economic development: The Turkish case', *Environment and Planning C: Government and Policy*, 24(1), pp. 117–38.

Perrot, S. *et al.* (2014), 'Introduction: Looking back at the 2011 multiparty elections in Uganda', in S. Perrot, S. Makara, J. Lafargue and M.-A. Fouéré (eds), *Elections in a Hybrid Regime: Revisiting the 2011 Ugandan Polls* (Kampala: Fountain), pp. 1–34.

Poteete, A. and Ribot, J. (2011), 'Repertoires of domination: Decentralization as process in Botswana and Senegal', *World Development*, 39(3), pp. 439–49.

Resnick, D. (2014), 'Strategies of subversion in vertically-divided contexts: Decentralization and urban service delivery in Senegal',

Development Policy Review, 32(1), pp. 61–80.

Reuss, A. and Titeca, K. (2017), 'When revolutionaries grow old: The Museveni babies and the slow death of the liberation', *Third World Quarterly*, 38(10), pp. 2347–66.

Schuurman, F. (1997), 'The decentralisation discourse: Post-Fordist paradigm or neo-liberal cul-de-sac?', *European Journal of Development Research*, 9(1), pp. 150–66.

Steffensen, J. (2006), 'Local government organization and finance: Uganda', in A. Shah (ed.), *Local Governance in Developing Countries: Public Sector Governance and Accountability* (Washington, DC: World Bank), pp. 93–136.

Steffensen, J. and Trollegaard, S. (2000), *Fiscal Decentralization and Sub-National Government Finance in Relation to Infrastructure Provision: Synthesis Report of 6 Sub-Saharan African Country Studies* (Copenhagen: DANIDA).

Steiner, S. (2006), 'Decentralisation in Uganda: Exploring the constraints for poverty reduction', Working Paper No. 31, Transformation in the Process of Globalisation Unit, German Institute of Global and Area Studies, Hamburg.

Titeca, K. (2014). 'The commercialization of Uganda's 2011 election in the urban informal economy: Money, boda-bodas and market vendors', in S. Perrot, S. Makara, J. Lafargue and M.-A. Fouéré (eds), *Elections in a Hybrid Regime: Revisiting the 2011 Ugandan Polls* (Kampala: Fountain), pp. 178–207.

Tripp, A. M. (2010), *Museveni's Uganda: Paradoxes of Power in a Hybrid Regime* (Boulder, CO: Lynne Rienner).

Tumushabe, G. *et al.* (2013), 'Uganda local government councils score card 2012/2013: The big service delivery divide', Acode Policy Research Series No. 60, Kampala, ACODE.

The Uganda Local Government Finance Commission. (2001), 'A case for continued collection of graduated tax', Kampala.

The Uganda Local Government Finance Commission. (2014), 'Transfers to local government', Kampala.

Uganda Radio Network. (2015a), 'Gov't asks to drop motion on creation of new districts', 13 August.

Uganda Radio Network. (2015b), 'Parliament approves 23 new districts', 4 September.

Uganda Revenue Authority (URA). (2011), *Taxation Handbook: A Guide to Taxation in Uganda* (Kampala: Fountain).

6
Neoliberal neverland: the Millennium Villages Project in Uganda

Japhy Wilson

'Welcome visitors, welcome today. We've all been waiting so long!'
Coming over the crest of the hill into the Millennium Village
of Ruhiira, Uganda, children's singing voices gradually become
louder, intermingled with bursts of clapping and laughter.
The long-awaited visitor, Jeffrey Sachs, is due to arrive at any
moment, and the anticipation is palpable ... For the people of
Ruhiira, the visit ... was a celebration of the fact that today, their
story is different. Today, the community was living proof to the
world that ... dreams can be made a reality as a result of effective
synergy between well-targeted aid and community empowerment.
'We haven't done it, you have', proclaimed Sachs, to tumultuous
applause and ululation from the crowd of hundreds ... Pledging
support to the community until 2015, [Sachs] promised that
when that day comes, Ruhiira will be 'a shining example to the
entire world ... having shown how this community achieved
all the Millennium Development Goals. (Millennium Villages
Project press release – Handa-Williams 2010)

Between 2006 and 2015, Uganda hosted one of the most ambitious and high-profile international development projects of recent
times. The Millennium Villages Project (MVP) was supported by the
United Nations Development Programme (UNDP), and the Earth
Institute at Columbia University, and aimed to achieve the Millennium Development Goals (MDGs) by their deadline at the end of
2015, in twelve clusters of villages with a combined population of
over 500,000 people, located in ten different countries across sub-
Saharan Africa, including Uganda; at the time of its launch, the
countries participating in the MVP were: Ethiopia, Ghana, Kenya,
Malawi, Mali, Nigeria, Tanzania, Rwanda, Senegal, and Uganda
(several other African countries have since adopted projects inspired
by the MVP model; MVP 2016). The MVP was conceived as a 'proof
of concept' for the development strategy set out by the Director of

the Earth Institute – the influential economist Jeffrey Sachs – in his best-selling anti-poverty manifesto, *The End of Poverty* (Sachs 2005). This strategy was codified in the Millennium Project, which was chaired by Sachs on behalf of United Nations Secretary-General Kofi Annan, and which published its final report in 2005 (Millennium Project 2005). Launched the following year, the MVP has made great claims of success (MVP 2010), and has been endorsed by numerous celebrities, including Bono, Madonna and Angelina Jolie. It has also received the financial backing of many of the world's wealthiest individuals and most iconic multinational corporations. George Soros has donated over US$70 million to the MVP, and GlaxoSmithKline, Monsanto, Novartis, PepsiCo and Pfizer are among over 200 partners of Millennium Promise, the foundation created by Sachs to finance the Project (Wilson 2014a).

Sachs has identified Ruhiira, in Uganda, as the 'flagship' Millennium Village (Divon and Bergstrom 2012: 88). In 2013, I visited Ruhiira, to assess the success of this 'flagship' project. With the help of a Ugandan research assistant, I conducted thirty-five household interviews, with five of these conducted in each of seven of the eight clusters of villages into which the Ruhiira MVP is divided. I also conducted nine interviews with implementers of the Project in the fields of health, education, and agriculture, and four telephone interviews with ex-administrators of the Project in Ruhiira. Household interviews in Ruhiira were predominantly conducted in Runyankole, with interpretation provided by my research assistant; interviews with implementers were conducted in English. The reality that I discovered was radically at odds with Sachs' celebratory assessment of the Project, and the utopian depiction of his visit to Ruhiira. In what follows, I argue that the MVP has staged a neoliberal fantasy of harmonious capitalist development, which has become entangled with the real processes of neoliberalisation already underway in rural Uganda. The conceptual erasure of the pre-existence of highly stratified class relations in the region has resulted in the elite capture of inputs, a lack of inclusive community participation and an absence of sustainability. I conclude that, in the case of Uganda, the MVP has only succeeded in deepening the antagonisms that this fantasy denies.

The staging of a development fantasy

The Millennium Villages Project begins from the premise that 'If every village has a road, access to transport, a clinic, and other essential inputs, the villagers of poor countries will show the same determination and entrepreneurial zeal of people all over the world' (Millennium Project 2005: 15). It includes a comprehensive range of interventions in agriculture, environment, health, nutrition, energy, infrastructure, communications, education, microfinance and business training (Konecky and Palm 2008). Everyday life is conceptually reduced to five forms of capital – human, social, natural, physical and financial, which are to be 'raised above a threshold level, beyond which the villages can move towards self-sustaining economic growth' (Sanchez *et al.* 2009: 2). US$120 is initially invested in each villager each year, with subsidies gradually phased out and replaced by credit, and communities organising to ensure the continuation of the services that the MVP has introduced, such as free school meals, community health workers and so on (Konecky and Palm 2008). The first phase of the Project, from 2006 to 2011, was aimed at raising the five forms of capital to the requisite levels. The second phase, from 2011 to 2015, was focused primarily on 'business development', including a broad array of participatory initiatives devoted to nurturing the 'entrepreneurial spirit', through business training, microcredit loans, the promotion of co-operatives, and partnerships with multinational agribusinesses (MVP 2011, Wilson 2014b). The MVP was originally planned as a five-year project, with subsidies phased out entirely by the end of this period (Konecky and Palm 2008: 38). According to Nina Munk, in her critique of the MVP, the decision was taken to extend the duration of the Project when it became clear that its objectives would not be met within the five-year time frame (Munk 2013: 136).

Conceptually, the MVP echoes Adam Smith's account of 'original accumulation', whereby capitalism originated through private smallholding farmers accumulating capital by dint of their own frugality. Capital investment in the process of further accumulation leads to the division of labour and the growth of trade, and results in the harmonious emergence of a commercial society of community-spirited entrepreneurs (Perelman 2000: 171–228). In *The End of Poverty*, Sachs reproduces this narrative, telling a story of the emergence of capitalism through the accumulative activities of 'a single farm household', which 'exemplifies Smith's insight' (Sachs 2005: 52–53). Through hard work, the household acquires some savings, moves from subsistence to cash crops, begins to specialise in a single crop, upgrades its capital inputs and acquires more land. Capitalism, Sachs concludes, is the aggregate outcome of this process operating 'through the interactions of thousands or millions of households linked together by markets' (*ibid.*: 54).

The MVP stages a faithful performance of this narrative, which begins from an erroneous representation of rural sub-Saharan Africa as a collection of 'sub-subsistence farmers' surviving precariously outside the market. With the assistance of the MVP, each individual farmer is expected to generate a surplus and accumulate capital, before joining the 'market economy' as a 'small-scale entrepreneur' (Sanchez *et al.* 2009). However, there are several conceptual problems with this development strategy. First, as Marx long ago observed, Adam Smith's narrative is historically inaccurate, and functions to obscure the violence of 'primitive accumulation' – the separation of the peasantry from the land through which capitalist social relations are actually established (Marx 1976: 873–940). Second, rural sub-Saharan Africa is not a collection of subsistence farmers longing to compete in the market. On the contrary, the process of primitive accumulation is already well underway across the continent. This process has accelerated in the context of structural adjustment, and is characterised by an increasingly stark differentiation between a small class of capitalist farmers engaged in global markets, and a growing population of wage labourers. The latter often retain small plots of land as an element of their survival strategies, and enter the labour market less motivated by 'entrepreneurial zeal' than by the decreased standards of living that have characterised their exposure to 'market forces' (Mueller 2011, Oya 2005). Third, the MVP abstracts from the complex power relations of rural African societies, which it conceptualises as homogenous and socially undifferentiated communities (see for example MVP 2010).

By failing to recognise the reality of local power relations, the MVP threatens to reinforce them. Equally, by abstracting from the multi-scalar political-economic dynamics of global capitalism, such interventions 'exclude structural sources of inequality from their technical domain and focus upon an incarcerated "local" in which properly guided villagers are expected to improve their own conditions by their own efforts' (Li 2007: 275, quoted in Golooba-Mutebi and Hickey 2010: 1216). In both respects, the MVP bears an uncanny resemblance to the World Bank's ill-fated Integrated Rural Development Programmes, which were implemented across Africa and Southeast Asia in the 1970s. The failure of these programmes offered several cautionary lessons that Sachs and the other MVP planners at the Earth Institute have chosen to ignore. Village committees were dominated by powerful networks; inputs were monopolised by these groups; and poverty rapidly returned to its previous levels once these projects had ended, albeit in the context of intensified inequalities and a consolidated class structure (Livingstone 1979, Ruttan 1984). As we will see, these tendencies have all been reproduced in the case of Ruhiira.

The Millennium Villages Project in Uganda

Ruhiira is a cluster of eight Millennium Villages located in southwest Uganda, near the border with Tanzania. Despite being called 'villages', the cluster actually covers a total of 140 square kilometres of mountainous land, with a population of approximately 50,000 people (Earth Institute 2009: 94). As with the countries chosen to host the other Millennium Villages, Uganda was selected by the MVP on the basis of its proven record of cooperation with the policy agendas of the World Bank and the IMF (Carr 2008: 335). In the 1990s, Uganda was celebrated as a rare case of successful structural adjustment in Africa. In marked contrast to most other African countries undergoing neoliberal reforms during this period, Uganda's economy grew rapidly and poverty declined, although it has been argued that Uganda's economic performance during this period had less to do with the reforms than with peasants returning to their land and resuming cultivation after fifteen years of civil war (Ellis and Bahiigwa 2003). Since then, the administration of President Yoweri Museveni has combined a continued adherence to privatisation and export-led development with limited social measures such as universal primary education, and the promotion of a transition from subsistence farming to export-oriented agribusinesses entirely consistent with the MVP (Hickey 2005, Bahiigwa et al. 2005).

For Jeffrey Sachs, Uganda is proof of the transformative potential of international aid. Sachs has worked as an economic advisor for Museveni, and has consistently praised him over the years for demonstrating 'the quality of leadership and governance [required] to achieve economic development' (Sachs 2004). Museveni has returned the compliment, publicly endorsing Sachs' failed campaign to be appointed President of the World Bank in 2012 (Museveni 2012). The two have developed a close personal relationship, visiting Ugandan factories together (Mulumba 2003), and sitting in Museveni's presidential offices discussing the end of poverty (Munk 2013). After one such meeting in 2003, Sachs reported that 'President Museveni ... was extremely engaged and interested in discussing ... the progress that Uganda has made towards the Millennium Development Goals ... We also talked about how the Earth Institute's

expertise can be useful to Uganda in its efforts to meet the Goals'
(Earth Institute 2003).

But Museveni's record is not quite as unblemished as Sachs would
seem to believe. Poverty reduction has stagnated since the turn of the
millennium, and inequality has grown dramatically (Hickey 2013). The
privatisation and liberalisation processes have been rife with insider
dealing, and corruption has reached epidemic levels, leading Uganda to
be identified by Transparency International as the most corrupt regime
in East Africa (Inzama 2012). Elections in Uganda have been rigged,
presidential term limits have been abolished and human rights organisations have accused the regime of systematic political brutality (Tripp
2010). A 2004 report by Human Rights Watch, for example, found
that 'abuses are not acknowledged by the Ugandan government that
instead fosters an enabling climate in which such human rights abuses
persist and increase while perpetrators of torture, rather than being
held accountable, act with impunity' (Human Rights Watch 2004: 4).

The MVP abstracts from these profound political and economic
problems, identifying Uganda as 'a fairly well governed country'
(Okario 2009). Ruhiira is presented as a place of 'deforestation,
environmental degradation ... high population density [and] land
shortages' (Earth Institute 2009: 94). We are told that Ruhiira is poor,
that malaria and HIV/Aids are rife, and that the village has one of
the highest rates of tuberculosis in the region. All this is true. But it
tells us nothing of Ruhiira's politics, history or class structure, all of
which are crucial to understanding the causes of its poverty. We do
not learn that the region was a focus of extreme violence during the
Uganda–Tanzania war of 1978–1979 and the subsequent civil war,
which destroyed past development achievements and traumatised the
population (Tankink 2004). The impact of patronage and corruption
on the political structure of the region, which is Museveni's birthplace
and power-base (Nganda 2009) are silenced. The intensification of
inequalities within the region, as land ownership becomes increasingly concentrated and peasant farmers are pushed into the labour
market, is not mentioned. By constructing an image of a place devoid
of human agency and abandoned to the natural vagaries of death and
disease such representations encourage an understanding of poverty
as a consequence of local environmental disadvantages, rather than
political and economic relationships of power, and legitimises development interventions by the very same governments and donors that
are responsible for the perpetuation of poverty and inequality.

In Ruhiira, the MVP claims '[a] significant proportion of the
community, which is estimated at between 40 [and] 50%, still live

in extreme poverty with an estimated annual per capita income of $250' (Millennium Promise 2010). It is this poorest 40–50 per cent, then, that the MVP should be providing with the greatest assistance. In practice, however, as we will see in the following section, the vast majority of the inputs provided by the Project have been appropriated by the better-off, while the poorest have been largely excluded. This is partly due to the Project's misrepresentation of rural Africa as a set of homogenous subsistence 'communities', in which there are no class relations or significant differences in assets and incomes (Konecky and Palm 2008). Like most of rural Africa, Ruhiira does not fit this representation, but is a stratified class society, in which differences in wealth are based on the ownership of land. The poorest farmers I interviewed had less than one acre of land, and in some cases no land at all. They were forced to rent land from wealthier farmers, and to sell their labour to these farmers for as little as 75 cents a day. The wealthiest farmers on the other hand owned as much as 250 acres of land, and employed twenty or more casual labourers. Differences of wealth and property ownership are also differences of power, in terms of political influence and the control of economic resources. A development project that refuses to acknowledge such differences is likely to exacerbate them, as the wealthier members of the society will be better positioned to appropriate its benefits. This has proved to be the case in Ruhiira, as the following section explains.

Not the end of poverty

The role that MVP has played in the exacerbation of existing inequalities in Ruhiira can be illustrated by the case of agricultural inputs. In terms of livestock, for example, individual farmers in Ruhiira could apply to the MVP to receive a cow or a goat, which were being provided in limited numbers. Several of the poorer farmers I interviewed had applied for a goat, but had been instructed by the MVP to construct shelters and plant grass before receiving one. Most did not have sufficient land or resources to do so, leading to their exclusion from the project at the expense of wealthier farmers. Cows, meanwhile, were perceived to be reserved for those with political connections. Only one of the households I spoke to had received a cow. The head of this household was the chairman of the local council, and already had forty cattle of his own (Cluster: Kisyoro, 2013). A poor farmer from a different cluster told a similar story:

'Those people who receive [things from the MVP]. Do you think they are the same as people who do not? The [local council] chairman received a cow. But you see a cow is such a big thing to come into the village. So you think a poor man would have been chosen to have it?' (Cluster: Ruhiira, 2013).

Seeds and fertilisers had been more widely distributed than live-stock, benefitting almost everyone. The quantity distributed to each farmer, however, depended on the amount of land that they owned (Konecky and Palm 2008: 35), which again meant that the wealthier farmers had benefitted disproportionately. Poorer farmers renting land were often unable to benefit from fertilisers at all, as their land-lords would not permit them to use fertiliser, on the assumption that it would impoverish the soil over time. Wealthier farmers also reported receiving seeds and fertiliser more regularly than poorer farmers. Again, many of the poorer farmers perceived this to be a consequence of political connections. One very poor woman living in an isolated area of the cluster told me 'For us this end, we don't get anything. For example, the third time [the MVP brought seeds and fertiliser], they were received by the leaders [i.e. the local elites]. But when we came, they told us ... you had to buy them' (Cluster: Kabuyanda, 2013).

The better-off farmers often acknowledged inequities in the distri-bution of fertiliser and other benefits, but explained this in terms of the supposed laziness and ignorance of the poor. One local council chairman told me, 'Those who have not benefited – maybe they don't want to ... Some people are just like that. They are just there. They don't want to go and get [what is offered to them]' (Cluster: Kanya-wameizi, 2013). In some cases, it was indeed the case that the poorest farmers were reluctant to collect seeds from the Project. But this was not due to lack of interest or motivation, but was instead a conse-quence of the material circumstances of their poverty. Some lacked sufficient land to make use of the seeds, and so did not collect them, while others had heard that the MVP was expecting repayment in kind following their harvest, and feared a poor harvest putting them into debt that would jeopardise their precarious survival strategies. This illustrates the difficulties that prevent the extremely poor from transforming themselves into the entrepreneurial 'risk-takers' envi-sioned by the Project. I found that the MVP was not catalysing any such transition in Ruhiira. Instead, it was boosting the accumulation strategies of the pre-existing entrepreneurial elite, while the poorest were increasingly pushed into wage labour on behalf of this nascent capitalist class. A major landowner and influential local politician, who was one of the wealthiest people I interviewed, explained this process in matter-of-fact terms:

> Now, there are some people who will benefit [from the MVP] according to their status. I'm saying this because you will find that someone will receive fertiliser, but he has nowhere to put it. And then you'll find someone else who has a lot of space and a lot of land benefitting more than the poor ... But those who do not have any land are beyond help. How can you help them? What can you do for those who have nothing at all? But they still benefit from ... working for other people and getting paid ... A poor person who lives around rich people ... If he is paid 3,000 [US$1.20 a day], that is something ... But some people cannot even look after themselves. (Cluster: Ntungu, 2013)

This casual description of primitive accumulation demonstrates the role of the MVP in the production of inequality in Ruhiira: the ownership of land determines access to agricultural inputs, the distribution of which exacerbates existing inequalities, leading to the consolidation of a class division between large land owners and impoverished people with nothing to sell but their labour. In the words of a poor farmer who rented land for subsistence, and who had just returned from a day's labour on one of the larger farms in the area, 'Those who have land – those people are getting ahead of us ... For the people with land, things are working well' (Cluster: Kabugu, 2013).

The failure of the MVP to acknowledge the existence of these stratified class relations ensured that its promotion of 'participatory community development' was transformed into a further opportunity for elite capture. The MVP had established 'groups' in Ruhiira, through which many of its inputs and activities are organised. But far from being inclusive and participatory, the majority of these groups were comprised almost exclusively of the more affluent and influential members of the 'community', and were functioning as a mechanism for the exclusion of the poorest. The daughter of an impoverished farmer who had received almost nothing from the MVP told me, '[The MVP] choose people to work with. Those people are well-off ... They call themselves to meetings – not everyone. So if [the MVP] have something to offer, they will organise themselves, and not tell others' (Cluster: Kanyawameizi, 2013; the daughter spoke English). Although many of the poorer people had heard of the groups, they felt unable to join them, either because they could not afford the membership fee, or because they felt that they lacked the necessary status. An agricultural extension officer working for the Project explained this:

> You see, to say that 'this is a group', it means someone who has a feeling to join with other people, and shares their view. And in that [sense], those poor farmers may feel that they can't afford to join with the rich people in forming a group. And in failing to join the groups, then we [the MVP] also fail to get them, because we will not know where they are. (Interview, MVP Agricultural Extension Worker, Kabuyanda, 2013)

This lack of inclusive participation reproduces the practical outcomes of Uganda's Poverty Reduction Strategy Programme (PRSP), which 'draws on the language of participatory planning, but, in the context of lack of resources and capture by local elites, is reduced to a ritualized performance with little meaningful citizen involvement' (Francis and James 2003: 326). It also casts serious doubt on the sustainability of the gains achieved by the MVP. By the time of its official conclusion at the end of 2015, subsistence farmers were supposed to have been transformed into small-scale entrepreneurs, and a process of intensive participatory development was supposed to have prepared the community to provide the services previously supplied by the Project. But many of the poorest people I interviewed were not even aware that the Project was due to end in 2015, and none were involved in collective preparations for driving it forward after this date. By the time I conducted my research in 2013, the MVP had started to charge for its seeds and fertiliser at a subsidised price, which was scheduled to move to full market rates once the Project finished. Even at the subsidised price, none of the poorer farmers were able to afford the fertiliser, and almost none of them could afford the seeds. By contrast, many of the wealthier farmers were buying the inputs, and expected to continue to do so once the subsidies were removed. In contrast to their optimism, the poorest households were almost unanimous in their assumption that the benefits that had trickled down to them – free school meals, more medicines, free seeds and fertiliser – would be lost once the Project came to an end.

'A shining example to the entire world'

In July 2013, the Ugandan government announced a scale up of the MVP model across the country, supported by a US$9.75 million

donation from the Islamic Development Bank. At the launch cere-
mony in Kampala, the Minister of Local Government praised 'the
success of Ruhiira ... which since 2006 has served as a proof of
concept of the benefits of an integrated, holistic approach to rural
development pioneered by the MVP' (Adolf Mwesigye, quoted
in MVP 2013). However, my field research, conducted only a few
months prior to this announcement, suggests that the MVP has failed
in its stated mission to provide a sustainable, scalable and participatory development model for the ending of extreme poverty. This is
not to say that the MVP has achieved nothing. On the contrary, even
the poorest and most marginalised people in Ruhiira have benefitted in some way from the MVP – from free seeds and fertiliser,
for example, or from improved healthcare, or free school meals. But
these benefits have at best provided temporary supplements to their
everyday survival strategies, and in most cases were already being
removed by the time of my field research, as the Project scaled back
its operations in preparation for its conclusion at the end of 2015.
Meanwhile, the wealthier and more influential members of Ruhiira
have generally done well from the Project. As we have seen, the
failure of the MVP to conceptualise inequalities of land ownership
and political power in Uganda ensured that its agricultural inputs
primarily benefitted local elites – as a consequence of their distribution on the basis of land holdings, and by virtue of the exclusionary
nature of the supposedly participatory 'groups' through which this
distribution was organised.

Further field research would be required to assess the sustainability of the development gains made in Ruhiira, following the
conclusion of the MVP at the end of 2015. Surprisingly enough,
despite their earlier claims of great success, neither the MVP nor
the Ugandan government has made any comment on this matter. In
practice, the promised scale-up of the MVP by the Ugandan government did not take place, and at the time of completing this chapter
(December 2016), the MVP had yet to provide any public statement
on the achievements of the project in fulfilling the MDGs by their
deadline, or in catalysing a sustainable development trajectory within
Ruhiira or any of its other villages. Notably, in 2014, the last official
MVP progress report announced that a final evaluation would be
published in 2016 (Millennium Promise 2014); yet, as of August
2018, there had been no activity on the MVP website since January
2016, suggesting that this evaluation may not be forthcoming.

Amidst this official silence, my findings strongly suggest that
the only sustainable gains of the MVP in Ruhiira will prove to be

those of the local elites. Far from transforming subsistence farmers into entrepreneurs, as was its stated intention, the MVP provided a generous subsidy to the 'entrepreneurs' who already existed in Ruhiira, with some of the benefits 'trickling down' to poorer farmers, while the class relations that ensure the reproduction of their poverty were only reinforced. Through its abstraction from the neoliberal policy regimes of Uganda and other countries in which it operates, and its endorsement of these policies in its background documents, the MVP has also helped to normalise and legitimate the political economy of global inequality that ensures the continuity of poverty in places like Ruhiira.

I have interpreted the MVP as a quixotic attempt to conceal primitive accumulation – the origin of capitalist social relations in the separation of the peasantry from the land – beneath a staging of Adam Smith's imagined history of original accumulation, in which capitalism emerges through the frugality and initiative of individual smallholding farmers. It is one thing to reproduce such an ideology in theory, however, and quite another to attempt to stage it in practice. In Ruhiira, the MVP's fantasy of capitalist development has collided with the reality of primitive accumulation that was already well under way across rural Uganda. Furthermore, its own ideological misconceptions have ensured that this collision has contributed to the further consolidation of this process, through which large farmers are expanding their agricultural production and diversifying into other sectors, while smaller farmers are increasingly forced into the labour market to survive. This peculiar entanglement of fantasy and reality can be given a final twist by returning to the utopian scene of Sachs' visit to Ruhiira, with which this chapter began. An American academic working with the MVP described the visit as follows:

> Everyone at the MVP office was immersed last week in
> preparations for the visit on Saturday of Jeff Sachs ... There
> were governmental officials, large staffs, armed police, and press
> people – maybe 50–80 people in a long line of UN white Land
> Rovers ... [And] there were children or community people at
> every stop lining the entrances, singing and clapping hands.
> (Powers 2010)

An official video of this neo-colonial spectacle shows Sachs being escorted through throngs of cheering villagers, from a pristine school to an overflowing warehouse and a gleaming water project (YouTube

2010). According to inhabitants of Ruhiira, the local MVP administration had even created a 'Millennium Band' for the occasion, which sang songs with lyrics such as 'Jeffrey Sachs/ You have done a lot/ God should bless you' (Member of the 'Millennium Band', interview. Ruhiira, 2013). Sachs' visit to Ruhiira was thus a carefully engineered occasion, in which every element of his experience was managed to provide him with an image of a flourishing development paradise, which bore very little resemblance to the reality behind the façade. Like Jim Carrey in *The Truman Show*, Sachs wandered around Ruhiira in a state of narcissistic bliss, unaware that his surroundings were being staged for his benefit, before taking to the stage to praise his own project as 'a shining example to the entire world' (quoted in Handa-Williams 2010). Welcome to Neoliberal Neverland, where fantasy is reality, and failure is success.

References

Bahiigwa, G. *et al.* (2005), 'Right target, wrong mechanism? Agricultural modernization and poverty reduction in Uganda', *World Development*, 33(3), pp. 481–96.

Carr, E. (2008), 'The Millennium Village Project and African development: Problems and potentials', *Progress in Development Studies*, 8(4), pp. 333–44.

Divon, S. and Bergstrom, C. E. (2012), 'Unintended consequences of development interventions: A case of diarrhoeal diseases, Ruhiira, Uganda', *Development in Practice*, 22(1), pp. 71–90.

Earth Institute. (2003), 'Earth Institute launches partnership with Ugandan stakeholders: President Museveni welcomes delegation', Available at: www.earth.columbia. edu/news/2003/story03-25-03.html [accessed 19 November 2016].

Earth Institute. (2009), *Infrastructure from the Bottom up* (New York: Earth Institute).

Ellis, F. and Bahiigwa, G. (2003), 'Livelihoods and rural poverty reduction in Uganda', *World Development*, 31(6), pp. 997–1013.

Francis, P. and James, R. (2003), 'Balancing rural poverty reduction and citizen participation: The contradictions of Uganda's decentralization program', *World Development*, 31(2), pp. 325–37.

Golooba-Mutebi, F. and Hickey, S. (2010), 'Governing chronic poverty under inclusive liberalism: The case of the northern Uganda Social Action Fund', *Journal of Development Studies*, 46(7), pp. 1216–39.

Handa-Williams, N. (2010), 'WFP director hails the "revolution of hope" in Ruhiira', Available at: www.millenniumvillages.org/ field-notes/wfp-director-hails-the-revolution-of-hope-in-ruhiira [accessed 22 March 2013].

Hickey, S. (2005), 'The politics of staying poor: Exploring the political space for poverty reduction in Uganda', *World Development*, 33(6), pp. 995–1009.

Hickey, S. (2013), 'Beyond the poverty agenda? Insights from the new politics of development in Uganda', *World Development*, (43), pp. 194–206.

Human Rights Watch. (2004), *States of Pain: Torture in Uganda.*

Inzama, A. (2012), 'Uganda: Oil, corruption and entitlement', *The Guardian*, 1 October.

Konecky, B. and Palm, C. (eds) (2008), *Millennium Villages Handbook: A Practical Guide to the Millennium Villages Approach* (New York, NY: Earth Institute).

Li, T. M. (2007), *The Will to Improve: Governmentality, Development, and the Practice of Politics* (Durham, NC: Duke University Press).

Livingstone, I. (1979), 'On the concept of 'Integrated Rural Development Planning' in less developed countries, *Journal of Agricultural Economics*, 30(1), pp. 49–53.

Marx, K. (1976), *Capital: Volume One* (New York, NY: Random House).

Millennium Project. (2005), *Investing in Development: A Practical Plan to Achieve the Millennium Development Goals* (New York, NY: United Nations Development Programme).

Millennium Promise. (2010), 'Ruhiira, Uganda', Available at: http://mp.convio.net/site/ PageServer?pagename=mv_ruhiira [accessed 19 November 2016].

Millennium Promise. (2014), *Millennium Promise Annual Report on the Millennium Villages Project* (New York, NY: Millennium Promise).

Millennium Villages Project. (2010), *Harvests of Development in Rural Africa: The Millennium Villages after Three Years* (New York, NY: Earth Institute).

Millennium Villages Project. (2011), *Millennium Villages Project: The Next Five Years: 2011–2015* (New York, NY: Millennium Villages Project).

Millennium Villages Project. (2013), 'Ugandan government launches scale-up of Millennium Villages Project', Available at: http://millenniumvillages. org/press-releases/ugandan- government-launches-scale-up- of-millennium-villages-project/ [accessed 6 September 2016].

Millennium Villages Project. (2016), 'Millennium Villages Project', Available at: http:// millenniumvillages.org/ the-villages/ [accessed 19 November 2016].

Mueller, B. (2011), 'The agrarian question in Tanzania: Using new evidence to reconcile an old debate', *Review of African Political Economy*, 38(127), pp. 23–42.

Mulumba, B. D. (2003), 'Museveni, Sachs on tour to boost textile producers', *The Monitor*, 5 March.

Munk, N. (2013), *The Idealist: Jeffrey Sachs and the Quest to End Poverty* (New York, NY: Doubleday).

Museveni, Y. (2012), 'Yoweri K. Museveni, President of Uganda' Available at: http://jeffsachs. org/2012/03/yoweri-k-musveni- president-of-uganda/ [accessed 19 November 2016].

Nganda, S. I. (2009), 'Corruption endemic in Uganda', *The Guardian*, 13 March.

Okario, J. (2009), 'Ruhiira MVP: Progress to date', presentation at Millennium Promise Partners Meeting, 21 September, Available at: https://academiccommons. columbia.edu/download/fedora_ content/download/ac:124730/ CONTENT/John_Okorio_ Lecture_Slides.pdf [accessed 27 July 2016].

Oya, C. (2005), 'Sticks and carrots for farmers in developing countries: Agrarican neoliberalism in theory and practice', in A. Saad-Filho and D. Johnston (eds), *Neoliberalism: A Critical Reader* (London: Pluto), pp. 127–34.

Perelman, M. (2000), *The Invention of Capitalism: Classical Political Economy and the Secret History of Primitive Accumulation* (Durham, NC: Duke University Press).

Powers, L. (2010), 'Lots of people visit Ruhiira', Available at:

http://lindapowers.blogspot.co.uk/2010/07/lots-of-people-visit-ruhiira.html [accessed 19 November 2016].

Ruttan, V. (1984), 'Integrated Rural Development Programmes: A historical perspective', *World Development*, 12(4), pp. 393–440.

Sachs, J. (2004), 'Doing the sums in Africa', *The Economist*, 20 May.

Sachs, J. (2005), *The End of Poverty: How We Can Make It Happen in Our Lifetime* (London: Penguin).

Sanchez, P. *et al.* (2009), 'The African Green Revolution moves forward', *Food Security*, 1(1), pp. 37–44.

Tankink, M. (2004), 'Not talking about traumatic experiences: Harmful or healing? Coping with war memories in southwest Uganda', *Intervention*, 2(1), pp. 3–17.

Tripp, A. M. (2010), *Museveni's Uganda: Paradoxes of Power in a Hybrid Regime* (London: Lynne Rienner).

Wilson, J. (2014a), 'Fantasy machine: Philanthrocapitalism as an ideological formation', *Third World Quarterly*, 35(7), pp. 1144–61.

Wilson, J. (2014b), 'The shock of the real: The neoliberal neurosis in the life and times of Jeffrey Sachs', *Antipode*, 46(1), pp. 301–21.

YouTube. (2010), 'Jeffrey Sachs and Josette Sheeran (UN WFP) visit Ruhiira, Uganda', www.youtube.com/watch?v=AbTffV-cEBI [accessed 19 November 2016].

Part II

Economic restructuring and social services

7
The impact of neoliberal reforms on Uganda's socio-economic landscape

Godfrey B. Asiimwe

Introduction

This chapter explores changes in Uganda's socio-economic landscape, which were a result of the neoliberal reforms introduced in the 1980s (see Kiiza *et al.* 2006). The Structural Adjustment Programme (SAP) reforms, which were introduced against the background of political instability and economic regression, re-configured the state in favour of the 'free market', and thus re-aligned economic, social and state–society relations (see Chapter 1). However, the reforms' policy precondition was often at variance with context-specific dynamics and realities (Khan 2012). Under the reforms, economic recovery and an up-swing in growth were reported, which were used to showcase Uganda as a successful model of neoliberalism (Ddumba-Ssentamu *et al.* 1999). By October 2005, the IMF had moved Uganda from the list of the poorest of the poor, which required financial help to maintain macro-economic stability, to the Policy Support Instrument Framework (PSIF) where it was largely given policy advice and endorsement. According to an IMF report of 2015, Uganda's economy continued to perform very well and was awarded a 'clean bill of health' (Muhakanizi 2015: 37). But how has the neoliberal model transformed state–society relations, livelihoods and development in Uganda?

We will analyse the impact of the reforms with regard to a wider spectrum of the complex interplay of socio-economic dynamics, rather than neoliberals' focus on economic growth per se. First, aid was the major driver of Uganda's economic recovery and growth. Yet aid is not sustainable, tended to serve particular donor interests, generated paternalism and dependence, and increased the debt burden (Moyo 2009). Meanwhile, major sectors of industry and agriculture stagnated while trade accelerated along the pathway of unbalanced deficit, thus increasing aid dependence. Second, in the neoliberal arena, many players entered from a weak position and encountered inherent imperfections and power asymmetries, which defied neoliberal assumptions of 'perfect competition and rational choice'. We note that neoliberal dynamics generated contradictions of 'imperfect' competition with trajectories of 'primitive accumulation' that engendered socio-political tensions and categories of winners and losers. While winners were largely facilitated by the restructured 'gate-keeping' state, neoliberal dynamics generated persistent poverty, widening inequality and unemployment for the majority losers. Under SAPs, the public sector contracted and many who entered the market from a weak position could not access and afford quality services, notably frontline services of health and education. The neoliberal model was, therefore, a paradox of growth without meaningful transformation.

Aid and growth

Neoliberal reforms have been credited for Uganda's recorded high annual GDP growth rate, which reached 11 per cent in 1994/9 and thereafter averaged 6.5 per cent up to 2015. First, Uganda's economic recovery and growth were contingent upon aid inflows. Aid inflows enabled an increase in public spending – hence the expenditure-driven growth trajectory – but with associated elite corruption (Asiimwe 2013). When corruption combined with reverse outflows, the debt burden increased. Second, the recorded growth and assumption of 'trickle down' were not reflected in transformed production and local capacity, but rather accelerated inequality, poverty and unemployment.

Aid in material goods coupled with liberalisation undermined the domestic production sectors of agriculture and industry. Subsequently, Uganda's aid-driven growth was largely through an expansion in services like transport, telecommunications, hair salons, hospitality/bars, imports including used commodities and consumables, speculative and circulative capital, real estate and construction that was largely fuelled by public expenditure.

Despite its initial reluctance, the National Resistance Movement (NRM) government adopted fully the neoliberal SAP conditionalities, which were in line with donor interests. As a reward for its commitment to the reforms, donors increased financial inflows in the form of aid and Uganda became the first country to benefit from the Heavily Indebted Poor Countries (HIPC) debt relief. Large amounts of aid inflows accounted for 50 per cent of Uganda's budget (Kasekende and Atingi-Ego 1999, Burnside and Dollar 2000, Fagernäs and Roberts 2004, Minoiu and Reddy 2009, Asiimwe et al. 2018). Budget support constituted a growing share of total aid receipts, rising from an average of 28 per cent during the 1990s to about 42 per cent, and reached 52 per cent in 2002 (Atingi-Ego 2006).

Aid was not free, yet stimulated both public expenditure and corruption, which increased indebtedness. Aid inflows enabled an increase in public spending as a ratio of GDP from 13 per cent in 2001 to 21 per cent in 2010, which contributed to the celebrated economic growth. Relatedly, as aid inflows increased, corruption in Uganda also increased. The 2005 World Bank (WB) survey estimated that up to $300 million were lost per year through corruption and procurement practices. With increasing corruption, donors threatened to cut aid, pointing out that a Corruption Perception Index (CPI) score below four was unacceptable (Ambassador Stig Barling, in Masumbuko 2005). Uganda's CPI remained below three, and even declined after 2009, yet aid inflows continued and even increased from 2005, despite the threat (Asiimwe 2016). The donors' failure to execute their threat led to questions about the underlying rationale behind, and interests of, giving aid.

Subsequently, most grants were channelled through non-governmental organisations (NGOs), which were presumably more effective than the state. It was estimated that 25 per cent of all official aid went to NGOs, some of which had a dependence rate of over 80 per cent on a single donor (Opoku-Mensah *et al.* 2007: 75). The channelling of aid through the NGO sector led to an increase in the number of NGOs from 200 registered in 1986, to over 7,000, of which only 20 per cent were reported to be operational (Baguma, 2009). However, channelling aid through NGOs did not necessarily reduce corruption (Asiimwe 2016). The aid system stimulated the growth of a network of a host of hierarchical international and local actors, some of whom used all sorts of means to access the money and to conjure up 'results' in order to justify 'good' work (Tvedt 1998, 2002). With increased inflows, public expenditure, corruption and outflows, Uganda's debt burden remained high as a percentage of GDP (Bank of Uganda, Annual Reports, 2003/2004, 2005/2006, 2006/2007, 2008/2009, 2010/2011, 2012/2013, 2015/2016 and 2016/2017). Table 7.1 and Figure 7.1 show the trend of Uganda's external debt.

Imbalanced trade

The largely aid-driven growth obscured the mutually beneficial and potentially sustainable trade which remained imbalanced. While

Table 7.1 – Total external debt (UGX billions)

Financial year	Total external debt (UGX billions)	Financial year	Total external debt (UGX billions)
00/01	13,662,730.56	08/09	12,727,603.97
01/02	14,606,191.50	09/10	12959951.72
02/03	16,754,877.40	10/11	16,810,339.47
03/04	17,466,312.04	11/12	18,118,912.01
04/05	19,113,909.65	12/13	21,573,599.74
05/06	19,222,541.18	13/14	25,724,695.14
06/07	14,183,746.57	14/15	31,157,211.16
07/08	10,788,987,2571	15/16	30,331,557.26

Source: Uganda Debt Network (2017: 4).

Figure 7.1 – Trend of Uganda's total external debt for the financial years 2000/01–2015/16 (UGX billions)

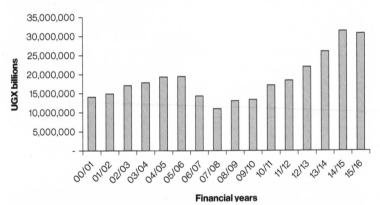

Source: Uganda Debt Network (2017: 3).

liberalisation opened the domestic market to imports from dominant multinational giants, Uganda's exports could not easily access international markets. Direct and indirect restrictions, poor terms of trade and a power structure that favoured powerful multinationals combined to tilt the balance against domestic exports compared to imports. Subsequently, low export earnings versus import expenditure had budgetary repercussions, driving the country into further aid dependence. Figure 7.2 shows the widening imbalance between imports and exports under the reforms.

Figure 7.2 shows that Uganda's import–export trade during the early period of the reforms was fairly balanced, but the gap progressively

Figure 7.2 – Uganda import–export trade

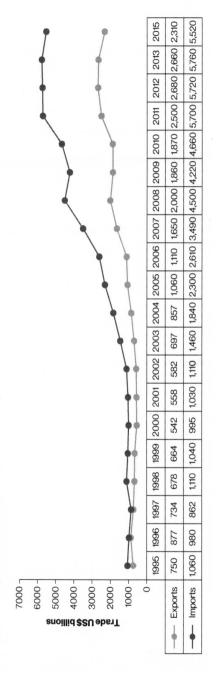

	1995	1996	1997	1998	1999	2000	2001	2002	2003	2004	2005	2006	2007	2008	2009	2010	2011	2012	2013	2015
Exports	750	877	734	678	664	542	558	582	697	857	1,060	1,110	1,650	2,000	1,860	1,870	2,500	2,680	2,660	2,310
Imports	1,060	980	862	1,110	1,040	995	1,030	1,110	1,460	1,840	2,300	2,610	3,490	4,500	4,220	4,660	5,700	5,720	5,760	5,520

Source: Author, data from Observatory of Economic Complexity (OEC) (2016).

widened as trade liberalisation took hold. In 2015, for example, Uganda's exports were $2.31 billion while imports were $5.52 billion, thus a deficit of $3.21 billion. This trade imbalance was also reflected in Uganda's major trade partners, whereby exports largely accessed regional markets rather than those of the major overseas trade partners. While over 45 per cent of Uganda's exports were to the regional markets of the East African Community (EAC) and the Common Market for Eastern and Southern Africa (COMESA), most imports were from overseas. The five major destinations of Uganda's exports were Kenya, Democratic Republic of the Congo (DRC), Sudan, Rwanda and Southern Sudan. Conversely, the major sources of imports were India, China, Kenya, United Arab Emirates and Japan, yet Uganda could not easily export to these countries. The imbalance was particularly pronounced with the Asian countries where Uganda's export value was only 11 per cent of the total value of imports from the Asia region (UBOS 2013).

Declining production

Uganda's major sectors of agriculture and industry were adversely impacted by policies of liberalisation and the removal of subsidies. These increased the cost of utilities like electricity, water, credit and inputs, and given the inadequate infrastructure, the cost of doing business escalated and productivity declined (UG 2014: 6). The contribution of total factor productivity (TFP) as a percentage of GDP growth, which was 34 per cent between 1990 and 2000, declined to 28 per cent between 2001 and 2010; and further dropped to 15 per cent during the 2011–2012 period. In turn, decline in major production sectors fuelled unemployment against a total labour force that had increased from 10.9 million people in 2005/06 to 13.4 million in 2009/10.

Agriculture

Agriculture was for long the mainstay of Uganda's economy. During the early period of the reforms, agriculture contributed 85 per cent of export earnings and employed over 66 per cent of the working population, and agricultural commodities constituted over 90 per cent of exports (MAAIF 2011, UBOS 2012: 17–18, NDP 2010: 12). However, agriculture's contribution to GDP started declining, from 43 per cent of GDP in the early 2000 to 21 per cent of GDP, and by 2007 accounted for 47 per cent of total export earnings (UG 2014: 45). From 2004 to 2008, agricultural growth slowed to an average of 1.1 per cent and in 2006 recorded a growth of -1.8 per cent. Cash crops declined by 16 per cent during the 2010/11 financial year, while the food crop contribution to GDP declined from 14.3 per cent in 2009/10 to 13 per cent during the 2010/11 year (MAAIF 2011, UBOS 2012: 17–18). Cash crops were particularly undermined by erratic world market prices, coupled with the policy of devaluation, which increased the volume and not the income from commodity exports.

While the National Development Plan (NDP) underlined low productivity in agriculture (NDP 2010: 15), official discourse blamed seasonal climatic vagaries like drought and *el nino*, thus obscuring the systemic structural problems inherent in the neoliberal model. The removal of subsidies, the degeneration and contraction of extension services after 'rolling back the state', constraints in accessing markets, unaffordable inputs and credit, and the collapse of cooperatives, all precipitated the decline in agriculture. Co-operatives used to offer Uganda's predominantly small-holder peasant producers collective power against shocks, market failures and price fluctuations. With liberalisation, the weak producers entered the marketing arena as individuals to buy market-driven inputs and sell products in largely imperfect transactions. In the marketing chain, producers encountered market failures, constraints and hierarchies of traders with transactions often replete with irregularities, and hence became 'price takers' (Asiimwe 2002, Wiegratz 2010, Wedig and Wiegratz 2017). Subsistence farming remained crucial for the producers' sustenance as it was a fall-back absorbent to monetary shocks. Producers also diversified into off-farm activities and non-traditional cash crops, and drifted into urban-based service and informal sectors. These changes underlay declining agricultural production, which thus increased unemployment, under-employment and socio-political unrest.

Conversely, developed economies maintained farm subsidies and direct and indirect protection for their powerful producers. For instance, some 25,000 US farmers who produced six-tenths of all the cotton in the world received $4 billion a year in subsidies. This enabled them to produce about 17 million bales and control 25 per cent of the total world export market. As a result, US cotton is exported at an average price of 57 per cent below the cost of production. Likewise, the EU commits 1.7 billion euros in annual export subsidies on dairy products (Stocking 2002).

Industry

Although liberalisation increased the volume of goods, it opened the domestic market to giant multinational companies whose products out-competed local products, thus leading to de-industrialisation. Such multinational giants enjoyed support and subsidies in their countries and had the advantage of economies of scale. For instance, massive imports of textiles and used clothes crippled Uganda's once vibrant textile industry, resulting in a multiplier effect travelling down through the domestic cotton and apparel sector including traders, designers and cotton producers at the grassroots level.

With privatisation, government aimed to attract foreign investors to revamp industry in the hope of realising the 'big-push' effect. When industry includes mining, quarrying, manufacturing, electricity, water, construction, electricity generation, transmission and distribution, its growth trajectory appears high. However, manufacturing remained marginal and stagnated and was largely in end-product assembling import substitution, basic low-value-added goods, extractive and processing rather than export-led value addition industrialisation. Ninety per cent of manufacturing is dominated by small and medium enterprises (SMEs), which generate over 80 per cent of the manufactured output and approximately 7 per cent of GDP (Royal African Society 2014).

Manufacturing, which constituted 6.3 per cent of GDP in 1982, before the reforms, did not significantly grow. It rose to 8.4 per cent of GDP in 1997, then declined to 6.7 per cent in the 2008/09 financial year, rose again to 8.8 per cent in 2012, and accounted for only 5 per cent of the labour force. Most activities were in food processing, beverages, tobacco and printing (UNCTAD 2008: 7, NDP 2010: 118, UBOS 2013). With privatisation and the removal of subsidies, Uganda's embryonic industrialisation was stifled by the high cost of utilities, including prohibitive energy costs that were aggravated by an erratic power supply under the assumed more efficient privatised electricity sector (Uganda Electricity Board/UEB was sold to UK's Globeleq and South Africa's Eskom, resulting in the formation of Umeme). Despite government inducements and incentives, most multinational investors preferred non-fixed capital investments like ICT, telecommunications and banking, which were easily transferable in case of unstable or unprofitable conditions. The Uganda case shows that investment capital under neo-liberalism is predicated on profit maximisation, thus can be speculative and unpredictable.

Entrepreneurs in the neoliberal arena

Despite prioritisation of the private sector, the policy environment and operational arena hindered the sustainable growth of local entrepreneurship (perhaps this was by policy design, as a strong indigenous middle class could be a political threat). Lack of affordable credit, 'imperfect' competition and systemic corruption were the major constraints on local entrepreneurs. Many were capital deficient and profits were undercut by the high cost of utilities, rent and manifold taxes. Such impediments drove some entrepreneurs into commonplace imperfection excesses that approximated primitive accumulation-cum-'fake capitalism', which impacted on transactions and quality services (see Wiegratz 2010). Most entrepreneurs operated SMEs and speculative short-term, quick-return types of commercial and consumer service ventures, and hence avoided long-term industrial and agricultural sectors. This was partly the cause of the slump in agriculture, and in the industrial sector small and medium-sized operations could hardly scale-up to benefit from economies of scale and break-even. In 2001/02, out of 11,968 manufacturing establishments, 9,519 (80 per cent) were small, employing one to four people (UBOS 2001/2002: 20). At the tail-end was the bulk of absorptive activities like vending/hawking, motorcycle taxis (*boda-boda*), hair salons, vehicle washing and other services that disguised employment yet hid under-employment. A 2010/11 census found that 70 per cent of businesses had an annual turnover of less than five million Uganda shillings (UGX) while only 10 per cent had an annual turnover of more than UGX 10 million (UBOS 2011).

The post-independence government had established the Uganda Commercial Bank (UCB) and Co-operative Bank to make affordable credit available to incipient African entrepreneurs and farmers. By the time UCB was privatised, it had appreciated and was making profits; hence, its controversial sale (see Aisu 1998, Uganda Parliament 2002). With privatisation, the financial sector was opened to networks of local and international commercial banks, moneylenders and micro-finance institutions (MFIs) that traded in high interest rates, largely short-term credit, with hardly any grace period for business growth. There was mistrust of MFIs in Uganda (Duggan 2016). Credit and capital became cyclical, interest rates of commercial banks and moneylenders were prohibitive, and there was an absence of long-term capital financing. The chairman of the Private Sector Foundation noted: 'MFIs charging 50% is day light robbery. It is killing these people who are investors of the world' (Daily Monitor 2005). By 2012, commercial bank lending interest rates had increased to 30 per cent and later averaged 24 per cent in 2013 and 22 per cent in 2015. Initially, commercial banks preferred salary loans, as they were easier to re-coup through re-payment arrangements with employers. Categories like small-holder producers, women and youth were handicapped by a lack of acceptable collateral or viable businesses to obtain loans, and thus remained capital deficient.

Meanwhile, government efforts to attract investors yielded all sorts of foreign investors that included petty retailers, 'fair-weather' investors and speculators in search of opportunities. Many substantial investors had a comparative advantage over local entrepreneurs, which included access to long-term credit in their countries. In addition to this, government extended inducements and concessions – including tax holidays – enabling them to invest, import, undersell and elbow-out local entrepreneurs. Yet they quickly flew in the face of vicissitudes.

The economic arena was, therefore, not level for the presumed 'perfect competition'. Contradictions in the liberal arena undermined the growth of entrepreneurship. This led to a cyclical trend that saw an increase in the number of local entrepreneurs followed by high drop-out rates, which were instead attributed to 'poor' business management and a lack of acumen in local entrepreneurs.

The 2000 Uganda Investment Authority Report noted that 39.1 per cent of the enterprises were wholly owned by Ugandans, 36.2 per cent foreign owned, and 24.7 per cent jointly owned. However, projects wholly owned by Ugandans had a higher rate of abandonment (79 per cent) and a slower rate of implementation. In comparison, the abandonment rate of foreign-owned projects was 8.7 per cent, while joint venture projects had an abandonment rate of 12.3 per cent (Uganda Investment Authority 2000: xii). The Director of Enterprise Uganda highlighted the high business failure rate (Nandudu 2010). The Deputy Governor of the Bank of Uganda noted that the failure of businesses was estimated at a rate of 26 per cent relative to the average of about 16 per cent for sub-Saharan Africa (Kasekende 2016). The UBOS business census shows that only 17 per cent of the businesses were more than twenty years old (UBOS 2011).

Growth against widening inequality and poverty

Under reforms, official data consistently projected an impressive decline in poverty – from 55.7 per cent in 1992/93 to 19.7 per cent in 2012/13 (UG-PSR 2014, UG 2014: 87). First, Uganda's GNP was only US$320 per capita, which was far below the regional average of US$600 per capita. Additionally, Uganda's per capita income has stagnated at about US$615 (World Bank, 2017).

Second, the reduction of poverty is predicated on the assumption of 'trickle down', which improves livelihoods (see Todaro 1981: 68, 131). On this note, neoliberalism quantifies income-based and wealth aggregates, which are generalised, thus hiding the realities of disparities, deprivation and marginalisation. In Uganda, the impressive economic growth was accompanied by increased inequality, poverty and unemployment, and thus generated social asymmetries of winners and losers. As income distribution widened, the increasing poverty for the majority was aggregated under the increasing wealth of the affluent few. Neoliberalism glosses over power structures and subsequent poverty and distribution disparities (Meier 1995: 537–538). Meanwhile, neo-Malthusian and modernisation discourses blamed the poverty on Uganda's high population growth, traditional practices and 'laziness'. However, this obscures the neoliberal structural architecture against the weak players in the arena.

During the reform period, the Gini index showed that the gap between the rich and poor rose from 33.0 in 1989/90 to 45.7 in 2002 and remained as high as 44.6 in 2012 (WB Group 2015). Household income or consumption share was only 2.4 per cent for the lowest 10 per cent of the population, while it increased for the highest 10 per cent of the population from 29.93 per cent in 1996 to 36.10 per cent in 2009 (WB Group 2015). When poverty had reportedly dropped to 33.8 per cent in 2000, the UNDP noted that income poverty still affected about 46 per cent of Uganda's population (UNDP 2000). Working with multiple methodologies, it was established that nearly 77 per cent of households in Uganda were in fact chronically poor (Lawson et al. 2006: 1236).

It is noteworthy that when non-income and expenditure approaches and capabilities are applied, more comprehensive forms of poverty emerge (see Sen 1999, Ellis 2000, Lawson et al. 2006). According to the 2011 UNDP Multidimensional Poverty Index (MPI) approach, which is based on multiple deprivations and living standards in the same households, up to 70.3 per cent of Uganda's population were multidimensionally poor while an additional 20.6 per cent lived near multidimensional poverty (UNDP 2015). In Uganda, it was noted that the consumption growth of the bottom 40 per cent was slower than the consumption growth of the top 60 per cent. Under the reforms, the reduction of public sector safeguards and subsidies increased the vulnerability of the general populace to shocks like prolonged illness and climatic vagaries, hence the tendency to fall back into poverty. It was, for instance, noted that between 2005 and 2009, for every three people who were lifted out of poverty, two fell back into it (WB 2015, WB 2016: x). Although Uganda's HDI improved, in 2012 its HDI was ranked low at 161 out of 187 countries and, in 2014, 163 out of 188 countries; below Kenya's position at 145 and Tanzania's at 151 (UNDP 2015). Life expectancy was estimated at only forty-seven years compared to sixty-five for all developing nations, and in 1999 about half of the population did not have safe water (Parkhurst *et al.* 2006, ADB/EOCD 2008).

According to the 2014 National Population and Housing Census, many people could not afford a basic need like food, as 63.2 per cent of the population was reportedly unable to have three meals a day. 'On average more than half of the household members aged 5 years and above consumed 2 meals a day … and 12% had one meal a day'. Fifty-two per cent of households used *Tadooba* (local paraffin candle) as their main source of energy; 71 per cent used firewood for cooking; 82 per cent of rural households obtained their livelihood from subsistence farming (UBOS 2016: 40, Mugerwa 2016). Although there was an increase and improvement of services, these were largely unaffordable and thus only accessed by the few winners.

The health and education sectors

Under the neoliberal reforms, frontline services of health and education were decentralised without adequate resources, which impacted on quality (Nystrand and Tamm this volume). This section specifically highlights increasing cost, corruption, and unequitable access and quality of health services under the reforms. With the policy of the removal of subsidies, expenditure on health as a percentage of GDP dropped to 2.2 per cent in 2007, while expenditure on health as a percentage of total government expenditure decreased from 16.2 per cent in 2011 to 11 per cent in 2014. The health sector budget allocation reduced from 8.6 per cent of the total budget in the 2013/14 financial year to 8 per cent in 2014/15. However, this was below the Abuja declaration of 15 per cent of national budget allocation to health by 2015 (WB 2016 and Uganda Budget Speeches). Meanwhile, government introduced user fees (cost-sharing) in public hospitals, but as Okuonzi noted, 51 per cent of the population living within walkable distance of health facilities did not use the facilities due to the prohibitive user fees. Although donors objected to the abolition of the user fees, government was compelled to revoke them in 2001 due to their unpopularity (Okuonzi 2007: 60).

Under decentralisation, corruption by local authorities increased and affected health services (*ibid.*: 66, Asiimwe 2016). In 2006, the

Ministry of Health noted that 73 per cent of the essential medicines destined to health units leaked, implying that only 27 per cent reached the target beneficiaries (Uganda Health Facilities Survey 2006). The auditor general's 'Value for Money Audit Report' (Office of the Auditor General 2006) noted that essential drugs were found lacking at 43 per cent of the health centres and there were no proper records for the medicine received and dispensed. Likewise, the 2004 Uganda Medical Survey Report found that the median availability of essential medicines at health units was 55 per cent at the public health facilities. Leakages also included gloves, syringes and wound dressings. According to the Poverty Eradication Action Plan (PEAP 2004–2007), the mean bribe in the health sector was about UGX 12,000. Degeneration of the public health sector forced many people to seek services from private providers, many of whom rendered better services to attracted 'clients'. However, fees of good private providers were prohibitive, and access for many was unequal. There were also rampant cases of fraudulent practices tailored at unethical profiteering among some private practitioners.

Uganda's health services, therefore, did not necessarily improve under the reforms (Okuonzi 2007: 89, Nystrand and Tamm this volume). By 2009, Uganda's healthcare performance was ranked 186 out of 191 nations by the World Health Organization – one of the worst in the world. Only 38 per cent of healthcare posts were filled and some 70 per cent of doctors and 40 per cent of nurses and midwives were based in urban areas, serving only 12 per cent of the population (Kelly 2009). There has been reported improvement in aspects like infant mortality rate (IMR) and life expectancy at birth (UBOS 2016: 40). However, such aggregate data obscure disparities and the real situation of the poor.

In education, reforms led to an increase of enrolment amidst quality deterioration and unequal access. At a higher level, reforms were underpinned by a paradigm shift from 'man-power planning' to market dictation and the monetary 'rate of returns' cost–benefit analysis (Samoff and Bidemi 2003) (during a meeting with vice chancellors in Harare in 1986, the WB argued that higher education in Africa was a luxury, Brock-Utne 2000). Consistent with the neoliberal discourse, there was a trend of restructuring university curricula towards applied skills that were 'relevant' for the market, and the prioritisation of natural sciences presumably for innovation for development and as a panacea to unemployment (Mamdani 2007).

Under reforms, expenditure on education as a percentage of total government expenditure dropped and impacted quality. Expenditure decreased from 12.1 per cent in 2011 to 11.8 per cent in 2013 and the percentage share of education was 13.3 per cent of the total budget in 2013/14 (WB 2016 and Uganda Budget Speeches). Ministry of Education allocations to the higher education sector ranged from 9 to 12 per cent since 1986 in comparison to the primary sub-sector which consistently received 60 per cent of its sector budget (Liang 2002). This imbalance was in tandem with the World Bank paradigm shift in favour of 'education for all', hence the increased funding to primary education. From 1990, funding for research and post-graduate studies was stopped (Kasozi 2006). At undergraduate level, government sponsorship was reduced to largely district quota allotments and the controversial State-House Scholarship Scheme. Meanwhile, many able students from poor backgrounds could not afford the payment of university dues. During the 2014/15 academic year, seventy students applied for withdrawal in the Schools of Liberal and Performing Arts and Languages and Communication where tuition averaged UGX 700,000 ($237) a semester (Joint Schools Board Withdrawal Cases, Schools of Liberal and Performing Arts 2014/2015). Many more students paid half tuition, or failed or defrauded payment (Deputy VC 2015).

Consistent with the shift in favour of 'education for all', the government instituted Universal Primary Education (UPE) in 2007, which was followed by Universal Secondary Education (USE) in selected schools. However, resources remained inadequate, as government committed a modest annual grant of up to UGX 141,000 ($52) per student, which was spread over three school terms, while parents were to provide uniforms, stationery and meals. Although both UPE and USE achieved increments of student enrolment, the quality of education deteriorated (Uwezo 2015, Nystrand and Tamm this volume). It was observed that: 'whilst there has been progress in improving equity in access to services, considerable inequities remain in the quality of education regionally, and across social groups' (Hedger *et al.* 2010: vii). On standards, Kavuma illustrates that whereas in 2006 before USE nearly 95 per cent of O-level candidates achieved at least the minimum pass rate to qualify for a national certificate, with a 54 per cent increase in candidates in 2010, those who qualified for the certificate dropped to 80 per cent (Kavuma 2011).

Liberalisation opened space for private players; however, most good private schools were situated around urban centres to attract middle- and higher-class 'clientele' rather than the rural poor. Additionally, good private schools were very expensive for the average citizen. At a higher level, many private and public universities were established and the private sponsorship scheme was introduced at Makerere in 1991. Despite the quality deterioration at lower levels, many students who could afford the costs were able to join universities. This increased enrolment and in many units beyond the official lecturer–student ratio and the few qualified staff. With lecture halls becoming chronically overcrowded, tutorials were suspended and intermittent strikes over poor pay prevailed; thus affecting the quality. In 2013, the National Council of Higher Education (NCHE) noted that academic staff numbers were not in sync with student enrolment; staff PhDs remained at 11 per cent; teaching and working space had not improved; student access to books was not impressive; and all public and private higher education institutions received less money than was needed for producing a graduate (NCHE 2013).

Conclusion

Under the neoliberal model, Uganda has been credited as a showcase of impressive economic recovery and growth. However, this chapter has highlighted contradictions that are deeply rooted in the structural architecture of the reforms. The dynamic interplay of the 'imperfect' market favoured few players, who became winners, while the poor, who were the majority, were marginalised. The chapter also showed the poor performance of major sectors of the economy amidst the recorded aid-driven economic recovery and growth. It was noted that the recovery and growth obscured deep contradictions of aid dependence, decline in major sectors, widening and persistent poverty, marginalisation, and the inequitable distribution, inaccessibility and unaffordability of major services vis-à-vis the poorer sections of society.

References

ADB/OECD. (2008), 'UGANDA', *African Economic Outlook*, African Development Bank (ADB) Group and Organisation for Economic Co-operation and Development (OECD).

Aisu, O. (1998), Parliament of Uganda, Select Committee on Privatisation, Report, Uganda Government, 8 December.

Asiimwe, G. (2002), *The Impact of Post-colonial Policy Shifts in Coffee Marketing at Local Level in Uganda: A Case Study of Mukono District, 1962–1998* (Maastricht: Shaker Publishing).

Asiimwe, G. (2013), 'Of extensive and elusive corruption in Uganda: Neo-patronage, power, and narrow interests', *African Studies Review*, 56(2), pp. 129–44.

Asiimwe, G. (2016), 'Progress and

constraints of civil society anti-corruption initiatives in Uganda, 2008–2015', in B. Davis (ed.), *Corruption: Political, Economic and Social Issues* (New York, NY: Nova Science).

Asiimwe, G. and Nahamya, K. W. (2011), 'Challenges of co-operative institutions in the post-colonial transformation of Uganda', *Mawazo*, Makerere University, 10(2), pp. 58–72.

Asiimwe, B. G., Mulyampiti, T. and Joyce, A. (2018), 'Uganda's post-independence development paradoxes through international aid architecture, 1962–2010', in R. T. Akinyele (ed.), *History and Diplomacy: Essays in Honour of Ade Adefuye* (Glassboro, NJ: Goldline and Jacobs), pp. 348–74.

Atingi-Ego, M. (2006), 'Budget support, aid dependence and the Dutch disease: The case of Uganda', in S. Koerberle, Z. Stavreski and J. Walliser (eds), *Budget Support as More Effective Aid? Recent Experiences and Emerging Lessons* (Washington, DC: World Bank).

Baguma, A. (2009), 'Have NGOs contributed to development', *New Vision*, 9 August.

Bank of Uganda. (2003/2004), Annual Report, Kampala.

Bank of Uganda. (2005/2006), Annual Report, Kampala.

Bank of Uganda. (2006/2007), Annual Report, Kampala.

Bank of Uganda. (2008/2009), Annual Report, Kampala.

Bank of Uganda. (2010/2011), Annual Report, Kampala.

Bank of Uganda. (2012/2013), Annual Report, Kampala.

Bank of Uganda. (2014/2016), Annual Report, Kampala.

Bank of Uganda. (2016/2017), Annual Report, Kampala.

Brock-Utne, B. (2000), *Whose Education for All? The Recolonisation of the African Mind* (New York, NY: Falmer Press).

Burnside, C. and Dollar, D. (2000), 'Aid policies and growth', *American Economic Review*, 9(4), pp. 847–69.

Daily Monitor. (2005), 'MFIs rates undermine business', Reporter, 7 October.

Ddumba-Ssentamu, J., Dijkstra, G. and van Donge, J. K. (1999), *What Does the Showcase Show?: Programme Aid in Uganda*, SIDA Evaluation Report, Stockholm.

Deputy VC, Finance and Administration. (2015), Correspondence to Staff, Makerere University webmail, 8 June, 10:05 am.

Duggan, S. M. C. (2016), 'Doing bad by doing good? Theft and abuse by lenders in the microfinance markets of Uganda', *Studies in Comparative International Development*, 51(2), pp. 189–208.

Ellis, F. (2000), *Rural Livelihoods and Diversity in Developing Countries* (Oxford: Oxford University Press).

Fagernäs, S. and Roberts, J. (2004), 'The fiscal effects of aid in Uganda', Working Paper No. 9, Economic and Statistics Analysis Unit (London: ODI).

Hedger, E. *et al.* (2010), 'Sector budget support in practice: Case study education sector in Uganda', Report (London: ODI & Mokoro).

Kasekende, A. L. and Atingi-Ego, M. (1999), 'Uganda's experience with aid', *Journal of African Economies*, 8(4), pp. 617–49.

Kasekende, L. (2016), Speech: 'Launch of the Orient Bank's financial literacy programme', The Orient Bank Business Academy, Kampala, 30 August.

Kasozi, A. B. (2006), 'Rethinking of our education system, Part 1: Higher education', Project Paper, MISR, Makerere University.

Kavuma, R. M. (2011), 'Free universal secondary education in Uganda has yielded mixed results', *The Guardian*, 25 October.

Kelly, A. (2009), 'Healthcare a major challenge for Uganda', *The Guardian*, Available at: www.

theguardian.com [accessed 5 June 2015].

Khan, M. H. (2012), 'Governance during social transformations: Challenges for Africa', *New Political Economy*, 17(5), pp. 667–75.

Kiiza, J., Asiimwe, G. and Kibikyo, D. (2006), 'Understanding the economic and institutional reforms in Uganda', in J. Mensah (ed.), *Understanding Economic Reforms in Africa: A Tale of Seven Nations* (Ottawa: Palgrave Macmillan), pp. 57–94.

Lawson, D., McKay, A. and Okidi, J. (2006), 'Poverty persistence and transitions in Uganda: A combined qualitative and quantitative analysis', *Journal of Development Studies*, 42(7), pp. 1225–51.

Liang, Xiaoyan. (2002), *Uganda Post-Primary Education Sector Report* (Washington DC: World Bank).

MAAIF. (2011), *Statistical Abstract*, Agricultural Planning Department, Ministry of Agriculture, Animal Industry and Fisheries, Government of Uganda.

Mamdani, M. (2007), *Scholars in the Marketplace: The Dilemmas of Neo-Liberal Reform at Makerere University, 1989–2005* (Dakar: CODESRIA).

Masumbuko, E. (2005), 'Donors will not tolerate Uganda graft – Ambassador', *The Daily Monitor*, 1 November.

Meier, M. G. (1995), *Leading Issues in Economic Development* (New York, NY: Oxford University Press).

Minoiu, C. and Reddy, S. G. (2009), 'Development aid and economic growth: A positive long-run relation', IMF Working Paper No. 09/118.

Moyo, D. (2009), *Dead Aid: Why Aid Is Not Working and How There Is Another Way for Africa* (London: Penguin Books).

Mugerwa, Y. (2016), 'Four million can't afford two meals', *Daily Monitor*, 28 March.

Muhakanizi, K. (2015), 'Finance chief welcomes IMF assessment report', *New Vision*, 19 May.

Nandudu, P. (2010), 'Uganda tops in failed businesses', *The New Vision*, 31 August.

NCHE. (2013), 'The state of higher education and training in Uganda 2011', Kyambogo, Kampala.

NDP. (2010), 'National Development Plan 2010/11–2014/15', Kampala: The Republic of Uganda.

Observatory of Economic Complexity (OEC) (2016), Uganda Trade Balance (https://atlas.media.mit.edu/en/profile/country/uga/ [accessed 3 July 2018].

Office of the Auditor General. (2006), 'Value for money audit report', Kampala.

Okuonzi, S. A. (2009), 'Free-market illusions: Health sector reforms in Uganda 1987–2007'. PhD Thesis, University of Bergen.

Opoku-Mensah, P., Lewis, D. and Tvedt, T. (2007), *Reconceptualising NGOs and Their Roles in Development: NGOs, Civil Society and the International Aid System* (Aalborg: Aalborg University Press).

Parkhurst, O. J., Ssengooba, F. and Serwadda, D. (2006), 'Uganda', in E. J. Beck and L. M. Holland (eds), *HIV Pandemic: Local and Global Implications* (New York, NY: Oxford: University Press).

Parliament. (2002), Adhoc Committee Minutes, 15 May.

Royal African Society. (2014), 'African economic outlook 2014: Global value chains and Africa's industrialisation', in collaboration with OECD Development Centre, the African Development Bank and UNDP, London.

Samoff, J. and Bidemi, C. (2003), 'From manpower planning to the knowledge era: World Bank policies on higher education in Africa', UNESCO Forum Occasional Paper Series Paper No. 2.

Sen, A. (1999), *Development as Freedom* (London: Oxford University Press).

Stocking, B. (2002), 'To them that hath ...: How world trade policies undermine poor producers', in J. Holden, L. Hawlad and D. Stedman (eds), *Food Staffs* (London: Demos), Issue 18.

Todaro, M. (1981), *Economic Development in the Third World* (New York, NY: Longmans).

Tvedt, T. (1998), *Angels of Mercy or Development Diplomats?: NGOs and Foreign Aid* (Oxford: James Currey).

Tvedt, T. (2002), 'Development NGOs: Actors in a global civil society or in a new international social system?', *International Journal of Voluntary and Nonprofit Organisations*, 13(4), pp. 363–75.

UG. (2014), 'Uganda Vision 2040', Kampala: Government of Uganda.

UG-PSR. (2014), 'Poverty status report: Structural change and poverty reduction in Uganda', Report, MFPED.

Uganda Bureau of Statistics (UBOS). (2001/2002), Statistical Abstract, Entebbe.

Uganda Bureau of Statistics (UBOS). (2011), Census of Business Establishments, 2010, 2010/11 Report, Kampala.

Uganda Bureau of Statistics (UBOS). (2012), Statistical Abstract, Kampala.

Uganda Bureau of Statistics (UBOS). (2013), Statistical Abstract, Kampala.

Uganda Bureau of Statistics (UBOS). (2016), 'The National Population and Housing Census 2014 – Main Report', Kampala.

Uganda Debt Network. (2017), 'A snapshot of Uganda's Public Debt Trends', Report, May, Kampala (www.udn.or.ug).

Uganda Health Facilities Survey. (2006), Ministry of Health Report, Kampala.

Uganda Investment Authority.

(2000), 'The Investors Survey 2000', Final Report, Kampala.

Uganda Medical Survey Report. (2004), Ministry of Health, Kampala.

UNDP. (2000), 'Overcoming human poverty', UNDP Poverty Report.

UNDP. (2015), 'Briefing note for countries on the 2015 Human Development Report', Available at: http://hdr.undp.org/sites/all/themes/hdr_theme/country-notes/UGA.pdf [accessed 16 April 2016].

United Nations Conference on Trade and Development (UNCTAD). (2008), 'Trade and development report', Geneva.

Uwezo. (2015), *Are Our Children Learning? Five Stories on the State of Education in Uganda in 2015 and Beyond*, Twaweza East Africa, Kampala.

Wedig, K. and Wiegratz, J. (2017), 'Neoliberalism and the revival of agricultural cooperatives: The case of the coffee sector in Uganda', *Journal of Agrarian Change*, 18(2), pp. 348–69.

Wiegratz, J. (2010), 'Fake capitalism? The dynamics of neoliberal moral restructuring and pseudo-development: The case of Uganda', *Review of African Political Economy*, 37(124), pp. 123–37.

World Bank. (2015), Project Information Document, Uganda Energy for Rural Transformation III, Project ID P 133312, Report PIDA 22274, Kampala.

World Bank. (2016), The Uganda Poverty Assessment Report: Assessing Poverty Reduction in Uganda from 2006 to 2013, Report No. ACS18391, Washington, DC.

World Bank. (2017), *Uganda Economic Update*, 8th edition, January 2017, Washington, DC.

World Bank Group. (2015), Global Poverty Working Group, Available at: indexmundi.com [accessed 1 June 2015].

8
Social service provision and social security in Uganda: entrenched inequality under a neoliberal regime

Malin J. Nystrand and Gordon Tamm

In this chapter we will discuss recent trends in the provision of social service delivery and social protection in Uganda, particularly as regards basic education, primary healthcare and social security. The framework of our analysis is the neoliberal reform process initiated in the 1990s by the Government of Uganda, supported by multilateral agencies such as the IMF and the World Bank as well as by the main bilateral donors. Our analysis shows that this reform, in particular through downsizing of the public sector, increase in private provision of social service and decentralisation, has led to increasing inequality in access to social service and social security for citizens, extensive reliance on informal social and kin support and a commodification of social service provision across the main social sectors. Donor dependency combined with donor preference for private and civil society social service provision also means that the sustainability of Uganda's social service provision systems is in question.

For the purpose of this chapter we have screened eighty-eight articles in international academic journals relating to social services and social welfare in Uganda, as well as relevant reports and country assessments by multilateral and bilateral agencies. As far as we have been able to ascertain there does not exist any thematic review of the social sectors covering the period since the reform process was initiated in the mid-1990s. The purpose of our review was to look for analytical discussions of social service provisions as embedded in the reform process, some of which have been used in this chapter. Equally important was the aim to look for longitudinal empirical data that depicted changes over time. However, it became clear that most empirical data found in the documents we reviewed were synchronic, site or project-specific or else driven by donor policies (e.g. evaluations). For longitudinal data we have therefore relied mainly on the Statistical Abstracts compiled by the Uganda

Bureau of Statistics (UBOS) along with relevant data from the World Bank, Unicef and WHO. With regard to personal social safety nets we use primary empirical material from a household survey on help within social networks conducted by one of the authors as part of a larger research project on social embeddedness of Ugandan business owners (Nystrand 2015).

The chapter will start with explaining our perspective on neoliberalism in Uganda and expanding on the aspects of neoliberal reform that are of relevance for our analysis. Thereafter the analysis of primary and secondary education, primary healthcare and formal and informal social security are presented respectively, followed by a concluding discussion where we draw out the overall conclusions with regard to the effects of neoliberal reform on social service provision and social security in Uganda.

Neoliberalism in relation to social service provision and social security in Uganda

As many scholars have argued, the concept 'neoliberal' has 'become something of a *rascal concept* – promiscuously pervasive, yet inconsistently defined, empirically imprecise and frequently contested' (Brenner *et al.* 2010: 184). (See also Harrison, 2005, and Harvey, 2007.) As emphasised in the Introduction, neoliberalism can be seen both as a project and as a process, and encompasses specific policies, discourses as well as ideologies. Our perspective is close to that of Brenner *et al.* (2010), who argue that neoliberalism or neoliberalisation is not a unitary project or one specific set of reforms, but rather an unevenly evolving process, which interacts with inherited institutional landscapes in specific contexts to produce different and constantly changing policy environments. Our understanding of the set of ideologically defined principles that is sometimes called 'deep' neoliberalism could be summarised as a preference for market mechanisms over state institutions and a conviction that commercialisation and commodification of various social practices produce the most efficient resource allocation. In the case of Uganda (as in many African countries), the implementation of neoliberal reform was primarily a consequence of heavy donor reliance and the dominance of neoliberal ideology among international financial institutions and bilateral donors, rather than a clear indigenous preference for neoliberalism over other ideologies. A consequence of this trajectory is that it is not necessarily the interests of various domestic groups that drive neoliberal reforms. Those who have gained from neoliberal reform are, for example, not primarily the Ugandan business sector at large – as the domestic private sector is very weak with the exception of a few large companies and individual businesspersons close to the ruling elite – but rather the ruling elite, who has been able to use donor funding to preserve their power through patronage (Whitfield *et al.* 2015).

There are of course more aspects of 'neoliberalism' that are frequently discussed with respect to Uganda, e.g. democratisation (Keating 2011), tariff and trade reforms (Jones *et al.* 2011), financial and fiscal reforms (Kuteesa *et al.* 2010), etc. In the context of this chapter we will confine 'neoliberal' to reforms affecting the social sector that involve: downsizing of the public sector, including retrenchment of staff; privatisation of social service and social protection; and decentralisation or devolution of state power.

Downsizing of the public sector forms part of the original neoliberal agenda both due to its focus on fiscal discipline and as a consequence of the ideologically driven preference for market over state. With the government's fiscal and administrative reforms rolled out in the mid-1990s the number of ministries were cut from thirty-eight to twenty-one and the number of employees on the public-sector payroll were similarly cut from 320,000 to 160,000 in just a few years. The purpose was not only to establish a balanced budget but equally important to push for a greater role of the private sector in service provision, including private–public partnerships along with introduction of user fees in health as well as education (Kuteesa *et al.* 2010, Mwine 2007). The increased role for private providers is central for creating the market-like conditions preferred in neoliberalism. The argument used is normally that competition between many actors and the consumers' free choice of providers will lead to the most efficient resource allocation. *Privatisation* in this context does not only include the increase in private sector providers of social service, but also the privatisation of responsibility for social protection to informal social groups, primarily the family level, rather than at the national level.

In Uganda, a *decentralisation* reform implemented gradually since the early 1990s came to strengthen the downsizing of state provision of social services. This reform was implemented through a succession of Local Government Acts, and was supported and largely funded by donors such as the World Bank and Danida. The decentralisation processes involved political, administrative and fiscal measures (Awortwi 2011) and meant in effect that Local Governments (District Councils) were responsible for education, health, veterinary services, etc. that were to be funded primarily by local taxes levied by the district authorities. From the start it received consistent political support, not the least by the political elite, and was lauded by donors as a show case for other countries to emulate (Green 2010).

However, parallel to the decentralisation there was also a proliferation of districts with the number going from thirty-nine in 1986 to 112 at present (2016). The official reason was an adjustment to provide marginal ethnic groups their own administrative and economic space (Awortwi 2011). However, the consequences of these two processes were several. First, very few districts have the resource base that could generate enough taxes to enable them to provide the services as required by the Local Government Acts. This resulted in the District Councils being provided with conditional central grants, largely funded by donors, which effectively meant a re-centralisation (Awortwi 2011; see also Naiga *et al.* 2015). Second, it provided a platform for political patronage with the election campaigns of local leaders in the new districts being increasingly financed directly from the state budget and controlled directly by the president, thereby consolidating the National Resistance Movement (NRM) and Museveni regime (Green 2010, Lambright 2014, Whitfield *et al.* 2015). In addition it meant a proliferation of non-governmental organisations (NGOs) and community-based organisation (CBOs), particularly in the social service sector, that were funded by bilateral donors directly or through international NGOs (INGOs) (Green 2010). All of these affected the quality and scope of social service provision at the local level, as will be shown in the analysis below, not the least because of rural districts as well as civil society organisations being unable to attract and retain good health workers or teachers.

Primary and secondary education

An important part of the reforms set in motion in the mid-1990s was the Education Strategic Investment Plan within which the policies of Universal Primary Education (UPE) and later Universal Secondary Education (USE) were launched in 1996 and 2006 respectively. Both also took place within the framework of the two main neoliberal reforms mentioned above, i.e. decentralisation, which meant that it is the responsibility of district councils to ensure that basic education is provided, and downsizing of the public sector and payroll.

It soon became apparent that the local governments did not have the resources to maintain or upgrade quality of teaching even if coverage and access expanded with the number of primary schools (public and private) increasing from 10.490 in 1997 to 18.408 in 2014 (Uganda Bureau of Statistics (UBOS) 2002 and UBOS 2015). The official drop-out rate in public primary schools was in 2003 estimated to be 14 per cent and in secondary schools 34 per cent (MoFPED 2003). An assessment made by Unesco Institute of Statistics indicated a much higher dropout rate in primary schools – 60 per cent in 2000 and 44 per cent in 2013 (World Bank 2016). As for the quality of education a study sponsored by the World Bank and carried out in 2013 estimated that less than one in five public school teachers fully know the curriculum they are supposed to follow, and 60 per cent of the teachers do not teach at any given time in a school day (Wane and Martin 2013). Similarly learning outcomes remain at abysmally low levels with the vast majority of primary education students never achieving functional numeracy or literacy skills (Uwezo 2014).

As the public schools lost ground, particularly in terms of quality, an increasing number of private schools were launched. This was in part both expected and promoted as part of the downsizing of the state and between 1998 and 2013 more than 4,600 such schools were started (UBOS 2002 and 2015). The school system was thereby cut in two – private schools for those that can afford the fees and public schools for the poor. Even so, private schools is the preferred choice of all with people seeking to mobilise resources through relatives (Nystrand 2015) or by creating rotating savings and credit clubs to pay for the fees (Vokes and Mills 2015).

However, even if private schools report lower drop-out rates and better outcomes there are signs that they are becoming more like public schools with big classes, deflated drop-out rates, and grades given that are better than the actual learning outcomes. In addition there have been reports that private schools have created 'ghost students' to get more government capitation fees which in turn has led the president to withdraw the capitation fee to private schools offering secondary education (*ibid.*).

The educational reforms set in motion in 1996 with the purpose of providing universal free quality education through public schools and by subsidising private schools through capitation fees have therefore not materially improved the educational system. Overall primary school completion rates have remained more or less static since 2000 at a national average around 54 per cent (African Child Policy Forum 2013).

In view of the above, our contention is that the neoliberal reforms of the education sector have improved neither the quality of nor access to the educational system and the outcome remains more or less the same as before the reforms. However, in one very important respect the situation has changed – a marked increase in inequality with a truncated system of public sector schools for the poor and private sector schools for the better off, an inequality which has manifested itself also between regions.

Primary healthcare[1]

As part of the structural reform programme and linked with the poverty eradication plan launched in 1997 Uganda adopted Universal Primary Health Care (UPHC) in 2002. This meant an expansion of the health infrastructure, particularly at the district and community level, with more than 900 additional facilities being established in the years between 2001 and 2014 (UBOS 2002 and UBOS 2015). As with basic education, primary healthcare is also part of the local governments' responsibility. By and large UPHC suffered from the same constraints as those facing education: resources and revenue being too small, staff too few and inadequately trained – all adding up to a low morale and low attendance rates, etc. In addition, medical supply chains are erratic and corruption rampant e.g. through pervasive demands for informal 'fees' (Kiguli et al. 2009).

It would be wrong to say that quality of the primary healthcare services have declined across the board and over time. Rather, it does not seem to have improved even if the coverage has, not the least through the establishment of an increasing number of private facilities (for-profit as well as not-for-profit). For example, in a review of the Education and Health Services in Uganda (Wane and Martin 2013) it was found that only 35 per cent of public health providers can correctly diagnose at least four out of five of the most common conditions, and only one out of five knew how to manage the most common maternal and neo-natal complications. Likewise non-attendance is a very serious problem at all levels of the healthcare system: more than 50 per cent of public health providers were absent on any given day (Ministry of Health and Makerere University School of Public Health 2012).

Of the three types of providers that form part of the overall system of primary healthcare, private for-profit generally scores best on all indicators used by the assessments reviewed by us (frequency of out-patient visits, staff attendance, medical supplies and qualified medical staff). They are also the facilities that are highest in demand, even by the poorest and even if the fees can be quite high (the fees are usually much less than the out-of-pocket expenses associated with a consultation at any health clinic such as travel, food, accommodation/overnight stay, etc.; Kiguli *et al.* 2009, Pariyo *et al.* 2009). One main reason for this is associated with waiting time – this is in many ways a proxy indicator for quality of health services. At private clinics it is in the interest of the owner/manager to ensure a high through-put of patients and consequently raise profits.

Private not-for-profit (e.g. missionary clinics, NGOs) score almost as high as the for-profit facilities. However, given a choice it appears that even the poorest prefer to consult a for-profit facility (Wane and Martin 2013). This is somewhat surprising but is in line with the argument put forward by Wiegratz and Cesnulyte (2015) about the 'neoliberalisation of moral economies' where the notion of money as an ultimate arbiter of social and moral values has percolated down even to the poorest segments of the population.

Lowest on virtually all scores are not surprisingly the public health facilities. The only exception is in terms of coverage and thereby access. However, even if more available and accessible (and thereby in principle entailing lower out-of-pocket expenses) they are the least preferred (Kiguli *et al.* 2009, Konde-Lule *et al.* 2010, Pariyo *et al.* 2009).

In comparison with the trends within the basic education sector it is clear to us that the neoliberal reforms embodied in the Universal Primary Health Care policy (encouraging and facilitating a larger private and civil society health service provision) have indeed led to improvements, also when viewed against the incidence and prevalence rates of the most common diseases (WHO 2015; see also Holvoet and Inberg 2014). But as with basic education the involvement of private and non-state actors, including public–private partnerships, have resulted in a health infrastructure that reflects the class structure: public facilities with very uneven service quality mainly used by the poor, and private for-profit with a (sometimes assumed) higher service quality mainly used by the better-of, with not-for-profit somewhere in-between (for an analysis of local perceptions of health service facilities, see Kiguli *et al.* 2009).

Social security

Uganda is a signatory of six international covenants and agreements related to social security, and has adopted fifteen policies and acts ranging from pensions, retirement benefits, workers' compensation, maternity leave to the national health insurance currently being final-ised. However, it lacks a coordinating framework such as a national social protection policy and the implementation of all these remain very weak and fragmented in addition to which virtually all social protection schemes only cover those who have employment in the public or formal sector (Bukuluki and Mubiru 2014; see also Kasente *et al.* 2002, particularly on existing non-formal arrangements).

Apart from the uneven implementation of those schemes that do operate, the limited coverage implies that less than 5 per cent of the adult population have access to any formal social security arrange-ment. Equally problematic is that the very few public pension or insurance funds are plagued by pervasive corruption and serve as sources of political patronage (Mwenda 2013, see also Chéne 2009).

Compared to the formal system there is no doubt that the informal social security systems prevailing in Uganda are more inclusive and more widely distributed even if their small capital base make them very vulnerable, particularly as one pervasive feature is weak manage-ment (rather than corruption as in the case of most formal systems). They include local self-help schemes, mutual burial groups, coop-eratives, market associations, etc. (Vokes and Mills 2015). However, these schemes are primarily geared to special events like sickness and burials, in some cases also support to primary and secondary schools. It has been estimated that more than 25 per cent of the total adult population is in one way or the other involved in such schemes (Kasente *et al.* 2002).

However, several observers are convinced that these voluntary and collectivist schemes are waning as the market-oriented and indi-vidualistic social transformation continues. Whereas previously most transactions and inputs to the mutual schemes were in kind (or by way of rendering a service such as shepherding) they are now exclu-sively in cash (Atekyereza 2001). This means that the very poorest are automatically excluded. Furthermore the lack of trust beyond the confines of the immediate family that came with the gradual intensification of the market economy well before the era of neolib-eralism and further underlined by the generalised violence during the Amin-Obote-LRA years has also tended to erode the notion of 'community' and to diminish the circles of mutual socio-economic cooperation (Dolan 2009). In sum, the formal social security system is essentially non-existent for the vast majority of the population. While this situation pre-dates and is not directly caused by neolib-eral reforms, the reforms have certainly not improved the situation.

Personal and family-based social safety nets

In light of the weak formal social service and security, social safety nets based on kin relations are important for Ugandans, in particular those based on the family and extended family. According to a household survey[2] conducted in 2009 by one of the authors (Nystrand 2015) in four Ugandan locations, 63 per cent of the respondents had either given help to fund education or medical treatment or had received help within these areas. Help with education entailed payment of school fees, primarily for primary and secondary education, and included funding whole or in part both the respondent's own education and the education for their children, while help with medical treatment included both medical fees and medicine. Other aspects of social responsibility in relation to extended family were explored in interviews with fifty-four Ugandan business owners[3] and over fifty other key informants (Nystrand 2015) and included support to elderly parents, general upkeep of children whose education was supported (often orphans), ad hoc assistance to various relatives with regard to transport, mobile phones and out-of-pocket expenses in connection to medical treatments as well as rather extensive contributions to burials and weddings.

Social responsibility in relation to the wider community was very rare among the interviewed business owners who almost entirely focused on the family and extended family. This again highlights the centrality of the family and extended family in the social security networks and the narrowing of social obligations to kin relations. Previously the community in which one lived played a much more important role in terms of social obligations, particularly in more remote areas that were not yet fully incorporated in the market economy, a fact that also predates the neoliberal transformation of the society (Vincent 1968).

The monetary aspect of responsibility for the extended family was estimated by some business owners to 5–10 per cent of their income. We would argue that this can be seen as an informal system of welfare provision, in line with Adelman and Fetini's (in Dia 1996) suggestion to call this type of informal redistribution a 'lineage tax'. However, kin-based social security often involves unpaid labour and other in-kind activities, which makes it difficult to estimate the value of the 'lineage tax'.[4]

It was clearly confirmed in the household survey that giving help is a socially desirable practice, in particular with regard to relatives. A total of 78 per cent of respondents supported the statement that individuals who are well off have an obligation to help poorer relatives (42 per cent strongly agreed), indicating that this is a strongly embedded norm. To help poorer community members was also supported by a majority, although by slightly less and with less strength (46 per cent agreed, and 20 per cent strongly agreed). However, the survey also showed that social security provided in family networks is not rights-based, i.e. the obligation to give does not translate into a right of the poorer to demand help, but is based on the good will of those who have resources.

Both the survey and interviews with business owners showed clearly that the burden of funding of education and medical treatment as well as social protection falls heavily on family and kin-based social networks in Uganda. Although the social desirability of giving help, especially among relatives, is a strongly held social norm, there are clear class-related problems attached to the practice. The heavy reliance on personal social safety nets creates strong dependency relations between extended family members, in particular a dependency on the good will of those with more resources. Obviously such dependencies risk entrenching power differences based on socioeconomic differentiation within the extended family. However, these relations might be more complicated than assumptions based on class interest would have it, as indicated in Nystrand's (2015) study, where the vast majority (85 per cent) of those having worked for a relative enjoyed the experience and saw the exchange as being of mutual assistance, while the business owners interviewed unanimously saw employing relatives as a social obligation that did not benefit their business and which they engaged in primarily for social reasons.

The reliance on informal social networks for social protection is not directly caused by neoliberal reform, as it is historically common and predates any type of reform at the nation-state level. However, the narrowing of social obligations, with responsibility limited primarily to the family and extended family rather than extending to the wider local community and even less the national level, risks having negative effects on the social cohesion within the nation. Furthermore it excludes those who belong to an extended family in which everyone is equally poor or where those who have more resources do not abide by the norm to share. Hence, the inequality in the formal system discussed above is further entrenched by dependence on informal, personalised social security, which is unequal in access as well as entails unequal power relations.

Concluding discussion

Based on our review of the trends in social service provision and social protection since the introduction of the neoliberal reform packages in the 1990s we see three main trends.

A   Commodification of service provision across the main
     social sectors. This is partly a consequence of the
     increased involvement of private actors and the increased
     emphasis on cost recovery for services provided as
     part of the fiscal reforms. This has entailed a gradual
     re-introduction of fees – whether formal such as in private
     for-profit actors and state–private sector partnerships,
     or informal (and accepted) under-the-table demands
     by teachers and healthcare providers to make up for
     erratic payment of salaries and maintenance. However,
     we contend that this commodification is linked to and
     reinforces a horizontal ongoing process that is not
     directly linked to neoliberal reforms induced from
     above: a widespread tendency to invoke money as a
     tool for redefining traditional idioms of reciprocity,
     interdependence and patronage as well as a yardstick
     for assessing what is 'good' (possibly forming part of
     what the Introduction refers to as the creation of a
     market society, and others the 'neoliberalisation of moral
     economies' (Wiegratz and Cesnulyte 2015)). This is
     exemplified through the preference of for-profit health
     and educational facilities across the entire range of the
     population regardless of the actual quality of service,
     through the acceptance of parents to provide 'fees'
     to teachers, and through the insistence in local social
     protection and support groups that participation requires
     payment in cash rather than as before in kind or labour.
B   An adaption to and reinforcement of the class dimension
     of the society as inherent in the nature and practice of
     formal social services and social protection. This goes
     for all the three sub-sectors reviewed above – basic
     education, primary healthcare and social security.
     Public schools and public primary health facilities are
     intrinsically serving those with least resources and/or
     from rural areas; non-profit facilities (usually run by civil
     society organisations) are in principal geared to the more

marginal segments of the population – socio-economically or location-wise – but are relatively few and critically dependent on external donor funding and therefore both vulnerable and probably unsustainable in the long run; and for-profit facilities intentionally catering to the more well-off to ensure the required revenue and income. Consonant with these trends in access to social services and social protection – formal or informal – are the personal and family-based social safety nets: dependency on richer relatives and patrons and reliance on the socio-cultural norms embedded in the concept of extended family.

C   Our analysis suggests that the combined effect of commodification and the inherent class dimension of social service provision and social security arrangements in Uganda implies that there is a category of (particularly the rural) population that are deprived of basic education and health services and are thus having their basic needs unmet. This part of the population is left in a limbo and make up the 'left-overs' of present Uganda – i.e. those with scarce resources and with no social networks or functional extended families to fall back on. This might explain why Uganda has the third highest rate of urbanization in the world and the highest of countries with a population of more than 35 million (CIA 2015) with a very large number of impoverished and unemployed youth migrating to the cities in search of jobs and income opportunities (World Bank 2015).

It should be noted that this chapter does not provide a before and after analysis of the effects of neoliberal reform in the social sectors. Instead it provides an overview of the effects of these reforms in terms of provision, assuming that the reforms aimed at improvements in access, quality as well as quantity of social services provided, where we find the results wanting, in particular with regard to quality and equality of access.

By way of concluding remarks we contend that: (i) The last three decades of neoliberal reforms have not materially improved the main social service or social protection provisions in Uganda except, as regards basic education and primary health, in terms of coverage. But inequalities that prevailed before the reforms in terms of access and scope remain and have been further strengthened to reflect socio-economic and spatial differentiation. (ii) The question of who is responsible for shouldering the financial and organisational burden for social service provisions in the Ugandan society – the state, local governments, private actors, civil society organisations, donors – has become increasingly unclear with the immediate and extended family being a window of first and last resort. It is, however, clear to us that those that stand to profit from this fragmentation of social service provision are primarily three: private sector providers, civil society organisations and the political elite. (iii) Much of social service provisions were an integral part of the Government of Uganda – donor interaction. But it was increasingly found to be plagued by a rampant corruption which meant that the main bilateral donors shifted their current support to civil society organisations. This also means that much of the support to poor and vulnerable groups is dependent on external funding. Overall we would conclude that the neoliberal dynamics in Uganda as regards social services and social security has come to underline a society that is more unequal (rather than poorer), more fragmented and with less social cohesion, and with serious deficiencies in terms of access to and quality of such services.

Notes

1 Healthcare reforms in Uganda are analysed more thoroughly in Ssali's chapter. The health section in this chapter focuses on primary healthcare and aims at summarising the main effects in relation to the overall analysis in the chapter, i.e. the effect of neoliberal reform on social service provision in general, of which healthcare is a crucial component.

2 The survey covered 386 households in total, from both urban and rural settings in and around Kampala in the central region, Mbarara in the western region, Mbale in the eastern region and Gulu in the northern region. Methodological details of the survey are described in Nystrand (2015).

3 The larger study drawn on here focused on social responsibility and social embeddedness of Ugandan owners of small and medium-sized enterprises (SMEs) and included not only the household survey but also interviews with fifty-four business owners as well as approximately fifty other key informants (Nystrand 2015).

4 The survey showed that 35 per cent of respondents had worked for a relative.

References

African Child Policy Forum. (2013), *The African Report on Child Wellbeing 2013: Towards Greater* *Accountability to Africa's Children,* Addis Ababa.

Atekyereza, P. R. (2001), *Critical*

Factors for Family Studies Analysis in Uganda: A Case Study of Changing Family Forms and Functions among Selected Ethnic Groups, PhD dissertation, Johannes Kepler University Linz.

Awortwi, N. (2011), 'An unbreakable path? A comparative study of decentralization and local government trajectories in Ghana and Uganda', *International Review of Administrative Sciences*, 77(2), pp. 347–77.

Brenner, N., Peck, J. and Theodore, N. (2010), 'Variegated neoliberalization: Geographies, modalities, pathways', *Global Networks*, 10(2), pp. 182–222.

Bukuluki, P. and Mubiru, H. B. (2014), *The Status of Social Security Systems in Uganda* (Kampala: Konrad Adenauer Stiftung).

Central Intelligence Agency. (2015), *The World Factbook* (Washington, DC: CIA).

Chéne, M. (2009), *Overview of Corruption in Uganda: U4 Expert Answer* (Bergen: U4/Transparency International).

Dia, M. (1996), *Africa's Management in the 1990s and Beyond: Reconciling Indigenous and Transplanted Institutions* (Washington, DC: World Bank).

Dolan, C. (2009), *Social Torture: The Case of Northern Uganda, 1986–2006* (New York, NY: Berghahn).

Green, E. (2010), 'Patronage, district creation, and reform in Uganda', *Studies in Comparative International Development*, 45(1), pp.83–103.

Harrison, G. (2005), 'Economic faith, social project and a misreading of African society: The travails of neoliberalism in Africa', *Third World Quarterly*, 26(8), pp. 1303–20.

Harvey, D. (2007), 'Neoliberalism as creative destruction', *The Annals of the American Academy of Political and Social Science*, 610(1), pp. 21–44.

Holvoet, N. and Inberg, L. (2014), 'Taking stock of monitoring and evaluation systems in the health sector: Findings from Rwanda and Uganda', *Health Policy and Planning*, 29(4), pp. 506–16.

Jones, C., Morrissey, O. and Nelson, D. (2011), 'Did the World Bank drive tariff reforms in Eastern Africa?', *World Development*, 39(3), pp. 324–35.

Kasente, D. *et al.* (2002), 'Social security systems in Uganda', *Journal of Social Development in Africa*, 17(2), pp. 157–83.

Keating, M. (2011), 'Can democratization undermine democracy? Economic and political reform in Uganda', *Democratization*, 18(2), pp. 415–42.

Kiguli, J. *et al.* (2009), 'Increasing access to quality health care for the poor: Community perceptions on quality care in Uganda', *Patient Prefer Adherence (Dove Medical Press)*, 3, pp. 77–85.

Konde-Lule, J. *et al.* (2010), 'Private and public health care in rural areas of Uganda', *BMC International Health and Human Rights*, 10(29), pp. 1–8.

Kuteesa, F. *et al.* (eds) (2010), *Uganda's Economic Reforms: Insider Accounts* (Oxford and New York, NY: Oxford University Press).

Lambright, G. M. S. (2014), 'Opposition politics and urban service delivery in Kampala, Uganda', *Development Policy Review*, 32(S1), pp. 39–60.

Ministry of Finance, Planning and Economic Development. (2003), *Uganda's Progress in Attaining the PEAP Targets – in the Context of the Millenium Development Goals: Background Paper for the Consultative Group Meeting Kampala, 14–16 May 2003*, The Republic of Uganda, Kampala.

Ministry of Health and Makerere University School of Public Health. (2012), *Uganda Health System Assessment 2011*. Kampala, Uganda and Bethesda, MD: Health Systems 20/20 Project, Abt. Associates.

Mwenda, A. M. (2013), 'Fighting corruption in Uganda', *The Independent*, 17 February.

Mwine, C. (2007), *Social Policy: Themes, Principles and Perspectives in Uganda* (Kampala: Makerere University Printery).

Naiga, R., Penker, M. and Hogl, K. (2015), 'Challenging pathways of safe water access in rural Uganda: From supply to demand-driven water governance', *International Journal of the Commons*, 9(1), pp. 237–60.

Nystrand, M. J. (2015), *The Rationale of Taking Social Responsibility: Social Embeddedness of Business Owners in Uganda*, Doctoral Thesis, University of Gothenburg.

Pariyo, G. W. *et al.* (2009), 'Changes in the utilization of health service among poor and rural residents in Uganda: Are reforms benefitting the poor?', *International Journal for Equity in Health*, 8(39), pp. 1–11.

UBOS. (2002), *Statistical Abstracts 2002*, Uganda Bureau of Statistics, Kampala.

UBOS. (2015), *Statistical Abstracts 2015*, Uganda Bureau of Statistics, Kampala.

Uwezo. (2014), *Are Our Children Learning? Literacy and Numeracy in Uganda 2014*, Kampala, Twawesa East Africa.

Vincent, J. (1968), *African Elite: The Big Men of a Small Town* (New York, NY: Columbia University Press).

Vokes, R. and Mills, D. (2015), '"Time for school"? School fees, savings clubs and social reciprocity in Uganda', *Journal of Eastern African Studies*, 9(2), pp. 326–42.

Wane, W. and Martin, G. H. (2013), *Education and Health Services in Uganda: Data for Results and Accountability* (Washington, DC: World Bank).

Whitfield, L. *et al.* (2015), *The Politics of African Industrial Policy: A Comparative Perspective* (Cambridge: Cambridge University Press).

Wiegratz, J. and Cesnulyte, E. (2015), 'Money talks: Moral economies of earning a living in neoliberal East Africa', *New Political Economy*, 21(1), pp. 1–25.

World Bank. (2015), *The Growth Challenge: Can Ugandan Cities Get to Work?*, Uganda Economic Update 5th edition (Washington, DC: World Bank).

World Bank. (2016), *Education Statistics*, Available at: http://datatopics.worldbank.org/education/wDataQuery/QFull.asp [accessed 9 January 2016].

World Health Organization (WHO). (2015), *Uganda: WHO Statistical Profile*, January 2015.

9
Neoliberal health reforms and citizenship in Uganda

Sarah N. Ssali

Introduction

This chapter critically examines the Ugandan healthcare sector decades after the neoliberal health sector reforms were introduced. It argues that what manifests as a corrupt and inefficient healthcare system (see Nystrand and Tamm this volume) is not just a problem of corrupt and unprofessional healthcare workers, but a symptom of the neoliberal-capitalist restructuring of Ugandan society, particularly healthcare provisioning. Unlike previous writings on neoliberal reforms in health which focused on the effect of the reforms on healthcare access and use, this chapter investigates the capitalist re-ordering of the health sector and its attendant effects on the nature of the state–citizen dynamics within a neoliberal context. By examining healthcare financing options undertaken by the state and the citizens, it shows that the promotion of market forces in healthcare had led to the delegitimisation of public healthcare services, manifesting as preference for private healthcare services, leading to a citizenship which did not make claims to the state but resorted to improvising for healthcare, eroding their ability to demand for accountability from the state (Katusiimeh 2015). The chapter uses Ministry of Health (MoH) Reports and policies and secondary data over the thirty-year period of the reforms to examine the healthcare system engendered by the reforms and what rights and entitlements citizens have therein. The chapter is organised into five parts. Starting with the discussion of citizenship, the chapter goes on to discuss the background to the health sector reforms, the specific reforms introduced, a review of the neoliberal health sector that has emerged and conclusions.

Citizenship rights and neoliberal health sector reforms in Uganda

The concept of citizenship has evolved over time and space (Shafir 1998). Originally restricted to civil and political rights for a privileged few, it later expanded to include social rights for all, including welfare state policies and institutions that guarantee social rights (Marshall 1998). By making the state responsible for guaranteeing social rights, these became universal and deemed fundamental for people's belonging as citizens, rather than subjects (King and Waldron 2010). Neoliberalism eroded this conception by creating socially excluded masses and a citizenship based on individual accomplishment rather than membership of a community (Somers 2008).

The neoliberal reforms cannot be solely blamed for the erosion of citizens' rights. Under colonial rule, the majority of Ugandans were treated as subjects, not citizens (Mamdani 2004), while after independence those who tried to exercise their newfound rights were quickly silenced, as the post-colonial state resorted to repression to contain criticism (*ibid.*). With the economic decline and informalisation that ensued and state repression of its critics, citizens learnt to adapt and innovate to fill the gap, instead of demanding services from the state. Hence, neoliberal health reforms were introduced in a context where the citizenry was compliant, neither questioning nor demanding rights and services from the state. It was a citizenry that did not look to the state for anything, but instead accepted to pay for healthcare formally and or informally, which to the World Bank (WB) communicated readiness for privatisation. The demand that the state reduce its role in healthcare provision compounded the state's abdication of its responsibility for healthcare provision on one hand and citizens' inability to demand services from the state on the other.

Background to the health sector reforms

Uganda inherited a colonial system in which the state was responsible for healthcare. Initially designed for European populations, the colonial government gradually expanded services to the native population. The first independence government of Milton Obote expanded access further, by constructing health facilities at the district level. In the 1960s, Uganda had one of the best healthcare delivery systems in Africa, characterised by the availability of free medicines and high access to public health facilities (Whyte 1991). However, with the economic decline that followed the civil and military unrest ushered in by Idi Amin's regime, the 1970s and 1980s saw a dilapidated health system, as the depleted national economy could no longer finance healthcare services (*ibid.*). The loss of skilled health professionals either to death, expulsion (as in the case of the

Ugandan Asians) or exile compounded the situation. The number of
doctors dropped from 978 to 574 and that of pharmacists from 116
to 15 between 1968 and 1974, and health facilities lacked medicines,
especially in rural areas (*ibid.*).

As the health services deteriorated, citizens became accustomed
to paying for health services from private facilities, paying illegal fees
to healthcare workers in public facilities to augment the poor services
being provided or even purchasing medicines and other requirements
needed by health workers to work on them. By the time the health
sector reforms were introduced in the 1990s, the Ugandan health
delivery system was public and free only in name. In reality, citizens
were paying for everything, be it in the private or public facilities.
Public health facilities were a 'shell', characterised by a dilapidated
physical infrastructure, lack of basics such as drugs and medical
equipment, low staff motivation and low patient attendance (Macrae
et al. 1996). Any remaining public facilities had become informal-
ised and the number of private providers had increased (Okuonzi
and Macrae 1995). The WB saw this as evidence of people's willingness and ability to pay for healthcare services, paving way for the
privatisation of healthcare services, within a larger context of several
neoliberal reforms in the wider economy (see Figure 9.1).

Health sector reforms were introduced globally as part of the
Structural Adjustment Programmes (SAPs), which dominated development policy in the 1980s (Lensink 1996). The WB recommended
reforms to improve the efficiency and effectiveness of the health sector
in developing countries. The problem was seen as one of misallocation
of resources, insufficient spending on cost-effective health activities,
internal inefficiency of public programmes and inequity in the distribution of benefits from health services (Akin *et al.* 1987, De Ferranti
1985). Similar concerns had been raised in the 1970s by the World
Health Organization (WHO) (Zwi and Mills 1995). However, while
the WHO in 1978 placed the burden of health services provision on
national ministries of health, the WB in the 1990s neoliberal context
sought to reduce their role, in preference for private providers and
individual consumers. The four main policy reforms the WB recommended, often as conditionality for aid, were: user fees, insurance,
decentralisation and a greater recognition for non-state actors (Akin
et al. 1987). Following concerns about how user fees constrained
access to healthcare, many countries abolished them. Nonetheless, no
country has recommended a return to the past when governments
were largely responsible for healthcare provision. The neoliberal
ideology continues to pervade all health sector reforms and policies.

Figure 9.1 – Context of neoliberal reforms in Uganda's healthcare

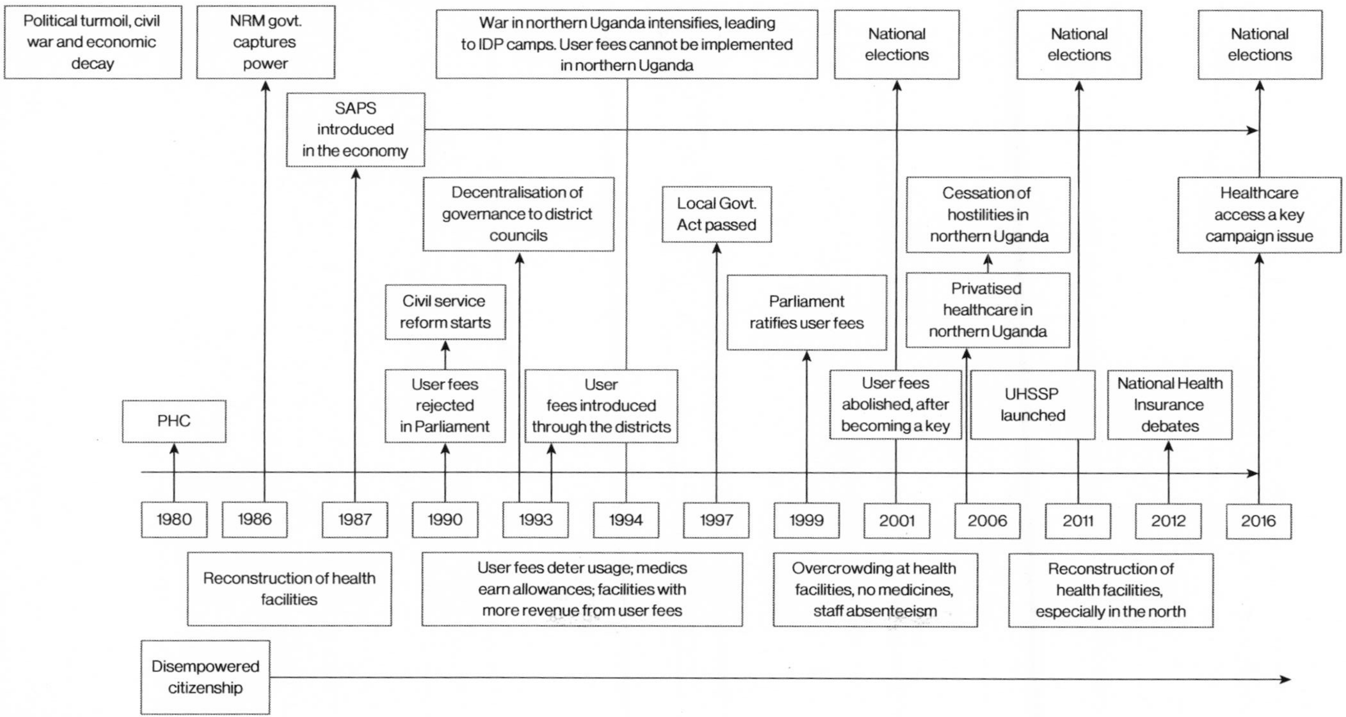

Source: The author.

In Uganda the WB did not insist on 'rolling back the state' due to the collapse of the Ugandan state and the mushrooming of the informal economy (Torrente and Mwesigye 1999). Even with SAPs under way, all sides, including the donors, agreed that the state needed rebuilding and its role in the economy needed to grow (see also WDR 1997).

Nonetheless, the WB's neoliberal stance and its basic recipe for reform (deregulation, privatisation and liberalisation) remained unchanged (Cornia 1998). Hence, in Uganda, rebuilding the state was simply a vital step in facilitating market reform, especially considering that the initial reforms, introduced in 1981, had to be abandoned due to the outbreak of guerrilla war. Rebuilding the state mainly addressed physical rigidities, such as reconstructing the infrastructure, which was considered one way of 'getting the basics right', the other being stabilisation (Torrente and Mwesigye 1999, Ochieng 1991).

Health sector reform in Uganda was equally modified. Instead of the government being required to cut expenditure on health services, state expenditure and foreign donations to the health sector actually increased from per capita expenditure of US$4 in the financial year (FY) 1997/98 to US$13.5 in FY 2014/15 (MoH 2014/15) because: (1) public health services hardly existed and (2) the WB realised that working through weakened government institutions would achieve minimal results (Torrente and Mwesigye 1999). Initially promoting only vertical programmes, donors quickly realised that restructuring the health sector was inevitable if they were to consolidate their gains (Macrae et al. 1996). The health sector had to be rebuilt and reshaped to improve the 'effectiveness' of health services delivery. However, restructuring the health sector to what it had been before the decline was out of the question (Torrente and Mwesigye 1999). Rather, it was to be restructured according to the prevailing neoliberal ideology of the WB. The state's role was restricted to policy making and supervision. Hence, despite increasing actual funding to the health sector, earmarking such funds for vertical programmes managed by donors, foreign or private organisations, or directly funding particular districts, meant that this funding undermined, rather than enhanced, the state's responsibility for healthcare and obligation to its citizens.

The specific health sector reforms

The specific health sector reforms recommended were in response to the following problems identified by the WB: (1) Limited funding, which was further constrained by the re-emergence of diseases such as tuberculosis and drug-resistant malaria, and the emergence of new ones such as AIDS (WB 1993a). (2) Less efficient government provision of health services compared to non-government organisation (NGO) provision. Physicians in NGO facilities handled five times as many patients as their counterparts in the public sector. Yet, spending in government facilities was approximately twice that of NGO facilities, most of which went on staff costs, medicines and food, leaving little or nothing for maintenance, equipment and supplies (WB 1993b). (3) Utilisation patterns, which demonstrated that recourse to non-government fee-charging facilities was high. (4) Skewed benefit, where public services benefited the affluent minority, leaving the majority with limited access to health services. Most MoH staff (67 per cent) were physically located in urban hospitals, which served only 13 per cent of the population, and health inspectors and health visitors were in short supply compared to physicians, nurses and clinical officers (WB 1993b).

To the WB the above constituted inequity and inefficiency, considering that the main burden of morbidity and mortality arose from preventable diseases and conditions. Hence there was need to invest in high-impact programmes, by shifting funds from relatively 'unproductive' areas such as curative care, to primary healthcare, where the economic and social returns were highest. The specific reforms implemented in the health sector were those considered fundamental to reducing the state's role in healthcare provision and increasing the role of non-state actors, particularly the market, in healthcare provision. These included: civil service reform, decentralisation, public–private partnerships and user fees.

Civil service reform was undertaken to rid the sector of ghost workers and reduce the work force, in order to free resources, which would be used to increase staff salaries, boost motivation and efficiency (Torrente and Mwesigye 1999). This reduced the work force in the health sector from 320,000 in 1990 to 64,632 in 1998. Although staff salaries were increased, they remained lower than the minimum living wage and lower than their private sector counterparts (Asiimwe *et al.* 1997).

Decentralisation aimed at radically transforming the power relations between the central government and the then forty-five district governments by devolving substantial administrative, political and financial authority to the districts (Torrente and Mwesigye 1999, Titeca this volume). Districts could now deliver and allocate health services, recruit and manage personnel for district health services, pass by-laws related to health and planning, budget for health services and mobilise additional resources (MoH 2000). The newly formed Health Unit Management Committees (HUMCs) comprised politically elected members who were charged with overseeing management planning activities, setting and supervising the utilisation of revenue from the user fees, providing public scrutiny and supervising the operations of health services at district level (MoH 1990). The assumption was that local ownership and control of public services was necessary to check the state, improve efficiency by limiting abuses and make provision more responsive to local needs (Torrente and Mwesigye 1999). While several modifications have occurred around the roles of districts and the centre, the principle of devolving power to the local level remains.

The WB also promoted public–private partnerships, arguing that whereas the state should remain responsible for the supply of public goods such as health, it was not necessarily its responsibility to provide healthcare services. Accordingly, these were better left to private sector and NGO agencies that had demonstrated capacity to provide them more efficiently (WB 1993b).

User fees were the prominent feature of Uganda's healthcare reforms and were introduced as a condition for negotiating the Community Health AIDS Project (CHAP) (Okuonzi and Macrae 1995). An earlier bill introducing them had been defeated by parliament in 1990, because it would deter healthcare access; people were already paying for healthcare through taxation; and the quality of care in public facilities was very poor (Okuonzi and Macrae 1995). Against this background, decentralisation empowered district authorities to introduce user fees (Okuonzi and Macrae 1995) and by 1999 user fees were being charged in forty-three of the fifty-two government hospitals and applied in forty-two out of forty-five districts (MoH 1999). The role of the MoH was confined to identifying uniform guidelines among the districts and include these in the national health policy (Konde-Lule and Okello 1998). Hence, in 1999, parliament ratified the user fees policy (MoH 1999). The rapid adoption of user fees suggests that districts prioritised their revenue needs, disregarding people's ability to pay (Okuonzi and Macrae 1995). By 1999, the reasons that had led parliament to reject fees in 1990 were still prevalent as poverty had increased in many rural areas (May 2001), user fees were regressive and unable to resolve healthcare related problems and people's inability to pay was high (MoH 1999, Konde-Lule and Okello 1998). The Inter Ministerial Task Force charged with reviewing user fees made similar observations, but still recommended to parliament that fees be adopted, albeit with some improvements to cater for the poor (MoH 1999).

Health sector review thirty years later: continuities and change

This section thematically reviews the implications of thirty years of reforms, as set out in 1987. Using available MoH and secondary data, it shows that the health sector, though with more resources, has not evolved to guarantee the rights of the majority of citizens. But rather, the neoliberal ideology remains present in all its aspects. For example, in spite of the abolition of user fees in 2001, the discourse of health and health services provision remains neoliberal. In the National Health Policy II (MoH 2010), cost-effectiveness rather than social needs remains the key driver of provision of the Uganda National Minimum Healthcare Package (UNMHCP). The health policy celebrates the private sector, which is the main agent for the implementation of UNMHCP. The persistence of the neoliberal discourse in health policy making, despite the reported regressive effect of privatisation, demonstrates government's reluctance to take back the responsibility of healthcare provision, which is likely to challenge the achievement of the equity concerns highlighted in the NHP II.

Financing for healthcare services

A look at health financing shows that despite some increment, total government expenditure (TGE) continues to be less than 10 per cent (or US$27 per capita) (see Figure 9.2), which is below the 15 per cent (or US$44 per capita) recommended by the Abuja Declaration (WHO 2016).

Figure 9.2 – GoU health expenditure as percentage of total government expenditure

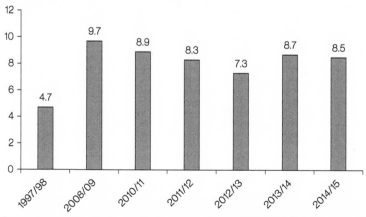

Source: Annual Health Sector Performance Report (AHSPR) (MoH 2014/15).

Moreover, the actual per capita government health expenditure is much less, as Figure 9.3 illustrates.

Figure 9.3 – Per capita health expenditure (US$)

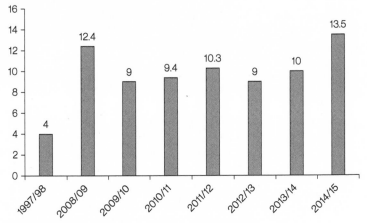

Sources: AHSPR (MoH 2014/15), NHA (MoH 1997/98).

Figure 9.3 reveals that the per capita expenditure on health has remained low, peaking at a mere US$13.5 in FY 2014/15.

The government is not the major source of revenue for the health sector, a trend that has persisted since healthcare was privatised (SIDA 2006, MoH 2012). In addition to being the lowest, government funding only peaked at 20 per cent in FY 1997/98 and has continued to decline ever since. Compared with other sources, Figure 9.4 shows that donors are the main sources of revenue for the health sector, which is not surprising given that donor reliance was the main reason the country adopted the neoliberal reforms (Nystrand and Tamm this volume).

The second main source of health financing is the private sector (constituting 90 per cent households), which also is one of the neoliberal goals. Unfortunately private funding also significantly declined after FY 2009/10 while that of donors increased after FY 2009/10, reducing slightly in FY 2011/12. With the exception of FYs 1996/7, 2008/9 and 2009/10, when the private sector surpassed that of donors, donors account for the largest contributions to the health sector budget. These two trends fall in well with the goals of the neoliberal project, of reducing state funding for health. However, the large contribution by households as out of pocket payments raises equity concerns with regard to those households with no ability to pay.

Figure 9.4 – Health funding sources

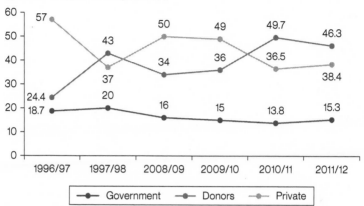

Sources: NHA (MoH 1997/98, Uganda Health Accounts Ministry 2010/11).

When initiating the reforms, the WB castigated the healthcare system for being curative and elitist, serving the interests of the urban populations and ignoring the majority poor in the rural areas (WB 1993b). The reforms were supposed to increase investment in public health, prominently preventive healthcare, which had high externalities. But thirty years later, health sector funding remains skewed towards curative services, as Figure 9.5 shows.

From the figure, funding for curative health services continues to be higher than that for preventive healthcare across the years

Figure 9.5 – Health financing by function

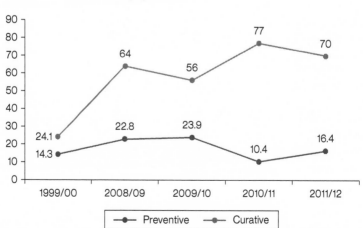

Sources: NHA (MoH 1997/98, MoH 2008/09–2009/10, Uganda Health Accounts Ministry 2010/11–2011/12), AHSPR (MoH 2014/15).

considered. Though the figures for later years were not readily available, the AHSPR for FY 2014/15 (MoH 2014/15) observed that funding for preventive care remains low, with most of the increment going to wages, with no increase in the non-wage primary health care (PHC) components (see Figure 9.6).

As Figure 9.6 reveals, wages take the biggest share of the PHC budget, followed by development. The general hospitals and NGOs which provide actual care take very little. Furthermore, the actual community programmes such as sanitation are newcomers in the PHC budget and are the least funded.

The limited funding for PHC activities could partly explain why several years after the reforms, preventable illnesses such as malaria, malnutrition, respiratory tract infections, AIDS, tuberculosis, perinatal and neonatal conditions remain the leading causes of the disease burden, as was the case in 1988. Malaria in particular remains the leading cause of under-five in-patient mortality ranging from 27.6 per cent in FY 2012/13 to 22.6 per cent in FY 2014/15. Their persistence indicates two things: (1) the rechannelling of public resources to prevention has not fully occurred, and (2) the private sector's investment in this area is not yet happening. Overall, fewer resources are being invested in PHC, which has the greatest externalities especially for the majority poor.

A focus on health expenditure by disease clearly shows the prominence of donor-funded disease control programmes. For example,

Figure 9.6 – Percentage allocation of the PHC budget

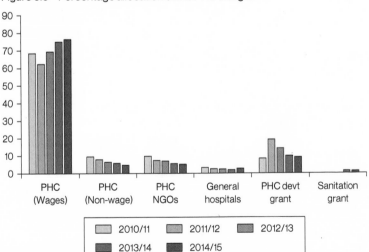

Source: AHSPR (MoH 2014/15).

Figure 9.7 – Current healthcare expenditure by disease/condition

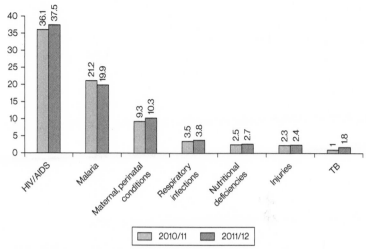

Source: NHA (Uganda Health Accounts Ministry 2010/11–2011/12).

the largest portion of health expenditure goes to HIV and malaria, leaving equally important health conditions such as non-communicable diseases and malnutrition – which are on the rise – unattended (see Figure 9.7).

Equally important conditions, i.e. non-communicable diseases included and not included in the figure, most of which are preventable, but which do not attract donor attention continue to be marginalised. This reinforces a therapeutic citizenship (Nguyen 2004) where only those with particular disease conditions – in this case HIV/AIDS and malaria – are entitled to healthcare. This picture is especially clear when one analyses government current health expenditure by recipients, as Table 9.1 illustrates.

As Table 9.1 shows, the biggest bulk of government healthcare spending went to hospitals, including regional referral hospitals, and not to the PHC providers. Moreover, even this is masked by the merging of vertical programmes funding such as Global Fund with the Healthcare System Administration (Uganda Health Accounts Ministry 2010/11–2011/12). If these were removed, the actual allocation from government revenue for preventive PHC is likely to be dismal.

Limited health insurance: whither equity concerns?

Health insurance was one of the four major recommendations of the WB's neoliberal restructuring of health to cater for those unable

Table 9.1 – Government current health expenditure by recipients

Provider	2008/09	2009/10	2010/11	2011/12
	Share (%)	Share (%)	Share (%)	Share (%)
Hospitals	31	27	33.8	37.1
Providers of ambulatory healthcare	—	—	11.1	14.5
Retailers and other providers of medical goods	—	—	3.9	2.6
Providers of healthcare system administration and financing	—	—	31.7	43.5
Rest of the world	—	—	19.5	2.3
Lower levels	34	35	—	—
Others	35	38	—	—
Total	100	100	100	100

Sources: NHA (MoH 2008/09–2009/10, Uganda Health Accounts Ministry 2010/11–2011/12).

to pay user fees (Akin *et al.* 1987). Even in Uganda, strategies of implementing insurance were studied, from the community insurance schemes of *engozi* (community-based insurance scheme based on the stretcher locally called *engozi* in the Rukiga dialect of Western Uganda) (Wiesmann and Jütting 2000, Carrin 2003) to the formal compulsory and voluntary schemes. In 2012, the Government of Uganda enacted the National Health Insurance (NHI) Bill 2012, whose aim was to 'ensure that Ugandans have financial access to affordable, equitable and quality healthcare services progressively to all residents in an efficient manner through health insurance' (Mugerwa 2013). However, to date, health insurance coverage in Uganda remains low, with no significant change over the years, as Figure 9.8 illustrates.

Figure 9.8 shows that there are hardly any prepayment schemes. Less than 3 per cent of the population is insured (mostly employees of the few active corporations). Insurance companies and other health financing institutions account for less than 10 per cent of private health funding, while households contribute more than 90 per cent of healthcare financing, peaking at 97.3 per cent in FY 2011/12. The much-lauded NHI scheme is yet to take off and may not address the equity concerns of reducing the household costs of care seeking for the poor (Orem and Zikusooka 2010). Moreover, the efficiency argument of neoliberalism is still pertinent in this scheme. The

Figure 9.8 – Health insurance financing by provider

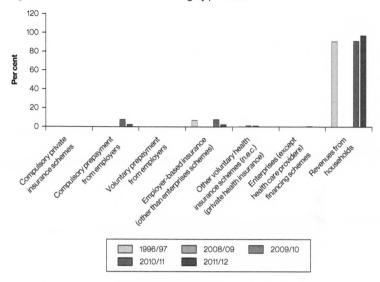

Source: NHA (MoH 1997/98, MoH 2008/09–2009/10, Uganda Health Accounts Ministry 2010/11–2011/12).

funding of the scheme is supposed to be largely private and market led, as opposed to state-led service provision.

Rising out-of-pocket and catastrophic household health expenditure

Out-of-pocket household health expenditure continues to rise, from 91 per cent (FY1996/97) to 97.3 per cent of private health revenue in FY 2011/12 (MoH 2014/15). This high household expenditure and limited insurance cover could explain the increasing cata-strophic health expenditures and subsequent household poverty and impoverishment that have been noted by the MoH. According to the AHSPR (MoH 2014/15), the proportion of households experi-encing catastrophic expenditures increased from 28 per cent in 2006 to 37 per cent in FY 2011/12. And, while the MoH had registered improvement in all impact factors, they were yet to register improve-ment in the percentage of households experiencing catastrophic expenditures on health (MoH 2014/15).

A breakdown of households' out-of-pocket payments shows that most of it went to medicines, followed by hospital clinic charges, consultations and traditional doctors' fees/medicines (see Figure 9.9). From the figure, the expenditure on medicines was the highest across

Figure 9.9 – Total household out of pocket expenditure by service

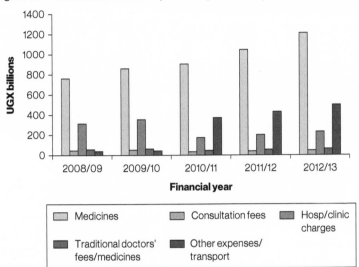

Sources: NHA (MoH 1997/98, MoH 2008/09–2009/10, Uganda Health Accounts Ministry 2010/11–2011/12).

all years under consideration and kept increasing, while that of other aspects was low and was declining.

This could suggest that more households are resorting to self-medication, probably either because they find consultation fees and hospital and clinic charges high, or because of poor quality care in public health facilities. For example, many households surveyed in 2008 reported stock outs, with only 33 per cent reporting experiencing adequate medicine availability in public health facilities (MoH 2008). Accordingly, the price households paid for medicines was a deterrent to adherence, with households with sick members reporting 65 per cent catastrophic expenditures on medicines as a proportion of non-food household expenditures; this ratio was observed to be similar across socio-economic groups countrywide. Relatedly, 58.12 per cent of household expenditure was spent in private clinics, compared to 13.3 per cent spent in government hospitals and clinics, with most of this expenditure being for medicines. Even the associated costs of healthcare masked under the category 'other expenses' such as transport could be a deterrent to accessing health facilities and an incentive to self-medication. The implication of increasing catastrophic expenditure implies households will not be able to access medicines, even by self-medication.

Figure 9.10 – Average out of pocket household expenditure on health by quintiles

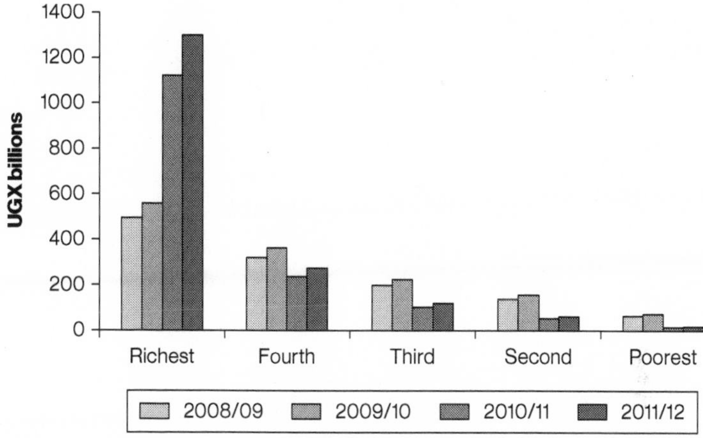

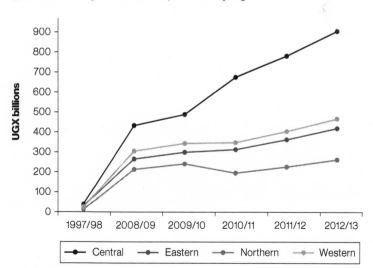

Sources: NHA (MoH 1997/98, MoH 2008/09–2009/10, Uganda Health Accounts Ministry 2010/11–2011/12).

Disaggregated by quintiles, household health expenditure was highest and increased for the richest quintiles, while it was much lower and even reduced for the other four quintiles from FY 2008/09 to FY 2011/12, as Figure 9.10 shows. This indicates that while the

Figure 9.11 – Average household expenditure by region

Sources: NHA (MoH 1997/98, MoH 2008/09–2009/10, Uganda Health Accounts Ministry 2010/11–2011/12).

richest Ugandans were able to cope with ever-increasing healthcare costs, the other quintiles could not, probably resorting to self-medication or cheaper public healthcare.

A regional disaggregation shows that household healthcare costs increased for all regions, as Figure 9.11 illustrates. However, the increment was highest in the central region, followed by the western, the eastern and lastly the northern region.

Figures 9.10 and 9.11 reveal that the rich and those residing in the central region, with more privileged access to income and healthcare, were more able to pay for the ever-rising costs of healthcare, than those residing in the more rural and post-conflict northern regions, indicating geographical location and socio-economic status as key determinants to accessing healthcare.

Limited health infrastructure

The Ugandan government embarked on reconstructing health facilities in two main phases, in 1986 and in 2011, as a strategy to expand universal health coverage (UHC). But three decades later, Uganda still has inadequate infrastructure to deliver health services. According to the *National Development Plan (NDP) 2010/11–2014/15*, the proportion of national referral hospitals is still low, at 1:30,000,000, against the standard recommendation of 1:10,000,000. The proportion of Health Centre IV (HC IV) is 1:187,500, against the desired proportion of 1:100,000, and HC III of 1:84,507, compared to the recommended 1:20,000 (Health Centres I to IV are different levels of primary healthcare units, with different competencies and catchments that form part of Uganda's healthcare system). Despite the increased investments in health facilities, especially private health facilities and diagnostic centres, most of these are constructed in urban areas, regardless of region, such as Gulu Independent Hospital in Gulu town, Mayanja Memorial Hospital in Mbarara, and Elgon Hospital in Mbale. Hence, most rural populations are reliant on government health facilities, which have quality concerns. For example the Access to Medicines Survey conducted in 2008 showed that 72 per cent of households lived more than one hour's travel away from a public hospital and 25 per cent lived more than one hour's drive away from any public health facility. Accordingly, many still lived more than five kilometres radius from a health facility. The situation is not any different for staff accommodation, causing absenteeism of healthcare workers at the facilities.

Inadequate staffing

Having the right number of staff, with the appropriate competencies is crucial for the delivery of healthcare. According to the *NDP (2010/11–2014/15)*, the ratio of doctors to patients remains high, at 1:24,725, which is in stark contrast to Kenya which is 1:7,100; Cuba at 1:169 and Malaysia at 1:1,430. The ratio of nurses to patients is similarly high, at 1:1,634, compared to Kenya at 1:877, Malaysia 1:740 and Cuba 1:134. These proportions greatly affect service delivery, as the government cannot have the requisite staff in all its facilities which most poor people visit. According to MoH (2010), 70 per cent of doctors/dentists, 80 per cent of pharmacists and 40 per cent of nurses are in urban areas serving 13 per cent of the population. From the AHSPR (MoH 2014/15), while health workers increased by 28 per cent, from 63,872 in September 2014 to 81,932 in August 2015, this is largely attributed to increased licensing. Moreover, these were all located in government health facilities and did not include community health workers.

Decentralisation: people power or elite capture

According to the WB, decentralisation of state power and resources offered the chance to match public services more closely with local demands, to build more responsive and accountable government from below (WDR 1997). The assumption was that decentralisation would make people monitor health facilities better, since they would now consider themselves stakeholders. With regard to healthcare, health unit management committees (HUMCs) were formed with the primary responsibility of regulating and monitoring health facility activities and budgets (MoH 2003). However, the extent to which this has been achieved remains questionable. First, the introduction of user fees as a strategy to raise revenue despite people's poverty was a clear sign that district leaders and their constituents had differing interests. Second, most HUMCs are dysfunctional, given that most rarely meet (MoH 2014/15). Moreover, Nystrand and Tamm (this volume) argue that in Uganda decentralisation came to strengthen the downsizing of state provision of social services, and not the empowerment of people to hold the state accountable as was popularly claimed. Consequently, decentralisation has not strengthened local accountability but rather it has become prone to elite capture, with local governments serving the interests of local elites in total disregard of the needs of the majority of the rural population (Bashaasha *et al.* 2011).

Conclusion: citizens vs clients; winners vs losers

Three decades after the reforms, Uganda's health sector still suffers from health systems challenges regarding financing, infrastructure, human resources and accountability. While the reforms did not find a perfect healthcare system, they eroded the little state responsibility in providing healthcare, leaving citizens to the vagaries of the market. The health sector that emerged continues to be elitist, urban based and serving those with the ability to pay. Citizens were re-fashioned into clients whose access to healthcare is determined by their own ability to pay, depending on location and socio-economic status. There are two categories of citizens: the winners, who with their newly acquired wealth can afford state-of-the-art diagnostic health-care in and outside the country from facilities whose consultations are not less than UGX 60,000; and the losers, the under-privileged, who cannot even access the most basic of health services without depleting their few household resources. The demographic majority of Ugandans are losers in this health system. They are stuck with poor quality services or can only access healthcare from private facil-ities by engaging in catastrophic expenditures. To conclude, if equity concerns are to be achieved, the state and not the market needs to be responsible for the citizens' health. Furthermore, citizens have to see health as a right and an entitlement to be demanded from the state.

References

Akin, J. *at al.* (1987), *Financing Health Services in Developing Countries: An Agenda for Reform. A World Bank Policy Study* (Washington, DC: World Bank).

Asiimwe, D. *et al.* (1997), 'The private sector activities of public sector health workers in Uganda', in S. Bennet, B. McPake and A. Mills (eds), *Private Health Providers in Developing Countries: Serving the Public Interest?* (London: Zed), pp. 141–57.

Bashaasha, B., Mangheni, M. N. and Nkonya, E. (2011), 'Decentralization and rural service delivery in Uganda', IFPRI Discussion Paper No. 01063, February 2011, IFPRI.

Carrin, G. (2003), 'Community based health insurance schemes in developing countries: Facts, problems and perspectives', Discussion Paper No. 1, WHO, Geneva.

Cornia, G. (1998), 'Convergence on governance issues, dissent on economic policies', *IDS Bulletin*, 29(2), pp. 32–38.

De Ferranti, D. (1985), 'Paying for health services in developing countries, an overview', World Bank Working Papers No. 721.

Katusiimeh, M. W. (2015), 'The non-state provision of health services and citizen accountability in Uganda', *Africa Today*, 62(1), pp. 85–105.

King, D. S and Waldron, J. (2010), 'Citizenship, social citizenship and the defense of welfare provision', in P. Bellamy and A. Palumbo (eds), *Citizenship* (Surrey: Ashgate), pp. 105–33.

Konde-Lule, J. K. and Okello, D. (1998), 'User fees in government health units in Uganda: Implementation, impact and scope', Small Applied Research Paper No. 2, Bethesda, MD.

Lensink, R. (1996), *Structural Adjustment in Sub-Saharan Africa* (London: Longman).

Macrae, J., Zwi, A. B. and Gilson, L. (1996), 'A triple burden for health sector reform: Post conflict rehabilitation in Uganda', *Social Science and Medicine*, 42(7), pp. 1095–108.

Mamdani, M. (2004), *Citizen and Subject: Contemporary Africa and the Legacy of Late Colonialism* (Kampala: Fountain).

Marshall, T. H. (1998), 'Citizenship and social class', in G. Shafir (ed.), *The Citizenship Debates* (Minneapolis, MN: University of Minnesota Press), pp. 93–126.

May, J. (2001), 'Lesotho, Uganda, Zambia and Maldives', in A. Grinspun (ed.), *Choices for the Poor: Lessons from National Poverty Strategies* (New York, NY: UNDP), pp. 231–51.

MoH. (1990), 'Introduction and operation of user-charges in government health units', MoH, Entebbe.

MoH. (1997/98), National Health Accounts 1997/98, MoH, Kampala.

MoH. (1999), 'Report on the review of cost sharing (user fees) in government health facilities', Draft Report of May 1999, MoH, Kampala.

MoH. (2000), Health Sector Strategic Plan 2000/01–2004/05, MoH, Kampala.

MoH. (2003), 'Guidelines on the Health Unit Management Committees', for Health Centre III, MoH, Kampala.

MoH. (2008), 'Access to and use of medicines by households in Uganda', Report of a survey conducted 2008, December, MoH, Kampala.

MoH. (2008/2009–2009/2010), National Health Accounts 2008/09–2009/10, MoH, Kampala.

MoH. (2010), The Second National Health Policy, MoH, Kampala.

MoH. (2012), National Health Accounts 2012, MoH, Kampala.

MoH. (2014/15), 'Annual health sector performance report (AHSPR) (2014/15)', MoH, Kampala.

Mugerwa, Y. (2013), 'Shelved health insurance plan gets new lease of life', *Saturday Monitor*, 20 July.

National Development Plan II (2010/11–2014/15), The Republic of Uganda, Kampala.

National Health Insurance (NHI) Bill 2012.

Nguyen, V. K., (2004), 'Antiretroviral globalism, biopolitics, and therapeutic citizenship', *Global Assemblages*, pp. 124–44.

Ochieng, E. S. (1991), 'Economic adjustment programmes in Uganda, 1985–1988', in H. B. Hansen and M. Twaddle (eds), *Changing Uganda* (Kampala: Fountain), pp. 43–60.

Okuonzi, S. and Macrae, J. (1995), 'Whose policy is it anyway? International and national influences on health policy development in Uganda', *Health Policy and Planning*, 10(2), pp. 122–32.

Orem, J. N. and Zikusooka, C. M. (2010), 'Health financing reform in Uganda: How equitable is the proposed National Health Insurance scheme?', *International Journal for Equity in Health*, 2010(9), pp. 1–8.

Shafir, G. (1998), 'Introduction: The evolving tradition of citizenship', in G. Shafir (ed.), *The Citizenship Debates* (Minneapolis, MN:

University of Minnesota Press), pp. 1–28.

SIDA. (2006), 'Use of National Health Accounts: The Case of Uganda', SIDA Health Division Document 2006:1 Issue Paper on NHA, March 2006.

Somers, M. R. (2008), 'Genealogies of citizenship: Markets, statelessness, and the right to have rights, book symposium', *Trajectories*, 22(2), pp. 8–33.

Torrente, N. and Mwesigye, F. (1999), 'The evolving role of the state, donors and NGOs providing health services in a liberal environment: Some insights from Uganda, Centre for Basic Research (CBR)', CBR Occasional Paper No. 2, CBR, Kampala.

Uganda Health Accounts Ministry. (2010/11–2011/12), National Health Expenditure Accounts 2010/11–2011/12, Uganda Health Accounts Ministry, Kampala.

WDR. (1997), *The State in a Changing World* (Washington, DC:

World Bank).

Whyte, S. R. (1991), 'Medicines and self-help: The privatization of healthcare in eastern Uganda', in H. B. Hansen, and M. Twaddle (eds), *Changing Uganda: The Dilemmas of Structural Adjustment and Revolutionary Change* (London: James Currey), pp. 130–48.

WHO. (2016), *The Abuja Declaration: Ten Years On* (Geneva: WHO).

Wiesmann, D. and Jütting, J. (2000), 'The emerging movement of community based health insurance in sub-Saharan Africa: Experiences and lessons learned', *Africa Spectrum*, 35(2), pp. 193–210.

World Bank. (1993a), *Uganda: Growing out of Poverty* (Washington, DC: World Bank).

World Bank. (1993b), *Uganda: Social Sectors* (Washington, DC: World Bank).

Zwi, A. B. and Mills, A. (1995), 'Health policy in less developed countries: Past trends and future directions', *Journal of International Development*, 7(3), pp. 299–328.

Part III

Extractivism and enclosures

10
Neoliberalism as Ugandan forestry discourse

Adrian Nel

Introduction

While colonialism was a hugely powerful territorialising force in Africa – instituting forms of the colonial state during a time of imperial expansion and mercantilist economic policy – neoliberal transformations since the 1890s have intensified modes of capital accumulation, value extraction and land use change in post-colonial Africa. In this context deforestation and agribusiness have become the foci of 'green economy' and green governance structures at a time when broader processes of intensification of land appropriations attendant to the globalisation of trade and investments are reshaping rural Africa (Fairhead *et al.* 2012). These processes culminate in part in increasing pressure to convert forests into various land uses such as for biofuels, and timber, pulp and paper, and agribusiness plantations (Mwangi and Wardell 2012: 341). In Uganda there has been, according to Martiniello (2012), a mushrooming of land grabbing and evictions, and localised struggles of resistance are daily reported by media and civil society activists in the central as well as western and northern regions, which were traditionally marginal in the colonial and post-colonial political economy; these have been no less prevalent in the forestry sector (Anti-Corruption Coalition Uganda 2010). In describing how this happens in places such as Uganda, it has been argued there is a need for critical scholars to locate the ecological and socio-economic significance of processes of commodification of nature within their broader discursive, historical and political economic dynamics (Arsel and Büscher 2012: 68). This approach is crucial in order to understand how many of the problems in the Ugandan forestry sector do not beset it 'from the outside', but are, if not intentional, derived from a neoliberal logic which externalises social and environmental costs, and stymies alternatives. This chapter takes up the call to critical scholarship by analysing neoliberal forestry discourse which circulates and transforms forestry management practice and governance.

Forests in Uganda are intimately anthropogenic, and have been involved in the co-production of the Ugandan landscape alongside its people. Forests were entwined in pre-colonial systems of ecological control and agrarian use (Doyle 1998), and have been estimated to support, directly or indirectly, approximately 23.42 per cent of Uganda's GDP and 65 per cent of its employment (World Bank 2011). They are perceived as cultural sites, 'sacred groves' and houses of ancestral spirits by some (UFRIC 1999), and interpreted by the colonial and post-colonial governments as sites of extraction and state formation (Cavanagh and Himmelfarb 2013), whilst at the same time the de jure protected areas and reserves that eventuated from state enclosure were seen as a source of 'empty land' for landless people, migrants and displaced peoples from the civil wars and beyond (Marquardt 1994). It is evident that forestry spaces in Uganda are inherently contested, and enwrapped with uneven development, increasing population pressure and the political economy of resource management (Mwenda and Tumushabe 2011). However, rather than leading to a questioning of the territoriality of the protected forest estate itself or its uneven access regimes (with privileged access for private timber planters, often at the expense of forest-adjacent communities), such tensions re-enforce the *urgent* governance imperative of forestry management. Finally, when described as degraded and embattled, forests and forest territories are seen as ripe for a variety of interventions, reforestation, care, investment and protection deployed by an apparatus of state, non-governmental and private governance.

The complex, messy realities of environmental damage and deforestation are translated into linear, unproblematic narratives by environmental agencies. Public and private agencies alike are pushing a neoliberal environmental discourse, where forest and carbon resources are presented as 'natural capital', to which economic calculation can be unproblematically applied. This chapter unpacks this discourse and the material implications it has had in Uganda. This endeavour sits well within the sub-focus of the book on neoliberal ideology and its impacts. Within the context of the periodisation in the introduction chapter, the neoliberalisation of the Ugandan forestry sector took place across the second and third decades of neoliberalisation in the country, with particular impetus from 2002; later than the restructuring of the Uganda Wildlife Authority for instance, but with carbon forestry in particular, representing a relatively recent and sophisticated form of neoliberal environmental restructuring. The chapter also dovetails well with Lyons' chapter

which examines the violence attendant to the activities of a particular forestry company in northern Uganda and its carbon offset
scheme; this articulates with the broader restructuring and discourses
set out in this chapter. The chapter begins by exploring how neoliberal discourses have transformed our understanding of conservation
and nature and how this is played out in the Ugandan conservation
scene.

Neoliberalism and fortress conservation in Uganda

The link between capitalism, colonialism, 'natures' and enclosure
in Africa (along with their associated social costs) has been made
explicit (Ranger 1989, Neumann 2004). Reflecting on the 'nature
as an entity worth protecting', Vaccaro *et al.* (2013: 246) describe
the emergence of the *fortress conservation* model (based around
the creation of exclusionary protected areas) at the moment when
colonialism, with its apparatus of remote authoritarian control, was
dominant. Such critiques argue that 'nature' was only integrated into
the service sector during the modernisation of Western societies and
the unfolding of nation-states and the capitalist market (Vaccaro *et
al.* 2013). This was to a large extent through the creation of a conservation apparatus (Peet and Watts 1996). Scott (1998), Neumann
(2004) and others attribute the British colonial administration's
efforts to re-order 'nature', production and human society within
its East African territories as a process of state building, entailing
an enclosure of the commons enacted under its 'civilising mission'.
These efforts to ensure resource access/control were embedded in
ideologies of racial and cultural superiority, and faith in Western
scientific achievements and mastery over nature. In this perspective
'Wilderness spaces' such as national parks or forest reserves should
not be perceived as vestigial 'pre-modern' spaces but are rather a
contested product of what Neumann calls the 'landscape of modernity' (2004), i.e. the outcome of capitalist restructuring/domination.

In the neoliberal era the uneven development of, extracting from,
polluting, conserving and restoration of 'nature' in Africa has become
increasingly intense and urgent (Brockington and Duffy 2010). In
forest conservation, neoliberal policies have created a new hegemony
on 'community participation' (McCarthy 2005), paradoxically transforming this potentially oppositional tool into a supplementary
intervention to neoliberal policies. Dressler and Büscher (2008)
reflect on the same practice in Community Based Natural Resource

Management (CBNRM) related to transfrontier conservation in southern Africa, where private and public sector delivery of devolved conservation and poverty relief projects support private sector interests rather than the resource base of rural livelihoods. Likewise, Dauvergne and Lister (2013) conclude that corporate social responsibility-linked sustainability initiatives in various guises, including those of timber companies, have the potential to restructure supply chains, but not for the good of the planet, rather for profits and market share in a volatile globalised economy, limiting the potential for deeper solutions. Finally, neoliberal attempts at climate change mitigation in places like Uganda through carbon sequestration have become a favourite tool in the global climate governance regime, but do not fundamentally restructure the production of carbon emissions, and can involve evictions of local communities (Nel 2015a).

In approaching neoliberal environments, Scholars have termed the varied processes of the neoliberalisation of nature as contingent, variegated and situated; less a thing than a bundle of processes which vary from location to location (Heynen and Robbins 2005). Accordingly, Springer (2012) notes that viewing neoliberalism through a discourse approach moves theorisations forward by recognising neoliberalism is neither a 'top-down' nor 'bottom-up' phenomenon, but rather a process of socio-spatial transformation. The next sections consider how such discursive constructions cohere in the Ugandan forestry context.

Uganda's neoliberal forestry context

Ugandan forestry is largely defined by a trend of deforestation and a dysfunctional forestry sector; while Indonesia and Brazil have higher gross losses of forest stocks, Uganda's *net* loss of forest cover is 2.6 per cent per annum, which is in the top five worldwide (FAO 2011). The leading drivers of forest loss and degradation include escalating timber trade, fuel-wood extraction – where there is a huge dependency (greater than 90 per cent of Uganda's energy supply) on charcoal made from woody biomass – and agricultural expansion, coupled with a largely uncoordinated, politically unsupported and poorly funded forestry management apparatus which is widely accused of corruption (Twongyirwe *et al.* 2015).

Uganda's period of structural adjustment, and ongoing external intervention, has seen a drive for the commercialisation and privatisation of the forestry sector, coupling weakened state management capacity with a focus on the creation of markets for timber, and, as a more recent novelty, carbon markets for the carbon stored in woody biomass. As already mentioned, the politics of a privatisation 'rush' for forestry resources echoes that in land: Uganda saw prospective commercial land deals to the extent of an estimated 14.6 per cent of the national agricultural land in 2009 (Friis and Reenberg 2010: 12). Since the creation of the National Forestry Authority (NFA) under donor pressure (see below), the purchase of leases to Central Forest Reserves (CFRs) has become standard practice by international forestry actors – including the 'big four', comprising New Forests (UK), Green Resources AS (Norway), Global Woods (Germany) and Nile Ply (Uganda) – who focus on monoculture plantations of timber and pine, and smaller private planters grouped under the commercial union the Uganda Tree Growers Association (UTGA). While access to 'fortress' CFR land may have changed for private sector actors, 'communities' and 'encroachers' are still predominantly excluded, with legislation in the national Forestry and Tree Planting Act (NFTPA) 2003 reinforcing this effect.

Uganda can be characterised as having a neoliberal forestry governance regime (Nel 2015b), in which the private sector lead in tree planting and offsetting described above came on the heels of major institutional restructurings in the forestry sector following the Forest Sector reforms of 2002. This has been overseen by the increased influence in Uganda's forestry governance of the private sector, non-governmental organisations (NGOs), donors and multilateral agencies such as the United Nations Framework Convention on Climate Change (UNFCCC). Mwenda criticises such external interventions, from what he terms the international 'cartel of good intentions', for the ways the National Resistance Movement (NRM) state apparatus has become reliant on the provision of donor resources. These, he argues, support non-democratic practices, and the perpetuation of a system that relies on corruption, violence and patronage to sustain itself (Mwenda 2007), and this is arguably the case in the context of Ugandan forestry (Nel 2015a, Cavanagh and Benjaminsen 2013). The forestry reforms split the previous Uganda Forestry Department into three associated units, to smooth the commercialisation of forest resources, namely: the National Forestry Authority (NFA), quasi-parastatal, designed to manage and lease out 'Central Forest Reserves' (CFRs) for commercial purposes; a District Forest Service (DFS) to oversee the remnant forests and woodlands excluded from the centralisation of commercial forestry in the CFRs, operating via a debilitated management apparatus tacked onto the local government reforms; and finally the Forest Sector Support Department (FSSD), ostensibly meant to provide oversight capabilities for the whole sector, but with very little 'teeth' to do so. These were complimented by the Sawlog Production Grant Scheme (SPGS), a powerful donor-funded NGO intended to facilitate private sector tree planting – predominantly on the part of elites, in the form of business leaders, former forestry officials, politicians and military personnel – and came to engage with the newly formed Climate Change Unit to co-ordinate policy alignment with UNFCCC principles. In part the reforms were sold to parliament by the reform secretariat based on the idea of a self-sustaining NFA, a claim the ex-SPGS director says was knowingly false, or rather that was only potentially feasible.

Turning to territoriality explicitly, the composition of the 'forest estate' was a key feature of the new forestry dispensation. In making up the forest estate, according to the NFA's national biomass study of 2003, the Protected Forest Estate (PFE) comprises 30 per cent (1,881,000 ha) of the forest resource, of which 1,145,000 ha (60.9 per cent) is managed by the NFA Forest Reserves (central and local); 38.8 per cent of the PFE, or approximately 15 per cent of the total stock in the forest estate is managed by the Uganda Wildlife Authority (UWA) in National Parks, and 5,000 ha (0.3 per cent) as Local Forest Reserves (LFRs), controlled by District Forestry Services (DFS). Thus, in terms of land ownership the bulk, 70 per cent, of the forested area, is on private and customary land, ostensibly under the control of the unfunded DFS (in conjunction with the LFRs mentioned) in a policy of decentralised forest management. This is significant because while previously the Uganda Forest Department had overseen the whole sector, cross-subsidising 'natural' forestry through its own commercial activities, this support has fallen away since the reforms, with local municipalities having to make up (though they mostly fail to do so) the budgets. If fact numerous local NFA managers attest that the forestry resources of the DFS are perversely used to supplement local budgets.

In this context woodland forests are being depleted rapidly, while there are restrictions on harvesting of wood and wood products from the gazetted protected areas (Jacovelli and Carvalho 1999). Furthermore, the protected forest estate itself is weak and contested, despite regular reformulations and revisions since the gazzettement of forest reserves beginning in the 1930s, 'it remains unclear whether these policies and laws are acceptable to the local people and appropriate to local situation' (Turyahabwe and Banana

2008: 641), and many forest territories are openly contested. It has been estimated by NFA officials that up to 90 per cent of CFRs are encroached (NFA Official Interviews, Kampala, 2012), and disputes over territory has arisen between the NFA, forestry companies and communities in multiple locations across the country (Tumushabe 2005, Mwenda and Tumushabe 2011). It is my contention that the neoliberal restructuring described above exacerbates these tensions. A lack of resources, funding, transportation and support on the part of the NFA is highlighted, while other managers speak of the problems of 'opening the boundaries' between the protected areas and community/private lands that resulted, and the opportunities for patronage and corruption – so-called forest-giveaways – that have been afforded (subsequent issues of corruption increased dramatically after 2009, according to a Uganda Anti-Corruption Coalition 2010 report which articles cases of 'forest giveaway' to politicians and illegal activities in the 'forestry sector' since 2000). An NFA official speaks of the 'big problem' of encroachment that has percolated from declining state support:

> First of all not all our boundaries are well demarcated. Ok, it is known, we have maps, but they are not opened or marked. You find many were opened ten or more years ago. So people take that advantage of encroaching … You are not exact and not sure where it will pass. If you know, it's easy; you know where the boundary is and people should stop, yet it's not sure. It's not exact. (Interview, 2012)

Such details set a critical context for the discussion to come, which considers the role of discourse in legitimising the institutional and territorial context just described.

Neoliberal discursive constructions in Ugandan forestry

The major focus of national forestry policy, codified in the National Forest Plan (NFP) of 2003, is on forests in government reserves, or the Permanent Forest Estate (PFE), to the detriment of a focus on forests outside of central forest reserves. This is dictated in part by the dominant discourse, that timber (pine and eucalyptus) is in short supply, due to a lack of planting in previous decades and a gap in supply before newly planted stock comes 'on-stream'. This was detailed in a SPGS timber supply–demand study in 2010, which sets out that 14,000 ha of plantations would need to be established annually to address local demand by 2030 (this demand is currently supplemented by exotic pine and cyprus wood from Kenya, Tanzania and South Africa and natural forests and woodlands in Uganda and the Democratic Republic of the Congo; SPGS 2011). While not inaccurate, this has come to predominate in policy efforts, which is seen as problematic by environmentalists in Uganda, because of the focus on 'production' and the privileging of public–private partnerships and private sector investment over conservation forestry. This approach has superseded the forms of state-based territorial management and biodiversity conservation that were the focus of policy through the 1980s and early 1990s. As a retired academic from Makerere University (active in environmental policy consultations in the 1980s and 1990s) put it:

> Before, we had biodiversity. Now there is sustainability, and
> the investigation of ways to harness biodiversity for production.
> So the forest of today is a plantation ... In the 1990s the elite
> were the vanguard of [forest] protection, but today it is seen as
> negative land, negative space. It is 'degraded' to be used for other
> purposes. (Interview, Paul Nusali, Kampala, 2012)

The institutional and territorial changes described above, including the roll back of the state and the effective deregulation of the District Forest Service (DFS), were legislated in the National Forestry and Tree Planting Act 2003 – as a response to the perceived climate and deforestation crises in Uganda. The changes were guided in part by a particular *industry builder's* discourse. This view called for the commercialisation of the NFA, the purported reduction in government 'meddling in the sector', reforestation and the rebuilding of a forestry industry with economies of scale, and market opportunities for private planting at reduced cost and better quality, which had been in decline after a lack of planting during the Amin years (the aims include building infrastructure such as the construction of sawmills for better recovery rates than local pit-sawing, treatment plants at different points in the country required for a cluster 'approach' to forestry, the development of opportunities for value addition to timber commodities, the establishment of growers and marketing associations, new biological and chemical regimes of production, the encouragement of private planting to augment the low capacity of government actors). This discourse was perpetuated through a number of predominantly expatriate actors working in the carbon forestry, donor and commercial forestry sectors (Nel 2014), who ascribed to ideals of 'efficiency' and minimalist state intervention in the sector. This discourse legitimised the externalisation of state management functions to non-state actors, like donors, NGOs and the private sector. In terms of timber stocks there were calls for the establishment of 150,000 ha of timber plantations by 2020 to address the shortfall in supply and (potentially) protect natural forests [sic] (Unique 2010). This imperative thus has an explicit association with a perception of scarcity, which is instrumental in advancing the interest/agenda of capital accumulation. In the Ugandan instance the imperative has stimulated the provision of incentives, through the Uganda Investment Authority and Uganda Revenue Authority, for plantations companies with the investment capacity required to advance the vision for commercial forestry. The overall direction in policy resulted a re-imagining of forestry as bio-economy, reducing complex ecosystems to biomass (including carbon and timber).

> It's not old forestry; it's a business. Keep Budongo [a prominent,
> biodiverse protected forest], put a fence around Mabira,
> that's another forestry; but here we are and I say consider this
> commercial agriculture, this is just what the country needs.
> (Interview, Former Director of the SPGS, Kampala, 2012)

Companion discourses: essentialism in Ugandan forestry

The neoliberal discursive constructions described above could not operate without articulating with other forestry discourses, which I argue function to naturalise the newly neoliberalised status quo, in much the same way that colonial discourses naturalised the enclosure of crown lands and forest reserves. In doing so these discourses depoliticise their local context, simplifying perceptions of forestry crisis to linear narratives that justify technical fixes and obfuscate the more complex socio-political explanations for – and nuanced responses to – deforestation.

A prominent essentialisation concerns 'forest natures', which are apprehended as pre-modern spaces to be conserved, gazetted and maintained through rules of access and exclusion. There is a common expression uttered by a number of actors involved in forestry governance in Uganda that evidences such naturalisation, the etymology of which I believe can be traced to one of the three wise white men fond of using it. It is voiced in relation to encroachment on forest reserves and national parks, and runs that 'you wouldn't find people encroaching onto Hyde Park' (notwithstanding that Hyde Park has its own history of contestation; Walford 1878). This utterance is a claim to the naturalness of forest areas, as normative, intrinsic conservation spaces which must inevitably be defended, rather than as socio-natural entities themselves, and products of exclusionary colonial and neoliberal regimes of production and conservation. Another example concerns how forestry actors take the institutional structure in Uganda as a given, inevitable container in which forestry interventions take place, and the 'national' scale as the most relevant for analysis. Yet research shows how, in the forests around Mount Elgon park, adjacent people deploy diverse 'weapons of the weak' (see Scott 1998) from guerrilla agriculture, boundary marker moving, negotiating and bribing officials and park enforcers, to legal claims and the occupation and repossession of territory (HURINET 2011, Cavanagh and Benjaminsen 2015, and for parallels in the Amuru district see Martiniello 2013). These activities, counter the authorities' narrative of 'illegal activities', should be understood in the manner colonial administrators understood it, as an anarchistic challenge to ongoing state formation itself (Cavanagh and Himmelfarb 2015), and to the neoliberalised forms of forestry accumulation that take place within hollowed out forest territories. Where contestations or complications such as these arise, they are erased from view, and smallholder or encroacher forest clearances are primarily blamed for forest degradation, and not macro and structural issues (wood-fuel usage, for instance, is one primary reason for forest loss) (Nakakaawa *et al.* 2010).

In mainstream forestry discourse, and in light of the above, the blame for deforestation and forest degradation could be characterised to fall on three idiomatic 'black men'. First, the *man with the axe* is seen by national forestry officials as the predominate cause of forest loss. This is the smallholder farmer or forest-adjacent individual who clears the forest resource for cultivation. The second, the '*man with the pen*', is a characterisation used by civil society actors in Kampala to accuse politicians, bureaucrats, forest managers and rangers of undermining the protected areas in different ways. This counter-narrative to the hegemonic 'view from Hyde Park' speaks of the incapacity of the state institutions such as the NFA to accomplish its mandate, and the openings for corruption afforded, but as argued above such failings are in part due to the reform of the sector, and they serve to increase the urgent imperative for more neoliberal interventions. Finally, the discourse of *encroachment* is used by forestry officials to describe individuals who are criminalised for 'degrading' protected areas on which they settle. These encroachers are perceived as illegal, are not extended civil rights, and are subject to expulsion when new investments take place on these leased CFRs, as they are often unable to prove continuous connection to the land for more than twelve years (which would ostensibly trigger their rights to land claims under the 1975 land act). However repeat encroachments and evictions over fundamentally contested territories occur over many decades, as in the case of the prominent New Forests evictions on the Namwasa and Luwunga CFRs in western Uganda (Grainger and Geary 2011). The powerful narrative of encroachment vilifies encroachers as environmental vandals and paints the private sector as saviours. In effect the encroachment and 'illegal activities' simultaneously establish the conditions of 'degradation' that incentivise 'more productive' use of the lands and perversely serve as the justification for eviction.

In dominant forestry discourses then, challenges and contestations are seen to beset the forestry management dispensation from 'the outside', leading to the impression that they can be fixed through more top-down intervention, and through more political will to 'operationalise, monitor and evaluate existing forest policies' and 'enforce rules and regulations' (Turyahabwe and Banana 2008). However, these challenges and contestations and tensions are not something that besets forestry governance from the 'outside', but are rather fundamental to it. In this light any discourse promoting a quick fix fails to take into account the structural inequalities at the 'local level' in which forestry politics is embedded. A piquant observation by the then Acting Director for Environment within the Ministry of Water and Environment shows how such simplistic understandings can miss out key local knock-on effects – such as the expansion of sugarcane or commercial farmland – as drivers for encroachment.

> If you analyse critically you will see we haven't reached that level of population that would really require resources to be degraded to the way they are. It has been partly mishandled, [for instance] someone comes and creates a commercial farmland and displaces some people over years, so people find no way but to get into CFRs. (Interview, Luzira, 2012)

Natural capital, carbon and climate security

Lastly there is a need to discuss changes associated with carbon forestry and market environmentalism – the extension of market mechanisms to the governance of 'nature'. Lyons (this volume), considers a particular instantiation of carbon forestry, but there is a need to attend to the general discursive constructions that carbon forestry entails, and the broad brushstrokes of interaction with neoliberal forestry in Uganda. Carbon forestry is emergent in Uganda following its integrations in carbon markets and international policy prescriptions. The former head of the national REDD steering committee stated, 'he who pays the piper calls the tune', to describe accountability in carbon forestry. In particular the UNFCC now holds a key position of authority in relation to the national environment sector and its relation to the global environment.

For market environmentalism to operate it requires an ontology of 'natural capital' as a point around which market mechanisms and decision structures can take purchase. The idea is that market value can be captured and quantified through pricing mechanisms and commodification pertaining to these services. Here the growing 'scarcity' of 'environmental services' increases the demand for the value provided by natural resources (Lohman 2009), such that their conservation is extracted from the public domain, becoming commodities in multi-factorial markets (Brockington and Igoe 2007). In such markets the focus is not on prohibiting or regulating dangerous climate-change-inducing activities such as fossil fuel emissions by particular entities, but rather concerns promotion of a reliance on the ability of the forces of supply and demand. This discourse of efficiency posits the potential to adjudicate or *securitise* climate 'risk' through the market allocation of environmental goods and bads, narrowly quantified in the form of and abstract homogenised carbon. The intervention comes in the form of carbon sequestration, where emissions in the Global North can be 'offset' on a project by project basis (see Table 10.1 for an explanation of differing project types) by storing carbon emissions elsewhere, often in the Global South in places like Uganda.

These interventions, and the discourse of efficiency and risk allocation that underpins them, constitute deeply political moves that reconfigure power structures, prioritising some industrial resource users, such as agro and forestry industrialists, over smallholders and subsistence farmers in project vicinities in ways that can entrench, rather than resolve, the crises it was designed to address (Cohen

Table 10.1 – Project distinctions and differentiation

Project acronym	Long title	Simple description of projects as pertaining to Uganda
REDD+	Reducing the Effects of Deforestation and Degradation, conservation and enhancement of forest carbon stocks, and sustainable management of forests	Predominantly INGO-implemented conservation projects with donor funds or finance from multi-lateral institutions[1]
A/R CDM	Afforestation/Reforestation Clean Development Mechanism	World Bank-funded projects by forestry companies seeking to reforest demarcated protected areas with exotic species
VCM	Voluntary Carbon Market	Private carbon providers implementing projects utilise payments from voluntary offsets to work with private forest owners on reforestation

1 Including the World Bank through its BioCarbon fund, NORAD, the African Development Bank, the Global Environment Facility and the Congo Basin Forest Fund.

and Bakker 2014). In an early 2007 study of carbon sequestration Payment for Ecosystem Services (PES) projects found PES mechanisms in Uganda to still be nascent, and moreover grossly mixed up with corporate social responsibility schemes, and alternative income generation channels for large corporate institutions such as sugar or forestry companies (Ruhweza and Waage 2011). The operative definition of 'forests', which includes monoculture plantations – sometimes termed 'green deserts' for their impacts on biodiversity (Bremer and Farley 2010) – has meant that reforestation initiatives to restore 'degraded forests' in the PFE are largely oriented towards plantation establishment with exotic pine and eucalyptus by the 'big four' plantation actors. Nine years later arguably not much has changed, with a further number of industrial plantations included, albeit with two newer REDD initiatives which seek the preservation of tropical high forest in national parks – but with other forest and woodlands biomes neglected in both discourse and practice, and with evidence of conflicts with local community interests in a number of projects across the country (Nel 2015a).

In the current carbon forestry dispensation, as in forestry more generally, there is a bias towards foreign investors seeking to justify novel, additional carbon finance revenue streams to supplement what they describe as narrow profit margins, and to a lesser degree multinational environmental NGOs and carbon developers seeking revenues from carbon markets. At best there are partnership linkages to local government, but there is only minimal or at times tacit acknowledgement of local indigenous actors or specific community groups. At the same time project boundaries are at times superimposed over de jure, contested protected area boundaries, or delineated over what are simplistically described as private/local 'forests'. The discourses of global emissions and natural capital, in conjunction with the market logics with predominate carbon offsetting schemes serve to further entrench the neoliberalisation of the forestry sector. Here the role of the state becomes limited to agenda setting and market facilitation in that it is involved in the creation of a context within which some objectives such as carbon sequestration and industrial tree planting are made simpler, while others are rendered inaccessible. The voices of 'encroachers', for instance, are precluded from having their stake in governance recognised, and non-commercial forestry is no longer the business of all but a number of forestry actors.

Conclusion

This chapter has argued that the discursively mediated reform and restructuring of the forestry sector has legitimated the enclosure of protected areas for plantation capital, the facilitated transfer of their management to private organisations or civil society (as is the case with carbon forestry, the subject of Lyons' chapter), a reshaping of security (be it timber supply or climate security) in ways that privilege calculable, technocentric interventions such as carbon forestry, and the proliferation of corruption in the sector.

References

Anti-Corruption Coalition Uganda. (2010), *Namanve Forest Report: Environmental Crisis Looms as Forests Come under Threat: Cases of Forest Giveaway and Illegal Activity* (Kampala: Anti-Corruption Coalition Uganda).

Arsel, M. and Büscher, B. (2012), 'Nature™ Inc.: Changes and continuities in neoliberal conservation and market-based environmental policy', *Development and Change*, 43(1), pp. 53–78.

Bremer, L. and Farley, K. (2010), 'Does plantation forestry restore biodiversity or create green deserts? A synthesis of the effects of land-use transitions on plant species richness', *Biodiversity and Conservation*, 19(14), pp. 3893–915.

Brockington, D. and Duffy, R. (2010), 'Capitalism and conservation: The production and reproduction of biodiversity conservation', *Antipode*, 42(3), pp. 469–84.

Brockington, D. and Igoe, J. (2007), 'Neoliberal conservation: A brief introduction', *Conservation and Society*, 5(4), pp. 432–49.

Cavanagh, C. and Benjaminsen, T. A. (2014), 'Virtual nature, violent accumulation: The "spectacular failure" of carbon offsetting at a Ugandan National Park', *Geoforum*, 56, pp. 55–65.

Cavanagh, C. J. and Himmelfarb, D. (2015), '"Much in blood and money": Necropolitical ecology on the margins of the Uganda protectorate', *Antipode*, 47(1), pp. 55–73.

Cohen, A., and Bakker, K. (2014), 'The eco-scalar fix: Rescaling environmental governance and the politics of ecological boundaries in Alberta, Canada', *Environment and Planning D: Society and Space*, 32(1), pp. 128–46.

Dauvergne, P. and Lister, J. (2013), *Eco-Business: A Big-Brand Takeover of Sustainability* (Cambridge: MIT Press).

Doyle, S. (1998), 'An environmental history of the Kingdom of Bunyoro in western Uganda, from c.1860 to 1940', PhD Thesis, University of Cambridge.

Dressler, W. and Büscher, B. (2008), 'Market triumphalism and the CBNRM "crises" at the South African section of the Great Limpopo Transfrontier Park', *Geoforum*, 39(1), pp. 452–65.

Fairhead, J., Leach, M. and Scoones, I. (2012), 'Green grabbing: A new appropriation of nature?', *Journal of Peasant Studies*, 39(2), pp. 237–61.

FAO. (2011), *State of the World's Forests 2011* (Rome: Food and Agriculture Organization), Available at: www.fao.org/docrep/013/i2000e/i2000e00.htm.

Friis, C. and Reenberg, A. (2010), 'Land grab in Africa: Emerging land system drivers in a teleconnected world', GLP Report No. 1, Global Land Project, Copenhagen.

Grainger, E. and Geary, K. (2011), *The New Forests Company and Its Uganda Plantations*. (Malden: Oxfam).

Heynen, N. and Robbins, P. (2005), 'The neoliberalization of nature: Governance, privatization, enclosure and valuation', *Capitalism Nature Socialism*, 16(1), pp. 5–8.

HURINET. (2011), *Resource Based Conflicts & Human Rights Violations in Uganda: A Rapid Assessment Report* (Kampala: HURINET-U).

Jacovelli, P. and Carvalho, J. (1999), *The Private Forest Sector in Uganda: Opportunities for Greater Involvement*, Forest Sector Review, Ministry of Water, Lands and Environment (Kampala: Uganda).

Lohman, L. (2009), 'Neoliberalism and the calculable world', in K. Birch and V. Mykhenkoto (eds), *The Rise of Carbon Trading* (London: Zed).

Marquardt, M. (1994), 'Settlement and resettlement: Experience from Uganda's national parks and reserves', in C. Cook (ed.), *Involuntary Resettlement in Africa* (Washington, DC: World Bank).

Martiniello, G. (2012), 'The accumulation of dispossession and resistance in northern Uganda', International Conference on Global Land Grabbing II, Land

Deals Politics Initiative, Cornell University.

Martiniello, G. (2013), 'Accumulation by dispossession, agrarian change and resistance in northern Uganda', Makerere Institute of Social Research (MISR) Working Paper No 12, Makerere University.

McCarthy, J. (2005), 'Devolution in the woods: Community forestry as hybrid neoliberalism', *Environment and Planning A*, 37(6), pp. 995–1014.

Mwangi, E. and Wardell, A. (2012), 'Multi-level governance of forest resources (editorial to the special feature)', *International Journal of the Commons*, 6(2), pp. 79–103.

Mwenda, A. (2007), 'Andrew Mwenda: Aid for Africa? No thanks', TED Talks. Available at: www.ted.com/talks/ andrew_mwenda_takes_a_new_ look_at_africa.html. [accessed 10 May 2014].

Mwenda, A. and Tumushabe, G. (2011), *A Political Economy Analysis of the Environmental and Natural Resources Sector in Uganda* (Kampala: World Bank).

Nakakaawa, C., Vedeld, P. and Aune, J. (2010), 'Spatial and temporal land use and carbon stock changes in Uganda: Implications for a future REDD strategy', *Mitigation and Adaptation Strategies for Global Change*, 16(1), pp. 25–62.

Nel, A. (2014), 'Sequestering market environmentalism: Geographies of carbon forestry and unevenness in Uganda'. PhD Thesis, University of Otago.

Nel, A. (2015a), 'The choreography of sacrifice: Market environmentalism, biopolitics and environmental damage', *Geoforum*, 65, pp. 246–54.

Nel, A. (2015b), 'The neoliberalisation of forestry governance, market environmentalism and re-territorialisation in Uganda', *Third World Quarterly*, 36(12), pp. 2294–315.

Neumann, R. (2004), 'Nature-state-territory: Toward a critical theorization of conservation enclosures', in M. Watts and R. Peet (eds), *Liberation Ecologies: Environment, Development, Social Movements* (London: Routledge).

Peet, R. and Watts, M. (1996), *Liberation Ecologies: Environment, Development and Social Movements* (New York, NY: Routledge).

Ranger, T. (1989), 'Whose heritage? The case of the Matobo National Park', *Journal of Southern African Studies*, 15(2), pp. 217–49.

Ruhweza, A. and Waage, S. (2011), 'The state of play: Payments for ecosystem services in East and Southern Africa', *The Ecosystem Marketplace*, Available at: www.katoombagroup.org/ documents/cds/uganda_2011/ PES%20in%20ESA/State%20 of%20Play%20PES%20 in%20ESA.pdf.

Scott, J. (1998), *Seeing Like State: How Certain Schemes to Improve the Human Condition Have Failed* (New Haven, CT: Yale University Press).

SPGS. (2011), SPGS Issue 33: Special Issue on Utilization, Markets and Adding Value, Sawlog Production Grant Scheme, Kampala.

Springer, S. (2012), 'Neoliberalism as discourse: Between Foucauldian political economy and Marxian poststructuralism', *Critical Discourse Studies*, 9(2), pp. 133–47.

Tumushabe, G. (2005), 'The theoretical and legal foundations of community-based property rights in East Africa', ACODE Policy Research Series No. 12, Advocates Coalition for Development and Environment, Kampala.

Turyahabwe, N. and Banana, A. (2008), 'An overview of history and development of forest policy and legislation in Uganda',

International Forestry Review, 10(4), pp. 641–56.

Twongyirwe, R. *et al.* (2015). 'REDD at the crossroads? The opportunities and challenges of REDD for conservation and human welfare in South West Uganda', *International Journal of Environment and Sustainable Development*, 14(3), pp. 273–98.

UFRIC. (1999), 'A site report prepared for presentation to the local people of Lwanika, Budhala and Forest Department Office, Iganga District', Uganda Forestry Resources and Institutions Centre (UFRIC), Research Note No. 3.

Unique. (2010), 'Report for SPGS on projected timber demand by 2020', Unique Forestry and Land Use, Kampala.

Vaccaro, I., Beltran, O. and Paquet, P. (2013), 'Political ecology and conservation policies: Some theoretical genealogies', *Journal of Political Ecology*, 20, pp. 255–72.

Walford, E. (1878), *Hyde Park*, 4 (London: Old and New).

World Bank. (2011), World Bank Indicators. Uganda – Agriculture. Available at: www.indexmundi. com/facts/uganda/agriculture.

11
Plantation forestry and carbon violence in neoliberal Uganda

Kristen Lyons

Introduction

I write this chapter as another environmental activist is murdered
for defending their land and environment, and their peoples' right
to say no to extractivist forms of development: environmental activists Berta Caceres and Nelson Garcia were murdered in Honduras
(Lakhani 2016), and Sikhosiphi 'Bazooka' Rhadebe in South Africa,
in March 2016; each of these activists were well known as being
outspoken against large-scale international development, including
hydroelectric power, logging and mining (Robertson 2016). Global
Witness (2015) documents natural resource conflict driving the
murder of activists around the world in record numbers, with 116
murders reported in 2014, and with indigenous peoples especially
vulnerable. Murder is at the extreme end. For many others, they
face physical violence, intimidation and restrictions of freedoms as a
result of being caught up in resource conflicts. Alongside these direct
forms of violence – which are often under-reported – global resource
conflicts are also tied to what can be understood as slow forms of
violence; delivering outcomes that place economic and political
constraints upon people's lives. While acknowledging the impacts
and suffering for those facing direct violence, this chapter focuses on
the diverse forms of slow violence tied to extractivist development,
with a specific focus on plantation forestry and carbon markets in
Uganda. The expansion of these markets in Uganda, and elsewhere,
is tied to what Adrian Nel has described in the previous chapter as
the neoliberalisation of Ugandan forestry which has come to characterise the global green economy.

The green economy, and associated green forms of governance,
have become the foci of global responses to climate change (Bond
2000). In Uganda, a regime of policies, practices and investments –
championed by international donors and development agencies, as
detailed in Lie's chapter, this volume – is driving (green) economic
development. Outcomes of this include increasing pressures to
convert forests (and other landscapes) into alternative land uses

related to green economic activities (Mwangi and Wardell 2012). In short, the globalisation of trade and investments in the green economy – in Uganda, and elsewhere – is driving the intensification of land appropriations and a radical reshaping of rural communities (Fairhead *et al.* 2012). These processes are directly tied to growing rates of slow violence.

To examine these links critically, this chapter explores the activities of industrial plantation forestry company Green Resources, in Uganda. The aim of this chapter is to make visible some of the diverse forms of slow violence associated with expanding plantation forestry and carbon markets. Drawing from in-depth research (alongside Peter Westoby, David Ssemwogerere, Connetie Ayesiga, and translators) in 2012–2013 with communities affected by Green Resources' plantation activities at Bukaleba and Kachung Central Forest Reserves, the chapter examines the processes and forms of violence on which expansion of this company's plantations has relied. While it is difficult to provide an accurate account of the number of people directly impacted by Green Resources' activities, estimates range from 8,000 up to 40,000 people (Lyons *et al.* 2014). Violence against local communities and ecologies appears tied to the burgeoning plantation forestry and carbon markets. In naming these diverse forms and processes as carbon violence, this chapter contributes to understandings of the local level impacts of neoliberal capitalist restructuring – including both the neoliberal project and processes – via carbon markets. The chapter concludes that diverse forms of local level resistance can be expected in these emerging zones of conflict, as communities express opposition to the mix of land enclosures and associated state violence.

Carbon markets, private plantation forestry and the new carbon colonialism

At the conclusion of the 2015 Paris Climate talks, and reaffirmed in Marrakesh in 2016, global agreement was reached to take action to keep global temperature rise in a climate-changing world to no more than 2°C (Davenport 2015). With this (non-binding) goal, national governments have some heavy lifting to cut emissions. The green economy, representing the commodification, commercialisation and marketisation of responses to climate change, including carbon markets and other payments for ecosystem services, are widely championed as central to meet this target. Reducing Emissions from Deforestation and Forest Degradation (REDD) and related projects, with a strong focus on developing countries, are a key part of this strategy. Premised on environmental modernist logic, these projects assume the episteme of market rule can deliver both appropriate economic and environmental outcomes (McMichael 2009). These market-based approaches, or what Sharife and Bond (in Fairhead *et al.* 2012) refer to as 'environmentally financialised markets', are demonstrative of the neoliberal turn that forms the focus of this book.

Demonstrating the growing significance of carbon markets, by 2011 the industry was valued at over $100 million, a figure that is predicted to rise in the coming years (Lohmann 2011). In the case of plantation forestry carbon market initiatives, investors from the Global North are frequently linked with smallholder and peasant farmers in the Global South. Calculative practices are engaged to measure and price the volume of carbon dioxide and other greenhouse gases (GHG) sequestered (or absorbed) from the atmosphere into wood, leaves, soil and organic matter in plantation forestry operations, thereby providing a market fix for atmospheric pollution (Bumpus 2011, Nel and Hill 2013). The premise of global carbon markets is that such sequestration activities can then offset GHG emissions in another part of the world (Lohmann 2011).

Plantation forestry and carbon offset markets are targeted by investors, with private actors playing a dominant role, and backed by government-enabled private-led industrial forestry and land management models (German *et al.* 2014). This expansion of privatised industrial forestry plantations occurs in the context of neoliberal capitalism (Amin 2012), and is enabled through the disassembling of national territories and their reassembling in the interests of private capital (Sassen 2013). The Food and Agriculture Organization (FAO) estimate industrial plantation forestry has grown by 48.1 per cent between 1990 and 2010, including dramatic growth on the African continent, giving rise to corporate forestry empires (Kroger 2014). In Uganda, since at least 2005, international private sector investment has established an estimated 100,000 hectares under forestry plantations, a figure the National Forestry Authority (NFA) aims to grow to 250,000 hectares by 2050. This expansion is backed by claims that plantation forestry will create on-going local employment and economic growth (NFA 2005, interview with National Forestry Authority Representative, Kampala, 2012). Despite these claims, local opposition to the Ugandan state's policies and laws gives rise to on-going tension between people, and people and the environment, a theme to which I return later in this chapter (see also Nel 2015).

The expansion of industrial plantation forestry has been enabled via policy initiatives established during the first decade of neoliberal interventions in Uganda, including by facilitating the entry of non-state actors into forestry management. This period marks the integration of Uganda's natural resource base into the industrial economy. The on-going transformation of Uganda's forestry sector, including during the second decade of neoliberalism, was further enabled by an array of 'business friendly' laws, alongside the influx of donor-led development initiatives. Examples of this enabling policy environment include the National Forestry Policy (2001) and the National Forestry and Tree Planting Act (2003), both of which have provided supports for private investment in forestry development. Meanwhile in terms of carbon markets, the Uganda Carbon Bureau (established in 2006) has a stated mandate to assist Uganda to 'continue to play a leading role in East African carbon markets' (Uganda Carbon Bureau 2013), meanwhile the Uganda Investment Authority was established to promote economic growth via international investor participation, including investment in carbon initiatives.

In combination, each of these has enabled the inclusion of private actors, with outcomes that have shifted power away from the state towards private sector and donor interests (Nel 2015). This de-territorialisation (Sassen 2013) has resulted in a mix of public and private sector actors driving the neoliberal governance of plantation forestry and carbon markets. Initiatives to price carbon and to drive participation in international carbon markets is also shaped by emerging national and international initiatives, frameworks and funding apparatus (Cavanagh and Benjaminsen 2014, Nel 2015). Importantly, this financialisation of land and natural resources – as part of their re-designation as new 'asset classes' – signifies the third decade in Uganda's neoliberal and extractivist forms of development.

Despite the euphoria amongst government and private sector actors, the spread of privatised plantation forestry and carbon offset initiatives is widely documented as introducing new constraints for local communities, including the rupture of historical land laws, with outcomes that drive the enclosure of land, thereby constraining local community usufruct rights to land and forest products (German *et al.* 2014). Research at Mt Elgon, Mubende and Kiboga, for example, documented the land grabs, forced evictions and subsequent constraints upon local peoples' resource access, as well as the militarisation of landscapes and other forms of violence (Tienhaara 2012, Himmelfarb 2012, Lang and Byakola 2006). The rupture in local communities' social, cultural and ecological connections to land also reinforces economic inequalities, with outcomes that often worsen life chances for affected communities. It is in this context that a 'praxis of everyday peasant resistance' has emerged, demonstrated in a wave of local struggles to oppose dispossession, displacement and violence (Martiniello 2015: 666).

The appropriation of local communities' land under the guise of plantation forestry, including for carbon offset, represents an extension of colonial and post-colonial expulsions from land and the associated appropriation of natural resources – a new form of capital accumulation through dispossession (Harvey 2005). It also demonstrates a neoliberal extractivist development approach, whereby ecologies and people represent frontiers to be enclosed by private sector actors (Klein 2014). A mix of conditions have converged, over a number of decades, to drive this carbon colonialism and extractivism, including national and international policies, alongside the influential power of donors, and the dominance of the ruling National Resistance Movement (NRM) (who have been associated over the long term with illegal activities, including during the 2016 presidential election) (Lyons and Westoby 2014a, Nel 2015). Discourses related to economic and environmental improvement have also been engaged as the basis for these appropriations, with the reconfiguration of forestry through the uptake of modern scientific industrial management practices, and integration into global forestry and carbon markets, centred as the pathway to development (Nixon 2007).

In addition to imposing cultural, economic and ecological constraints upon local communities, this neoliberal expansion of plantation forestry and carbon markets is also characterised as enabling industrialised countries to maintain high levels of carbon emissions on the basis of their offsetting activities (Bottazzi *et al.* 2013). This occurs at the same time as human-induced climate change disproportionately affects communities in the Global South, including in Uganda, who are least responsible for the emissions associated with climate change.

Carbon violence – as a form of structural and slow violence

This chapter began by highlighting the brutal violence that has too often become associated with environmental and land disputes. There is a growing body of work that documents this violence, rendering visible the casualties of colonial development trajectories.

In the context of plantation forestry and carbon markets, and the carbon colonialism characterised by the enclosure of lands, particular forms of violence that are engendered can be understood as carbon violence. In explaining what is meant by carbon violence, a brief review of the violence literature is necessary.

Violence has been conceptualised in different ways, including with a focus on what can be thought of as either direct, referring to embodied, immediate and material violence, and slow violence, referring to the gradual and insidious ways violence can occur, with outcomes that are invisible, or at least not immediately apparent (Scott 1998, Watts 2001, Bohle and Fünfgeld 2007, Allen 2013). While there is often direct violence associated with development conflicts in the Global South, including related to expanding plantation forestry and carbon markets (alongside other extractive industries, hydropower and a broad range of development interventions), the conceptual focus in this chapter – drawing from in-depth fieldwork over two years – places importance on the slow and structural forms of violence associated with these industries (Galtung 1990, Nixon 2007).

Nixon (2011) defines slow violence as those fatal threats whose affects may be delayed over space and time, while Galtung (1990) describes it as referring to non-spectacular forms of violence. While slow violence might be difficult to recognise for its immediate adverse impacts, the spectacle lies in its significant effects over the long term. Galtung also refers to slow violence as structural, to demonstrate its ties to processes – including the strategic manipulation of the economy and power relations – with outcomes that impose economic and/or political constraints upon peoples' lives. While some of these constraints may be immediate, the impacts often play out in slow ways. In other words, structural violence should be understood as both subtle, and often slow; with outcomes only realised over the medium and long term. For example, while the enclosure of lands for plantation forestry is frequently associated with the forced removal of local communities – an example of direct violence – it also drives slow forms of structural violence in the form of food insecurity; by disconnecting community members from land that is vital for food growing. Perhaps even more difficult to comprehend are the long-term social, cultural and economic impacts for those displaced from land to make way for industrial forestry plantations.

The opaque nature of slow, or structural violence (Nixon 2007), is further bolstered by cultural factors, including in this case of global carbon markets, with buyers of carbon credits disconnected via a

metabolic rift (McMichael 2009) from those directly affected by the
material and discursive ways in which carbon credits are produced.
In this sense, the green economy, and carbon markets in particular,
must be seen as giving rise to specific forms of cultural violence.
Naming such violence 'carbon violence' renders visible the diverse
forms of violence on which plantation forestry for carbon markets
relies (see Lyons and Westoby 2014b). Carbon violence provides an
analytical framework to examine the forms and forces that expose
people to new forms of vulnerability now and into the future, as
well as for making sense of their sensitivities and coping capabilities
(Bohle and Fünfgeld 2007).

Research methods

Green Resources provides the case study to explore the carbon
violence associated with private sector plantation forestry and
carbon offset in Uganda.[1] Green Resources is a private Norwegian
company engaged in forestry plantations, carbon offset, forest products and renewable energy. It is engaged in activities in Mozambique,
Tanzania and Uganda, and claims to have planted more trees than
any other private company in the last ten years – with over 40,000
hectares of standing plantation forestry – and to have invested over
$125 million in tree planting in Africa (Nel and Hill 2013, Green
Resources 2017).

In Uganda, Green Resources has obtained licences to engage in
plantation forestry in two degraded Central Forest Reserves: the
Bukaleba Forest Reserve in Mayuge District, and the Kachung
Forest Reserve in Dokolo District. The Bukaleba plantation covers
4,500 hectares, is certified by the Forest Stewardship Council,
and was validated and verified as an Afforestation and Reforestation project under the Verified Carbon Standard in 2012 (Green
Resources n.d.; the current volume of carbon credits at Bukaleba Forest is 25,350 VCUs, and the project is expected to deliver
100,000 t CO_2 from 2012 to 2015; Green Resources have also
recently established a charcoal plant using timber from Bukaleba,
with funding from the Nordic Climate Initiative, and claim this will
enable a further reduction of 15,000 t of CO_2 each year through
more efficient charcoal production). Meanwhile the Kachung
plantation (covering 2,221 hectares), is validated under both the
Clean Development Mechanism (CDM) and the Climate Community and Biodiversity Standard (CCBS), and with carbon credits

worth over US$4 million sold to the Swedish Energy Agency (SEA). In 2015, however, and on the basis of concerns related to Green Resources conduct at its Kachung site, the SEA put a halt on these payments.

Research methods included interviews with representatives from central and local government, environmental non-government organisations, journalists and company representatives. It also included two field visits to both Bukaleba and Kachung Central Forest Reserves, and was split over a year between 2012 and 2013. At each of these sites focus group discussions were undertaken in nine villages (with between seven and thirty people in attendance at each focus group). Three of these villages are located in the licence area at Bukaleba, while six villages are located on the edges of the plantations at Bukaleba and Kachung. In total, at least 150 community members living in or adjacent to the plantation forestry sites were included in this research. This primary data was supplemented with the analysis of documents, including annual reports, policy documents and company publications.

Findings: diverse forms of slow and structural violence

Violence has been a historical feature at each of the sites licensed to Green Resources; with outcomes that have provided the legal, economic and cultural grounds (albeit contested), for Green Resources' acquisition of land in Uganda for plantation forestry and carbon offset activities (see Lyons *et al.* 2014, Lyons and Westoby 2014b). While acknowledging the complex and contested history of land use in the current licence areas, this chapter focuses specifically on the diverse forms of violence experienced in the contemporary lives of those living in, and adjacent to, Green Resources' forestry plantations.

Enclosure of licence areas and erosion of food security

Many people living in and adjacent to both sites of Green Resources' industrial forestry plantations report practising cultivation and animal grazing within, as well as nearby, the licence areas over the long term. Parts of the licensed areas were widely described as vital to ensuring sufficient food supplies for households. Historical constraints to land rights, including access and utilisation, alongside the more recent arrival of Green Resources, has had profound impacts for local food security, with local leaders describing 'a coming food crisis'.

Local people explained how the arrival of Green Resources resulted in their denial to access to land vital for food growing, with some describing their crops being destroyed and animals confiscated by company staff and local police. Sometimes this has occurred on land demarcated within the company licence area, but in many instances it was described as occurring on land made available for community use by Green Resources as part of their community development initiatives (Westoby and Lyons 2016). A number of villagers believed this to be a deliberate strategy by Green Resources to intimidate local communities, thereby driving them away from the licence area. One elected leader described this as a culture of fear that led local people to 'worry[ing] from day to day'.

Numerous community members also reported food crops being sprayed with chemicals by those they believed to be company staff. One elderly woman explained: 'some crops were slashed down, and they used chemicals to spray crops. Even the animals fed on the crops (that were) sprayed died'. In a different village, a community member described the company as having no interest in the on-going viability of the villages, and argued, 'the company doesn't care about killing animals, they only care about killing weeds'. Another woman explained: 'We are now struggling with life. We are forced to eat sweet potato from others … Life has become more difficult now. It is more difficult to survive, we survive on handouts'. Many people also described the '*taunga* system', referring to the mixed cultivation of food crops amongst the plantations (a form of agro-forestry), as allowed in the early days of Green Resources' arrival to the regions. The company concurred with this, but explained they later phased out the practice due to concerns that human intervention in the plantation might cause fire, or introduce weeds that may jeopardise carbon sequestration and Forest Stewardship Council (FSC) compliance. In its efforts to remove activities that might disrupt compliance with various certification systems, including FSC, CDM and CCBS, or reduce carbon sequestration (that is, through damage or loss of trees), Green Resources enclosed its licence areas, thereby excluding communities from land vital to local food provisioning.

Local communities redefined as trespassers and the livelihood impacts

The allocation of licences to Green Resources in Central Forest Reserves has provided a legal framework to enable the removal of people and livelihood activities. In so doing, it has transformed people with access and use rights upon state lands into 'trespassers' and 'encroachers'. Land tenure arrangements have literally changed underneath people's everyday livelihood activities. This change in land access has led to the labelling of local communities as trespassers, resulting in the forced removal of people in some cases, as well as the erosion of rights to engage in livelihood activities. This has occurred via the police and Green Resources' security officers, both of whom were described as defending the border of areas licenced to the company. This carries profound impacts for local communities, with many describing having become 'the enemy' of the state and 'non-citizens', and living in 'fear' for their families' future.

In demonstrating this, one man explained how he had once generated an income through the collection of sand from within the central forest reserve, which enabled him to provide for his family through the sale of the sand. In losing access rights to the forest, however, he described losing his income, lamenting 'for me, I am now the poorest'. Others described losing access to forest products (including medicines and firewood) as well as watering holes for animals. One man articulated this powerfully, describing current circumstances as 'very dangerous', and if the current conditions prevail '(our) life will be gone'.

While company representatives acknowledged the struggles facing some community members as a result of being fortressed out of state land, they expressed little tolerance to what they understood to be illegal activities within their licensed area. One company staffer demonstrated his growing impatience with those he described as 'trespassers' on company land:

> These are poor people. So, we are trying to encourage them, once they have finished their season of planting, to go back from where they came, as much as possible. We will try everything possible to make sure they don't come back.

The non-citizen status of those living in and adjacent to the forestry plantations was also frequently utilised to justify the poor (and often non-existent) service provision and depressed living conditions in many of the villages adjacent to the plantations. For example, villagers described having no sanitation or electricity, limited water access, as well as little or no transport options (with many villages having no means of public transportation). A government-employed community development officer explained the area now licensed to Green Resources was not recognised as home to any permanent communities, and therefore did not fall under the mandate of government. This officer lamented that villages did not receive adequate services from the district, a concern repeatedly raised by residents themselves.

The labelling of local communities as trespassers – a form of cultural violence – is driving the slow destruction of life and livelihoods.

Slow destruction of culture

The privatisation of central forest reserves to establish forestry plantations has also constrained, and in some cases denied, local people's access to sites of cultural significance. Demonstrating this, a number of villagers described Green Resources as imposing limits upon access to places of ancestral worship, as well as sacrifice and other cultural sites. Some community members also described cultural sites as being disrupted or destroyed by Green Resources' plantations, including the removal of indigenous trees. As a result, one man explained despairingly 'there are (now) no places to pray to our gods', while another lamented 'the original set up (of cultural sites) was disorganised and disturbed'.

In Mayuge District, a giant Mvule tree – referred to as the 'Walumbe Tree', based on the belief it houses the spirit of Walumbe (meaning death in the local language Lugandan) – is believed to be an important ancestral place of worship. The Walumbe Tree was regularly cited as having been disrupted by Green Resources' plantation activities. Disruptions included the planting of trees in close proximity to the Walumbe Tree, as well as the relocation of local communities that had previously resided nearby, thereby reducing access. A number of local leaders described communities as now distant from the sacred site, including one local youth leader who stated he could not remember when he last visited the tree. More broadly, he described a trend of declining importance of cultural practices amongst young people in the district, and saw this as connected to the social and ecological disruptions associated with the arrival of the company.

The impacts associated with constrained access to cultural sites are profound, and represent part of the slow destruction of cultural life for those affected by Green Resources. Many people lamented they were no longer able to engage in cultural practices, including manhood and blessing initiations. This was understood as having significant adverse impacts on family health and happiness, as well as for the environment.

Slow environmental violence

Despite Green Resources' engagement in forestry plantation operations in Uganda since 1996, the Environmental Impact Statement (EIS) was only approved in 2008. And while the EIS requires Green Resources to work to a Forest Management Plan, a local environment officer (and others with whom we spoke) lamented that the company was in breach of this plan – and the broader EIS – on a number of substantive issues.

Those interviewed cited a number of examples of poor environmental management. For example, numerous villagers and local journalists described Green Resources regularly encroaching into fragile ecosystems, spraying chemicals and tree planting within the 200-metre buffer zone adjacent to Lake Victoria, as well as in other riparian zones. Such practices stand in direct breach of the Forest Management Plan. Chemical use was also described by community members as causing runoff into rivers and lakes, creating adverse downstream impacts, as well as killing vegetation and animals. In one village, community members had documented the deaths of 32 goats and seven cattle in recent years, claiming it as an outcome of what they believed to be chemicals sprayed by the company.

Concerns were also raised about Green Resources' reliance upon two non-indigenous tree species (pine and eucalyptus), planted in large monoculture stands. Some community members cited the company as clearing indigenous (and culturally significant) trees to make way for their monoculture plantations. A local environment officer described this practice as imposing 'environmental shock'. Similar wide-scale clearing and environmental destruction is also reported in other parts of Uganda, including alongside the expansion of oil palm plantations in the Ssese Islands in Lake Victoria. After clearing the land to make way for the monoculture plantations, the company then imposes further shocks by proceeding to cut down plantation timber; thereby constraining options to establish diverse and resilient ecosystems that could provide habitat for insects, birds and other animals.

Discussion and conclusions

This chapter has documented some of the diverse forms of slow and structural violence, including the forms and processes of violence connected to the expansion of industrial forestry plantations and carbon offset projects. Structural violence, like cultural and direct violence, is a relatively established concept. However, this chapter's focus on slow violence provides a framework to describe the often invisible and slow processes associated with structural violence. Slow violence is indicative of forms of violence that are not necessarily spectacular or visibly obvious. Instead, it represents the insidious, and often well-hidden forms of violence that occur over a long period of time.

Carbon violence, as a way of analytically describing the diverse forms of violence (structural, cultural, direct and slow) required for carbon trading, is a particular case in point, by demonstrating the impacts for local communities associated with structural processes (policies, programmes and procedures, e.g. certification) that drive direct forms of violence over a long period of time. In and of themselves, each action of Green Resources – e.g. calling local people trespassers, or stopping the *taunga* system, has adverse impacts on local people's lives in the immediate term. But as part of a broad set of corporate practices – and enabled via the neoliberalisation of plantation forestry and carbon markets – these signify long-term violence towards local people, landscapes and livelihoods.

The case study of Green Resources examined in this chapter demonstrates the slowly growing rates of hunger, slow destruction of cultural expression, of livelihood activities, and environmental problems, as part and parcel of the violence underpinning resource extractivism and neoliberal market-based development taking place in Uganda. While not always sensational in terms of visuals, these forms of violence are structured into industrial plantation forestry and carbon markets. Yet often the Global North (as buyers of carbon credits) are disconnected from the Global South (communities impacted by the creation of carbon credits) and the impacts of these green economy initiatives.

The findings presented in this chapter also demonstrate the extent to which national-level policy changes across three decades of neoliberalism in Uganda has provided an enabling environment for private sector actors to gain access to public lands for green forms of development. In Uganda, the neoliberal policy context, and backed by the militarisation and enclosure of land and resources, has been a key enabler for private international investment. This case study therefore highlights the need to carefully scrutinise how such policies and practices 'play out' on the ground for local and marginalised communities.

The case study also demonstrates the multiple ways in which local people and other actors act in resistance to these various forms of violence, including in both covert, overt, including militant ways. As documented elsewhere (Martiniello 2015, Atkinson this volume) many rural producers reject the enclosure of their lands, and their incorporation into capital labour process. In this case, there are various forms of local resistance to this carbon violence (Lyons and Westoby 2014a, 2014b), including moving food growing and animal grazing onto steep slopes or riparian zones, continuing to grow on land licensed to Green Resources, and burning trees planted by the company. Importantly, these forms of local resistance, along with international actions that have exposed the diverse forms of violence associated with Green Resources' practices, have occurred along-side the Swedish Energy Agency halting its payment to the company in 2015. In this context, the future of global carbon markets that produce structural violence – including diverse forms and processes of violence that are often rendered invisible – remains uncertain. While privately owned industrial forestry empires continue to expand, the case study of Green Resources in Uganda demonstrates how the neoliberal roll out of market environmentalism in Uganda, and elsewhere, is contested, resisted and in some cases, rejected. Resistance movements point to the instability and uncertainty facing future plantation forestry and carbon markets, and the neoliberal project and policies that underpin them.

Note

1   This research was funded by Australian Research Council Discovery Grant dP110102299, The New Farm Owners: Finance Companies and the Restruc-turing of Australian and Global Agriculture. The author would like to thank Peter Westoby for feedback on this chapter.

References

Allen, M. (2013), 'Melanesia's violent environments: Towards a political ecology of conflict in the western Pacific', *Geoforum*, 44, pp. 152–61.

Amin, S. (2012), 'The surplus in monopoly capitalism and the imperialist rent', *Monthly Review*, 64(3), 1 July.

Bohle, H. and Fünfgeld, H. (2007), 'The political ecology of violence in eastern Sri Lanka', *Development and Change*, 38(4), pp. 665–87.

Bond, P. (2000), 'Economic growth, ecological modernisation or environmental justice? Conflicting discourses in post apartheid South Africa', *Capitalism Nature Socialism*, 11(1), pp. 33–61.

Bottazzi, P. *et al.* (2013), 'Carbon sequestration in community forests: Trade-offs, multiple outcomes and institutional diversity in the Bolivian Amazon',

Development and Change, 45(1),
pp.105–31.

Bumpus, A. (2011), 'The matter
of carbon: Understanding the
materiality of tCO2e in carbon
offsets', *Antipode*, 43(3),
pp. 612–38.

Cavanagh, C. and Benjaminsen, T.
(2014), 'Violent accumulation:
Unpacking the "spectacular"
failure of carbon offsetting at a
Ugandan national park', *Geoforum*,
56, pp. 55–65.

Davenport, C. (2015), 'Nations
approve landmark climate accord
in Paris', *New York Times*, 12
December.

Fairhead, J., Leach, M. and Scoones,
I. (2012), 'Green grabbing: A new
appropriation of nature?', *Journal
of Rural Studies*, 39(2), pp. 237–61.

Galtung, J. (1990), 'Cultural
violence', *Journal of Peace Research*,
27(3), pp. 291–305.

German, L., *et al.* (2014), 'Shifting
rights, property and authority in
the forest frontier: "Stakes" for
local land users and citizens', *The
Journal of Peasant Studies*, 41(1),
pp. 51–78.

Global Witness. (2015), *How Many
More? Global Witness*, 20 April.

Green Resources. (2017), 'Green
Resources merges with GSFF to
create leader in African forestry',
Available at: www.greenresources.
no/News [accessed 1 September
2017].

Green Resources. (n.d.), *Bukaleba
Forest Project*, Uganda.

Harvey, D. (2005), *The New
Imperialism* (Oxford: Oxford
University Press).

Himmelfarb, D. (2012), 'In the
aftermath of displacement: A
political ecology of dispossession,
transformation, and conflict
on Mt. Elgon, Uganda', PhD
Dissertation, University of
Georgia, Athens, GA.

Klein, N. (2014), *This Changes
Everything* (London: Penguin).

Kroger, M. (2014), 'The political
ecology of global tree plantation

expansion: A review', *The Journal
of Peasant Studies*, 41(2),
pp. 235–61.

Lakhani, N. (2016), 'Fellow
Honduran activist Nelson Garcia
murdered days after Berta
Caceres', *The Guardian*, 17 March.

Lang, C. and Byakola, T. (2006),
*A Funny Place to Store Carbon:
UWA-FACE Foundation's Tree
Planting Project in Mount Elgon
National Park, Uganda* (Frankfurt:
World Rainforest Movement),
Available at: www.wrm.org.uy/
countries/Uganda/Place_Store_
Carbon.pdf [accessed 11 January
2014].

Lohmann, L. (2011), 'Capital and
climate change', *Development and
Change*, 42(2), pp. 649–68.

Lyons, K., Richards, C. and Westoby,
P. (2014), *The Darker Side of Green:
Plantation Forestry and Carbon
Violence in Uganda. The Case of
Green Resources' Forestry-Based
Carbon Markets* (Oakland, CA:
Oakland Institute).

Lyons, K. and Westoby, P. (2014a),
'Carbon colonialism and the new
land grab: Plantation forestry
in Uganda and its livelihood
impacts', *Journal of Rural Studies*,
36, pp. 13–21.

Lyons, K. and Westoby, P. (2014b),
'Carbon markets and the new
"carbon violence": A story from
Uganda', *International Journal of
African Renaissance Studies*, 9(2),
pp. 77–94.

Martiniello, G. (2015), 'Social
struggles in Uganda's Acholiland:
Understanding responses and
resistance to Amuru Sugar Works',
The Journal of Peasant Studies,
42(3–4), pp. 653–69.

McMichael, P. (2009),
'Contemporary contradictions of
the global development project:
Geopolitics, global ecology
and the "development climate"',
Third World Quarterly, 30(1),
pp. 247–62.

Mwangi, E. and Wardell, A. (2012),
'Multi-level governance of forest

resources', *International Journal of the Commons*, 6(2), pp. 79–103.

National Forestry Authority. (2005), 'Uganda's forests, functions and classification', June 2005.

Nel, A. (2015), 'Zones of awkward engagement in Ugandan carbon forestry', in M. Leach and I. Scoones (eds), *Carbon Conflicts and Forest Landscapes in Africa* (London: Earthscan).

Nel, A. and Hill, D. (2013), 'Constructing walls of carbon: The complexity of community, carbon sequestration and protected areas in Uganda', *Journal of Contemporary African Studies*, 31(3), pp. 421–40.

Nixon, R. (2007), 'Slow violence, gender, and the environmentalism of the poor', *Journal of Commonwealth and Postcolonial Studies*, 13(2), pp. 14–37.

Nixon, R. (2011), *Slow Violence and the Environmentalism of the Poor* (Cambridge, MA: Harvard University Press).

Robertson, J. (2016), 'Australian mining company denies role in murder of South African activist', *The Guardian*, 25 March.

Sassen, S. (2013), 'Land grabs today: Feeding the disassembling of national territory', *Globalisations*, 10(1), pp. 25–46.

Scott, J. (1998), *Seeing Like a State: How Certain Schemes to Improve the Human Condition Have Failed* (New Haven, CT: Yale University Press).

Tienhaara, K. (2012), 'The potential perils of forest carbon contracts for developing countries: Cases from Africa', *Journal of Peasant Studies*, 39(2), pp. 551–72.

Uganda Carbon Bureau. (2013), Available at: www.ugandacarbon. org/index.php [accessed 25 November 2013].

Watts, M. (2001), 'Petro-violence: Community, extraction, and political ecology of a mythic commodity', in N. Peluso and M. Watts (eds), *Violent Environments* (Ithaca, NY: Cornell University Press).

Westoby, P. and Lyons, K. (2016), '"We would rather die in jail fighting for land, than die of hunger": A case study examining the ambiguous role of corporate-led community development in the bio-green economy', *Community Development Journal*, 50th Anniversary Special Issue, 51(1), pp. 60–76.

12
Neoliberal oil development in Uganda: centralisation, accumulation and exclusion

Laura Smith and James Van Alstine

Introduction

In early 2017, after ten years of slow progress, Uganda appears to be back on track towards achieving first oil. The awarding in August 2016 of production licences to Tullow Oil and Total E&P provided forward momentum to Uganda's oil development since discoveries were made in 2006. The potential for oil to transform the economic base of the country and generate billions of dollars in revenue provides an opportunity to address challenges of mass poverty and inequalities, but does not guarantee it. Trends in Uganda's journey to an oil state are not encouraging. On the one hand, there are signs that the government is placing oil central to the national development vision; to lift the country to middle-income status. On the other, oil has intensified some of the more regressive tendencies of the regime even before the first drop is produced.

The history of globalised oil and gas demonstrates that there are close links between oil and grievances based on class and ethnic identities (Watts 2005). Struggles over the share of benefits from oil wealth often become caught up in longstanding issues of inclusion/exclusion, social identity struggles and complex relationships to land and resources (McNeish and Logan 2012). A neoliberal agenda of good resource governance, which attempts to tackle these so-called development deficits, is being implemented in Uganda in a fragmented and ad hoc manner, partly through norms and standards espoused by non-governmental organisations (NGOs) and donors, and corporate social responsibility (CSR) implemented by international oil companies. Such interventions are unlikely to lead to a more even distribution of the costs and benefits of extraction. These voluntary and discretionary approaches championed by international oil companies, international financial institutions, international NGOs and Western donor countries do little to address power imbalances between state, corporations and communities (Van Alstine *et al.* 2014).

This chapter reflects on the social and political reconfigurations of oil development in Uganda, which defines the third decade (2006–2016) outlined in the Introduction of this book. The government's ambitions to achieve middle-income status by 2020 are largely predicated on revenues from oil and gas; and the 'shared prosperity' and 'local content' discourse espoused by the National Resistance Movement (NRM) is further propagated by international oil company partners.

In particular we look at (1) the configuration of the role of the state as 'extra-economic force' and (2) the oil multinational corporation (MNC) as provider of social investment to mitigate the social impacts of oil; two key features unique to neoliberal oil development. The chapter first examines the socio-political dynamics taking place in Uganda as the country moves towards first oil. We explore (i) the re-regulatory role of the state through processes of dispossession, increased surveillance and securitisation of the oil region, and the centralisation of control of the oil resource, and (ii) private resource governance, specifically CSR activities carried out by international oil companies. Our findings are from data gathered during a study in the oil-bearing regions (especially in Hoima District) between 2012 and 2015. We interviewed local community residents, local government officials, oil company representatives and civil society organisations on their perceptions of the emerging oil industry.

The expanding extractives frontier

Uganda has undergone extensive neoliberal reform over the last twenty years. In the late 1990s the country opened to oil exploration and as of 2014 had attracted an estimated $2.8 billion investment from international oil capital (MEMD n.d.). Initial exploratory activity in the remote shores of Lake Albert saw resounding success rates and surpassed the threshold for commercial viability in 2006. These finds attracted investment from major players in the oil industry; in 2012 Chinese state-owned China National Offshore Oil Corporation (CNOOC) and the French oil major Total SA entered into a joint venture partnership with the independent UK/ Irish Tullow Oil plc to share one-third interests in blocks 1, 2 and 3A. CNOOC was awarded the production licence to develop the

Kingfisher basin (block 3A) in 2013, while Total and Tullow Oil received their licences in August 2016. In early 2017 Total announced the purchase of a further 21.75 per cent interest from Tullow Oil for $900 million, making Total the lead partner in the project. The three joint venture partners (JVPs) expect to invest as much as $14 billion developing Uganda's oil fields over the next several years

The discovery of oil in Uganda boosted the NRM's modernisation plans. In his State of the Nation address in 2009 Museveni promised Ugandans that because of their oil resource: 'No one, in Uganda or internationally, can now doubt the country's steady and deliberate path to a middle-income country status in the near future' (Museveni 2009). A Global Witness (2014) analysis estimates that Uganda will receive roughly US$3.3 billion per year over a twenty-year period, which although is subject to change depending on the global oil price, holds the potential to transform the economy and bring millions of Ugandans out of poverty. Expectations to this end were significantly raised during campaigning for the 2016 presidential elections. All three contenders for the presidency made promises regarding oil revenue sharing in their campaign. Museveni's victory was secured despite waning political legitimacy of the regime, and domestic agitation against high unemployment, slow economic growth and Museveni's thirty-year rule. During his next term, 2016 to 2021, it is imperative for Museveni's continued grip on power that the oil industry delivers. The central bank expressed concern that Uganda may struggle with debt unless the country begins exporting crude oil in the next few years (The Africa Report 2016). The government has set its sights on 2020 for first oil, which is an ambitious timeline considering the slow progress so far. Protracted negotiations between the Government of Uganda and oil companies, first over the domestic refinery project and then over the terms of the production licences (Hickey *et al.* 2015), took place in the context of falling oil prices and delayed the schedule for first oil for almost a decade.

The government needs to ensure continued capital investment to bring the resource to production and export. The sixty bpd oil refinery, which has been central to Museveni's vision for the industry, and the 1,300 km crude oil export pipeline needed to transport the oil through Tanzania to the Indian Ocean, are huge capital investment projects and will necessitate a close alliance between the state and international capital. The developments necessary to transform Uganda into an oil producing nation also mean continued impact in the oil-bearing regions.

Oil, accumulation and displacement in the Graben

Uganda's oil deposits lie in the Albertine Graben, which forms part of the East African Rift System in the western region of Uganda. This region is physically isolated, and one of the poorest and most marginalised in the country with limited state presence. The Albertine Graben is being transformed into a site of international capital investment and resource extraction, which involves a new role for the state. The transformation requires the expansion of state power into this peripheral region, to secure the conditions for capital and to manage the dispossession that occurs as communally owned property such as land is turned over to private industry use. As Bridge explains, in facilitating the development of petro-capitalism the state retains a key role as 'extra-economic force' (Bridge 2007). This means that the state manages the displacement of local communities through the enclosure and privatisation of land to enable investment and production to take place (Glassman 2007, Bridge 2013). Although neoliberalisation is commonly understood to be deregulation, involving a withdrawal of the state, in frontier contexts such as Uganda neoliberalisation can be understood as 're-regulation'. The role of the state is not necessarily reduced, but comes to play a new role, for example to facilitate private accumulation. Re-regulation takes place through the granting of exploration licences by the state to international oil companies, which convey an exclusive right to prospect for oil for a given period, affirm property rights and render the resource an exploitable space (Bridge 2007). Thus, although the global prospecting and exploitation of natural resources is not unique to the neoliberal era, the recent stage of capitalist expansion involves the 'neoliberalisation of access regimes to mineral resources' (*ibid.*: 76). Through processes facilitated by the state's re-regulatory role peripheral resource regions are enclosed into sites linked to the strategic objectives of non-localised capital, creating what Ferguson has called enclaves, which are quite literally walled off from national society. Ferguson (2006) argues that rather than flow to the locality, capital hops from point to point, connecting secured resource enclaves in the Global South to metropolitan centres in the Global North. The enclave nature of resource extraction also means that communities close to the site of resource extraction largely are excluded by this process, and restricted from accessing land and resources depended on for livelihoods. These processes are not unique to oil, for example the chapter in this volume by Wedig shows, in a similar way, the privatisation of Uganda's fishing grounds excludes and threatens local people's livelihoods.

Although communities are situated close to extractive enclaves they remain separated physically, culturally and economically. Indeed, the main way that re-regulation is taking place in Uganda is through land reform and acquisition and enclosure. The development of the industry requires the temporary and permanent acquisition of land, most of which is under customary tenure. Uganda has a complex land tenure system, and there was no comprehensive land policy prior to 2013. The process of translating customary land into freehold titles for communities in the oil regions is taking place in some instances. However, this is a complicated, long and expensive process, with no clear legal guidelines meaning that citizens' land rights are being sidelined (Oil in Uganda, 2012, 2014a, 2014b, 2014c). Further, processes of dispossession in the Albertine Graben region are leading to the physical displacement of local communities from communal lands.

In 2012 over 7,000 people were moved from their homes and land by the government to make way for the oil refinery site. The Constitution allows for the compulsory acquisition of land for public use, providing that there is prompt payment of fair and adequate compensation (Constitution of the Republic of Uganda 1995). The residents of the refinery site were offered the choice between compensation and relocation, yet at the time the area of relocation was not disclosed. Rumours circulated that some families could be moved as far as Karamoja, a region in the northeast of Uganda, approximately 500 km from Hoima, which suffers extremely high poverty levels, underdevelopment, insecurity, drought, famine and marginalisation (Kaduuli 2008). Largely due to the fear of being moved far away to a challenging and different environment and separated from their community, most residents chose compensation (Global Rights Alert 2015). However, the compensation process was delayed and hindered by administrative problems. Many of the displaced residents consider that the amount of compensation does not reflect the value of their land and crops (interviews). As of August 2016 the few residents opting for relocation still had not been re-housed, almost four years after the eviction. The constitutional right of the residents to prompt, adequate and fair compensation has not been upheld. Livelihoods have been considerably interrupted for the last few years, and this has had a knock-on effect impacting food production in the region (interviews). As Global Rights Alert writes, 'Since majority [sic] of people who opted for cash compensation left, what were once vibrant communities appear deserted today' (Global Rights Alert 2015: 5). Around seventy families affected by the refinery formed the Oil Refinery Residents Association and with the support of civil society groups have organised peaceful local demonstrations and lobbied the government for recognition of their plight.

Displacement is also occurring because of land fraud, land grabbing and land conflict, which are increasing as the oil industry develops. In August 2014 201 families in Hoima District were forcibly evicted and their homes burned to the ground by a local businessman with the help of the Uganda police force (Daily Monitor 2014). According to local news sources the land was purchased fraudulently to lease to an American company for the construction of an oil waste treatment plant (Oil in Uganda 2014a). The case is now with the District court in Masindi, which recently ruled in favour of the communities; however, the families remain in temporary camps and have lost their homes and means of livelihood (interviews).

In this way, hydrocarbons development can be seen as a continuing and dynamic process of 'accumulation by dispossession' (Harvey 2003), whereby wealth is transferred to capital and/or state elites through actively dispossessing the public of their wealth, often land. The re-regulatory role of the state facilitates these processes. The transfer of property from communally owned and used land to private investor owned is the dominant form of accumulation in the neoliberal era (Glassman 2006, 2007), and often involves the use of coercion and force (Harvey 2003). Kampala-based civil society organisations (CSOs) have documented several cases of land dispossession, which appear to be a result of collusion between District officials and politicians, and local/national elites (Bashir and Brophy 2015). Local people claim that customary land in the oil region is being registered in other people's names, usually by business people connected to District leaders and national elites, who later use the fake titles to evict them (Oil in Uganda 2016). In Buliisa District Area Land Committees and local leaders are said to be involved in facilitating such land grabs (Oil in Uganda 2014c). The Uganda Human Rights Commission (UHRC) reports allegations that a Kampala-based businessman native to Buliisa owns 80 per cent of the land where the oil wells in Buliisa District are located (UHRC 2014). Locals claim that he acquired prior knowledge about the location of oil wells through connections to politicians with seismic survey results (*ibid.*).

Inward migration has been increasing to the oil regions, which also adds to land and livelihoods pressures. According to a 2009 research study about conflict dynamics in the Albertine Graben, the migration of pastoralists to the oil regions is rumoured to be a pretext for land grabbing by officials at the top levels of government (International Alert 2009).

The Uganda Land Alliance (ULA) reports that communities are facing tremendous pressure from local and national political elites and wealthy individuals to relinquish their rights to land (Uganda Land Alliance 2011). They found that most new land acquisitions involved people from outside the oil bearing region purchasing land from local land holders and local leaders. Our research found that land grabbing both by local and national political elites and business people is more acute in the Bunyoro region where the oil project is in a more advanced stage of development (see Manyindo *et al.* 2014). Forty per cent of land in Bunyoro comprises wetlands, forests and gazetted areas for national park and wildlife reserves, leaving a relatively narrow corridor for use by the population (Oil in Uganda 2012). Historical grievances over lands lost during colonialism have been linked to the Bunyoro Kingdom's demands for 12.5 per cent of oil revenues (settled at 1 per cent in the 2015 Public Finance Act) and a percentage of pre-oil production monies (Daily Monitor 2015). Unsurprisingly, land is already a point of tension, and is being exacerbated by oil. Local people express concern that they will be 'chased away' as the oil industry develops. As Lyons' chapter demonstrates in relation to local level resistance to the expansion of neoliberal carbon markets, resistance to oil-related land grabbing and displacement is also likely to increase.

Centralisation and exclusion in the control of oil

Re-regulation processes also involve surveillance and securitisation, which have impacted the lives and livelihoods of communities in the oil-bearing regions. The Ugandan state has deepened its control and surveillance of the region, and the Albertine Graben has become increasingly militarised and securitised since oil exploration began. The oil deposits are located close to the border with the Democratic Republic of Congo (DRC) where an ongoing border dispute occasionally leads to violent clashes. Already this has proved to be high risk for oil companies; in 2007 a British oil worker was shot dead by DRC troops (Reuters 2007). The security threat justifies restrictions to access and movement in the oil regions and the continued presence of the military and private security companies. The elite 'Special Forces Group' of the Ugandan Peoples' Defence Forces is mandated to protect the president and also provides security to Uganda's oil investments (Patey 2015).The increased securitisation of the oil region is impacting the movement of local people on communal land, as one female respondent told us:

> When we go to fetch firewood, security personnel always ask for identification letters from our LC Chairperson. If you don't have it you are stopped. We are not used to these things, this is our community land.

The quote highlights the tensions between the operations of the new industry, and the daily lives of local people. Indeed, the process of enclosure and transformation involves considerable upheaval for communities as land and resources with social, economic and cultural importance are surrendered to the needs of industry. International Alert's (2013) study notes that more than half of respondents reported increased restrictions to fishing activities during exploration. ULA also noted that communities were excluded from accessing grazing lands, watering points for animals and important cultural sites without compensation (ULA 2011). As the industry moves to the next stages it is likely that the trends seen so far – of collaboration between state and private interests, restrictions to movement and conflict over land – will intensify in Uganda, leading to more cases of dispossession and displacement of local communities.

As the state extends its reach in terms of re-regulating the frontier to enable enclosure and transformation to take place, the control of oil is centralised. In recent years the state has used repressive measures when this control is challenged. The contestations around Uganda's oil bills in 2012 revealed the increasing authoritarian nature of the state and highlighted the interplay of political and economic interests. Clause 9 in the Upstream Oil Bill grants sweeping powers to the Oil Minister, including those to negotiate, grant and revoke exploration and production licences, and to issue policy and regulations. The Clause was hotly contested by MPs with the support of CSOs that considered the clause to be an obstacle to transparency in the sector (Daily Monitor 2012). Eventually the Clause was reinstated due to Museveni's strong arming, despite lobbying by MPs. The president responded to the MP's rebellion by accusing MPs and Ugandan CSOs of 'working for foreign interests', which he claimed were providing funding to MPs to oppose the Oil Bill (New Vision 2012).The implication of the clause is that the control of oil is highly centralised, the power of the executive is bolstered and opportunities for elite rent seeking are increased. There is already evidence that the oil industry has added new incentives for graft and corruption, seen in the alleged collusion between oil MNCs and state elites. For example, in 2011 Tullow Oil senior executives became embroiled in a scandal after they were accused of bribing senior ministers (BBC 2011). Other exposés of high-level corruption between senior ministers and oil companies surfaced around the 2009 Tullow Oil / Heritage deal (Platform 2010), and then around the 2012 farm down deal.

The state also reacted against civil society's attempts to organise around issues raised by the refinery resettlement in 2013. Again, CSOs lobbied MPs about the resettlement process, which they claimed lacked transparency and provided unfair compensation rates to the affected residents. The government accused CSOs of mobilising communities against the state and effectively attempting to sabotage the refinery project (Daily Monitor 2013). Subsequently, the Public Order Management Bill was passed in August 2013 which requires police approval for more than three people to gather to discuss political issues, a law which CSOs working in oil see as directly targeting their work (interviews). Amnesty International criticised the Bill as 'designed to intimidate civil society and shrink Uganda's diminishing political space further still' (Amnesty International 2013). In 2015 parliament passed the NGO bill, which further obstructs civil society activities. In July 2015, the increased powers of the executive were exercised to close a meeting in Hoima District between CSOs, regional leaders and the Ministry of Land about land conflict a few hours before it was due to start (interviews). Pressure on CSOs relaxed in the lead up to the 2016 elections; however, organisations working on oil issues are required to share their work plans with government security representatives, which is seen as an attempt to silence those voices representing the common interest. However, the contestations around the oil bills and the refinery resettlement revealed the capacity of Ugandan civil society to challenge and influence political outcomes. In this way oil is bringing to the fore some of the fractures in state–society relationships which increase as political and economic interests coincide.

Another feature of the re-regulatory role is the centralisation of oil information. Interviews revealed that local leaders and civil servants were largely bypassed by central government. Information was deliberately centralised, preventing local leaders from informing local communities about the industry. The lack of information at community level has resulted in increased suspicion and mistrust of the industry, and anxiety about future livelihoods. CSOs are attempting to provide local communities with a channel through which to voice their concerns and interests in oil, but have been restricted by the state in physically accessing the oil-bearing regions to carry out their work. The close collaboration between state and oil capital in Uganda and the withholding of information about oil blurs accountability relationships, and excludes communities and civil society. The increased state authoritarianism is directly linked to oil and the state's re-regulatory role, and reflects the strong link between economic and political interests.

Sharing prosperity? Oil MNCs and CSR during the exploration period

Besides increased authoritarianism and a re-regulatory state which facilitates processes of accumulation by dispossession, self-regulation by oil MNCs through CSR is another key feature of the neoliberal era of petro-capitalism. CSR is a term which refers to the voluntary initiatives aimed at improving the social and environmental impact of a company's business activities (Jenkins 2005). Below we discuss CSR trends during the oil exploration period.

Forms of private resource governance such as CSR have grown during the neoliberal era. Resource governance is understood to be the hard rules (e.g. regulations and enforcement mechanisms) and soft rules (e.g. norms and standards) that influence the way the extractive industries contribute to inclusive and equitable modes of sustainable development (Van Alstine *et al.* 2014, Van Alstine 2014). The term has been employed to capture the reconfigurations in resource decision making away from state-centric models of resource regulation (Himley 2010). This reflects the wider shift from government to governance which has occurred under economic and political reform associated with neoliberalism. So, although the state plays a significant role in 're-regulation' to enable the development of the oil industry, the governance of the industry itself is diffused among state and non-state actors at different scales. The activities and initiatives implemented in extractives contexts under the banner of CSR or 'corporate responsibility', are a key part of the resource governance agenda.

The World Bank has been a key champion of CSR in extractives contexts. The Bank's current focus for Africa's extractive industries is on boosting shared prosperity and ending poverty. In the wake of the 2003 Extractive Industries Review, which questioned the

Bank's continued involvement in extractives, the Bank called for 'a new generation of extractives projects' based on 'transparency, environmental and social accountability, and a sharp focus on development results' (World Bank 2013). This implicitly passes regulation to private and semi-private actors, and is based on the idea that if managed correctly extractives projects can be mutually beneficial. Indeed, the Bank's ideas of 'creating shared prosperity' (Tullow) and 'win–win' (CNOOC) are mirrored in oil company rhetoric regarding their CSR operations in Uganda. In this way, the neoliberal approach to resource governance becomes involved in the national discourse around managing the oil sector. One of the objectives of Uganda's National Oil and Gas policy calls for self-regulation and monitoring by oil MNCs and the implementation of CSR (NOGP 2008: 29). Thus, whilst the state facilitates investment through its re-regulatory role, oil MNCs self-govern through CSR.

Tullow Oil and Heritage Oil have provided what are essentially state functions in terms of education provision through the construction of three schools in the oil regions and supplementing teachers' salaries during the exploration stage of the industry.

Indeed, some civil society groups report that CSR projects have brought vital social services to some marginalised communities in the Albertine Graben region (ULA 2011). The new schools, plus new health centres and a hospital constructed by Tullow are some of the benefits from oil reported by respondents in some villages. Other respondents noted health initiatives implemented by Tullow and CNOOC in villages, such as HIV awareness raising and testing, and donations of equipment to local schools.

As illustrated above, the CSR rhetoric of Tullow and CNOOC centres on the idea that the benefits of oil extraction can be distributed fairly between capital and the Ugandan population for a win–win outcome. Although there is evidence of some benefits to some communities in terms of improved infrastructure and social service investment as outlined above, there are other villages close to the areas of operation that have received no CSR investment at all. This is because CSR is voluntary and discretionary, and investments in communities must meet business objectives ('win–win'), therefore CSR tends to be strategically linked to developments in the industry and the project cycle. CSR investment had been promised to host communities by oil exploration companies during the initial exploration stages, but was not delivered when oil was not found in these locations. In another case, we found that equipment and materials for CSR projects implemented by one company were taken away from communities with apparently no explanation. The timing of the disappearance of the projects coincided with the industry downturn and the shift of the oil company camp to another location, which highlights the way that CSR is linked to the needs of the industry and impacted by its short-termism.

Now that oil development is moving into the production phase, CSR is driven towards 'impact mitigation and social issues management' and addressing key operational requirements (Tullow interview). Similarly, CNOOC's on the ground CSR is geared towards social impact mitigation. CNOOC's initial CSR projects around health and education were aimed at 'gaining entry into the community' (CNOOC interview), or in other words, gaining the social licence to operate in that community. Most of the CSR projects implemented by Tullow and CNOOC are subject to review and evaluation by external consultancies. The requirement to demonstrate impact and justify the business case is a significant limitation on the potential of projects to deliver benefits. We found that some projects, such as HIV testing and scholarships for vocational skills training, were on hold waiting for review, or waiting for the 'second phase', which had not materialised.

Although community leadership had been consulted on some CSR projects, community respondents stated that there had been no consultations or needs assessments carried out in communities. CSR projects are ad hoc and discretionary and are not incorporated into the local government planning cycle. Thus, any long-term or equitable distribution of benefits to local communities from CSR are compromised by the oil companies' win–win strategy, which is ultimately tied to strategic business decisions and the exigencies of capital.

Win–win and shared prosperity are neoliberal discourses which in practice mean very little for the local communities impacted by the dynamics of land acquisition and displacement taking place in the Albertine Graben. CSR spending is not focused on addressing the challenges faced by the fishermen and women whose livelihoods are interrupted during exploration. In this way, there is a disconnect between the ideas of 'win–win' and what that might mean in practice. CSR approaches which are geared towards the business case inevitably fail to address the micro-politics of how impacts and benefits are distributed at the local level (e.g. Gilberthorpe and Banks 2012). CSR as a neoliberal form of governance in extractives contexts can be a way of ensuring the management of grievances and containment of contestation and struggle by MNCs rather than providing substantive benefits to local populations (Himley 2013, Bebbington 2009). Although CSR and the oil industry in Uganda are in the early stages, trends towards management can be identified as CSR is geared more towards ensuring that oil companies maintain their social licence. In this way, the state's role as re-regulator and manager of dispossession in the oil communities is complimented by private resource governance approaches through CSR.

Conclusion

This chapter has shown that oil developments in Uganda are characterised by accumulation by dispossession, the centralisation of control of the oil resource, close alliance between state and capital, and a narrowing of political and policy space for citizens and civil society organisations. Public resources are being transferred into private hands through land speculation, land acquisition and land grabbing by elites. Oil companies are delivering CSR activities in the oil regions which are influenced by the rhetoric of neoliberal approaches to governance, and geared towards business goals. Such interventions are unlikely to lead to a more even distribution of the costs and benefits of extraction. This is because CSR relies on a voluntary and discretionary approach, and the win–win rhetoric promoted by oil companies, international institutions and Western donor countries does not address power imbalances between state, corporations and communities, nor the overall distribution of benefits which are skewed towards oil MNCs and local and national elites. (Re-)regulation by the state is primarily carried out to facilitate investment and manage processes of displacement, whereas the primary purpose of CSR is to establish and maintain the social licence to operate. As the companies begin to scale up their operations in Uganda towards production closer alliances between state and capital are to be expected. The experiences of the refinery residents are spreading anxiety about the upcoming oil pipeline developments, and this is likely to be the next flashpoint between the state, oil companies and local communities aligned with civil society groups.

References

The Africa Report. (2016), 'Uganda central bank warns of "debt distress" if oil revenues delayed', 21 July.

Amnesty International. (2013), 'Uganda: Public Management Order Bill is a serious blow to open political debate', Available

at: www.amnesty.org/en/latest/
news/2013/08/uganda-public-
management-order-bill-serious-
blow-open-political-debate/.

Bashir, T. and Brophy, K.
(2015), '"Up against giants":
Oil-influenced land injustices
in the Albertine Graben in
Uganda. Case study research
findings presented by CRED in
partnership with TIU and DGF',
CRED, Kampala.

BBC. (2011), 'Uganda MPs block
oil deals after corruption claims',
BBC, 12 October.

Bebbington, A. (2009), 'Extractive
industries and stunted states:
Conflict, responsibility and
institutional change in the Andes',
in R. Raman (ed.), *Corporate Social
Responsibility: Discourses, Practices
and Perspectives* (London: Palgrave
Macmillan), pp. 97–115.

Bridge, G. (2007), 'Acts of enclosure:
Claim staking and land conversion
in Guyana's gold fields', in N.
Heynen *et al.* (eds), *Neoliberal
Environments: False Promises and
Unnatural Consequences* (London
and New York, NY: Routledge).

Bridge, G. (2013), 'Resource
geographies II: The resource-state
nexus', Progress report, *Progress in
Human Geography*, 38(1), pp. 1–13.

Constitution of the Republic of
Uganda. (1995), State House
Uganda, Available at: www.
statehouse.go.ug/sites/default/files/
attachments/Constitution_1995.
pdf [accessed 10 April 2016].

Daily Monitor. (2012), 'Oil Bill
passed but 198 MPs didn't vote',
9 August.

Daily Monitor. (2013), 'Oil
compensation splits Hoima
residents', 21 August.

Daily Monitor. (2014), 'Oil refinery
compensations: A mixed bag of
hope, despair for residents', *Daily
Monitor*, 4 March.

Daily Monitor. (2015), 'Bunyoro
demands share of pre-production oil
cash', *Daily Monitor*, 27 December.

Ferguson, J. (2006), *Global Shadows:
Africa in the Neoliberal World Order*
(Durham, NC: Duke University
Press).

Gilberthorpe, E. and Banks, G.
(2012), 'Development on whose
terms? CSR discourse and social
realities in Papua New Guinea's
extractive industries sector',
Resources Policy, 37(2),
pp. 185–93.

Glassman, J. (2006), 'Primitive
accumulation, accumulation by
dispossession, accumulation by
"extra-economic" means', *Progress
in Human Geography*, 30,
pp. 608–25.

Glassman, J. (2007), 'Neoliberal
primitive accumulation', in N.
Heynen *et al.* (eds), *Neoliberal
Environments: False Promises and
Unnatural Consequences* (Oxon:
Routledge).

Global Rights Alert. (2015),
'Acquisition of land for the oil
refinery: Tracking progress in
resettling project affected persons
who opted for land for land
compensation', Global Rights
Alert, Kampala.

Global Witness. (2014), 'A good
deal better? Uganda's secret oil
contracts explained', Global
Witness, London.

Harvey, D. (2003), *The New
Imperialism* (New York, NY:
Oxford University Press).

Hickey, S. *et al.* (2015), The political
settlement and oil in Uganda,
ESID Working Paper No. 48,
University of Manchester.

Himley, M. (2010), 'Global mining
and the uneasy neoliberalization
of sustainable development',
Sustainability, 2(10), pp. 3270–90.

Himley, M. (2013), 'Regularizing
extraction in Andean Peru:
Mining and social mobilization
in an age of corporate social
responsibility', *Antipode*, 45(2),
pp. 394–416.

International Alert. (2009),
'Harnessing oil for peace and
development in Uganda', Investing
in Peace Briefing Paper No. 2,

London, September.

International Alert. (2013), 'Governance and livelihoods in Uganda's oil-rich Albertine Graben', Kampala, March 2013.

Jenkins, R. (2005), 'Globalisation, corporate social responsibility and poverty', *International Affairs*, 81(3), pp. 525–40.

Kaduuli, S. (2008), '"Forced migration" in Karamoja Uganda', Africa Leadership Institute, Kampala.

Manyindo, J. *et al.* (2014), 'The governance of hydrocarbons in Uganda: Creating opportunities for multi-stakeholder engagement', Research Report, Maendeleo ya Jamii, Kampala.

McNeish, A. and Logan, O. (2012), *Flammable Societies: Studies on the Socio-economics of Oil and Gas* (London: Pluto).

Ministry of Energy and Mineral Development (MEMD). (n.d.), 'The oil and gas sector in Uganda'.

Museveni, Y. (2009), State of the Nation Address, 9 October, Radio Kikoni.

New Vision. (2012), 'NGOs hit back at President Museveni over oil', *New Vision*, 15 December.

NOGP. (2008), National Oil and Gas Policy for Uganda, February 2008.

Oil in Uganda. (2012), Newsletter, August, issue 2.

Oil in Uganda. (2014a), 'Hoima evictions: One woman's horror', 1 October.

Oil in Uganda. (2014b), 'Reinforce citizens' land rights first, satisfy commercial interests after', 21 October.

Oil in Uganda. (2014c), 'Oil fuels land grabs in the Albertine Region', 12 September.

Oil in Uganda. (2016), 'Land fraud on the rise in Bunyoro', 12 July.

Patey, L. (2015), 'Oil in Uganda: Hard bargaining and complex politics in East Africa', Oxford Institute for Energy Studies Paper WPM 60.

Platform. (2010), 'Cursed contracts: Uganda's oil agreements place profit before people', February.

Reuters. (2007), 'Congo says shot at Heritage Oil boat, killed worker', *Reuters Business*, 9 August 2007.

Uganda Land Alliance (ULA). (2011), 'Land grabbing and its effects on the communities in the oil rich Albertine Graben of Uganda: The case of Hoima, Buliisa and Amuru', Kampala.

UHRC. (2014), 'Oil in Uganda: Emerging human rights issues', Uganda Human Rights Commission, Kampala.

Van Alstine, J. (2014), 'Transparency in resource governance: The pitfalls and potential of "new oil" in sub-Saharan Africa', *Global Environmental Politics*, 14, pp. 20–39.

Van Alstine, J. *et al.* (2014), 'Resource governance dynamics: The challenge of "new oil" in Uganda', *Resources Policy*, 40, pp. 48–58.

Watts, M. (2005), 'Righteous oil? Human rights, the oil complex, and corporate social responsibility', *Annual Reviews*, 30, pp. 373–407.

World Bank. (2013), 'World Wildlife Fund and World Bank sign memorandum of understanding on Africa's extractive industries', Press Release, Washington, DC, 28 May.

13
Water grabbing or sustainable development? Effects of aquaculture growth in neoliberal Uganda

Karin Wedig[1]

Introduction

Uganda's fisheries resources are facing unprecedented pressures from overfishing driven by a lack of alternative income sources for a growing local population and rising international demand for fish from Lake Victoria. Since 2000, aquaculture on Uganda's share of Lake Victoria grew rapidly (FAO 2016), promising regenerated fish exports and increased incomes for fishers and fish-workers ('fisherfolks', henceforth), despite declining wild fish stocks. However, access to fisheries is highly unequal across Lake Victoria (Béné 2003), and inequalities may intensify as more of the lake is allocated to large-scale cage fish-farming. Worldwide, aquaculture expansion has created conflicts of interests with small fishers, often pushing them out of business (Franco *et al.* 2014). In Uganda, recent processes of primitive accumulation in fisheries and aquaculture are paralleled in agriculture and the extractive industries (Suárez 2013b, Wass and Musiime 2013, FoE 2012). In their chapter on Western Uganda's expanding oil industry, Smith and Van Alstine illuminate the role of the state in realising land enclosures – which often entail displacements – to enable oil exploration. In agriculture, the far-reaching neoliberal reforms of the early 1990s have led to large-scale corporate land deals, whilst no legislation prevents similar processes in fisheries. The Government of Uganda's (GoU) strategy to expand cage aquaculture in response to declining wild fish stocks entails the establishment of large aquaculture parks (Mugabira *et al.* 2013). This will end access to sizable water areas for local fishers and introduce exclusive use rights on the lake, which is officially still managed by an open-access system.

Aquaculture can relieve pressures on wild fish stocks and create new income sources for fisherfolks if it is guided by sufficient knowledge of local ecological dynamics and economic needs. A recent study of small-scale fisheries (SSF) on Lake Victoria indicates, however, that cages are often installed without consulting local fishers, while scholarly information about the dynamics of the lake's wild fish stock is still limited (Wedig 2016b). Furthermore, socio-economic mobility from capture fisheries to aquaculture is minimal, because the capital requirements for establishing cages exceed the means of most local fishers. This chapter examines how Ugandan and international fisheries governance strategies, which promote aquaculture growth as a pathway for the sustainable and inclusive development of the sector, may shape access to fisheries resources for the local people who depend on them. I argue that current policies are unlikely to protect fisherfolks' political, economic and cultural rights. Uganda's Beach Management Units (BMUs) – a co-management system that also exists in Kenya and Tanzania – fail to allow fisherfolks to shape local fisheries resource management (Lawrence and Watkins 2011) and mainly focus on curbing illegal fishing methods (Wedig 2016b).[2] The GoU's focus on cage aquaculture requires more secure tenure rights to the lake's water, but an introduction of Rights-Based Fisheries (RBF) – the private-property-based approach to fisheries management that is promoted by the World Bank (2014) – will almost certainly advance concentrated corporate control over fisheries resources. The RBF discourse blames weak and/or illiberal property regimes for the worldwide degradation of fishing grounds. However, as Nakayi's chapter in this volume shows with regard to land tenure reforms, property rights in aquatic systems may not reflect existing social relations of access and use of fisheries resources. As with land, exclusive use rights of water are a site of social struggle (Campling and Havice 2014, Campling et al. 2012) and the privatisation of Lake Victoria's water may prioritise big capital interests over fisherfolks' needs.

As the growth of cage aquaculture in Uganda starts to infringe upon Lake Victoria's open-access policy, the World Bank, supported by other donors, is positioning its 'Global Partnership for Oceans (GPO)' as a universal policy framework for fisheries resource management (World Bank 2014). The GPO promotes RBF as a win–win instrument for small-scale fishers and agro-industries and is becoming a central funding mechanism for fisheries reforms in aid-receiving countries. In Uganda, as elsewhere, aquaculture growth means that corporations appropriate highly productive and easily accessible water areas to install cages, while small-scale fishers compete for access to fishing grounds in more remote and often less productive areas. In addition to obstructing access to fishing grounds, cage operations can damage them through water pollution.

Given the relatively higher capital requirements for cage aquaculture, only the largest fishers have the opportunity to become cage owners (Wedig 2016b), and the resulting primitive accumulation on Lake Victoria may deprive fisherfolks of access to fisheries resources. Thus, rather than contributing to local food/nutritional security, the expansion of cage aquaculture may intensify levels of destitution in SSF.

The following discussion draws on a large face-to-face survey in Uganda's Lake Victoria basin (Wedig 2016b), a literature review and an analysis of Uganda's National Fisheries Policy (NFP) (MAAIF 2004), Agriculture Sector Development Strategy and Investment Plan (DSIP) (MAAIF 2010) and the GPO framework (World Bank 2014). Our analytical starting point is the assumption – as laid out in this book's introduction – that a better understanding of the dynamics of capital accumulation in neoliberal Uganda depends on an examination of the under-studied linkages between economics, politics and civil society. Thus, I aim to illuminate how global political-economic structures of power and the associated global strategies for fisheries development may impact the ability of Lake Victoria to provide incomes for large numbers of people. Wiegratz *et al.* (Introduction to this volume) describe changes in Uganda's political economy that advance the country's reorganisation as an (agro-)extractive economy. Whether the growth of cage aquaculture will increase local incomes or restructure fisheries into a sector characterised by highly concentrated corporate power and few linkages to the local economy will depend on how fisheries resources are co-managed and how cage development is regulated and supported by the state. Concepts about how to organise access to water (and fish) will shape these processes in fundamental ways.

The neoliberal restructuring of fisheries

The recent history of Uganda's fisheries starts with the introduction of five exotic fish species in the 1950s (four Tilapia species and the Nile perch), to increase the sector's economic value. By the early 1980s, Uganda's fisheries had been transformed: one of the four introduced Tilapia species had established itself and Nile perch stocks had exploded, causing the extinction of approximately 200 of the 500 low-value indigenous Haplochromisfish species (Reynolds *et al.* 1995). The Nile perch boom drove the expansion of export-oriented fish-processing (Nyeko 2004, Harris *et al.* 1995), causing intensified fishing efforts and declining fish stocks. The associated structural transformation of Uganda's fisheries created production patterns that are controlled by fishing fleet owners and processing factories, with many fishers becoming boat crew members. By the late 1990s, Uganda's fisheries had changed from a sector 'dominated by fishermen ... who owned their labour and their fishing gear', to one 'divided between gear- and boat-owners and labourers' (Geheb et al. 2008: 86–87).

This process of class differentiation through accelerated capital penetration created highly insecure and poorly-paid jobs, expanding accumulation structures that allow for increasing capital concentration. As processing factories expanded, the numbers of casual workers and subcontractors grew (Eggert et al. 2015, Asowe-Okwe 1996). Boat crew work for individual boat owners or factories that maintain fleets to deepen their supply chain control (Nyeko 2004: 17). Subcontractors are frequently indebted to boat owners, factories or middlemen for fishing gear and thus forced to supply fish at below-market prices in a tithe system that regulates repayments (Geheb et al. 2008). Middlemen consolidated their position in the sector by allowing factories to buy at remote landing sites.

The transformation of Uganda's fisheries reflects SSF development trajectories elsewhere: export-oriented fishing increasingly contributes to GDP growth, but fails to improve fisherfolks' incomes. In Lake Victoria, increased fishing efforts have caused a substantial decline of fish stocks, which reduces fisherfolks' incomes and creates poverty-driven social-ecological traps, which further intensify stock decline. Against this background, policy makers and international donors promote aquaculture as a solution to the fisheries crisis (HLPE 2014, AFSPAN 2015). Aquaculture, it is assumed, can meet the triple challenge of increasing export earnings from fisheries while improving food/nutritional security and ensuring sustainable production. The next section critically examines these assumptions.

Aquaculture growth: opportunities and threats to fisherfolks

The promotion of aquaculture as a solution to the fisheries crisis largely ignores the ecological limits of fish-farming and the unequal distribution of benefits from cage aquaculture as a protein and income source. A key argument for aquaculture highlights the economic and ecological efficiency of animal protein production through fish, rather than meat (HLPE 2014). Given the global decline of wild fish stocks, aquaculture thus enables a sustainable increase in food production. This assumption, however, ignores the degrading effects of fish farming on aquatic ecosystems and the persistence of widespread poverty in SSF worldwide, despite extensive aquaculture. Large-scale aquaculture also increases competition over water bodies and lower-value fish (as feed for farmed fish), thereby reducing fisherfolks' access to resources. Intense spatial competition may violate fisherfolks' customary access rights to land and water, a situation aggravated by the fact that profitable water areas for cage aquaculture are often a nursery habitat for wild fish. Aquaculture investors seek exclusive use rights of such areas, and large investors may make preferential access a condition for investing. The GoU depends on agricultural foreign direct investment (FDI) to boost GDP growth and increase state revenues, and the associated employment creation potential of such investments, even if jobs are low skilled and poorly paid, legitimises the state's promotion of large-scale cage aquaculture as a win–win pathway to prosperity. In Uganda, the ecological threats posed by aquaculture receive relatively little attention, and socio-economic problems are often ignored, as is the case when dispossessions have occurred under state protection (Wedig 2016b).

Worldwide, the promotion of large-scale aquaculture has been used to legitimise the privatisation of oceans, inland water bodies and mangrove forests, thereby dispossessing small-scale fishers of customary fishing rights (Franco et al. 2014). Data on the effects of aquaculture-induced spatial competition in Uganda is still unavailable, but the Uganda Fish and Fisheries Conservation Association (UFFCA) states that at least half of all municipalities around Lake Victoria have lost access to coastal lands due to government transactions to investors from the tourist, cut-flowers and (pond-) aquaculture industries (TNI 2014: 9). One recent example of aquaculture-related water grabbing describes how a private investor, who encountered local resistance when establishing cages near Bukakata, was supported by security forces to realise his operations (Kifuko 2015). The investor felt he was the rightful owner of the lake area after being granted permission by the government, but fisherfolks felt displaced as they were deprived of their livelihoods. Studies of land grabs for agricultural investment (FoE 2012, Kandel 2015, Suárez 2013b), often driven by diverse definitions of land ownership (Doss et al. 2014), indicate that Uganda's government may grant exclusive use rights to lake areas without consulting and reimbursing fisherfolks.

Dispossession is not a necessary outcome of aquaculture development. Aquaculture operations that are ecologically sustainable and
owned by fisherfolks' associations can help prevent poverty-driven
social-ecological traps in fisheries and potentially raise local incomes.
To achieve this, cage development needs to follow context-specific
socio-economic and ecological needs by integrating local ecological knowledge and resource use strategies into fisheries resource
management, rather than prioritising big capital interests. Trans-
local environmental knowledge can provide detailed information on
local ecosystems and the socio-economic consequences of resource
depletion (Reichel and Frömming 2014). So far, Uganda's regulatory framework for aquaculture growth does not integrate such
insights. The GoU thus risks rendering inaccessible lake areas with
important social-ecological value, thereby reducing much-needed
adaptive capacities to environmental changes and further increasing
destitution among fisherfolks.

Fisheries development policies

Uganda's agricultural development strategies shape the struggle over
fisheries resources by emphasising the need to reduce overfishing.
Overfishing is largely framed as a problem in SSF, while the behaviour of big investors is perceived as more manageable. However,
effective regulation of big investors may be eroded by elite-driven
political settlements between economic and state elites, which are
a defining feature of Uganda's economic development (Kjaer 2015,
Tripp 2010, Wiegratz 2010). The policy emphasis on overfishing by
small-scale fishers ignores the role played by industrial fishing and
large-scale cage aquaculture in over exploitation and in pushing
small-scale fishers into destructive resource use. As Finley (2011:
8) notes, blaming the over-exploitation of Lake Victoria's stocks on
a tragedy of the commons scenario ignores the effort-intensifying
effects of international capital accumulation on new sources of
extractable resources and labour:

> To argue that fisheries have collapsed because individual
> fisherman failed to control their behavior is to whitewash the role
> of government and science in establishing policies that encourage
> the building of the ultimate industrial system, the global fishing
> industry. (Finley 2011)

One response to overfishing is restricting the numbers of fishers allowed on the lake (Waters 1991), but without alternative employment creation this approach disregards distributive justice and rights to food (Allison *et al.* 2012). Thus, restricting local fisherfolks' access to fish – in the absence of sufficient alternative income sources – violates second- and third-generation human rights to food, social and economic development, and natural resources (UN 1992). Under Lake Victoria's open-access policy, access restrictions cannot easily be imposed on people, but are imposed on fishing gear and practices. Due to lax enforcement, these restrictions have proven insufficient to halt fish stock decline (Benkenstein 2014). The limited success of top-down legislation advanced a decentralised co-management scheme that promotes partnerships between officials and fisher-folks through BMUS (MAAIF 2003a). In 2003, BMU membership became mandatory for fishers, but they seem to have achieved little as a basis for adaptive governance. Instead, BMUs are widely used as a top-down instrument to control illegal fishing and seem to be vulnerable to corrupt practices (Wedig 2016b).

Overall, BMUs have succeeded in reducing overexploitation by small fishers, but with a mandate so narrowly focused on SSF, they are unlikely to influence national resource management strategies for aquaculture and industrial fishing. To promote community participation, BMUs have created local consultation mechanisms to allow fisherfolks to voice their interests to local governments, but there is no veto mechanism to allow them to stop restrictions on fish-erfolks' lake access or large-scale water leases to big investors. The scheme has a narrowly-defined mandate of democratic representa-tion: controlling over exploitation through participation, due to the state's inability to patrol hundreds of landing sites along Uganda's 1,750 km-long lake coastline. There is no transfer of legal power to fisherfolks through BMUs and existing power asymmetries in fish-eries remain essentially untouched. Thus, heterogeneous fishing communities, despite being represented by BMUs, are unlikely to assert their interests if in conflict with those of big investors.

Uganda's policies for agriculture and fisheries reflect a neolib-eral ideological pattern: the positioning of private sector investment as the main driver of growth and the belief that investment flows that are driven by short-term profit maximisation will simultane-ously produce corporate gains and social benefits. The Agriculture Sector Development Strategy and Investment Plan (DSIP) (MAAIF 2010) and its predecessor, the National Plan for the Modernization of Agriculture (PMA) (MAAIF 2000), emphasise poverty reduction through agricultural productivity increases, and they attempt to achieve this by creating favourable conditions for private-sector investment. They acknowledge the need for greater public investment in rural production infrastructures, but fail to commit to strategic public investment that addresses the needs of small producers/fishers. A key objective is to commercialise subsistence farming, which is expected 'to raise rural household incomes and improve the food and nutrition security of all Ugandans' (MAAIF 2010: i). The underlying assumption that most small-scale farmers/ fishers produce for subsistence (*ibid.*, MAAIF 2000: 30) disregards advanced labour diversification in agriculture/fisheries, which is characterised by exploitation and driven by constrained access to capital and natural resources.

The DSIP continues the policy focus on owners of means of production at subsistence, small-scale and export levels by emphasising favourable conditions for private-sector entrepreneurs, based on the assumption that targeted investment in wealth creation will alleviate poverty. If the state provides the infrastructure necessary for private investors to make profits, redistribution is not necessary in this scenario, because most actors are expected to be capable of seizing existing business opportunities, or of achieving these capacities through limited state services, such as education/ training and microcredits. The misrepresentation of the sector's dominant relations of production promotes the advancement of GDP growth based on wealth accumulation and concentration. The achievement of 'extended GDP growth' (Stiglitz *et al.* 2009) – a rise in net national disposable income and a more equal distribution of income, consumption and wealth – receives no attention.

The proletarianisation of fisherfolks through progressive dispossession and increased dependence on capital is necessary to allow for concentrated wealth accumulation and has been long underway in Uganda's fisheries. By the mid-2000s, few small-scale fishers owned their means of production, and boat crew members faced high income inequality (Geheb *et al.* 2008). According to one study on revenue distribution in Uganda's Nile perch value chain, factories appropriated 63 per cent of the total catch value, compared to 10 per cent respectively for factory agents and middlemen and 17 per cent for boat owners who pay boat crews out of their share (Nyeko 2004). With every additional boat owned, the income gap between boat owners and crew widens, advancing class differentiation that is triggered by accumulation. Fishers' indebtedness ensures revenues for middlemen and factory agents and their incomes are also more scalable due to higher mobility and buying choices (*ibid.*). Due to limited access to transport, fishers sell their fish directly at their beach and are forced to accept price deductions (Heck *et al.* 2007). Agents and middlemen at bigger landing sites interface with countless actors to identify profitable transactions without significant travel, and even those who service remote landing sites usually have more choice than fishers. As casual labourers, boat crews also face high economic uncertainty. To secure their employment, they travel ever further in search of fish, accepting long periods of separation from their families and uncertain economic returns.

DSIP's four key programmes exclusively address the needs of entrepreneurs and seemingly ignore workers' grievances. Program One, aimed at enhancing production and productivity, acknowledges capital constraints and poor public infrastructure as growth barriers for small-scale actors, but declares overcoming these challenges as 'well beyond the MAAIF mandate' (MAAIF 2010: 24). Program Two, aimed at improved market access and value addition, notably signals support to agricultural/fisheries cooperatives. This is significant, given that recent evidence from Uganda's coffee sector shows how democratically organised cooperatives can improve their members' economic prospects (Wedig 2016a). However, it remains unclear whether broad-based support to large, democratically organised cooperatives in agriculture/fisheries will be realised, given that conflicting political interests between state elites and cooperatives have led to cases of antagonistic state–cooperative relations in agriculture (Wedig and Wiegratz 2017). Program Three, aimed at creating an enabling investment environment, focuses on harmonising policies and improving intra- and inter-sector communication, coordination and data availability. No mention is made of public support to reduce investment risks for small-scale producers/fishers, or how an enabling investment environment may strengthen their competitiveness vis-à-vis big investors. Program Four, on institutional constraints, emphasises the need to strengthen MAAIF's capacities to achieve the above-described goals.

Overall, the DSIP focuses on removing constraints to and creating opportunities for private sector investment, but pays little attention to state interventions necessary to build a level playing field for all actors in agriculture/fisheries. As an investment strategy, the DSIP creates conditions that are conducive to state interventions on behalf of big capital, and the first reported cases of state-protected water grabs for aquaculture development may therefore not remain exceptions. For aquaculture growth, the open-access policy essentially means that anyone with sufficient capital and state/police support can appropriate lake areas for cage development. Establishing cages in ecologically sensitive areas will permanently alter local ecosystems and affect the availability of ecosystem services in ways that are not yet fully understood. Under Uganda's Fish Aquaculture Regulations (MAAIF 2003b), permission for aquaculture development is given by the Chief Fisheries Officer, who is advised by the Aquaculture Inspector. Fisherfolks have limited indirect access to the Chief Fisheries Officer: through BMU committee members, who work with lower-level fisheries officers who report to the Chief Officer. There are not direct communication channels and thus no opportunities – other than protest – to voice resistance against cage developments on lake areas that are economically and/or culturally significant for fisherfolks.

Like the DSIP, Uganda's Fish Aquaculture Regulations fail to address access and redistributive concerns, and emphasise attracting large investments for aquaculture parks. To this end, the state must provide secure water tenure rights for investment areas, in addition to supporting (i) the management of natural/biological risks, (ii) functional markets for reliable feed supply and (iii) the enforcement of food safety regulations to help avoid export bans. Further, the GoU needs to negotiate and regulate the size, location and ways of operations of cages to protect fisherfolks' human rights, facilitate access to a healthy environment and foster inter-generational equity. In contrast to DSIP and the Fish Aquaculture Regulations, Uganda's National Fisheries Policy (NFP), legislated in parliament in 2004, strongly focuses on poverty reduction. It recognises the importance of SSF for local wellbeing and emphasises broad-based access to the benefits of growth in capture fisheries and aquaculture (MAAIF 2004). A major objective of the 2005 Draft Fisheries Bill was the establishment of a semi-autonomous Fisheries Authority to strengthen fisheries-specific institutional capacities. However, the bill remains pending and no fisheries bill has been implemented to date.

Private property regimes in fisheries management

So far, Lake Victoria's riparian states' open-access policy prevents the introduction of a private property regime to manage fisheries resources, but the GoU's goal of attracting investments for large-scale aquaculture will require more secure tenure rights. The emerging RBF agenda and the World Bank's GPO (World Bank 2014) provide the rationale for managing fisheries resources on the basis of private property rights. The GPO framework provides a basic, single argument for RBF as the superior way of achieving sustainable fisheries management: private ownership of resources provides incentives for environmentally responsible behaviour by investors and therefore protects the resources on which local people depend (*ibid.*). The common property dilemma in fisheries has supported the view that RBF offers solutions to overexploitation (Beddington *et al.* 2007, Hannesson 2004). However, this view misrepresents corporate investment strategies, because the mobility of transnational capital allows for deplete-and-move-on-strategies that prioritise short-term profits over sustainability, especially in the context of weak regulatory systems and the possibility of regulatory incentives granted by the host government. RBF proponents furthermore seem to ignore that fisherfolks, who cannot readily move on after resource depletion, have incentives – and the knowledge – to operate sustainably (Suárez 2013a).

A privatisation of Uganda's fishing grounds – whether explicitly through the introduction of RBF or implicitly through government leases of water to aquaculture investors – threatens fisherfolks' access to fishing grounds. It will disadvantage heterogeneous fishing communities vis-à-vis firms and corporations, because the latter have superior market information and, in case of corporations, large capital assets. As legal entities designed to operate on markets, firms are better positioned than small fishers to buy and trade in fishing quotas. The argument that under a private property regime, small-scale fishers could become competitive actors that buy fishing quotas and lease water areas hinges upon the existence of permanent fishers' organisations and powerful non-market institutions that create a level playing field between small-scale fishers and big investors. However, the level of organisation of Uganda's SSF is extremely low (survey results), and access to loans is insufficient to compete with corporate investments. Furthermore, the creation of equal conditions, measured against needs, not opportunity costs, necessitates the reservation of lake areas for SSF. Instead, the GoU prioritises big investors in the allocation of water leases to boost GDP growth and supposedly create employment by attracting FDI (MAAIF 2010). GoU policies largely ignore the low quality of agricultural wage jobs and the failure of agricultural FDI to significantly increase net national disposable income. The result is a piecemeal privatisation process that allows corporations to establish control over fisheries resources even before a market-based trading system is introduced.

The above discussion of Uganda's fisheries sector clearly shows that RBF would create a double disadvantage for SSF. First, small-scale fishers and fish farmers lack the capacities to compete with big investors in a market-based system. The GPO's focus on private property as a pathway to poverty reduction is based on a weakly defined notion of fishing 'communities' as largely homogenous groups that may effectively function as firm-like legal entities in a capital-driven market-based resource management system. Second, big investors will appropriate particularly productive lake areas and thereby destroy or limit access to valuable fishing grounds for capture fisheries. Due to spatial competition, even a limited intro-duction of RBF for aquaculture threatens local fishing rights and enables commercial exporters to outcompete SSF operations.

Evaluations of RBF elsewhere point to the exclusion of small-scale fishers from the sector and the vanishing of sustainable SSF practices. In South Africa, only 10 per cent of fishers received fishing quotas, and these applied to a single species, which ended existing sustainable practices of multi-species fishery (Isaacs 2011).[3] RBF was abolished in 2005 and the government invested in re-teaching sustainable practices (High Court of South Africa 2005). Chile's RBF system, established 2012, allocated 92 per cent of all fishing quotas to four companies (Praca 2012). Despite this extreme concentra-tion of resources, the system is described to end open-access systems 'while still considering community-level ties to the local resources' (Afflerbach *et al.* 2014), but this has been disputed (WFFP and WFF 2013). In New Zealand, small-scale fishers who do not own non-fisheries assets against which to borrow cannot access credit to buy quota allotment (*ibid.*). These results echo Chile's experience, where few companies own most quotas. In Iceland, the RBF system equally led to the exclusion of small-scale fishers, but legal action against the government, on grounds of human rights violations, let to its abol-ishment (*ibid.*). Unsurprisingly, the concentration of quotas in the hands of few foreign firms can cause capital flight, as reported from Namibia (Rey and Grobler 2011).

The GPO framework claims to focus on ensuring access to income for small-scale fishers while providing incentives for environmentally responsible behaviour (World Bank 2014). Thus, it promises to 'work exclusively to empower local ocean users – the owners of this public resource – to take a long-term stake in the health of those resources and will help them to reap the benefits from them' (*ibid.*: 12). This is expected to be achieved by ending open-access in fisheries to incen-tivise 'owners' to operate sustainably. There is no discussion of how existing inequalities in access to capital will affect fisherfolks' access to fisheries resources under RBF. Overall, arguments for the world-wide introduction of RBF have ignored country-specific empirical realties. Thus, Hannesson (2004: 57) assumes that tradable quotas will 'rationalize a fishery plagued by overcapitalization' because more efficient fishers will buy quotas from less efficient fishers, who take the 'rational' decision to leave the sector; to where remains unclear.

Conclusion

Uganda's current strategies for its fisheries sector lack a focus on equitability and ecological sustainability. First attempts at achieving ecological sustainability of new cage developments are made, but too little is known about local aquatic ecosystems. Moreover, the concentration of power in the hands of the Aquaculture Officer is unlikely to promote adaptive governance of fisheries resources. The GPO's global influence indicates that Uganda's future strategies for fisheries/aquaculture development are likely to follow an RBF- approach. The existing evidence on the socio-economic and ecological effects of RBF-regimes worldwide indicates that the commodification of fisheries will increase corporate power and exclude large numbers of small-scale fishers from their source of income. In less well-regulated contexts, it may push more people into illegal fishing practices due to a lack of alternative income sources.

The human rights approach (HRA) that is supported in conjunction with RBF is unable to solve the incompatibility between exclusive use rights and non-exclusionary human rights. In the context of ecological degradation and increasing economic pressures on Lake Victoria, third-generation human rights stand in conflict with the interests of large-scale cage aquaculture. The protection of customary rights to fisheries resources and the simultaneous commodification of aquatic systems creates conflicts of interests between highly unequal groups. Substantial state intervention on behalf of fisherfolks could create a more level playing field, but is unlikely as long as relevant regulations of aquaculture investments are not part of Uganda's development strategy. The active role of economic and state elites in the political settlements that shape economic development in Uganda (Hickey 2013, Kjaer 2015, Tripp 2010) further reduces the viability of an HRA approach to challenge investors' interests.

The lack of attention paid to unequal access to fisheries resources by national and international sustainability standards has been acknowledged (FAO 2015, HLPE 2014), but there are few studies about accumulation by dispossession and water grabbing as a state-supported instrument of development (Franco *et al.* 2014, Doerr 2016, WFFP and WFF 2013). Whether aquaculture expansion on Lake Victoria can improve economic opportunities for fisherfolks depends on improved ecological knowledge, state capacities and elite support for sustainable resource management, legal protection of fisherfolks' access to resources and the enforcement of labour rights in agriculture/fisheries. In Iceland and South Africa, small-scale fishers have successfully sued their governments against RBF (Human Rights Committee 2007, High Court of South Africa 2005), but it remains to be seen whether Uganda's political and economic conditions will provide similar opportunities for Lake Victoria fishers in the future.

Notes

1 I thank Hunter Stoehr for his contributions to this chapter.

2 In 2015, Museveni disbanded BMUs, despite Uganda's commitment to BMUs as a member of the Lake Victoria Fisheries Organization (LVFO). The new management structures installed by the GoU grant less power to community members but are otherwise similar. Some fisherfolks and local government officials continue to refer to their co-management structures as BMUs (Wedig 2016b).

3 Fishers alternate between species depending on availability (migration patterns) and breeding seasons.

References

Afflerbach, J. C. *et al.* (2014), 'A global survey of "TURF reserves": Territorial use rights for fisheries coupled with marine reserves', *Global Ecology and Conservation*, 2, pp. 97–106.

AFSPAN. (2015), 'Aquaculture for Food Security, Poverty Alleviation and Nutrition (AFSPAN) final technical report', Seventh Framework Programme, European Commission.

Allison, E. H. *et al.* (2012), 'Rights-based fisheries governance: From fishing rights to human rights', *Fish and Fisheries*, 13(1), pp. 14–29.

Asowe-Okwe, C. (1996), 'Abavubi: An examination of the living and working conditions of fish labourers of Lake Kyoga and Victoria (Uganda)', in M. Mamdani (ed.), *Uganda: Studies in Labour* (Dakar: Codesria).

Beddington, J. R., Agnew, D. J. and Clark, C. W. (2007), 'Current problems in the management of marine fisheries', *Science*, 316, pp. 1713–16.

Béné, C. (2003). 'When fishery rhymes with poverty: A first step beyond the old paradigm on poverty in small-scale fisheries', *World Development*, 31(6), pp. 949–75.

Benkenstein, A. (2014), 'Development, sustainability and social justice: The elusive balancing act of African fisheries governance', Saiia Policy Note No. 3: Governance of Africa's Resources Programme.

Campling, L. and Havice, E. (2014), 'The problem of industrial rights in industrial fisheries', *Journal of Peasant Studies*, 14, pp. 707–27.

Campling, L., Havice, E. and Howard, P. (2012), 'The political economy and ecology of capture fisheries: Market dynamics, resource access and relations of exploitation and resistance', *Journal of Agrarian Change*, 12, pp. 177–203.

Doerr, F. (2016), 'Blue growth and ocean grabbing: A historical materialist perspective on fisheries in East Africa', Colloquium Paper No. 18. 'Global Governance/ Politics, Climate Justice and Agrarian/Social Justice: Linkages and Challenges', An International Colloquium, International Institute of Social Studies (ISS), The Hague, 4–5 February 2016.

Doss, C., Meinzen-Dick, R. and Bomuhangi, A. (2014), 'Who owns the land? Perspectives from rural Ugandans and implications for large-scale land acquisitions', *Feminist Economics*, 20(1), pp. 76–100.

Eggert, H. K., Greaker, M. and Kidane, A. (2015), 'Trade and resources: Welfare effects of the Lake Victoria fisheries boom', *Fisheries Research*, 167, pp. 156–63.

FAO. (2015), 'Securing sustainable small-scale fisheries: Update on the development of the voluntary guidelines for securing sustainable small-scale fisheries in the context of food security and poverty eradication', SSF Guidelines, Food and Agricultural Organisation, Rome.

FAO. (2016), *Figis Fishstat Database* [Online]. Available at: www.fao. org/fishery/statistics/software/ fishstatj/en.

Finley, C. (2011), *All the Fish in the Sea: Maximum Sustainable Yield and the Failure of Fisheries Management* (Chicago, IL: University of Chicago Press).

FoE. (2012), 'A study on land grabbing cases in Uganda', National Association of Professional Environmentalists, (FoE–Uganda), Kampala.

Franco, J. *et al.* (2014), *The Global Water Grab: A Primer* (Amsterdam: Transnational Institute (TNI)).

Geheb, K. *et al.* (2008), 'Nile perch and the hungry of Lake Victoria: Gender, status and food in an East African fishery', *Food Policy*, 33, pp. 85–98.

Hannesson, R. (2004), *The Privatization of the Oceans* (Cambridge, MA: MIT Press).

Harris, C. K., Wiley, D. S. and Wilson, D. C. (1995), 'Socioeconomic impacts of introduced species in Lake Victoria fisheries', in T. J. Pitcher and P. J. B. Hart (eds), *The Impact of Species Change in African Lakes* (London: Chapman & Hall).

Heck, S., Béné, C. and Reyes-Gaskin, R. (2007), 'Investing in African fisheries: Building links to the Millenium Development Goals', *Fish and Fisheries*, 8(3), pp. 211–26.

Hickey, S. (2013), 'Beyond the poverty agenda? Insights from the new politics of development in Uganda', *World Development*, 43, pp. 194–206.

High Court of South Africa. (2005), Equality Court Order. File No: EC1/2005. The Republic of South Africa. Available at: www.lrc.org. za/docs/judgments/george_fishers_ order_2may2007.doc.

HLPE. (2014), 'Sustainable fisheries and aquaculture for food security and nutrition', High Level Panel of Experts Report. UN Committee on World Food Security, Rome.

Human Rights Committee. (2007), *Erlingur Sveinn Haraldsson and Írn Snævar Sveinsson v. Iceland*. World Courts.

Isaacs, M. (2011), 'Individual transferable quotas, poverty alleviation and challenges for small country fisheries policy in South Africa', *Mast*, 10, pp. 63–84.

Kandel, M. (2015), 'Politics from below? Small-, mid- and large-scale land dispossession in Teso, Uganda, and the relevance of scale', *The Journal of Peasant Studies*, 42, pp. 635–52.

Kifuko, R. (2015), 'The state of cage fish farming in Uganda: Actors, enabling environment, challenges and way forward', *International Journal of Education and Research*, 3(3), pp. 483–88.

Kjaer, A. M. (2015), 'Political settlements and productive sector policies: Understanding sector differences in Uganda', *World Development*, 68, pp. 230–41.

Lawrence, T. J. and Watkins, C. (2011), 'It takes more than a village: The challenges of co-management in Uganda's fishery and forestry sectors', *International Journal of Sustainable Development and World Ecology*, 19(2), pp. 1–11.

MAAIF (Ministry of Agriculture Animal Industry and Fisheries). (2000), *Plan for the Modernisation of Agriculture: Eradicating Poverty in Uganda* (Entebbe: Republic of Uganda).

MAAIF. (2003a), Fish Beach Management Rules, 2003, Republic of Uganda, Entebbe.

MAAIF. (2003b), Fish Aquaculture Rules 2003, Republic of Uganda, Entebbe.

MAAIF. (2004), National Fisheries Policy for Uganda, Republic of Uganda, Entebbe.

MAAIF. (2010), Agriculture for Food and Income Security, Agriculture Sector Development Strategy and Investment Plan: 2010/11–2014/15, Republic of Uganda, Entebbe.

Mugabira, M., Borel, P. and Mwanja, W. (2013), *National Investment Policy for Aquaculture Parks in Uganda* (Dakar: Uganda Investment Authority and Trustafrica).

Nyeko, I. (2004), 'Co-management and value chains: The role of Nile perch exports in poverty eradication in Lake Victoria fishing communities', The United National Fisheries Training Paper, United Nations University, Reykjavik.

Praca, A. (2012), 'Chile intenta privatizar el mar', *equaltimes.org*, 25 September.

Reichel, C. and Frömming, U. (2014), 'Participatory mapping of local disaster risk reduction knowledge: An example from Switzerland', *International Journal of Disaster Risk Science*, 5(1), pp. 41–54.

Rey, M. G. and Grobler, J. (2011), 'Spain's hake appetite threatens Namibia's most valuable fish', *Public Integrity*, 4 October.

Reynolds, J. E., Greboval, D. F. and Mannini, P. (1995), 'Thirty years on: The development of the Nile perch fishery in Lake Victoria', in T. J. Pitcher and P. J. B. Hart (eds), *The Impact of Species Changes in African Lakes* (London: Chapman & Hall).

Stiglitz, J. E., Sen, A. and Fitoussi, J.-P. (2009), 'Report by the Commission on the measurement of economic performance and social progress', Available at: www.stiglitz-sen-fitoussi.fr.

Suárez, S. M. (2013a), 'The human rights framework in contemporary agrarian struggles: Recognizing a rights-based approach to development in fisheries (by J. Sunde and C. Sharma', *The Journal of Peasant Studies*, 40(1), pp. 280–85.

Suárez, S. M. (2013b), 'The human rights framework in contemporary agrarian struggles: The struggle of the Mubende Community against land grabbing, Uganda. A testimony of Peter Baleke Kayiira',

The Journal of Peasant Studies, 40(1), pp. 253–58.

TNI (2014), *The Global Water Grab: A Primer*. Amsterdam: Transnational Institute.

Tripp, A. M. (2010), *Museveni's Uganda: Paradoxes of Power in a Hybrid Regime* (Boulder, CO: Lynne Rienner).

UN. (1992), *Report of the United Nations Conference on Environment and Development, Rio De Janeiro, Brazil, 3–14 June* (New York, NY: United Nations).

Wass, G. and Musiime, C. (2013), *Business, Human Rights, and Uganda's Oil Part I: Uganda's Oil Sector and Potential Threats to Human Rights* (Antwerp and Kampala: International Peace Information Service (Ipis) and Actionaid International Uganda).

Waters, J. R. (1991), 'Restrictive access vs. open-access methods of management: Towards more effective regulation of fishing effort', *Marine Fisheries Review*, 53(3), pp. 1–10.

Wedig, K. (2016a), 'Towards inclusive rural development? Effects of governance on economic equality in Uganda's coffee cooperatives', in J. Bijman, R. Muradian and J. Schuurman (eds), *Cooperatives,*

Economic Democratization, and Rural Development (Cheltenham: Edward Elgar).

Wedig, K. (2016b), Lake Victoria Fisheries Survey. A Socioeconomic Assessment of Living Standards, Labor Relations, and Fisheries Resource Use Strategies. Date of Collection: April–November 2016, Unpublished data set.

Wedig, K. and Wiegratz, J. (2017), 'Neoliberalism and the revival of agricultural cooperatives: The case of the coffee sector in Uganda', *Journal of Agrarian Change*, 18(2), pp. 348–69.

WFFP and WFF. (2013), 'A call for governments to stop supporting the Global Partnership for Oceans (GPO) and rights-based fishing (RBF) Reforms', World Forum of Fisher Peoples (WFFP) and World Forum of Fish Harvesters and Fish Workers (WFF).

Wiegratz, J. (2010), 'Fake capitalism? The dynamics of neoliberal moral restructuring and pseudo development: The case of Uganda', *Review of African Political Economy*, 37(124), pp. 123–37.

World Bank. (2014), *Global Partnership for Oceans: Framework Document for a Global Partnership for Oceans* (Washington, DC: World Bank).

14.
The politics of land law reforms in neoliberal Uganda

Rose Nakayi

Introduction

Uganda has experienced a number of constitutional, legal and policy reforms aimed at, among other things, liberalising land ownership and markets. Issues of ownership and access to land are very critical in a number of processes of accumulation and dispossession. They also offer 'current state of affairs' on discourses of natural resource allocation and susceptibility to dispossession based on the mode of land ownership, social class and at times access to power, as presented in other chapters in this book. Reforms have aimed at (re) ordering Uganda's legal regime and society to suit the market fabric. The reforms are largely shaped by global politics and the global political economy. They have to an extent facilitated a class society and trends of acquisition/accumulation by high-class groups and increased the propensity for dispossession for low classes of people. The reforms are initiated in the Constitution of 1995, embedded in the Land Act Cap. 227[1] (of 1998) and policy frameworks such as the National Land Policy of 2013.

The above has taken place against a backdrop of a complex multiple tenure system, influencing the options of reform and its outcomes. The customary system of land holding is the widest and highly informal tenure (Hapwood 2015). Customary tenure is not homogenous across the country. It differs from community to community, and at times within the same community; it may differ among clans, subclans and families. Broadly, it is categorised as communal ownership (predominant in northern Uganda and among pastoralist communities), and individual ownership (where land use rights are regulated within the family) (Lastrarria-Conhiel 2017). Customary norms are the primary source of rules regulating customary tenure, although the Land Act further delimits their application by subordinating them to the human rights principles of gender equality and equal treatment towards disabled persons (sections 3(1) and 27). Leasehold tenure is where one acquires rights to land by contract or provisions of the law on specified terms and conditions (section

3(5)). It is considered the most appropriate tenure through which non-citizens may acquire rights to land (section 40). Also important is the freehold tenure, a replica of the English freehold that denotes perpetual ownership of land within the context of Uganda's law (section 3(2)). Lastly is the mailo land tenure: Uganda's current law on mailo tenure accommodates the holding of land in perpetuity and recognises the rights of tenants (lawful and bona fide) on registered land (sections 3(4) and 29).

Mailo land tenure is, to a great extent, a product of Uganda's political history, and has in contemporary times been used to condition outcomes of political significance (Meiner and Kjaer 2016). The mailo land tenure offers good examples of using land as a political tool to empower people by giving them land, and to disempower others by removing it from them. By signing the 1900 Buganda Agreement between the British and the King of Buganda, land customarily occupied in Buganda (and Bunyoro) was certified and gifted to individuals, thereby creating dual rights to land – for the customary occupiers and the new landlords with titles (Buganda Agreement 1900). The beneficiaries were mainly Baganda chiefs, king and elites. This led to a conflictual relationship between the given and the dispossessed, and thereby a need to streamline their relationship (Busulu and Envujjo Law 1928). Through history to date, land issues arising from dual rights under mailo tenure have been politicised (Joireman 2007). Issues such as protection from eviction still take centre stage in political events such as the most recent 2016 elections (Meiner and Kjaer 2016).

Beyond attempts to clarify land tenure in Uganda, the Land Act and the constitution herald the new waves of land law reform, affecting the tenure system. These reforms promote demarcation, registration of land and formalisation of title (Manji 2014). They aim to secure land rights and promote land markets (Manji 2014). Adoption of land law reform as a conduit through which the above can be achieved ignores a lot of pertinent social and political debates (Kennedy 2003). Law, per se, is not always for the protection of those on the lower rungs of society. Philosophical conceptualisation of law in relation to property per Marxist political economy is that it is a tool that is used by the bourgeoisie to entrench private property using state institutions (Marx 1977). The poor may lose land in the process. The land law reforms in Kenya's Constitution of 2010, for example, ignored pertinent debates about redistribution of land irregularly acquired by elites and the powerful from the poor (Kennedy 2003).

Land tenure reforms have aimed at formalising customary claims to land through certification and conversion to freehold titles, streamlining the relationship between landlords and tenants on (mailo) land and regulation of land ownership by non-Ugandans. The formalisation of customary titles falls within a broader neoliberal agenda, supported by the donors' community and especially the International Financial Institutions, towards the strengthening of property rights. Secure land rights and competitive land markets are presented as a win–win for both Ugandan interests and foreign interests (Manji 2014).

This chapter looks at the debates on land, law and power with a specific focus on how this plays out on mailo land. Although seemingly formal to a substantial level, mailo land has an agrarian social structure and regulating norms. Official rhetoric in justification of legislative reforms on mailo points to an agenda to improve the tenure for the people, but processes and outcomes also show other political agendas. Legislative reforms have been a domain of power play in processes of negotiation for legal reforms on mailo and intended among other things to streamline relationships between landlords and tenants. This makes mailo tenure unique and a good case study for this chapter. This chapter interrogates the reforms touching the mailo land tenure to highlight the gaps and contradiction between the discourse and the reality of neoliberal reform. It makes the argument that mailo land reforms are anchored in legislative rhetoric that is neither sufficiently enforced nor supported by social realities, creating an environment for hidden political and economic agendas to thrive in shaping action in regulation of mailo land. In the end, the reforms do not get rid of tenure insecurities.

Land tenure reforms have prevalently been top-down (Mamdani 1986), with very selective and strategic participation of specific interest groups. Neoliberal agendas and trends have reshaped law and, to some extent, its role in society (Grewal and Purdy 2014). Law offers differentiated protection to people of varying classes. Neoliberal dynamics tend to 'support market imperatives and unequal economic power in the context of political contest' (*ibid.*). In Uganda, this has contributed to class formation around land property and access (Mamdani 1986). High on the neoliberal agenda are markets/capital and not necessarily social redistribution/equity, but the argument of reformers is that the promotion of capital in the long run leads to social equity (Mamdani 1986, Hont and Ignatieff 1983).

Law, therefore, becomes a very important tool for neoliberalism as long as it delimits the precincts of power and rights on land. The nature and extent of land rights to own or access are set out in the law, and so are the roles of all institutions of land administration, management and courts that enforce laws (Grewal and Purdy 2014). The question of what role law should play in land reform experimentation remains relevant (Manji 2006). Neoliberal market-oriented agendas on land are strengthened when inserted in laws, for they may be shielded from political interference or criticism (Leys 2001). This is more so where lawful processes of law making were adhered to. If passed as law, it may not matter that there is evidence that reforms such as those aimed at commodifying land may have far reaching negative consequences on communities, including dispossession of the poor (Manji 2006). Law becomes a useful tool for pushing neoliberal agendas as exemplified by the 'third wave' of land law reforms in East Africa. Joireman (2007) has argued that land law reforms have been aimed at promoting trade; they are market driven and the market has shaped their approaches. To Shivji, in Tanzania 'customary law has had very little presence except as a nuisance which ought to be modernized' (1998: 60). Law reform in the East African countries has therefore been about increased land registration and regulation of dual rights – statutory and customary (*ibid.*: 62, McAuslan 2013: 9–23).

Implications of the reforms are varied. Privatisation of land rights impacted on the rights of women for example; a few benefited from commodification while others lost out (Englert and Daley 2008). In Tanzania, in around 1996, the space for agitation for participation in land decision making was opened, leading to democratic arrangement, increased role in management of rural lands in village councils, security of tenure and equal rights for women (Shivji 1998, McAuslan 2013). In Uganda, the Land Act had similar agendas of reforming tenure for market imperatives while simultaneously targeting customary tenure to remove its perceived antithetical nature to development (McAuslan 2003: 1–2).

The evolution of mailo land tenure is shaped by a number of factors among which are cultural trajectories, social dynamics, political processes and economic structures. These create contradictions between the existing social norms and the principles of the law reforms shaped by neoliberal agendas. A close analysis of some of the reforms on mailo land shows that they have, however, had an effect of locking up land in multiple layers of conflicting claims that make it unattractive to 'the market' (i.e. commercial land transactions). To this end, de Soto's (2003) thesis on the formalisation of property as a tool towards economic development does not necessarily hold true for mailo land in Uganda. For example, a title holder might not be able to sell his/her land, because the tenant on it has occupancy rights recognised under the Land Act.

This chapter analyses some of the politics behind legal and policy framework reforms in the regulation of mailo land in Uganda at the national level, focusing mainly on the Land Act. Analysis of secondary sources and of the land law was compared with social realities on the ground, on which the author conducted interviews (thirty-four respondents) in Wakiso District in May and July 2015 among land tenants and members of the local government. The chapter highlights the drivers and justifications for the reforms and maps the contestations arisen at the local level, as a result of the new legal and policy framework.

These are used to show how the 'third wave' of land reforms re-shaped old and/or produced new patterns of contestations regarding mailo land and also reshaped relations of power over that land. As much as the reforms may have been officially intended to promote tenure security for the tenants on mailo land, they have, to some extent, had an effect of entrenching social inequality against the subaltern poor tenants – more so when they are ignored by the landlords – in a bid to sell land and benefit from its ever-increasing value. This raises an important question as to whether law reform per se can provide a solution to the inequality entrenched in the mailo land tenure system, which is embedded within the broader inequality issues and class divisions in Buganda.

Power centres and actors in the land law and policy reforms

Post-1986 land reforms in Uganda have evolved in response to global trends. During this period, IFIs aimed at privatisation and increased marketability of land (Joireman 2007). These institutions are therefore power centres, with regard to land law reforms. As big global lenders, a number of countries such as Uganda and Ghana had to heed the above market-oriented agenda, with others such as Tanzania engaging in pilot projects to formalise land rights (de Soto 2003).

Reincarnation of mailo land tenure or introduction of a new form?

Historical shape and nature of mailo land tenure

Revisiting of the mailo land tenure system in the historical sense conjures up a number of issues touching hierarchies of power among the British colonial government, the King of Buganda and his clan leaders, chiefs and subjects. The mailo land tenure system has its origin in the 1900 Buganda Agreement. In effect, notables, chiefs and significant individuals acquired private property rights to land. Incongruities arise from the fact that most of the distributed land was removed from the commons, whereby everyone had a right to access it from the supreme landlord (*sabataka*)/king who held it in their trust (Batungi 2008). Below the king's supreme title were the chiefs' landlords, directly under whom some people enjoyed rights to land in return for a meagre rent (*busuulu*) and property tax on harvests (*envujjo*). The distribution to the chiefs and others under the 1900 Agreement left the tenants susceptible to exploitation by the land-lords (Mafeje 1973). Eventually, inequality was entrenched in the structure of property and defended through the dual legal system, whereby the tenants' claims are customary while the landlords' titles confer statutory rights. This differential status builds on an implicit hierarchy, not least because customary rights are informal (not from written land title), while statutory rights are formal and defended by a written land title (Mamdani 2013). The relationship between a landlord with formal title and tenant without title subsisted in a customary/social setting less regulated by the state. This provided a fertile ground for powerful landlords to exploit the tenants with impunity. Removing land regulation from the private customary spaces into spaces of state control is among the tools of the state to extend its power centres and patronage. The dual system legiti-mises the process of land dispossession of the subaltern poor by the powerful elites (1962 Constitution of Uganda article 17 (c)). It does this by protecting the dispossessor as opposed to the dispossessed, further skewing social relationships (Okuku 2006) and legitimising the creation of classes: the landless and landlords.

Current legislative land law reforms in Uganda are premised on a desire to undo the 1975 Land Reform Decree which converted all land into public land, held by the Uganda Land Commission on behalf of the government, assisted by decentralised centres of power such as the District Land Boards. Leaseholds were preferred over all other tenure systems on the belief that they were amenable to productivity on land and therefore development (Mugambwa 2007: 44). Mailo land, according to the 1900 Buganda Agreement, bestowed perpetual ownership rights to land title holders. Titles for individuals were converted into contractual leaseholds of ninety-nine years (199 years for religious institutions). The state maintained an upper hand in removing land from those who did not meet the development conditions upon which leases were granted and granted new leases to those with potential to meet such conditions, which were often the rich and powerful. To some extent this evened out the micro-level inequality between former landlords and tenants; technically everyone's rights were ceded to the state.

Further there is an unspoken intention deducible from the circumstances that land needed to be removed from the poor that merely used it for subsistence or non-monetary ends. The Decree annihilated security of occupancy for customary tenants by reducing them to tenants at sufferance. To Mamdani, the agenda for some of the reforms in the Decree was to elevate the status of the state to 'landlord' and render the peasants as tenants of the state to further skew patterns of class and create room for patronage (Mamdani 1987). The powerful landlords of the pre-1975 era were put in a lesser position (they lost perpetual ownership and acquired periodic lease-holds) whereas the tenants on land suffered twice: they remained secondary and were susceptible to eviction if an investor wanted the land they occupied. The government would only pay compensation for developments on the land (Land Reform Decree 1975, Mugambwa 2007). The Decree was never implemented due to the political context of the time, characterised by dictatorships and also the high cost of its implementation (MISR & Land Tenure Centre 1989). It remained, however, the reigning law until initiation of land law reforms under the NRM government.

Entrenchment of neoliberal reforms

The early 1980s saw the promotion of new agricultural policies and land tenure reforms oriented towards economic development. This was during the first decade of neoliberalism in Uganda. To international consultants, the driving factors behind land law reform should be facilitation of agricultural modernisation geared towards economic development, not least to diminish Uganda's donor dependence (MISR/LTC 1989). The 1995 Constitution (chapter 15) provided a general framework for land reforms and basic principles that would guide the process. A pertinent question is: if constitutional and legal reforms were mainly driven by the argument of a need to promote agriculture, how effective or appropriate would they be to address other issues such as conflicting rights on land, tenure insecurity and eviction of subsistence agriculturalists by large-scale commercial agriculturalists?

The constitution did not address a number of the pertinent issues, leaving details such as the specific rights of the tenants on mailo land to parliament (Article 237(7)). The Constituency Assembly that drafted the Constitution failed to agree about such details (Bosworth 2003). Although the Land Act 1998 and its subsequent amendments try to deal with some detail, not all that needed to be addressed was addressed, leaving many grey areas on matters within the mailo land tenure system. For example, the co-ownership clause, which was advocated for by women, was left out for lack of consensus, but there was agreement on the consent clause – to the effect that women had a right to grant consent to transfers and sale of family property (Land Act s. 39). The ambivalence of the law creates room for political manoeuvre using conflicts on land (Kjær 2017).

Some scholarly arguments are to the effect that reforms have overly concentrated on tenure security as a way to address historical tenure problems (Bosworth 2003). This, to some extent, reduces the space for addressing current and future land-related issues, which are not necessarily connected to tenure security but are imbued in the social nature of relationships on mailo land. On the other hand, there is agreement across the scholarly divide that the reforms were driven by the desire for individualisation of land rights for land market promotion (convert land into property that can be transferred, mortgaged, etc.) and also preservation of the status quo on mailo land (Joireman 2007, Bosworth 2003). The timing of the reforms in the Land Act 1998 (during the second decade of neoliberalism) in which there is preoccupation with entrenching neoliberalism by for example making pro investment laws, may explain the reforms on (mailo) land which is a key factor for investment and production. Consequently, law is used as a tool to place the subaltern poor in the market (and all its vagaries), without providing sufficient protection for them, leaving them susceptible to exploitation. This is through a number of reforms on mailo land as detailed below.

Streamlining the relationship between tenants and landlords

The dual-carriage rights on mailo land presents a challenge, particularly against a backdrop that sees land law regulation as part of the realm of property law. Property law is about regulating the relationship between people based on their respective differential control over a thing (property). This goes beyond merely regulating the relationship between an individual and the thing (property) (Cohen 1927, Gray and Gray 1998). Property owners have the power to determine who accesses their property, and the terms on which they do. Under mailo land tenure, landlords whose land is occupied by tenants have had their power vitiated as a result of law reforms

empowering the tenants (Land Act 1998 s. 31). With the colliding
rights of landlords and tenants, landlords resort to power to diminish
the rights of tenants. Efforts to reassert power on the part of the
landlords led to increased evictions of tenants, hence the need to
streamline their relationships with the tenants. The term 'streamline'
points to the modernisation and update of those (cordial) relationships. This is happening in a neoliberal context of less government
involvement and more market orientation in the land sector. The
Constitution of Uganda article 237 (3) reinstates land tenures (freehold, customary and mailo) that were abolished by Idi Amin in
1975. Together, with leasehold, the four are the recognised tenures
in Uganda. The gaps left by the Constitution are filled by the Land
Act, under which mailo land holders enjoy freehold-type rights, as
set out in the Act (section 3 (2)), with perpetual claims to the land
subject to some restrictions/limitations stipulated by law (section 3
(4) (a) and (c), and section 3 (2)). The Act endorses the historical
position of dual rights on mailo land. Among the limitations is that
the enjoyment of ownership rights is subject to the statutory rights of
lawful or bona fide occupants (tenants) on the land and their successors in title (section 3 (4) (c)). The landlord owns the land and not
the developments on it made by the occupants (Land Act 1998 s.
3(4) (b)). The landlord can only fully control land if there are no
occupants/tenants.

The law reforms delimit the category of 'tenants' by definition
under section 29. Lawful occupants include historical tenants that
claimed their tenancies under the Busuulu and Envujjo Law of 1928,
Toro and Ankole landlord and tenant laws of 1937, persons occu-
pying land with the consent of the registered owners and purchasers.
Bonafide occupants include persons who occupied and used land
without any challenge by the owner or his/her agent for twelve years
or more before the passing of the Constitution in 1995. Recognition
of the tenants changes the power dynamic for the owner to control
the land, since the lawful and bona fide occupant is guaranteed security of occupancy (section 31(1)) and can pass his/her interest to
another person that inherits all the privileges of the tenant. Courts
of law have upheld this position.[2]

It has been argued that mailo land has always been *monarchised*
in the sense that regulation of mailo is an attempt to regulate the
Buganda monarchy (Batungi 2008). It would not be accidental that
the recognition and protection of tenants' right to pass on their
title to land to some extent decongests the power in the historical
high social class of landlords (and their successors in title) with an

inextricable linkage to the monarchy. Ultimately, the monarchy's control over land is reduced. Regulating such issues by market to some extent reduces possibilities of exertion of (monarchical) and political power on land matters (Cohen 1927: 10).

Law as a tool of social change: symbolic busulu (ground rent)

Tenants on mailo land only pay a nominal non-commercial ground rent to the landlord in return for utilising the land (Land Act section 31(3) and Land (Amendment) Act 2004 section 14(3c)). The District Land Board has mandate to set the annual nominal ground rent (*ibid.* and 31 (3a)). This role is subjected to political supervision of the minister. Rent set by the Board has to be approved by the minister, to ensure that it is affordable for the poor (*ibid.*). In essence, the law allows that executive power is evoked to interfere in matters concerning nominal ground rent, which can be effectively handled by the board in accordance with the rule of law.

The rent is non-commercial, which means it is subsidised/not for profit. In 2012, for example, the lands minister set the annual rent for land within the city at UGX 50,000, and UGX 5,000 for rural areas (both were less than $20) (New Vision 2012). For the city, this is not at all comparable to the market rate rent which is normally of five to six digits monthly (above $300). The non-commercial rent is only a symbolic gesture of appreciation to the landlord for letting the tenants occupy and use his/her land. It is not determined in accordance with competitive market rates. The rent is not uniform; it is fixed in accordance with a number of factors including the location of land and its size (*ibid.*). This stipulation removes regulation of the landlord–tenant relationship from the market forces which would determine a competitive market rate. The exclusion of the market logic and other provisions excluding eviction, except for non-payment of rent and upon court order, shifts the pendulum more in favour of the tenant (Land (Amendment) Act 2010 section 32A). Even where there is default in payment of rent, the landlord is obliged to give the tenant notice to give reasons why the tenancy should not be terminated for non-payment, and termination can only take place where rent is outstanding for a period exceeding one year (Land (Amendment) Act 2004 section 31(6), *ibid.* section 1(b)). By reducing the circumstances under which the landlord can evict the tenants, the landlord's power is reduced in favour of the tenant.

There is no economic reward for the government from the above, but it carries strong political statements in favour of protecting a majority poor (with the votes) that keeps government in power. Issues on mailo land tenure have been used by the National Resistance Movement (NRM) government for political reasons (Hunt 2004: 176, McAuslan 2003). It is a game of votes in exchange for protection on mailo land. Yet field findings have revealed that protection might only be nominal, as some of the reforms have very limited application in practice. For example, nominal ground rent is not attractive to the landlords. In Wakiso and other parts of the country, landlords defy the law and sell the land to powerful individuals with capacity to evict the tenants with impunity. Within an environment of limited knowledge about the protections of the law and, limited ability to enforce the legal provisions, tenants remain at risk (Nakayi 2015).

Option for landlord to sell the land to the tenant and vice versa or land sharing

Neoliberalism promotes pro-market policies and reforms and sees the state as the enabler of competitive market dynamics (Harrison 2005). The 'third wave' of land law reforms have not aimed at transforming social relations through rebalancing land property structures, but rather supported the notion that land markets and 'willing-buyer willing-seller' logics would suffice to address the land question (Musembi 2007). Some reforms on mailo land that are embedded in the Land (Amendment) Act 2010 are to some extent contradictory to the above. A landlord who wishes to sell land must give the first option to purchase to the tenant and if the tenant wishes to assign his/her tenancy, must give the first option to the landlord (section 35 (1) and (2) respectively). This is no matter whether each of them will offer the other a competitive market price.

Our findings show that the landlords have better leverage to buy out the tenant than the tenant to buy out the landlord. This implies hierarchy in power to condition terms of the sale in favour of the landlord. In some cases, the landlords coerced the tenants to sell their interests to the landlord (*ibid.*). This is possible due to the skewed economic patterns between the landlord and the tenant. Most times, when the landlords want to sell, they do not offer to sell to the tenant, but to other people who are in a position to pay competitive market prices (*ibid.*). A landlord who violates the legal requirement to sell to the tenant and sells to someone else commits no offence, although the purchaser takes the land subject to the existing rights of tenants (*ibid.* section 35 (8)). The law sets a harsher criminal penalty for the tenant who violates it: a fine or imprisonment for four years and the invalidation of the transaction (Land (Amendment) Act 2010 section 35 (1a)).

Neoliberal traits are also identified in reforms in the Land Act, which makes provision for mutual agreements between the landlord and the tenant to either subdivide the land and hold one piece each as exclusive owner, or hold it jointly with clear percentages for each (*ibid.* section 36 (1) and (2)). By this, a tenant can acquire a certificate of title to land, which, in neoliberal terms, is a better title than an unregistered interest (de Soto 2003). The certificate, besides being a good status symbol of ownership, creates confidence in the purchasers of land on the market.

Our findings from Wakiso revealed that, although the law envisages negotiations in such situations of mutual agreements, poverty, lack of information on the part of tenants and skewed power patterns between tenants and landlords inhibit equal bargaining power. Some tenants mentioned that their landlords asked them to either buy their interests in the land at market value or share it with the landlord. The complaints made by the tenants included: landlords taking bigger chunks and leaving the tenants with smaller portions of the land; landlords taking the most fertile land leaving the tenants with less productive land; landlords not compensating the tenants for loss of crops and other developments on land; landlords hiring personal surveyors who did inaccurate surveys hence cheating the tenants; also, selective enforcement of the law, whereby pro-poor provisions are not enforced.

The Land Act provides for a land fund which the government can use to facilitate getting rid of dual rights on land (section 41 (4)(a), (5)(a)–(c)). It is noted elsewhere that the 'third wave' of land reforms is averse to redistribution (Kennedy 2003). For Uganda, the land fund may promote redistribution: the government can utilise it to purchase/pay off landlords and issue titles to tenants. All respondents in Wakiso and Kampala did not benefit from the land fund, to acquire title. Local media has recently carried stories alleging selective application of the fund to benefit the elites and politically connected individuals (Bukedde 2017).

Role of courts

Uganda's constitutional and legal frameworks stipulate a robust structure of courts to deal with land disputes and other institutions for land management (Constitution articles 129–41). Under Article 50 of the Constitution, courts of law have powers to protect people's rights from violation. It further establishes bodies to assist in land matters: the

Uganda Land Commission (article 238), district land boards (article 240) and the defunct land tribunals (article 243).[3] Other institutions include local council courts, magistrates' courts and land committees (Land (Amendment) Act 2010 section 64). Establishment of the robust institutional framework on the ground has been hampered by lack of funds, leaving people to go to defunct but accessible and available institutions (Deininger and Castagnini 2006).

The institution one can access for justice is determined by a number of factors, including one's ability to afford the expenses that come with it. Fieldwork revealed that the tenants are financially constrained and most can only access local council courts, whereas the landlords undermine these courts and therefore bypass them for better options such as magistrates' courts and the High Courts, which offer enforceable decisions. The poor are conscripted for lesser quality of outcomes from these institutions, which are, at times, influenced by corruption. Just like it is stated in the literature, vulnerable groups such as women face double jeopardy as a result of poverty and vulnerability in such lower institutions of justice (Khadiagala 2001, Nakayi 2015). It is argued that there is more competition rather than cooperation among institutions, which means that those that start in the lower institutions are clouded out of those that are higher (Mwangi 2010).

On the other hand, neoliberal Uganda has embraced international human rights frameworks and standards intended to promote justice and fairness through properly constituted democratic institutions such as courts of law. On-the-ground realities, however, reveal that in some instances justice and fairness is not an automatic outcome of courts for the subaltern poor.[4] There are also instances where political expedience has led to exercise of presidential discretion to create parallel institutions such as the state house land desk/unit, and also the once popular 'committee on illegal land evictions' chaired by Hon. Elios Nantaba (New Vision 2013). These, to some extent, have undermined decisions of judicial institutions (Daily Monitor 2012). In the same vein, community popular dissent through courts of law against large-scale land acquisitions supported by government is hampered by the government's indirect control of judicial power (Martiniello 2015).

Conclusion

Although seemingly inclusive, the neoliberal land tenure reforms driven and controlled by the government and development partners have mainly benefited elites and the ruling class. The Land Act makes an effort to take care of the social significance of mailo land tenure by protecting/securing tenure for the tenants in return for nominal rent. In a way, this is a response to a call to make reforms that 'transcend economic reasoning and prescription', by introducing a social dimension (Okuku 2006). That notwithstanding, within the wider context of individualisation and formalisation of title to land, the socially driven protections for the tenants which promote continued dual rights are oftentimes defeated by demands for exclusive rights by landlords. The 'third wave' of land law reforms on mailo land has, in the above context, reshaped old patterns of conflict over land and reproduced new ones, mainly with a political and power dimension which disregards tenants' rights and is sanctioned and promoted by evoking connections to power or exerting it from land-lordism. The wider contextual situation of power play limits the available options for the subaltern poor to defend their rights against the powerful who are locally and/or at times internationally connected, thereby entrenching the existing cleavages of division among the rich and the poor in relation to land.

Notes

1   Which has a number of amendments, such as of 2004, 2007 and 2010.

2   *Kyepaka Francis & Another vs. Rwakarongo & others*, Land Division Civil Suit No. 289/ 2007.

3   *Sarah Nakku vs. Commissioner for Land Registration*, HCCA No. 064/2010.

4   *Hon. Michael Ocula and others vs. Amuru Sugar Works Ltd and others*, HCT No. 126/2008.

References

Batungi, N. (2008), *Land Reform in Uganda: Towards a Harmonised Tenure System* (Kampala: Fountain).

Bosworth, J. (2003), 'Integrating land issues into the broader development agenda: Uganda', in P. Groppo (ed.), *Land Reform: Land Settlement and Cooperatives*, 2003 (3), Special Edition, FAO Corporate Document Repository, Economic and Social Development, pp. 233–48.

Bukedde. (2017), 'Abanene baguzizza gavumment ettaka [Prominent people have sold land to government]', 10 January.

Cohen, M. R. (1927), 'Property and sovereignty', *Cornell Law Review*, 13(1), pp. 8–30.

Daily Monitor. (2012), 'State House, police accused of land grabbing tendencies', 6 May.

de Soto, H. (2003), *The Mystery of Capital: Why Capitalism Triumphs in the West and Fails Everywhere Else* (New York, NY: Basic Books).

Deininger, K. and Castagnini, R. (2006), 'Incidence and impact of land conflicts in Uganda', *Journal of Economic Behavior and Organization*, 60(3), pp. 321–45.

Englert, B. and Daley, E. (eds) (2008), *Women's Land Rights and Privatisation in East Africa* (New York, NY: Boydell and Brever).

Gray, K. and Gray, S. F. (1998), 'The idea of property in land', in S. Bright and J. Dewar (eds), *Land Law: Themes and Perspectives* (Oxford: Oxford University Press), pp. 15–41.

Grewal, S. D. and Purdy, J. (2014), 'Introduction: Law and neoliberalism', *Law and Contemporary Problems*, 77(1), pp. 1–23.

Hapwood, J. (2015), 'Women's land claims in the Acholi region of northern Uganda: What can be learned from what is contested', *International Journal on Minority and Group Rights*, 22(3), pp. 387–409.

Harrison, G. (2005), 'Economic faith, social project, and a misreading of African society: The travails of neoliberalism in Africa', *Third World Quarterly*, 26(8), pp. 1303–20.

Hont, I. and Ignatieff, M. (1983), 'Needs and justice in The Wealth of Nations', in I. Hont and M. Ignatieff (eds), *Wealth and Virtue: The Shaping of Political Economy in the Scottish Enlightenment* (Cambridge: Cambridge University Press), pp. 133–44.

Hunt, D. (2004), 'Unintended consequences of land rights reform: The case of the 1998 Uganda Land Act', *Development Policy Review*, 22(2), pp. 173–91.

Joireman, S. (2007), 'Enforcing new property rights in sub-Saharan Africa: The Ugandan Constitution and the 1998 Land Act', *Comparative Politics*, 39(4), pp. 463–80.

Kennedy, D. (2003), 'Laws and developments', in J. Hatchard and P.-K. Amanda (eds), *Law and Development: Facing Complexity in the 21st Century* (London: Cavendish), pp. 9–17.

Khadiagala, L. S. (2001), 'The failure of popular justice in Uganda: Local councils and women's property rights', *Development and Change*, 32(1), pp. 54–76.

Kjær, A. M. (2017), 'Land governance as grey zone: The political incentives of land reform implementation in Africa', *Commonwealth & Comparative Politics*, 55(4), pp. 426–443.

Land Reform Decree (1975) (Laws of Uganda).

Lastarria-Cornhiel, S. (2003), 'Uganda country brief: Property rights and land markets', Land Tenure Centre, Available at: www.nelson.wisc.edu/ltc/docs/ ugandabrief.pdf [accessed 13 February 2017].

Leys, C. (2001), *Market-driven Politics: Neoliberal Democracy and the Public Interest* (London: Verso).

Mafeje, A. (1973), 'Agrarian revolution and the land question in Buganda', ISS Occasional Papers No. 32, The Hague.

Mamdani, M. (1986), 'Contradictory class perspectives on the question of democracy (the case of Uganda)', *Eastern Africa Social Science Research Review*, 2(1).

Mamdani, M. (1987), 'Extreme but not exceptional: Towards and analysis of the agrarian question in Uganda', *The Journal of Peasant Studies*, 14(2), pp. 191–225.

Mamdani, M. (2013), 'The contemporary Ugandan discourse on customary tenure: Some theoretical considerations', MISR Working Paper No. 13, Kampala.

Manji, A. (2006), *The Politics of Land Reform in Africa: From Communal Tenure to Free Markets* (London: Zed).

Manji, A, (2014), 'The politics of land reform in Kenya 2012',

African Studies Review, 57(1), pp. 115–30.

Martiniello, G. (2015), 'Social struggles in Uganda's Acholiland: Understanding responses and resistance to Amuru Sugar Works', *The Journal of Peasant Studies*, 42(3–4), pp. 653–69.

Marx, K. (1977), *A Contribution to the Critique of Political Economy* (Moscow: Progress).

McAuslan, P. (2003), 'As good as it gets: Politics and markets in the making of Uganda's Land Act, 1998', in P. McAuslan (ed.), *Bringing the Law Back In: Essays in Land, Law and Development* (Farnham: Ashgate), pp. 275–309.

McAuslan, P. (2013), *Land Law Reform in Eastern Africa: Traditional or Transformative?* (London: Routledge).

Meinert, L. and Kjaer, A. M. (2016), 'Land belongs to the people of Uganda: Politicians' use of land issues in the 2016 election campaigns', *Journal of East African Studies*, 10(4), pp. 769–88.

MISR and LTC, University of Wisconsin. (1989), *Land Tenure and Agricultural Development in Uganda* (Madison, WI: University of Wisconsin).

Mugambwa, J. A. (2007), 'Comparative analysis of land tenure law reform in Uganda and Papua New Guinea', *Journal of South Specific Law*, 11(1), pp. 39–55.

Musembi, N. (2007), 'De Soto and the land relations in rural Africa: Breathing life into dead theories about property rights', *Third World Quarterly*, 28(8), pp. 1457–78.

Mwangi, E. (2010), 'Bumbling bureaucrats, sluggish courts and forum-shopping elites: Unending conflict and competition in the transition to private property', *European Journal of Development Research*, 22, pp. 715–32.

Nakayi, R. (2015), 'The perceived protection of tenants on registered land against evictions: An assessment of the legal challenges faced by victims of land evictions in Kampala and Wakiso District', PILAC Working Paper No. 4.

New Vision. (2012), 'Government sets ground rent amid mixed reactions', *New Vision*, 12 June.

New Vision. (2013), 'Nantaba land committee awaits new mandate', *New Vision*, 21 October.

Okuku, J. A. (2006), 'The Land Act (1998) and land tenure reform in Uganda', *Africa Development*, 31(1), pp. 1–26.

Shivji, I .G. (1998), 'Contradictory perspectives on rights and justice in the context of land tenure reform in Tanzania', *Tanzania Zanami*, 4(1), pp. 57–96.

Part IV

Race, culture and commoditisation

15
African Asians and South Asians in neoliberal Uganda: culture, history and political economy

Anneeth Kaur Hundle

Introduction

This chapter explores the re-emerging role of 'Asian' presence and capital under neoliberal economic conditions in the post-1986 Museveni-led National Resistance Movement (NRM)-era in Uganda. Attention to 'processes of capitalist restructuring and change in Uganda' must be analysed in relation to the racialised Asian minority and both old and emerging forms of Asian capital in Uganda. Indeed, the ongoing 'neoliberalisation' of the urban Ugandan economy, society and culture presents new opportunities for 'racialised class formation' and social inequality today. In the following pages, I examine African Asian and South Asian sources of capital, labour and accumulation in the urban economy, noting that 'Asian' is a homogeneous category of ethno-racialisation that masks an extremely heterogeneous population marked by divisions in class, community and migration histories, ethnicity, language, religion and caste. Here, it is important to note that 'Asian' was an ethno-racial category developed and mobilised by the British colonial administration to govern individuals from pre-Partition British India in East Africa. Thus, it is an important category of analysis and practice that continues to be mobilised by individuals who can also refer to themselves as 'East African Asians'. I use 'South Asian' to refer to more recent migrations of Indians and Pakistanis from contemporary South Asia. In general, I use 'Asian' to refer to the colonial political economy, and 'South Asian' to refer to the contemporary political economy of neoliberal Uganda.

In order to examine the role of African Asian and South Asian labour and capital in the contemporary neoliberal economy, I focus on the effects of the 1972 Asian expulsion on Uganda's national economy, and then shift to the late 1980s and early 1990s return migration of 'ex-Ugandan Asians' from exile and diasporic locations in the West to address their repossession of private property

and businesses in the country. I will also examine the liberalisation of Ugandan national borders in a post-Africanisation context,
exploring the role of recent transnational South Asian migration
to Uganda (from the early 2000s onwards), and in particular the
relationship between the contemporary Indian state and new South
Asian migrants in East Africa. Since the late 1990s, the Museveni-
led Ugandan government and complementary statecraft have been
engaged in a neoliberal project of creating an ethno-racialised 'foreign
investor' urban class and community of post-expulsion 'Asians' in
Uganda. This foreign investor 'business community' is the normative and hegemonic model of Asian presence in the country and
in the context of post-expulsion indigenous nativism. The foreign
investor/business community model helps to maintain and legitimise
'Asian' presence in the nation via both inclusionary and exclusionary
logics of economic citizenship. In doing so, it conflates communities
carrying complex migration histories, class divisions and regional
differences; it also often invisibilises the gendered aspects of African
Asian and South Asian productive labour (the work of women in the
domestic and informal economy) in the nation.

In essence, I argue that an approach to Ugandan political economy
that highlights urban neoliberal processes expands the scope of studying 'Asian' capital and labour exclusively. Rather, contextualising
African Asian and South Asian presence, capital and labour in an
era of neoliberal economic globalisation lends itself to new questions
about governance, citizenship, subjectivity and the reproduction,
maintenance and legitimacy of racialised economic inequality by
the state and elite interests and classes. Indeed, while colonial-era
racial and class hierarchies continue to reproduce themselves in
Kampala, racial and class analysis must be concerned with the political dynamics of neoliberal governance and management on a global
scale, thus compelling us to ask new questions about governance,
citizenship, subjectivity, inclusion and ethno-racial difference in an
era of accelerated transnational capitalism.

The information I offer here is based on secondary sources,
general estimates, informal observations, interviews and ethnographic research carried out roughly from 2008 to 2015 – these are
all anthropological approaches that are limited in their ability to
provide precise community-based or population-wide data. There is
an urgent need for more in-depth empirical data collection on African
Asian and South Asian communities – including both formal migration and informal migration processes, the scope of their trading and
labour activities, the extent to which migrants of different classes are

able to appropriate other migrant and indigenous African labour and accumulate capital, and the role of remittances. Emerging scholarly attention to the dynamics of 'South–South' migration, as well as new funding initiatives on the role of transnational capital and migration in East Africa may help to increase interest among researchers on these issues.

It is also important to note that the study of Asian labour, capital and accumulation processes in the colonial-era economy is easier, and yields much richer data, because of the role of the colonial state in record-keeping and the researcher's easier access to archival material in the Uganda National Archives and in the UK. Studying the South Asian political economy in the post-colonial context is more challenging because of the important role of the informal economy in periods of post-independence political and economic instability; and second, because of the multiple sources of capital and processes of capitalist accumulation in a complex transnational global economy. Finally, it is important to note that the 1972 expulsion of Ugandan Asians and its aftermath continues to produce an environment of racialised insecurity and political repression for East African Asians and South Asians in the country (Hundle 2013a, 2013b). Thus, many East African Asians and South Asian migrants have real or imagined fears about anti-Asian sentiments from the indigenous urban population. They can also be suspicious and nervous around researchers, particularly if they were complicit in illicit economic activities after the expulsion, or are unauthorised/informal migrants in Uganda today (see more on this in Hundle 2013b).

Mapping community and migration: periodising South Asian presence and capital

In mapping the shifting and transforming role of South Asian capital and labour in Uganda, periodising South Asian presence in the region across three key temporal frames is important: (1) in the era of British empire, the creation and colonisation of the Uganda Protectorate and the role of Indians in the British metropolitan economy of capitalist accumulation, (2) the decolonisation, Africanisation and nation-building period which led to the expulsion of Ugandan Asians from the independent Ugandan nation and (3) the post-1990s era of neoliberal globalisation, foreign direct investment (FDI) from India, and the role of transnational South Asian migration and capital in the nation (much of the data that I possess is based on the experiences of Indian nationals; more research is needed to determine the role of Pakistani migrants in Uganda). What is important to note here is that historically, 'Asians' played a significant role in British capitalist accumulation in the context of imperialism, as well as the 'underdevelopment of the Ugandan economy' (Mamdani 1976: 71). Mamdani explains,

> the eventual dominance of Indian over African commerce represented a qualitative change in the very nature of both trade and production in Uganda, a change from internal trade that linked domestic production to an externally oriented export– import trade that gradually divorced the two ... from the outset, the thrust of the colonial policy was to keep Africans in the agricultural economy and out of the marketplace – thus keeping them away from activities (such as commerce) that would give them the skill, the vision and the opportunity to organize the colonial masses – while allocating the trading function, through administrative encouragement, to an alien community that could easily be segregated from the mass of the colonized and thus rendered politically safe. The petty bourgeoisie in the colony had for political reasons to be an ethnically alien petty bourgeoisie. (*ibid.*: 65–71)

Of course, the interests of more autonomous Indian commercial manufacturers, traders and firms often competed and conflicted with the imperatives of British capitalist accumulation at certain moments in colonial history. Nonetheless, British metropolitan and Indian capital were both critical in the constitution of the 'commer- cial' and 'petty' Indian bourgeoisie (a comprador colonial class) and the making of the colonial economy (*ibid.*).

In the decolonisation period, post-colonial African leaders attempted to rectify racialised economic inequality through projects of national, economic and social 'Africanisation' or 'indigenisation'. Indeed, the socialist 'Move to the Left' policies of Milton Obote (1969–1970) and the eventual expulsion of Asians from the country in 1972, led to an objective and empirically documented economic crisis in the nation (Mamdani 1976). In addition to what Mamdani (1996) has called the 'de-racialization of civil society', in the post- independence period, Ugandan leaders often sought to 'de-link' from British capitalist interests, or the 'neocolonial economy'. The post-independence governance regimes of Milton Obote, Idi Amin and Yoweri Museveni are all instructive here (Barongo 1984,

Museveni 1997). By the late 1980s, the national economy was co-opted by international capital or left with little alternatives to global capitalist norms. Finally, the restructuring of African nations' economies in the 1980s and 1990s according to hegemonic international economic norms resulted in Uganda's more aggressive shift to both global financing, donor aid/debt relations and to the liberalisation of borders and tariffs – all alongside the embrace of global capital investment from a range of sources (Collier and Reinikka 2001). It is here, in the early 2000s that Indian capital (some from British Ugandan Asian sources) has become relevant to the Ugandan economy once again. Indeed, the story of 'Asian' capital in Uganda, told from the vantage-point of an older generation of British Asian and Ugandan Asian businessmen and entrepreneurs, cross-cuts their experiences of engaging with imperial British metropolitan markets, informal and illicit economies during periods of national economic decline, and more recent neoliberal global markets.

How might we understand this periodisation of Asian capital in terms of South Asian presence on the ground in Uganda? In terms of demographics, the Ugandan Asian population reached its zenith during the late colonial and independence era. In 1969, Uganda's Asian population was at about 75,000 (Read 1975). By the time of the expulsion decree in late 1972, estimates from a range of sources suggest that about 55,000 Ugandan Asians made their way out of the country (Hundle 2013a). In terms of population distribution, Ugandan Asians constituted 1 per cent of the population (a total population of 8 million in 1972), but disproportionately dominated 67 per cent of the *urban* economy (everything except the peasant economy; including trade, industry, agricultural processing; as well as the service economy including the civil service, artisans and professionals) (Jamal forthcoming).

A small population of about 500 Ugandan Asian men, traders and civil servants continued to remain in Uganda post 1972 during the Amin regime, crafting spaces of inclusion for themselves in the 'de-racialised' environment (Hundle 2013a). Milton Obote's coup in 1982 marked the first return of major Ugandan Asian businessmen (family firms such as the Madhvani's Kakira Sugar and Mehta's Lugazi Sugar). The years 1993–1995 marked another important moment as Ugandan Asians, who had resettled in the UK, Canada and the US, were invited by President Museveni of the NRA/M to return to Uganda to repossess properties (see more below).

In Uganda today (2015), the population of new South Asians – post-colonial Indian and Pakistani nationals – are estimated at between 25,000 to 30,000 individuals (no official census has been taken, but these are preliminary estimates based on personal communication with representatives at the Indian Association of Uganda). In addition, about 2,000 original Ugandan Asians (second-, third-, fourth-generation Ugandan Asian families who were or are descended from British subjects of the Uganda Protectorate) returned and have re-settled in Uganda (Jamal forthcoming). These Ugandan Asian returnee individuals and families are rather elite, mobile and transnational citizens (i.e. they possess a variety of citizenship statuses, in some cases dual citizenship with the United Kingdom. This is an outcome of their expulsion and refugee resettlement in countries such as the UK and Canada in the 1970s). This flexibility in their formal citizenship statuses allows them to conduct business in Uganda but also live outside the country for parts of the year.

Significantly, newer South Asian migrants in Uganda are a much more transient and precarious population that do not necessarily have historical ties to East Africa. While many have become long-term residents in Uganda, very few have taken on Ugandan citizenship because most seek to emigrate to other Western destinations such as Europe, the US and Canada. Among new migrants, the majority are Indian nationals (often referred to as 'NRI', or Non-Resident Indian by the Indian state and embassies), with fewer numbers of Pakistanis, Bangladeshis and Sri Lankans (see Hundle 2013b for a list of communities by nationality, ethnicity and religion). Most migrants arrive on visitor visas and travel as individual, unmarried single men. If they decide to settle in Uganda for a longer time, migrants will formalise their visa status and return to their homes in South Asia for marriage, applying for a spousal visa for their wives (in some cases, partners and kin are informal and migrants might remain with overstayed visas). Significantly, new generations of South Asian-origin children are being born, raised and educated in Uganda as migrants attain upward social and class mobility to join the new South Asian urban bourgeoisie.

With Uganda's total population having jumped to almost 38 million (based on statistics from 2013), South Asians (in general) constitute less than 0.0001 per cent of the total population. Nonetheless, given the colonial and political formation of the urban–rural divide in the nation (Mamdani 1996), and the concentration of African Asians and South Asians in urban areas and their role in the urban economy, it is important to understand the dynamics of newer South Asian communities in Uganda after the expulsion. As I discuss more below, they have a visible, ethno-racialised presence in urban areas, they provide insight into how the Ugandan state manages and racialises minority communities; and they inform both the elite and underclass in a new era of racialised economic inequality and neoliberal economic globalisation.

The significance of historical political economy on the 'Asian question' in Uganda

In Uganda studies, Africanisation and the 1972 Asian expulsion compelled the East African intelligentsia to produce extensive scholarship on the role of 'Asians' in Ugandan society. One trajectory of this scholarship tended to use historical Marxist analysis to undercut analyses of the Asian expulsion as an unexpected and aberrant 'event'. This was also a reactive stance to tropes of the exceptional, erratic and primitive violence of Idi Amin (Peterson and Taylor 2013). Scholarship by Mahmood Mamdani (1975, 1976) and Issa Shivji (1976), for example, understood colonial class formation among 'indigenous' and 'alien' groups, as well as the larger underdevelopment of the colony, as the cause of African and Asian racial tensions in decolonising East Africa. Indeed, in *The Politics of Class Formation in Uganda* (1976), the focus of Mamdani's scholarship was historical *process and structure*, not the event of the expulsion itself, which was more or less understood as an outcome or consequence of nativist populism and the visibility of the Indian petty bourgeoisie, class mobility, wealth accumulation and consumption that characterised Kampala and other urban areas of Uganda from the 1950s to the 1970s. In a non-settler colony, Indians were the dominant and visible 'territorially based class' and thus, scholars stressed that what seemed to be a racial or ethnic problem was, in fact, class. In East Africa, Uganda was exceptional in the sense that race and class had coincided to produce the need for a resolution to the Asian question in postcolonial Uganda. The resolution would begin in the 1960s through the 'Move to the Left' policies aimed at the Indian capitalist class (both the commercial and the petty Indian bourgeoisie) by President Obote; it would culminate in Amin's Immigration (Amendment) Decree on 5 October 1972, which resulted in the expulsion of Uganda's Asian population within a three-month time frame.

In the realm of formal economic analysis, one should note that the expulsion of Ugandan Asian skilled professionals and the trading classes led to economic crisis and further political and social violence in Uganda (Hansen and Twaddle 1988, 1991). Yet it is also true that most analysts have marginalised and neglected the economic activities of urban indigenous African traders, entrepreneurs and businessmen in the years both before and after the expulsion. They have also largely ignored the production of other forms of value and capitalist accumulation in the informal economy via mercantile trade, as well as the production of value in the domestic sphere and through indigenous subsistence farming practices of Ugandans in both rural and urban areas (for new information on the informal coffee trading business and other arenas of *magendo* see Asiimwe 2013, Hundle 2013a). Because of the biases of formal economic analysis, and the excision of subsistence agriculture and the informal economy, the contemporary state and popular economic discourses continue to construct 'Asians' as model economic entrepreneurs, businessmen and 'drivers' for the national economy (therefore often casting them as politically ineffective citizens). On the other hand, and particularly in the context of the FDI regime of economic investment, indigenous Africans' capacity for contributing to national development is consistently devalued and marginalised. Significantly, these processes reproduce colonial ethno-racial ideologies and urban ideologies of 'hardworking' Asians and 'lazy' Africans: colonial racial projects that were utilised to import Indians as indentured labourers in East Africa when colonial administrators failed to capture the labour of the African peasantry in capitalist accumulation processes.

Thus, while the earlier generation of scholars argued that the 'racial consciousness' of Indians and Africans was a reflection of deeper class divisions ('racial consciousness' was a 'superstructure' or a 'false consciousness' in a Marxist sense), the classical historical political-economic analysis did not account for the ways in which material and ideological/symbolic relations constituted each other, or the ways in which formations of class and race, ethnicity, gender, culture and caste intersected to establish social practices and meanings in urban areas – including the social production of *both* ethno-racial and class hierarchies in contemporary Uganda. Indeed, the earlier scholarship bordered on a Marxist functionalism that studied urban Indians *only* through the logic of capitalist accumulation, avoiding the ways in which human activities, ideologies and processes give social structures their reality. This critical take on classical class formation, one that I have begun to shift through the analytic of 'racialised class formation', informs this study of 'neoliberal Uganda'.

The Ugandan state and the post-expulsion South Asian landscape: family firms, mercantile networks and corporate capital

The 1972 expulsion of the Ugandan Asian population resulted in the displacement of the Indian commercial and petty trading classes as well as several elite family firms that had dominated the commercial, industrial and plantation sectors of the economy in Uganda. Popular and scholarly narratives of Ugandan Asians' *return* to the country tend to begin in the Museveni-era, or post-1986 Uganda. Yet, it is important to note that a small group of about 500 Ugandan Asians and other long-term residents were able to remain in the country, allying themselves with the Amin regime (Hundle 2013a). Mostly engaged in trade or working under government contracts, some would emerge as important business entrepreneurs who were able to negotiate space within various regimes. They took advantage of trading monopolies and the *magendo* (illicit or informal) economy that proliferated in Amin's regime to create individual wealth (Hundle 2013a). These 'tycoons' did not necessarily come from prominent industrial families; some were not even descended from historical Ugandan Asian families but newer trader-migrants from India. Thus, entrepreneurs who gained wealth from the Amin era are perceived as 'new money' business families in Kampala. Discussions about wealth earned through ill-gotten ways are rampant in Kampala; they are also subject to a range of moral and ethical interpretations about the possibilities and limits of 'staying on' after the expulsion. Indeed, these discussions reflect contemporary popular discussions of moral decline that occurred among Indian and African businessmen in the 1970s; they also help to explain the 'architecture of silence' surrounding business and entrepreneurship among Asians and Africans associated with the Amin regime in the 1970s (Hundle 2013a).

Certainly, most entrepreneurs, whether African or Indian, took advantage of the informal economy and engaged in some form of profiteering through government contracts in the Amin era. As Mamdani observes, 'it is surely an irony of the post-1972 period that it created a multi-racial group of African and Asian capitalists in Uganda' (1993: 272). The transition to NRM governance has allowed wealthy Indian businessmen who prospered during the 1970s to re-invent themselves in the context of the trappings of a more normative, liberal, political moral order. Today's Indian 'tycoons' are community, business and industry leaders; at times they are even solicited for political advisorship roles. All of them have close ties to President Museveni and the NRM leadership. Because of their formal political exclusion and reliance on clientelist relations with African leaders across several regimes, new money Indian tycoons exemplify the political culture that flourished under precarious political regimes (studying patronage practices between South Asians and the state in the context of post-expulsion political insecurity is very difficult; this information is based on long-term relationships and informal conversations).

While 'new money' businessmen and entrepreneurs are critical to understanding the transition to NRM governance, so are 'old money' family firms. My use of 'family firms' here refers to the traditional model of Indian business enterprise that emerged in colonial East Africa and the Indian Ocean: commercial trading networks, based on family and extended-family kinship ties, which gradually expanded into corporate firms in which members of nuclear and extended families were partners and majority shareholders. After the 1979 coup that displaced Idi Amin, the UNLF government, led by President Obote, invited the Madhvani and Mehta business families, two of the most important Gujarati Lohana family firms in Uganda, to return. Both family firms had owned the two largest sugar plantations in Buganda and Busoga (called Lugazi and Kakira, respectively). Significantly, neither family firm returned as a Ugandan company, but as subsidiaries of multinational companies that expanded over the intervening years since the expulsion (Ahluwalia 1995: 215). The Madhvani Group, for example, had already shifted its base of operations to the tax havens of Bermuda and the Isle of Man prior to Ugandan independence in anticipation of Africanisation policies and political unrest in the new nation (Madhvani and Foden 2008: 99). Thus, in order to increase their profits and the security of their investments, as well as to minimise capital risks in an unstable political environment, family firms sought to rehabilitate Uganda's sugar industry on a joint-venture basis with the government. Because the state was an active participant in the sugar industry, both firms were able to utilise significant amounts of capital borrowed from international donors and agencies, further minimising risks to capital investments in the new regime (Ahluwalia 1995: 215). In the process, business leaders of both family firms re-established personal relationships with President Obote.

Furthermore, Ugandan Asians, resident in the UK and North America, travelled to Uganda during this period in order to reclaim property from the Departed Asians Property Custodial Board

(DAPCB) through a legal act called the Expropriated Properties Act, passed by Obote in 1982 (1983 Expropriated Properties Act, Cap. 87; Amin established the DAPCB in 1973). Significantly, the vast majority of Ugandan Asians who left in 1972 (the petty bourgeoisie class) were renters and owned no fixed property in Uganda – those who did own fixed assets were small proprietors (Mamdani 1993: 272). Expelled small-time proprietors in the diaspora were largely interested in compensation rather than the repossession of their properties (Mamdani 1993; only 2,000 small-time proprietors filed repossession claims with the Uganda High Commission after the passage of the Expropriated Properties Act in 1982, Mamdani 1993: 272). Thus, those who did return were interested in repossession and re-investing. They owned large-scale property: industrial, commercial and residential in Kampala and many small district towns scattered across Uganda.

While the 1982 Act was largely unsuccessful in bringing back most expelled Ugandan Asians to settle and re-invest in the country, it was re-invigorated in the early years of the Museveni-led NRM regime. This time the government was more successful in processing paperwork and returning property and assets back to its original Ugandan Asian owners. In the process, Museveni sought to attract foreign investment back to Uganda by exhorting expelled Ugandan Asians to return to the country, repossess their property and invest in the nation (Abidi 1996: 53). He did this by travelling to the embassies of the adopted countries of expelled Ugandan Asians and by re-establishing diplomatic relations between Uganda and India through a memorandum of understanding (*ibid.*: 57). The NRM regime effectively dealt with the problem of graft and violence connected to Asian properties and the Departed Asians Property Custodial Board, although many lingering problems remain (interviews with Ruth Oligio, Lawyer for the Indian Association of Uganda, in 2010 and 2011; interview with Morde Mwerinde in 2011; all Kampala). In sum, although the government was successful in returning properties to various landlords, they were not so successful in enticing Ugandan Asians (original property owners) in the diaspora to return and re-settle in the country (the repossession process began in 1983 and culminated in 1997 with the handover of 4,063 properties to Ugandan Asians in Uganda and abroad; interview with Mwerinde in 2010, Kampala). With the departure of small businessmen, artisans and salary earners during the expulsion, the population of Ugandan Asians who have remained or returned has been able to accrue wealth (see more below).

After repossession, returnee family firms were more deeply aligned with the developmental state, Museveni and the NRM. Although they were less invested in formal political inclusion through legal citizenship, they were critical to the national reconstruction process. The president's cultivation of a host–guest model of economic citizenship for returnees allowed transnational business leader to advocate for reforms and concessions that were amenable to a modern liberal business environment and that would help them reconstruct their businesses. In doing so, Ugandan Asian family firms began to reinvest in the manufacturing sector, agricultural processing, banking and foreign exchange dealings, insurance, the hotel and restaurant industry, pharmaceuticals, and the printing and publishing sectors (Abidi 1996: 54–55). In addition, the Aga Khan Fund for Development (a religious community organisation) played a major role in the reconstruction of Uganda's economy by investing in a number of large-scale development projects (Abidi 1996). Finally, a more recent wave of Ugandan Asian business families returned from the UK or other parts of East Africa and were able to repossess properties and assets, reinvesting capital in them.

Thus, Ugandan Asian family firms who returned are a transnational, bourgeois class of 'tycoons' who reside both in the country and abroad. With enormous political influence, particularly during elections, returnee family firms are regional economic machines, often employing hundreds to thousands of indigenous Ugandan workers. Capital accumulation is often accompanied with philanthropic practices such as funding local development projects or subsidising school fees and providing college scholarships for the children of workers in the towns that factories and offices are located. Significantly, returnee business families are able to legitimise themselves as contributors to the nation through discourses of shared colonial oppression with Ugandan Africans, their personal experiences of the expulsion, and claims to an African Asian or Ugandan national identity. Claims about their role in Ugandan national development and a high proportion of tax contribution to the state allow them to make further political claims for their presence in the nation. In sum, Ugandan Asians who remained and returned view themselves as a distinct group of African Asian entrepreneurs markedly different from new Indian businessmen, firms and trader-migrants who arrived in the country from the early 2000s onwards.

In addition to returnee family firms that invested in agriculture, manufacturing, tourism, industry and the service sector, South Asian trader-migrants revived trading networks that had been destroyed in the expulsion and migrated into Uganda from the 1980s onward. From the 1990s onwards, economic liberalisation reforms, open immigration policies and networks of information, resources and credit among Gujarati traders (largely Patel, Lohana and Ismaili communities) – but also Punjabi traders – made it fairly easy for a newly arrived trader to open a small retail shop in Uganda once again (the state instituted an open licensing system for traders in the 1980s; Rubongoya 2007). Shop owners, in turn, could easily convince extended family members from their home villages in India to work in shops. These shops quickly fanned out into networks of retail businesses, often expanding into the former colonial towns of Ugandan Asian settlement.

Increasingly, however, informal migrant-traders are travelling to East Africa outside of traditional ethnic-based chain migration networks. They may begin by working unskilled jobs or trades, but are usually successful in finding jobs in established Indian firms, where business owners like to employ Indian men in order to shore up political security and where they are likely to be trusted if they share the same race, ethnicity, religion, caste and/or language. In addition, young men who are petty traders and work as shopkeepers may eventually move into salaried employment at a more-established Indian firm and formalise their stay in Uganda through work permits and permanent residency certificates.

This new wave of informal trader-migrants working in Uganda is connected to broader neoliberal economic globalisation that has re-structured the economies of both India and Uganda into new collaborative partnerships in the private sector. During the late 1990s and throughout the 2000s, for instance, multinational Indian firms began to expand their investments into Uganda. TATA Uganda Limited, which engages in the import and sale of motor vehicles and pharmaceuticals, is one example. These new firms employ Indian expatriate labour for upper-level management, as well as Indian employees for semi-skilled labour such as management, accounting and IT (information technology). It is significant to note here that multinational Indian firms like the TATA Group in Uganda operate at the level of commercial sale, and have not invested in the production of machinery or vehicles in Uganda itself. Thus, while Indian multinationals have a presence in Kampala city, their capital investment is limited to low wage, unskilled African labour (with some clerical and management positions) and the rent of commercial space in urban areas. Moreover, both multinational firms and family businesses in Uganda often seek Indian employees using websites such as www.monstor.com or www.nokri.com to hire chartered accountants or other skilled professionals. Returnee Ugandan Asian family firms often follow suit and seek Indian professionals through similar employment sites (communication with interviewee from Rafiki Ltd., 2009).

Thus, while Ugandan Asian family firms are still recognised as the most important and (historically) committed investors in the country, and while Indian trading and commercial networks have revived in the country, new 'Indian investors' are also increasingly part of the Ugandan scene. These new entrepreneurs do not have a historical relationship to Uganda and are not integrated into the Gujarati ethnic networks of returnees and more traditional traders. Rather, the state is soliciting FDI to the country in a more general-ised way. In the past decade, African nations have shifted towards a new development strategy that is focused on the growth of the private sector through foreign investment and trade, and this has occurred in the context of the economic growth of India and China. Emboldened by critiques of Western neo-imperialism (foreign aid, donor/debt relations and the development priorities set by Western nations), India and China have 'stepped in to fill the investment gap left in emerging economies by more cautious Western investors, and have heavily prioritized building South–South relationships over the past several years' (Gowda 2015: 1). In Uganda specifically, I have examined the ways in which ties between Uganda and India have been re-invented through 'Africa/Asia Rising' discourses, exploring the importance of diplomatic visits, trade conferences, and the prac-tices of the Uganda Investment Authority (a state agency) in the global re-branding of Uganda as a foreign investment destination (see Hundle 2013b).

In 2008, during the height of rising Global South celebrations, Uganda had received $77 million in FDI from India and $44 million in investment from China in various economic sectors (UIA news-letter 1(3); a focused 'investment policy reform agenda' occurred among policy makers from 2000 to 2006; in general, average FDI inflows increased to $204 million in 2001–2005 from $127 million in 1996–2000 (UNCTAD 2007: 1); figures from 2014–15 suggest 'planned' investment from China at $529 million and $58 billion from India; UIA Status of Investment Press Release). In general, IT or telecommunications, tourism, entertainment, agribusiness, construction and property development are flagged as sectors attrac-tive for FDI 'projects' for investors. FDI projects possess important symbolic and material weight in the urban context: during my fieldwork period between 2008 and 2011 at least six different telecom companies competing for the Ugandan market, and five new luxury hotels appeared in the city – helping to legitimise the neoliberalisation of the Ugandan economy.

In today's Uganda then, it is not returnee Ugandan Asian family firms who are the most important 'investors' on the Ugandan scene. Rather, a new topography of Indian and Chinese state and corporate capital and individual businessmen has been foisted upon an older dispensation of colonial African Asian commercial relations, plantation and peasant economies, and the informal *magendo* economy of 1970s Uganda. In concert with global and neoliberal policies of investment, the state discursively defines all foreigner populations (especially those from South Asia and East Asia) as 'foreign investors'. Thus, the colonial category of 'Asians' has now been transformed into a racialised and social category of foreign investor regardless of one's historical, regional, national or ethnic affiliations, or even, as I observe below, the amount of capital that one might possess. This new inclusivity is based on a foreigner's potential economic contribution to the country, whether they are an actual 'investor' or not. As a mode of recognising the bodies of racialised minorities, it is also based on a liberal, global multicultural discourse that promotes urban cosmopolitanism and promises economic and bodily security for foreigner populations. Finally, and most significantly, four decades after Africanisation policies that culminated in the expulsion, the state is now engaged in a generalised search for investment and recruitment of 'Asian' investors without any clear resolution of historical and ongoing nativism, racial inequality and economic inequity.

It is still not clear what the long-term effects of FDI and the focus on the private sector for development will be. Indeed, capital investments to Africa, in general, are extremely idiosyncratic and tend to be specialised within certain enclave economies (Ferguson 2006). In the Ugandan context, unlike China's interest in natural resource markets, Indian FDI projects include more diverse and smaller kinds of investments, particularly in healthcare/medicine, agriculture, IT and telecommunications (Gowda 2015). Indian investments also have the added advantage of building networks with Ugandan Asian family firms and integrating relatively easy into the local African indigenous economy. Existing South Asian communities in Uganda provide a base to promote Indian interests in the country.

While Indian foreign investment seems to have had some noticeable effects on Kampala city, the same cannot be argued for the rest of the country. Ugandan commentators on 'cosmetic development' critique the unstable and sudden appearance of new real estate properties in the city, particularly since real estate investments are often used as a cover for kick-backs and investments made by politicians in collusion with wealthy businessmen. In addition, Indian investors have been critiqued for undercutting wages and excluding indigenous labour from the local market in their hiring practices. Finally, there have been numerous complaints about working conditions and the abuse of African workers in Indian firms, shops and other places of employment. Much more research needs to be conducted in all of these arenas to understand the (re)production of racial and class inequity, Asian anti-Black/African racism and anti-Indian xenophobia and nativist sentiments in the context of new urban investments from India.

What is new and different about the new phase of South Asian capitalist accumulation in Uganda? The 1972 expulsion continues to affect processes of community formation – a small number of elite, original Ugandan Asian families returned to the country, and along with a few other successful business entrepreneurs, have become extremely wealthy (according to one source, a majority of Asian properties once expropriated by Idi Amin have fallen into the hands of ten to twelve landlords, including indigenous Ugandan businessmen; see Jamal forthcoming). But they are outnumbered by a larger population of more transient, informal migrants who work in trade and other forms of petty entrepreneurship. New migrants are in the process of establishing their own communities, both alongside and in conflict with the older generation of Ugandan Asian businessmen. Practices of migration, securing work and establishing families in Uganda (processes of social reproduction) are all characterised by a high amount of insecurity and informality, particularly in the context of formal political exclusion after the expulsion. Finally, Indian corporate capital and the professionals who work in these firms are also engaged in community-building processes. The NRM government has taken advantage of the precarity of newly emerging South Asian communities, often promising ethno-racial and political security to community leaders in exchange for economic patronage, particularly during election seasons. The Ministry of Interior Affairs, whose immigration officers benefit from the informality and increasing visa and work permit fees applied to foreigners in the country, is also implicated in the logics of inclusion and exclusion of different classes of South Asians in Uganda (see Hundle 2013b).

Conclusion: revisiting the 'Asian question' in neoliberal Uganda

This chapter has attempted to weave together historical, cultural and political-economic frameworks to understand African Asian and South Asian presence and capital in Uganda over time and in the contemporary era in order to shed light on the neoliberal transformation of Uganda. The new era of neoliberal capitalist accumulation and the state's emphasis on the search for FDI capital from numerous global sources, particularly Asia, suggests new openings for racialised, elite class formation in the country today. On the other hand, the precarity that characterises neoliberal global capitalist accumulation and a liberalised economy demands attention to the practices of informal and mobile trader-migrants – including their links to more established African Asian firms and businesses in Uganda. The multi-racial and ethnic scene in Uganda is complex and requires attention to the shifting relations of the Ugandan and the Indian state to new migrants, investors and businessmen (for instance, the extent to which borders and business opportunities are variously opened and closed to different classes and kinds of South Asians based on connections to or exclusion from the Ugandan and Indian state). In addition, analysing urban Uganda in the context of neoliberal economic globalisation requires a deeper understanding of the relations among Asian capital accumulation and labour, the state, governance, citizenship and subjectivity. As urban inequality increases, it will become increasingly important to pay attention to the relations between African Asian / South Asian and indigenous capitalists, traders and entrepreneurs; indigenous and Asian class formation, and the production, reproduction and internalisation of ethno-racial hierarchies and ideologies in contemporary Uganda.

References

Abidi, S. (1996), 'The return of Asians to Uganda', *Africa Quarterly*, 36(3) pp. 45–58.

Ahluwalia, D. (1995), *Plantations and the Politics of Sugar in Uganda* (Kampala: Fountain).

Asiimwe, G. (2013), 'From monopoly marketing to coffee *magendo*: Responses to policy recklessness and extraction in Uganda, 1971–79', *Journal of Eastern African Studies*, 7(1), pp. 104–24.

Barongo, Y. R. (1984), 'The de-embourgeoisement of Ugandan society: The first stage in the break with international capitalism', *Journal of African Studies*, 11(3), pp. 100–09.

Collier, P. and Reinikka, R. (2001),

Uganda's Recovery: The Role of Farms, Firms, and Government (Kampala: Fountain).

Ferguson, J. (2006), *Global Shadows: Africa in the Neoliberal Order* (Durham, NC: Duke University Press).

Gowda, S. (2015), 'China and India in Africa: Implications of new private sector actors on bribe paying incidence', *The Developing Economist*, 2(1), Available at: http://www.inquiriesjournal.com/articles/1397/china-and-india-in-africa-bribe-paying-private-sector.

Hansen, H. B. and Twaddle, M. (eds) (1988), *Uganda Now: Between Decay and Development* (London: James Currey).

Hansen, H. B. and Twaddle, M. (eds) (1991), *Changing Uganda: The Dilemmas of Structural Adjustment and Revolutionary Change* (London: James Currey).

Hundle, A. K. (2013a), 'Exceptions to the expulsion: Violence, security, and community among Ugandan Asians, 1971–1979', *Journal of Eastern African Studies*, 7(1), pp. 164–82.

Hundle, A. K. (2013b), 'The politics of (in)security: Reconstructing African-Asian relations, citizenship and community in post-expulsion Uganda', Dissertation, University of Michigan, Ann Arbor, MI.

Jamal, V. (forthcoming), *Uganda Asians: Then and Now, Here and There*.

Madhvani, M. and Foden, G. (2008), *Tide of Fortune: A Family Tale* (London: Manubhai Madhvani Bermuda Trust).

Mamdani, M. (1975), 'Class

struggles in Uganda', *Review of African Political Economy*, 4(2), pp. 26–61.

Mamdani, M. (1976), *Politics and Class Formation in Uganda* (New York, NY and London: Monthly Review Press).

Mamdani, M. (1993), 'The Ugandan Asian expulsion: Twenty years after', *Journal of Refugee Studies*, 6(3), pp. 265–73.

Mamdani, M. (1996), *Citizen and Subject: Contemporary Africa and the Legacy of Late Colonialism* (Princeton, NJ: Princeton University Press).

Museveni, Y. (1997), *Sowing the Mustard Seed: The Struggle for Freedom and Democracy in Uganda* (Oxford: Macmillan).

Peterson, D. R. and Taylor, E. C. (2013), 'Rethinking the state in Idi Amin's Uganda: The politics of exhortation', *Journal of Eastern African Studies*, 7(1), pp. 58–82.

Read, J. (1975), 'Some legal aspects of the expulsion', in M. Twaddle (ed.), *Expulsion of a Minority: Essays on Uganda Asians* (London: Athlone), pp. 193–209.

Rubongoya, J. (2007), *Regime Hegemony in Museveni's Uganda: Pax Musevenica* (New York, NY: Palgrave Macmillan).

Shivji, I. (1976), *Class Struggles in Tanzania* (London: Heinemann).

UNCTAD (United Nations Conference on Trade and Development). (2007), *Report on the Implementation of the Investment Policy Review: Uganda* (New York, NY and Geneva: United Nations).

16
Religious economies: Pentecostal-charismatic churches and the framing of a new moral order in neoliberal Uganda

Barbara Bompani

Introduction: thirty years of Museveni's Uganda

Much academic analysis has focused on the impact of thirty years of neoliberal interventions in Uganda from a political, economic, social and legal perspective (Tripp 2010, Harrison 2006, Wiegratz 2010, Goodfellow 2014); meanwhile relatively little scholarly attention has focused on social and structural transformation (see Introduction this volume), and within that on religious transformation as new religious actors have emerged in the public sphere. Given the central role that religion has always played in Ugandan public, social and political life it is important to understand those changes and their interplay with the broader transformative process listed above. Indeed, in the Ugandan context the Church is inextricably bound to the political and economic conditions of the nation since colonial times with Catholic missions fighting with Anglican missions over their connections and sway over the political sphere, while trying to establish their influence on society through schools, hospitals and through the shaping of the new elites (as discussed in the following section). Note, in 2010 the Ugandan population included an estimated 28,980,000 Christians, 3,840,000 Muslims, 100,000 Hindus and 170,000 unaffiliated to any religion (www.pewforum. org/2015/04/02/religious-projection-table).

This chapter will map the political economy of religion in Uganda over the past thirty years (following section) and will then trace the emerging public prominence of the Pentecostal-charismatic community as the most active, and in some ways successful religion (Marshall-Fratani 2009), engaged in providing a reassuring moral order in times of neoliberal uncertainty caused by rapid structural and social changes, free competition, insecure employment, individualisation and hyper-responsibilities as defined by Comaroff and

Comaroff (2000). If neoliberal restructuring in the Global South had a strong impact in 'freeing' new actors and creating a free market (Harrison 2005) that was also true for the religious arena. In fact the apparatus of globalisation, with the opening up of markets, the establishment of global networks, flows of ideas, opportunities and people, the spread of technologies and media contributed to the emergence of new forms of religions – like Pentecostal-charismatic groups – that with their global networks, focus on technology, ideas of accumulation and prosperity, mobility and religious competition (to list just a few of their traits), were better equipped to deal with and address the challenges of newly established socio-economic environments. Pentecostalism, in the charismatic form that we discuss here, started to gain popularity in sub-Saharan Africa towards the end of the 1970s (Coleman 2002) as part of a global phenomenon that thrived alongside the spread of neoliberal capitalism and the consumerist opportunities offered by the market (as explained in Comaroff 2009). Moving from a minority religious expression, it is obvious that in the past two decades those forms of Christianity are becoming relevant public and political voices that deeply shape the life of citizens in many African countries.

This chapter will use the definition of Pentecostal-charismatic churches (PCCs) to highlight their belonging to the so-called 'third wave' of Pentecostalism. This kind of Pentecostalism has a strong emphasis on the prosperity gospel, deliverance and spiritual warfare. In Uganda members of these churches are also frequently defined as 'born-agains' or Balokole (as per the communities during the East African Revival in the 1930s; although the original Balokole are loyal to the Church of Uganda and do not self-identify as Pentecostal charismatic). Drawing from empirical material collected across five PCCs in Kampala, the chapter will argue that in the second part of Museveni's era, PCCs became extremely active public actors with political ambitions (Marshall-Fratani 2009: 11). The overarching message that emerges from these churches, and that makes them 'furiously' active (Berger 1999: 2) in their mission to convert the public, is that there is no scope for 'better' politics and economics if not through a moral regeneration of the country through religious conversion. This is not dissimilar from the argument of the Ugandan state – that the nation is suffering from the lack of a strong moral fibre that protects its own citizens from 'immoral' dangers like divorce, corruption, lack of respect towards authority and gender roles, homosexuality etc. – all dangers perceived as 'brought in by new global forces' and which are approached in the public sphere and in public debates with the same seriousness as the economy and politics (see Bompani and Terreni Brown 2015). One of the main themes that, for example, constantly emerges from the Ugandan press is that the state of the nation reflects the state of morality. In this message usually the Church is indicated as the starting point for nation building and reconstruction (New Vision 2012). By extension, Pentecostal-charismatics understand themselves as the only force able to reconnect Ugandan citizens with the Ugandan state because only their strong morally informed public attitudes can 'save' the country from failure. Thirty years of neoliberal interventions, institutional disenchantment and the opening up of a religious market has fundamentally transformed the old dynamic of a public sphere predominantly dominated by the Anglican and the Catholic Church (Ward 2005), and created the conditions for Uganda's new religiously inflected moral economy and a new religiously framed public action (this public moralisation and religiously driven public action does not only belong to PC churches but PC found a terrain to unify themselves and become extremely vocal around the issue of public morality and the moralisation of the country; Bompani 2016).

New religious actors and their public work within the Ugandan state

When Museveni was sworn in as president on 29 January1986 the nation was in ruins and his administration was determined to rebuild non-functioning institutions and a divided society. The National Resistance Movement (NRM) assured the Ugandan public that it was a movement of fundamental change for the country (see Museveni Inauguration Speech 1986, Daily Monitor 2010). With a strong emphasis on reconciliation and tolerance, the early policies of the NRM attempted to bring together people with different political, ethnic and religious affiliations. One of the NRM's first promises for transformation was to put an end to religious and sectarian divisiveness that has defined the Ugandan public sphere since pre-colonial times, when Christianity first took hold in the Buganda monarchy (Mockler-Ferryman 1903). In the colonial and post-colonial history of Uganda, organised religion has played an inextricable role in national politics with the Catholic and the Anglican traditions negotiating a blurred boundary between material and spiritual realms. Historically both the Anglican and Catholic church have held a near duopoly on Ugandan Christianity. Colonial rule also reinforced religious divisions as the British favoured Protestant chiefs (Buganda remained an exception and after the expulsion of the Kabaka (king) in 1966, Baganda Anglicans became deeply suspicious of UPC) to access land and retain authority, leading to grievances amongst the Catholics, the biggest religious group in the country, and Muslims (Kasozi *et al.* 1994; Islam in Uganda arrived in the second part of the nineteenth century through traders; its political and public role became only briefly relevant during the Idi Amin era when he established a narrow minority regime based on a Nubian-Kakwa core group and Muslims more generally (Lindemann 2011)). Religious sectarianism and religious divisiveness continued to characterise the post-independence period. During the decade before independence political parties began to form based largely along Catholic and Anglican divides (Ward 2005: 112). While Milton Obote, a Protestant and the nation's first post-independence president, 'endeavored to create a secular state, in which religion did not obtrude into the political sphere [in reality he] entrenched religious loyalties, which he himself could not transcend, mak[ing] it hard for him to succeed' (*ibid.*). For Gifford it was at this time that the rivalry between Anglicans and Catholics became institutionalised in their respective political parties; Obote's UPC (Ugandan People's Congress) became intrinsically linked to the Anglican Church of Uganda, and the DP (Democratic Party) to the Catholic Church (Gifford 2000: 105) and this established the Anglican Church as the direct ally of the state in the post-independence period.

Under Museveni, by contrast, the emphasis on national unity and the elimination of divisive political and religious forces was so strong that in their rise to power the NRM espoused an anti-multiparty stance, first visible in the 1986 ban on political parties (Lindemann 2011: 387). The political system under the NRM constructed a vision of a unified Uganda under the Movement 'where party activity was banned and elections were held between individual candidates' (*ibid.*: 395). Museveni argued that political parties in the Ugandan context would exacerbate the ethnic, regional and religious affiliations that had characterised Ugandan politics in previous decades and that a transitional period without political parties would help create a less polarised political environment. In 1988 an Anti-Sectarian Law promised the formation of a broad-based government comprising people from all ethnic groups (*ibid.*). Local elections were held in 1989 alongside the drafting of a new Constitution. By 1993 a tentative draft of the Constitution was published which permitted the continuation of the 'non-party' system, and extended the ban on political parties for an additional seven years (Gifford 1998: 115). In 1994 a Constituent Assembly was elected through 'an innovative process in which sectors of the public were heard for suggestions [on the Constitution] ... all churches participated actively, including the newer 'born-again' [or Pentecostal] ones' (Freston 2004: 141). This process of active 'reintegration' of religion into public affairs almost ten years after Museveni's first election, signalled the recognition that, amongst the absence of other non-governmental actors, churches were playing a fundamental role in connecting the state to its citizens and that the initial post-liberation suspicions towards the divisive power of religion were starting to vanish. The new Constitution was ratified in 1995 and the following year presidential elections were held, with Museveni receiving 70 per cent of the vote (Hansen and Twaddle 1995). The 1995 Constitution banned multiparty democracy, relying instead on a participatory system through an association of Resistance Councils that oversaw local affairs (Freston 2004: 141). Only nearly twenty years later, in July 2005, was multiparty politics re-instituted in Uganda (Mwenda 2007). According to Makara *et al.* (2009) though, the reintroduction of a multiparty system was not so much the result of donors or civil society's pressure but was primarily stimulated by internal conflicts between NRM factions. The decision to move to multiparty politics was made contingent on other constitutional changes and manoeuvres that enabled the executive and the central political leadership to remain in power (*ibid.*).

While in the first half of his thirty-year mandate Museveni positioned religion at odds with creating a unified public, the dismissive way of conceiving of religion only as a negative force was gradually replaced by a different attitude when both Museveni and the NRM recognised that churches were such 'a prominent part of the fabric of Ugandan life that they cannot be ignored' (Ward 2005: 115) and that they could become important actors in mediating ruptures and dissatisfaction between the state and society. Ultimately their public role, especially around issues of development and public health interventions, could no longer be ignored; the material realties of the HIV epidemic proved to be an overwhelming factor in integrating churches back into the realm of politics. The United States President's Plan for Emergency AIDS Relief (PEPFAR; a US government initiative to tackle HIV – but also tuberculosis and malaria – around the world) was instigated in Uganda in 2004 and redirected national strategies around HIV to 'morally' informed campaigns and religious organisations. In four years PEPFAR allocated around US$650 million to

Uganda (Gusman 2009: 68). Churches and Christian organisations capitalised on PEPFAR funds that were 'channeled into Faith-based organisations working on HIV/AIDS prevention issues, particularly those concerning abstinence and faithfulness' (*ibid.*). Due to their theological and organisational parallels with US conservative Christian donors, Ugandan PCCs were among the primary beneficiaries of PEPFAR funds (Cooper 2014, Patterson 2011), helping to institutionalise the Pentecostal-charismatic presence in Ugandan public and political realms in the past decade (Bompani and Terreni Brown 2015, Boyd 2015). Yet the increased prominence of faith-based actors is not solely the result of US interventionism but also the results of broader global changes in development approaches. The turn to religion in international development and relief, in fact, reflects the growing reliance on non-state actors in sub-Saharan Africa where non-governmental organisations (NGOs) and in particular faith-based organisations (FBOs) play an increasingly prominent role in the provision of services (Cooper 2014: 4). This change of strategy towards privileging faith-based organisations over secular NGOs and government bureaus in the international development community greatly affected a country like Uganda over-reliant on donors' funding.

Global factors contributed to the proliferation of PCCs in Uganda as well as in many other sub-Saharan contexts (Anderson 2013). Within Uganda, politically and ideologically these churches also benefited from existing outside the old political-religious divides of the Anglican and Catholic churches, and increasingly proved to be in harmony with the goals of the NRM. PCCs reflected several elements of similarity with the NRM's discourse of unity. They transcend ideas of identification with specific ethnic groups or political parties as per the Anglican and the Catholic Church – and reconstruction – with their strong ethos on the future and shaping the youth, economic advancement and development, while they have never challenged the existing political establishment (Freston 2004: 142, Gusman 2009). Thus churches ostensibly remained in line with Museveni's consistent stance and preoccupation that religious and cultural leaders should not interfere with politics. In part this explains their rapid growth throughout the entirety of the Museveni regime and their increased political clout.

As per the rest of East Africa, early Pentecostal churches began to take root in Uganda in the late 1950s and 1960s but during the 1970s the Amin regime banned and persecuted evangelical churches. According to Ward, Amin – the only Muslim to serve as president

– 'was not against Christianity as such. But he greatly feared the churches as centres of opposition to his rule. He prohibited altogether the small evangelical and Pentecostal churches which have proliferated in the 1960s' intensifying the powers of the Catholic and Anglican traditions (Ward 2005: 115). Museveni and the NRM, in contrast, provided legal and social protection to the existence of these churches as they began to experience rapid growth since the 1990s. The narrative of Museveni as the leader who guarantees protection and the flourishing of PCCs in Uganda is dominant and unquestioned across the religious community:

> In fact, it is a common criticism of the Pentecostal leaders in Uganda, that they do not criticise the political leaders at all. This is because these churches, the *Balakole* [from the East African Revival, commonly used to identify PCCs in Uganda], they have a history of oppression in Uganda, and were hidden for many years. So under the current government, they have been free to worship, and they like this a lot, so they do not criticise the government at all. In fact, they praise it! (Interview, member of the Uganda Workplace Fellowship Network, Kampala, 2013)

It is equally true that PC churches gained from the alliance with Museveni not only in terms of protection, safety and opportunities to express themselves in the public space, but also in terms of power and money-making possibilities that allowed churches to become centres of economic accumulation and navigating political networks for gaining more public visibility and getting access to several centres of power.

According to Epstein (2007) and Gusman (2009) in recent years nearly one-third of Ugandans have converted to Pentecostal-charismatic Christianity and its growth is also reflected in the influence it is having in the public space. For example it is common to see Pentecostal-charismatic preachers in the street of Kampala reading passages from the Bible and shouting through megaphones words of conversion and repentance; members of congregations distributing flyers inviting participation in church events and services; massive advertisements to attend new Christian fellowships and posters promoting lunch-hour and breakfast prayers; on a weekend there is loud music and singing coming from PCCs; in front of mega churches like Watoto and Miracle Centre traffic jams caused by churchgoers waiting to park in the church yard obstruct traffic. PCCs have their own radio stations and leaders are often invited to present their opinion on local and national radio and TV programmes as well as in the print media (Bompani and Terreni Brown 2015; the importance of owning radio stations, as the main vehicle of opinion making in Uganda, is also represented by the fact that many NRM politicians own their own radio and that Pro-NRM channels are the great majority in the country). Links between the political establishment through the president's wife Janet Museveni, a sort of spiritual leader of the Ugandan Pentecostal-charismatic movement, and her daughter Patience Museveni Rwabwogo, pastor and founder of her own church, the Covenant Nations Church (CNN), are interpreted as signs of benevolence for the advance of Pentecostalism in both the spiritual and the political realms. The connection between civil servants and the Pentecostal community is very visible with many politicians and bureaucrats publically associated with these churches. This is win–win: politicians associated with PCCs can draw from the churches' allure of incorruptibility and becoming more trustworthy public figures, while they can also take advantage of important political networks established between PCCs, and the political elites. These networks are particularly appealing to 'younger' government officials who were not involved in the liberation war and the old NRM cadre and therefore have greater need to develop their relation and establish themselves within the ruling party. As one of the participants said:

> I know that in parliament, there are many that are saved
> [Pentecostal-charismatics]. The ex-minister [James Nsaba]
> Buturo, he is saved. Then there is the First Lady and Ondoa and
> Bahati. Also Jennifer Musisi at KCCA [Kampala Capital City
> Authority]; and at the URA [Uganda Revenue Authority] there is
> Allen Kagina. They are both Watoto [one of the biggest PCCs in
> Kampala] people. Even in the police force and the army there are
> many who are born again, like Maj Gen Angina and Gen Tumine.
> I think these people really know the lord. (Interview, church
> leader, Kampala, 2013)

As discussed above, part of the recent advancement of PCCs in terms of public presence and influence in Uganda can be explained through the developmental role they acquired during the HIV crisis and through their strategic positioning as new and non-aligned religious actors in line with the NRM discourse of national unity. However, their success also needs to be understood in light of the corresponding social restructuring that followed the neoliberal transformation that began in 1986. Beyond material implications, this transformation affected people's subjectivities, sociability, relationships, practices, orders and understandings of what is acceptable and what is not (see Introduction). In this context, PCCs proved to be adept in providing people with new interpretative tools to navigate those structural changes and create social cohesion and social networks despite the 'institutional deficit' caused by the neoliberal global order (Martin 1998: 18).

Pentecostalism and the framing of a new moral order

In similar ways to the Protestant Calvinist ethic – that in Weberian terms (Weber 1930) supported and had as its counterpart the development of early forms of modern capitalism – we can perhaps view Charismatic-Pentecostalism as the religion for the modern economic world. The Pentecostal-charismatic 'prosperity gospel' operates to condone the pursuit of wealth for its adherents; a 'theology of consumption' is added to a strong 'work ethic' as central to this form of Christianity, which had led to PCCs as ideal receptors and interpreters of neoliberal transformations (Meyer 2007, van Dijk 2009). Another attractive dimension of Pentecostalism for new members is its notion that the 'Holy Spirit' can provide lasting protection from malignant spirits; including spirits that cause economic hardship, lack of access to relevant networks and centres of power, spirits that prevent access to jobs and financial security, spirits of corruption, spirits that bring immoral behaviours and dangerous social changes (Gauthier and Martikainen 2013). In short, in the structurally changed Global South, PCCs proved to be formidable mediators equipped to navigate the limitations and hardships of unequal wealth redistribution of neoliberal restructurings but also successful cultural mediators that offer meanings and trusted networks in the mutated social order.

As Wiegratz (2010: 130) stated in Museveni's Uganda reforms, 'undermine, delegitimise, overwrite and displace pre-existing non-neoliberal norms, values, orientations and practices'. In this way, the new 'neoliberal subject' developed a vision of the world that is different from the past. This provides the premises to approach neoliberalism as a 'cultural programme' (*ibid.*) that not only affects the material but also norms, beliefs, perceptions, social-behaviours and understandings. 'Notwithstanding the official rhetoric and statistics of reform success, many people actually experienced the day-to-day manifestations of neoliberal pseudo-development' (*ibid.*: 134) and unmet promises of change and progress (Mbembe 2001). This generates a set of worries and anxieties that need to be taken seriously in order to understand drivers and perceptions that motivate the Ugandan citizen to look for alternative sources for public interventions and public change beyond the state and the international development community.

From an analysis of print media (Bompani and Terreni Brown 2015) and from fieldwork across four PCCs between November 2012 and July 2013 in Kampala it emerged that there is a pervading sense that 'people lost their morals' and that corruption and indecent behaviours are polluting Uganda at different socio-political and economic levels and through all structures, from police to politics, society, bureaucracy and financial institutions (fieldwork, Kampala, November 2012 to July 2013); this is also supported by other analyses, for example Wiegratz's (2010) study in rural Uganda. More precisely Ugandan society is projected as morally corrupt based on the influence of the West and conditions of poverty. Articles from the major newspapers explore themes of financial gain and sex, and highlight the perception of moral degradation of the youth (Bompani and Terreni Brown 2015). Discourses on the moral degeneration that is deeply affecting the country and most of all influencing Ugandan youth and the future are extremely popular in public as well as in private spaces. In one of the many discussions on the pervasive immorality of the country, all with a similar thread of falling apart and then regaining morality and a newly flourishing life through religious conversion, a newspaper article for example explores one woman's experience of having a 'sugar daddy'. She described that she was young, poor and vulnerable, and became pregnant because of the relationship. Yet her 'sugar daddy' wanted nothing to do with the pregnancy. She concluded her intervention quoting the Bible and the need to repent in order to find, through the Church, a way to regain a moral life that will then translate into a better material life (Daily Monitor 2013).

The permeating and powerful sense of anxiety towards the future of the country and the incapacity of the untrusted leadership to break this spiral of immoral behaviour is also summarised in several debates to 'reform' legislations aimed at controlling non-normative and (so perceived) 'immoral' sexual behaviours such as the Anti-Pornography Bill (also known as the 'miniskirt ban' for its ban on 'indecent' and 'provoking' clothing), which was passed by parliament in December 2013; the Marriage and Divorce Bill that covers a wide range of marriage, divorce and gender issues and the Anti-Homosexuality Act (AHA) approved by parliament on 20 December 2013 and then nullified and declared unconstitutional by the Constitutional Court in August 2014.

In an extremely religious country with 85 per cent of the population belonging to Christianity (National Census 2012), churches have always played a fundamental role in shaping and defining moral orders and public behaviours. Yet in recent years it seems that this role has been played mainly by the very vocal and active PC communities. Ugandan Pentecostal-charismatics elaborated a very clear idea of what kind of social world they want to shape (Haynes 2012) and who they want to include – moral citizens – and who they want to exclude – people considered sinful, for example non-conforming sexual minorities against whom PCCs are waging a very public battle (Bompani 2016). Their vision and understandings of a regained moral (and therefore Pentecostal) society is widely debated in public, even in not-necessarily Pentecostal circles.

As Ferguson pointed out, meanings of production and accumulation in most of the African continent are 'interpreted in fundamentally moral terms' and the same is frequently true for consumption and exchange (Ferguson 2009: 72). If economics and financial actions have always been framed in moral terms, then neoliberal changes produced a vacuum in terms of eroding old networks, kinship, trust and transforming social behaviour. This vacuum of course then needs to be filled with new moral understandings of social and economic interactions. Pentecostalism seems to be a very successful form of religion in contemporary Uganda to respond to the need of providing meanings, new moral orders and to create trustworthy interpersonal connections. Indeed, through the use of a moral language and moral behaviours Pentecostal-charismatics have provided theological legitimation to the idea of progress, development and prosperity and earthy reassurance that everyone can aspire to salvation (through prosperity) and that a new secure order with moral trustworthy subjects will be re-established. In this way Ugandan Pentecostalism was able to give a morality to economics and public discourses that structural adjustment reforms transformed into technical jargon and neutral bureaucratic principles 'in the name of pragmatism and efficiency' (Ferguson 2009: 80). Against the reality of persistent political and administrative malfunctioning determined by 'corrupted', 'immoral' and 'untrustworthy' public figures and the system, Pentecostal-charismatics are always represented in the public sphere as 'moral agents' that can be trusted and that can deliver. For example, the recent Research World International (RWI) poll showed that 41 per cent of Ugandans thought corruption and embezzlement of government funds were the most detrimental problems for the country. Corruption was ranked second after poverty in the poll (RWI 2014), where poverty was perceived as a consequence of the incapacity of the state and international community to produce positive change and generate progress. In contrast, the moral strengths and successful public action of Pentecostals has been clearly articulated by public observers.

> There is a crop of Pentecostal women in particular who are
> very keen on these churches. It offers them something that the
> traditional churches [meaning mainline churches] cannot offer,
> and perhaps that is something to do with support for women in
> positions of leadership. There is Allen Kagina, Ondoa, Musisi.
> There is an increasing belief that these people can be looked to get
> things done, but they can get things moving, especially because
> they are seen as trustworthy people. (Interview with reporter and
> online editor of *The Independent* magazine, Kampala, 2013)

And again:

> There is an increasing belief that public service offices should be
> occupied by born-agains. It has happened hugely at the Uganda
> Revenue Authority. The president is convinced that born-again
> people do not steal. It is like he did a pilot study with the Uganda
> Revenue Authority [Allen Kagina served as general director between
> 2004 and 2014] and he is now moved to KCCA [Kampala Capital
> City Authority; Jennifer Musisi is the executive director]. And also
> to State House. State House is hugely Pentecostal. I get the sense
> that with the Pentecostal movement there is a consolidation of the
> National Resistance Movement's politics. (Interview, Director of
> Marketing and Digital Media, Red Pepper, 2013)

As has been articulated several times in interviews, this understanding of Pentecostals as moral citizens who are impermeable to vices and corruption, influences also common perceptions that if politicians were becoming Pentecostals, then that would ensure their ethical and moral behaviour. For example, a PCC congregant stated:

> our country must be connected with God. Even our politicians,
> I have what is going on here in Uganda, a lot of corruption,
> bribing, and people are giving away big money. We really need

to know God. We really need Him here in the country. It is
important for politicians to express their faith. I think it would
mean they were more trustworthy, then they would be not so easy
to steal money. (PCC congregant, Kampala, June 2013)

Conclusion

As this chapter has demonstrated, in contemporary Uganda Pentecostal-charismatic expressions are providing new moral frameworks
to understand and interpret neoliberal tenets and the political, social
and economic uncertainties that neoliberal reforms have generated
in the country. In particular, during the second part of the Museveni
era, which is characterised less by a narrative of successful transformation and much more by uncertainty and social anxiety, PCCs
have started to produce their own interpretation of a pathway to
reconstruction through Pentecostal conversion and a Pentecostal
way of life. For Ugandan Pentecostals salvation is no longer a private
and individual issue as it was at the origins of the movement, but
has evolved into something public and a possibility offered to the
entire nation. This leads to a new PC conception of the nation as a
unit of (biblical) redemption (O'Neill 2010). In line with neoliberal
ideologies that aim to radically change societies, in order to fulfil this
project PCCs need to actively change the entire Ugandan nation
(Comaroff 2009) through their religiously inspired struggle. Through
ostensibly concrete examples that conversion to a Pentecostal-charismatic life brings material and spiritual benefits like success, trust,
networks, prosperity and a better life for the individual as well as
for the community, PCCs have attempted to position themselves as
catalysts of multi-dimensional change within and through Ugandan
society. Their message of hard work and taking individual responsibility in order to gain a more prosperous future resonates well with
neoliberal ideologies and the neoliberal restructuring project undertaken throughout the country (see Introduction this volume). PCCs
seek to convince Ugandans of the validity of their project to create
a new moral society with moral citizens, which means Pentecostal-
charismatic citizens. The rate at which this movement has been
gaining traction across the Uganda population, especially the youth,
has been extraordinary. Pentecostal-charismatic groups have grown
from a tiny persecuted minority in the 1970s to the moral arbiters
of contemporary Uganda, shaping and offering guidance to a transformed, and transforming, Ugandan neoliberal society.

References

Anderson, A. (2013), *An Introduction to Pentecostalism: Global Charismatic Christianity (Cambridge: Cambridge University Press)*.

Berger, P. L. (eds) (1999), *The Desecularization of the World: Resurgent Religion and World Politics* (Grand Rapids, MI: Eerdmans Publishing).

Bompani, B. (2016), '"For god and for my country": Pentecostal-charismatic churches and the framing of a new political discourse in Uganda', in A. van Klinken and E. Chitando (eds), *Public Religion and Issues of Homosexuality in Contemporary Africa* (London: Ashgate).

Bompani, B. and Terreni Brown, S. (2015), 'A "religious revolution"? Print media, sexuality and religious discourse in Uganda', *Journal of Eastern African Studies*, 9(1), pp. 110–26.

Boyd, L. (2015), *Preaching Prevention: Born-Again Christianity and the Moral Politics of AIDS in Uganda* (Athens, OH: University of Ohio Press).

Coleman, S. (2000), *The Globalisation of Charismatic Christianity: Spreading the Gospel of Prosperity* (Cambridge: Cambridge University Press).

Comaroff, J. (2009), 'The politics of conviction: Faith on the neo-liberal frontier', *Social Analysis*, 53(1), pp. 17–38.

Comaroff, J. and Comaroff, J. L. (2000), 'Millennial capitalism: First thoughts on a second coming', *Public Culture*, 12(2), pp. 291–43.

Cooper, M. (2014), 'The theology of emergency: Welfare reform, US foreign aid and the faith-based initiative', *Theory, Culture and Society*, 32(2), pp. 1–25.

Daily Monitor. (2010), 'Museveni 24 years later', 29 January.

Daily Monitor. (2013), 'What it means to date a sugar daddy', 30 January.

Epstein, H. (2007), *The Invisible Cure: Africa, the West and the Fight against AIDS* (New York, NY: Farrar, Straus and Giroux).

Ferguson, J. (2009), *Global Shadows: Africa in the Neoliberal World Order* (Durham, NC: Duke University Press).

Freston, P. (2004), *Evangelicals and Politics in Asia, Africa and Latin America* (Cambridge: Cambridge University Press).

Gauthier, F. and **Martikainen,** T. (2013), *Religion in the Neo-liberal Age: Political Economy and Modes of Governance* (London: Ashgate).

Gifford, P. (1998), *African Christianity: Its Public Role* (Indianapolis, IN: Indiana University Press).

Gifford, P. (2000), 'Pentecostalism in Museveni's Uganda', in A. Corten and A. Mary (eds), *Imaginaires politiques et pentecotismes* (Paris: Karthala), pp. 103–17.

Goodfellow, T. (2014), 'Legal manoeuvres and violence: Law making, protest and semi-authoritarianism in Uganda', *Development and Change*, 45(4), pp. 753–76.

Gusman, A. (2009), 'HIV/AIDS, Pentecostal churches, and the "Joseph generation" in Uganda', *Africa Today*, 56(1), pp. 67–86.

Hansen, H. B. and Twaddle, M. (1995), *From Chaos to Order: The Politics of Constitution-Making in Uganda* (London: James Curry).

Harrison, G. (2005), 'Economic faith, social project, and a misreading of African society: The travails of neoliberalism in Africa', *Third World Quarterly*, 26(8), pp. 1303–20.

Harrison, G. (2006), 'Neoliberalism and the persistence of clientelism in Africa', in R. Robison (ed.), *The Neoliberal Revolution: Forging the Market State* (London: Palgrave), pp. 98–113.

Haynes, N. (2012), 'Pentecostalism and the morality of money: Prosperity, inequality, and religious sociality on the Zambian copperbelt', *Journal of the Royal Anthropological Institute*, 18(1), pp. 123–39.

Kasozi, A., Musisi, N. and Sejjengo, J. M. (1994), *The Social Origins of Violence in Uganda: 1964–1985* (Montreal: McGill-Queen's University Press).

Lindemann, S. (2011), 'Just another change of guard? Broad-based politics and civil war in Museveni's Uganda', *African Affairs*, 110(440), pp. 387–416.

Makara, S., Rakner, L. and Svåsand, L. (2009), 'Turnaround: The National Resistance Movement and the reintroduction of a multiparty system in Uganda', *International Political Science Review*, 30(2), pp. 185–204.

Marshall-Fratani, R. (2009), *Political Spiritualities: The Pentecostal Revolution in Nigeria* (Chicago, IL: University of Chicago Press).

Martin, B. (1998), 'From pre- to postmodernity in Latin America: The case of Pentecostalism', in P. Heelas, D. Martin and P. Morris (eds), *Religion, Modernity and Postmodernity* (Oxford: Blackwell).

Mbembe, A. (2001), *On the Postcolony* (Oakland, CA: University of California Press).

Meyer, B. (2007), 'Pentecostalism and neo-liberal capitalism: Faith, prosperity and vision in African Pentecostal-Charismatic churches', *Journal for the Study of Religion*, 20(2), pp. 5–28.

Mockler-Ferryman, A. F. (1903), 'Christianity in Uganda', *Journal of the Royal African Society*, 2(7), pp. 276–91.

Mwenda, A. (2007), 'Personalizing power in Uganda', *Journal of Democracy*, 18(3), pp. 23–37.

National Census. (2012), 'Counting for planning and improved service delivery', Available at: www.ubos.org/UgCensus2012/census2012.html [accessed 15 August 2015].

New Vision. (2012), 'Museveni hails church on economy', *New Vision*, 10 December.

O'Neill, K. L. (2010), *City of God: Christian Citizenship in Postwar Guatemala* (Berkeley, CA: University of California Press).

Patterson, A. S. (2011), *The Church and AIDS in Africa: The Politics of Ambiguity* (Boulder, CO: Lynne Rienner).

Research World International (RWI). (2014), 'Opinion poll report series: Three years into the 4th term', Available at: http://researchworldint.net/storage/app/uploads/public/571/b68/cce/571b68ccebda0907844047.pdf [accessed 16 August 2015].

Tripp, A. M. (2010), *Museveni's Uganda: Paradoxes of Power in a Hybrid Regime* (Boulder, CO: Lynne Rienner).

Van Dijk, R. A. (2009), 'Social catapulting and the spirit of the entrepreneurialism: Migrants, private initiative and the Pentecostal ethic in Botswana', in G. Hüwelmeier and K. Krause (eds), *Traveling Spirits: Migrants, Markets and Mobilities* (London: Routledge).

Ward, K. (2005), 'Eating and sharing: Church and state in Uganda', *Journal of Anglican Studies*, 3(1), pp. 99–119.

Weber, M. (1930) *The Protestant Ethic and the Spirit of Capitalism* (London: Unwin Hyman).

Wiegratz, J. (2010), 'Fake capitalism? The dynamics of neoliberal moral restructuring and pseudo-development: The case of Uganda', *Review of African Political Economy*, 37(124), pp. 123–37.

17
Youth as 'identity entrepreneurs': emerging neoliberal subjectivities in Uganda

Julia Vorhölter

This chapter focuses on the post-1986 generation in northern Uganda which plays a significant role in rebuilding Acholi society, both economically and politically, after the twenty-year war between the Lord's Resistance Army (LRA) and the Museveni government (1986–2006). I study how members of this generation engage in the wide-ranging debates on (northern) Uganda's post-war future and how they position themselves as economic and political actors. Based on ethnographic data gathered during eleven months of field-work in Gulu in 2010/2011, I show that young people's social and political positioning is often characterised by strategic switching between competing ideologies and groupings rather than based on stable, long-term convictions and alliances. I argue that this reflects a particular kind of neoliberal subjectivity which has emerged and spread in Uganda where – after three decades of neoliberalism (see Introduction) – much of social and political life has become reduced to economic cost–benefit calculations; ethics are increasingly based on individualism, consumerism and self-promotion; and people have come to be regarded as, and forced to be, entrepreneurial subjects. Drawing on Jean and John Comaroff's (2009) work on the commodification of culture and identity as one aspect of contemporary neoliberalism, I show how – in a context where few have access to capital, land or meaningful employment – youth actively take on the role of entrepreneurs by 'selling' their cultural and political identity/ies.

In the first part, I give examples from my work with two different sorts of youth groups in Gulu – traditional dancers and hip hop artists (Vorhölter 2014). On the surface, both seemed to represent homogenous collectives which positioned themselves at opposite ends of the ongoing discourses on the future of Acholi society: the former aimed to revive what they considered to be traditional Acholi culture and claimed to reject what they called modern or Western values, especially individualism, materialism and consumption. The latter often stated that they wanted to overcome the conservativeness in Acholi traditions and explicitly oriented their styles and behaviour towards what they associated with Western modernity, usually wealth, (economic) progress and individual freedom. In practice, however, quite a number of youth participated in both groups and switched between competing discourses and styles depending on the situation, audience and expected benefits of identifying with one or the other.

In the second part, I discuss a similar strategic attitude in debates among youth on national politics during the 2010 pre-election campaigns. While in former times, region, ethnicity, religion or party affiliation had figured highly in people's political reasoning and voting behaviour, especially in northern Uganda, members of the young generation cited more short-lived, individualist and utilitarian motives when engaging in political discourses.

As stated in the Introduction of this volume, the restructuring of peoples' subjectivities towards purely transaction-based arrangements forms a key process of neoliberalisation in Uganda. However, such a view risks perceiving youth mainly as opportunistic, profit-maximising and depoliticised actors who compromise their ideals for economic desires and necessities. Therefore, one has to contextualise the socio-political eclecticism of youth by taking into account the uncertainty and ambivalence which has characterised their generation's life for the past three decades.

Youth uncertainty in northern Uganda

For people in northern Uganda, the rise of the Museveni regime marked the beginning of a two-decade-long civil war which is widely perceived to have caused a fundamental 'break-down' of Acholi cultural, economic and political life and social relations (Vorhölter 2014: 113ff.). The massive forced displacement during the war and related land dispossessions in the post-war era have led to the deterioration of people's material base for social reproduction (Branch 2013: 3160ff.). Whereas the majority of Acholi before the war had been subsistence farmers, today there is a growing mass of people who have neither access to land nor employment and who struggle for livelihood and a meaningful existence. Many of these have come to settle in Gulu, where their 'total incorporation' into the monetary economy (*ibid.*: 3157) means that they have to pay for everything (rent, food, school fees etc.) – a task that, given the precarious state of employment, hardly seems possible. Parallel to the influx of this new landless and marginalised population, Gulu has seen the rise of a small elite, mainly Acholi who returned from the diaspora, who publicly display their investments and conspicuous consumption. This has led to a growing awareness of inequality which fuels frustrations and conflicts between different societal groups: men and women, youth and elders and, increasingly, rich and poor (*ibid.*: 3163).

In this context, the urban youth I worked with during my fieldwork (most of whom were in their late teens/early twenties in 2010/11) occupied a highly ambivalent social position. Many had come to Gulu as children and spent most of their life in town. They had become used to town lifestyle, and despite their often precarious situation, few could imagine resettling to the village and becoming farmers. In local discourses they were thus often blamed – especially by elder generations – for 'losing' Acholi culture, for disrespecting long-established norms and orders and for 'Westernising' Acholiland. However, they were also seen as bearers of hope for the future who would have to re-establish social order, stability as well as the reputation of Acholi society after the troubled war years. Placed in this pivotal position, the young people I met experienced feelings of uncertainty and ambivalence. Many dreamed of a 'modern' life, characterised by living in town, having a well-paid job, being able to provide for a family and to afford small luxuries – which for most, however, seemed unattainable. At the same time, youth were also confronted with and fascinated by the societal discourse on retraditionalisation, which strongly idealised the past as a time of stability, morality and communalism, and appealed to the young generation to participate in the revival and maintenance of Acholi traditions. Most of my interlocutors were caught in between moralised societal expectations and individual dreams and 'expectations of modernity' (Ferguson 1999) which were shaped by global discourses and images of consumption and individual liberties.

The way youth tried to deal with this situation of moral and economic uncertainty is intrinsically linked, both to the war (which I will not discuss here) and the neoliberalisation of Uganda since 1986. I understand neoliberalism, following Foucault (2006[1979]: 331ff.), as the profound economisation of all fields of social and political life. Linked to this is the conceptualisation of individuals as entrepreneurial subjects who feel the imperative to be self-reliant and view relationships as flexible alliances rather than long-term stable solidarities (Comaroff and Comaroff 2009: 50). When analysing the social actions of youth in Uganda, I also draw on Weber's distinction between instrumental rationality and value rationality. According to Weber (1961: 1063f.), social action is *instrumental* when it is oriented to attain discrete personal ends by weighing the ends, means and secondary results in order to achieve maximum results at minimum cost. Social action is *value-rational*, when it is oriented to an 'absolute value of some ethical, aesthetic, religious, or other form of behaviour, entirely for its own sake and independently of any prospects of external success', and when it is motivated by the fulfilment of unconditional 'commands' or 'demands' (*ibid.*). Weber acknowledges that most action is not purely one or the other. Nevertheless, these ideal types might be usefully applied to the situation in Uganda where the social actions of today's youth seem less continuous and less oriented to ultimate, stable ethical values and ideologies, and are rather characterised by a means–end rational calculation of practical self-interests.

Hip hop and traditional dance as moral and economic practices

In the northern Ugandan context described above, being a traditional dancer or a hip hop artist also means *symbolically* positioning oneself in the highly moralised discourse on Acholi culture, whereby the former signals being 'pro-tradition' and the latter 'pro-Westernisation'. In addition to serving as moral signifiers, both practices can also serve to generate small amounts of often desperately needed money. However, while engaging in traditional dance or hip hop for moral or political reasons requires a (performed) commitment to absolute values, pursuing one or the other for economic benefits requires certain flexibility and willingness to compromise 'absolute positions' and switch between different 'cultural styles' depending on the situational context (Vorhölter 2014: 205ff., cf. Ferguson 1999). The way youth in Gulu strategically 'produce' particular identities to suit particular audiences is reminiscent of Comaroff and Comaroff's (2009) discussion of the commodification of culture or identity. In their book *Ethnicity Inc.* they describe a worldwide expansion of what they label 'identity industries' which are 'born of a time in which ... the sale of culture has replaced the sale of labour in many places' (*ibid.*: 24). In the absence of employment opportunities and in constant need of money for school fees or consumer goods, 'selling' their identities became one of the few income-generating strategies available to youth in Gulu. However, one should not see these 'identity entrepreneurs' as simple dupes of the market, nor regard their performed and changing identities as less 'real' or valuable. As Comaroff and Comaroff (*ibid.*: 27) state: 'Even if the transaction of cultural products and practices *were* entirely reducible to cash, it does not necessarily mean that they would be denuded of all auratic, affective, or social worth'.

Traditional dance

In northern Uganda today, traditional dances are regarded as one of the most important and widely known cultural practices of the Acholi, representing the richness and vivacity of their culture. According to my older interlocutors, Acholi dances have always been a vital part of social life. In the past, children and adolescents used to learn the dances from their elders and there were many social or ritual occasions (funerals, weddings, political ceremonies etc.) where people from different villages came together for dancing. Nowadays, traditional dances are mainly performed for entertainment purposes and children are introduced to it through school. Dance and music classes are a compulsory part of the primary school curriculum and there are nation-wide competitions between schools. Outside the school setting, at least in urban areas, traditional dancing is mainly practised in the more or less institutionalised context of so-called cultural groups whose members (usually children and youth of different ages) come together for training, to participate in competitions, or to perform at weddings, tourist functions or other public events.

It seems that in their current form, cultural groups have only existed in northern Uganda since the late 1990s. During this time, international donors involved in peacebuilding had been eager to support youth activities – because youth were seen as particularly vulnerable members of society who had suffered tremendously during the war, but also because they were regarded as important peacebuilding actors for the future. Due to donors' provision of funding (and attributable to their need to have local partners), many community-based organisations were founded and several youth projects started. These projects were seen as a means for healing youth from war traumas and for normalising social relations (Branch and Yen this volume). Traditional dances were further regarded as a means to support the revival of Acholi culture and the re-establishment of 'traditional society' (Vorhölter 2014: 164ff.), and thus became especially prominent. Soon, a new 'culture industry' started to develop in which local actors were paid (or otherwise rewarded) to perform rituals and dances which conveyed a (positive) image of Acholi culture and identity. In the absence of other employment opportunities, becoming a 'cultural entrepreneur' proved to be one of the few cash-generating practices that were available, especially for people without other forms of (social) capital. Accordingly, youth involved in cultural groups often saw their activities not as leisure but as a kind of work which enabled them to access school fees, donor networks and sometimes food or other material benefits. Many also saw their engagement as a way to comment on social affairs and to claim a respected position in society. This may partly explain why cultural groups have prevailed, although funding has been phased out for most.

During my research, I interacted with different cultural groups and gained some insights into the traditional dancing scene. I regularly met one group, in particular. I visited their practice sessions and public performances, and also conducted interviews with some of the members in which we discussed the meaning and value of 'Acholi culture'. My interlocutors stated that without cultural groups, youth (especially those in town) would simply forget about Acholi traditions. They lamented that many of their peers only knew the 'Western culture' and that the urban lifestyle was spoiling their generation. The following quotations are exemplary for the strong moral claims made in these conversations:

Young people today who are not in cultural groups no longer know their culture, because they lead this life like Westerners. ... They prefer going for clubbing, they like [disco] music better than this cultural group. Yet cultural group, it has more value than going for clubs. (Innocent, 21)

We are lucky, because we are in a cultural group. We don't go in for other things like stealing ... But other people are idle. They are so many ... mostly youths, taking drugs, those kind of things ... You'll find that people who are in cultural groups, their lifestyle is different from people who are outside. Because they teach you morals, behaviour, how to conduct yourself, and the way you should behave to the whole community. So you find that their behaviour is quite different to people who are outside. (Odong, 19)

Despite this rhetoric, many members of cultural groups, including the two interviewees above, also went to nightclubs and lived lives which were not much different from those of their peers. Further-more, although their strong desire to contribute to 'cultural revival' was by no means insincere, being in a cultural group also had 'real' (economic and social) benefits. It provided opportunities to enter social realms that were normally not accessible for young people of a poorer background, like travelling to exclusive and/or distant places, and offered the chance to gain recognition and prestige (cf. Pier this volume). When I asked one of my interviewees *whether Acholi traditions were still important for him,* he answered:

> I never used to know those big people ... But when they hire
> us for dances, that is the opportunity, we get to see them and
> talk to them, like [mentions names of Ugandan politicians].
> In 2008, German President Horst Köhler came to Gulu, we
> appeared in the newspaper with him, we went in Bouma Hotel
> [one of the most expensive hotels in Gulu], and we danced. He
> shook my hand and we talked ... I get the opportunity of seeing
> where I would not see if I was not in the [cultural] group ... If
> the other deal works out well, we are going up to Sweden for a
> show ... When I was in O-level [secondary school] I was elected
> entertainment prefect, simply because of the traditional dances I
> do. (Simon, 18)

Apart from gaining new experiences and social acknowledgement, successful cultural groups had the chance to raise money which was often used to pay for members' school fees or given out as cash. Performances at business functions, weddings or tourist locations, earned UGX 150,000 (approximately 50 euros) or more. Even more profitable were the cash prizes offered in big dance competitions, for instance by beer-brewing company Senator (see chapter by Pier, this volume) or Radio Rupiny (local radio station). According to my interlocutors, the winner of these competitions received between one and six million UGX, i.e. up to 2,000 euros.

I sometimes had the impression that the prospect of winning so much money paralleled or even superseded the primary motivation of being cultural ambassadors. The following extract from my field notes deals with this issue:

> We talk about the Senator competition: Odong tells me that
> some years ago their group was second at the National finals and
> received 1.5 million shillings. He says the winner received six
> million and adds that the money is the main reason why everyone

likes Senator so much. 'At least they pay you well unlike in other competitions'. The three guys tell me about a competition that used to be sponsored by the Italian government and held in Kampala every year. One cultural group from each district performed, the whole event took a week. All groups received free food, transport and accommodation. 'But', so the guys complain, 'there wasn't any money to win and therefore it was really a waste of efforts to participate. Even the winners only got trophies'. Surprised I say that staying in Kampala for free is not such a bad deal, whereupon Odong replies that they 'perform to get money, not just for fun'. (3 January 2010)

This extract shows that the highly moralised claims and seemingly 'pure' attempts to revive Acholi culture were paralleled and sometimes determined by material interests. The decision to enter a competition, for instance, was often based on instrumental rationality rather than absolute values. The prospects of economic and social rewards were also a reason for the fierce competition between cultural groups who often accused each other of foul play or corruption. Irrespective of the enthusiasm and the genuine motivation to 'revive' Acholi culture of many involved in these groups, their performances were always *also* opportunities to make money and to gain status and respect which was denied to youth in other contexts.

Hip hop

Since the late 1980s, hip hop or its local variants (like BongoFlava or LugaFlow) have become increasingly popular among youth in the urban centres of East Africa (Ntarangwi 2009). In Uganda, despite its local adaptation, hip hop is still commonly regarded as a cultural import. Critics see it as a sign of 'Westernisation', while supporters take the US 'original' as a prime source of inspiration. As in other places across the globe, hip hop has a double-edged reputation. On the one hand, it is often represented (in the media) and used (by young people) as a means of resistance and political criticism, for instance to speak out against marginalisation, corruption and inequality. On the other hand, hip hop has also become a symbol of ravenousness, chauvinism and conspicuous consumption. The latter, with its typical portrayals of money, sex and (male) power, is sometimes referred to as 'gangsta rap' or 'bling bling' and it is this form which shapes critics' imagination of and aversion against hip hop.

In northern Uganda, hip hop started to become popular among youth in the early 2000s. In the context of humanitarian interventions and the subsequent internationalisation of Acholiland during the war years, it spread via radio, (informal) trade of CDs and video clips played in bars and video halls, and soon became a symbol of 'Westernisation'. As in the case of traditional dancing, albeit to a lesser extent, donors initiated a number of youth projects which centred around breakdance and hip hop and which aimed to provide positive leisure spaces for youth, usually combined with educational activities (like peace-training or HIV/AIDS sensitisation, cf. Branch and Yen this volume). Over time, a local hip hop industry emerged which was driven by youths themselves and only loosely tied to the aid industry. During the period of my fieldwork, local hip hop production was rapidly growing and record studios with a 'producer' and basic recording equipment were springing up everywhere. Recording a song was a popular youth activity for those who could afford it. Prices which covered the creation of a beat by the producer, the recording and one copy of the song on CD ranged somewhere between UGX 50,000–70,000 (approximately 20 euros), with video productions starting from UGX 100,000 (approximately 30 euros).

When I asked my interlocutors about their motivation to do hip hop, many stressed that it was a meaningful form of social participation and political critique. They saw hip hop as a chance to communicate their life experiences and struggles; and as a means of criticising the current conditions in Gulu, where prospects for most youth were bleak. For example:

> I really like hip hop, because ... it got discovered by people who were very frustrated in my view, you know black Americans, they experienced a lot of things so they discovered it. I see it like they were doing a strike in a modernised way, because they could talk about things like ... how they were mistreated. (Elima, 20)

Many of my interlocutors saw hip hop as a symbol of modernity and a way to contest 'outdated' social hierarchies and values. 'Rebelling' against older generations who saw hip hop as the embodiment of Westernisation and moral decay was evident, at least in the artists' self-presentation, although it seemed that quite a few of them were, in fact, also passionate traditional dancers. Besides its ideological function, however, many stated that their motivation for making music was also driven by the hope to earn some money and 'become big'. While the prospects of becoming rich or famous were very small, making music was indeed becoming a source of income for some youth in Gulu, not only those who worked as producers.

Most local clubs had hip hop contests in which many of my inter-locutors participated regularly and in which small prizes (sometimes money up to UGX 100,000, but usually much less) could be won. Some artists also tried to market their services and to write (praise) songs for politicians or other 'big people' – a strategy which some-times played out during election times, but which usually required changing the music style to a more 'traditional' one. One producer I knew had the idea of writing hip hop songs for the aid industry on issues like HIV/AIDS or poverty reduction. In these contexts, then, selling one's youth identity (which was highly valued both in poli-tics and humanitarian contexts) and performing a particular kind of ideological subjectivity to suit elite actors became a way to profit, even if this meant compromising one's own political convictions.

Those who had already managed to record a song tried various strategies to promote it. They sold copies of (pirated) CDs on the street, which included their own song (and video) but, importantly, also those of more well-known artists. Some marketed their songs via radio which, however, required paying a fee that many could not afford. During my fieldwork, Gulu was still heavily frequented by foreign aid workers and researchers. Hip hop artists targeted these groups, especially younger internationals, in the hope of attracting sponsors and connections with international producers.

All in all, although most artists saw themselves as critical commentators and many tried to perform a 'bad boy' image, they were usually willing to compromise their style of music and/or their appearance when this meant getting cash. Rather than reading this as inconsequential or fake, it was a sign of their often very precarious economic situation as depicted in the following quote:

> I have to cope up and do something at least, so I wrote some kind
> of lyrics. [But I have] no money to record, the biggest problem
> in Africa is money and – I have told you before: unemployment!
> ... The biggest problem which affects the youth – you can have
> finished your course, finished your studies: no job! (Martin, 26)

This shows that while many of the youth involved in music and tradi-tional dancing attributed profound meanings to their activities, the need to make money overshadowed everything else. In a situation where (regular) formal employment was not a realistic perspective, all social activities were turned into potential cash-making activities and thus lead to an on-going economisation of the social. However, youth not only found themselves in a precarious economic situation, but also in a highly moralised and politicised context in which contested visions for a future post-war Acholi society were being negotiated. Thus, activities like traditional dancing or hip hop were seen as moral and even political signifiers. Paradoxically, while the situation of economic uncertainty necessitated youth to be flexible and take advantage of any cash-generating opportunity, the moralised context required them to authentically convey their belief in the absolute and exclusive values associated with either retraditionalisation or modernisation. Subsequently, moral claims and political visions themselves were becoming economised as different elites (humanitarian actors, politicians, 'traditional leaders' etc.) were seeking publically visible support for their positions and programmes – a development which, I argue, can also be observed in the broader context of Ugandan politics and voting behaviour.

'Opportunistic youth'? The economisation of politics

During a recent stay in Uganda, I read the following letter, entitled 'Opportunistic Youth', in the daily newspaper, *Daily Monitor*:

> As Uganda changes politically, there is a determined group of opportunistic youth taking advantage of political activities for basically materialistic and not ideological causes. A case in point is a group of youth that make it to the media for switching from one side of the political divide to the other where they think the bread is more buttered. This is evidence it was their survival at heart and not our country. (Kasumba 2015)

Another comment in the same newspaper stated: 'My sense is that today, Ugandan youth make their broader political decisions in a highly relativistic context, not in absolute terms like their parents' (Oyango-Obbo 2015; the author claims that while older generations, following the independence of Uganda in 1962, had strong political visions based on a nationalist ethos and pan-Africanist aspirations, the younger generation lacks such aspirations and judges the National Resistance Movement (NRM) performance mainly by comparing it to other, often worse, African or previous Ugandan regimes).

These two statements encapsulate a hypothesis I want to propose here but cannot develop in detail. Namely that (youth) political engagement in neoliberal Uganda, and especially after the end of the war in the north, is increasingly driven by the pursuit of individual economic interests (like profit or survival) rather than a belief in and commitment to ideologies, programmes and alliances. Similar hypotheses have been put forth by others. Ojok and Kabassa (2016), for instance, argue that there has been a broader shift from stable, collective (e.g. ethnic, regional, religious) loyalties to a candidate or party (what they label 'old clientelism') to more individual voting rationalities whereby individual 'clients' exchange their vote for benefits which are offered or promised to them by political 'patrons'.

Northern Uganda is an interesting case in this regard. Ever since Museveni came to power, Acholiland in particular has been an opposition stronghold. In the first multiparty presidential elections, in 2001, around 80 per cent of the voters in the three Acholi districts voted for the main opposition-candidate Kizza Besigye (votes for Besigye: Gulu: 81.8%; Kitgum: 72.4%; Pader: 80.7%; all data provided by the Ugandan Electoral Commission; www.ec.or.ug, accessed 20 May 2016). A similar pattern occurred in the 2006 elections (votes for Besigye: Gulu: 82.4%; Kitgum: 75.5%; Pader: 77.4%). The 2011 elections, however, have not only seen a sharp decline in actual votes (from 69% in the two previous elections to 59%) but also a surprising increase of support for Museveni, in Agago and Lamwo over 50% (the former three Acholi districts have now been subdivided into seven. Museveni received the following percentage of votes: Amuru: 36.75%; Gulu: 29.64%; Nwoya: 26.69%; Lamwo: 50.21%; Kitgum: 38.82%; Agago: 59.57%; Pader: 46.12%)! This trend was to some extent confirmed in the recent 2016 elections where support for Museveni even increased in a number of northern districts (from 29.64% to 32.74% in Gulu, from 38.82% to 41.84% in Kitgum and from 26.69% to 41.64% in Nwoya), although he lost supporters in Pader (from 46.12% to 38.86%) and Amuru (from 36.75% to 31.52%).

The growing support for Museveni in the north is surprising because in local discourses and debates most people remain highly critical of him. The majority of my interlocutors in Gulu (in 2010/11, but also during recent fieldwork in 2015) were convinced that he was corrupt and, more importantly, blamed him and his party for the war, the suffering of the Acholi and the marginalisation of the north.

Drawing on my conversations with Acholi youth during the pre-election campaigns in 2010, I suggest a few aspects which could shed light on this gap between how people perceive the NRM regime and how they vote. Most of my interlocutors were eligible to vote for the first time in 2011. When talking about the elections, most of them stated that they wanted to get a voter's card (which also figured as a national ID), but that they would not actually use it to vote. Asked for their reasons, many stated that Ugandan politics was highly corrupt and that they did not believe that voting would actually make a difference. First, because Museveni would remain in power no matter what, either because he was able to 'buy' enough votes by generously giving out alcohol, soap and other 'gifts' during his campaigns, or simply by rigging the election results. And second, because even given the unlikely case of a regime change, politicians would operate according to the same logic (i.e. corruption) and it would not change anything for the people on the ground. For my interlocutors, politics was largely about individuals fighting for money and influence rather than about ideas, as this statement reveals:

> Museveni is a very sharp [clever] old man. … But the way he runs the government is so fake. These guys are so corrupt, they want to take what does not belong to them, equality is not there. Those guys, a brother and a brother, could kill themselves because of money. (Joseph, 20)

Despite the general anti-Museveni climate in Gulu, some of my interlocutors stated that, if they voted at all, it would probably be for Museveni and the NRM – not because they believed he was a good politician or his party had a good political programme, but because they thought that demonstrating loyalty to the regime might bring personal benefits for them, for instance when applying for jobs. Some also said that they had never known anyone else in power and although Museveni surely had not done much good to the north, there might still be politicians who would do worse. However, also older people who in the past had never voted for Museveni sometimes wondered whether shifting their alliance to the NRM would prove beneficial for them. It seemed that increasing frustration with and disbelief in Ugandan politics and politicians changed people's motivation to vote from wanting to make a political and ideological statement to seeking best-possible *individual* advantages. The increasingly repressive political climate and intimidation of opposition supporters added credibility to the widespread assumption that being pro-NRM or completely disengaging from politics were the most viable options (cf. Branch 2013: 3165), although, as outlined in the Introduction, there are also several examples of popular protests against the current regime.

A compelling example of the commodification of political loyalties is the increasing practice of 'party-switching', also mentioned in the comment at the beginning of this section. Party-switching occurs at all political levels – among 'simple' voters just as among high-ranking politicians (Daily Monitor 2015). It is commonly part of campaigns, where people who have supposedly changed their party loyalty are publically 'paraded' and symbolically given t-shirts or other items with the new party's logo.

While party-switching already occurred during the Obote I regime, it has increased dramatically since the re-establishment of multiparty politics in 2005. According to Ojok and Kabassa (2016: 41–43), it is now being practised by a majority of Ugandan voters, whereby party affiliation and voting function as rent-seeking strategies, emerging out of people's need to survive and/or establish clientelistic networks. Thus, many citizens 'shop' (*ibid.*: 51) around for the party which can provide the most incentives. This is undoubtedly the NRM due to its position as the ruling party and its related ability to access and distribute money and other resources on a much larger scale than other parties. It is therefore no surprise that crossovers from other parties to the NRM are the most common.

In public discourses, 'party-switchers' are often accused of 'selling their soul' for short-term economic profits. More significantly, the increased incidence of party-switching among established politicians seemed to suggest that party alliance is no longer a strong indicator of a person's political convictions and values. In short, it contributes to the economisation of politics whereby both politicians and voters increasingly make choices based on instrumental rationality rather than absolute values.

Conclusion

This chapter has discussed some of the key processes of neoliberalisation in Uganda since 1986, namely the widespread economisation of social practices, moral values and political beliefs, and the commodification of cultural and political identities. I have shown how youth, in particular, (are driven to) perceive themselves and act as entrepreneurial subjects rather than members of collectives, and how they have internalised the need to be self-reliant, flexible and to take advantage of any situation which offers a chance of making money. Their positioning must be seen against the background of their upbringing in a context where Uganda, on the one hand experienced unprecedented levels of economic growth and capitalist expansion and, on the other hand saw increasing inequality and the foreclosing of economic and political opportunities for members of younger generations, especially in the north. As one of my interlocutors put it:

> The older generation had better opportunities than us. [Then] the population was small and there were few educated people. By the time you reached Senior 4 [fourth year of secondary school], you were big. That is why most of them are in the government ... Those guys had opportunities, but for us it is a little bit closed now and the competition is very high. So if you are not fit, man, you are missing out, that is it. (Joseph, 20)

Like Joseph, the majority of youth I spoke to felt that there were few chances for members of their generation to gain access to the (consumerist) lifestyle they witnessed in their daily lives and in the media. Furthermore, due to their experience of Ugandan politics which since their birth had been dominated by a small, established and apparently corrupt elite, few believed that a more democratic and just political system was possible, leading to widespread disillusionment with politics and mistrust of politicians' programmes and claims. In this context, youth had come to learn that in order not to 'miss out' one needs to be able and willing to strategically adapt ones convictions and loyalties. This erosion of beliefs in and commitment to absolute values and long-term loyalties among the young generation is maybe one of the most profound, but often unacknowledged, consequences of Uganda's neoliberalisation.

References

Branch, A. (2013), 'Gulu in war ... and peace? The town as camp in northern Uganda', *Urban Studies*, 50(15), pp. 3152–67.

Comaroff, J. and Comaroff, J. (2009), *Ethnicity, Inc.* (Chicago, IL: University of Chicago Press).

Daily Monitor (2015), 'Former Kilak Legislator Ocula crosses to NRM', 23 March.

Ferguson, J. (1999), *Expectations of Modernity: Myths and Meanings of Urban Life on the Zambian Copperbelt* (Berkeley, CA: University of California Press).

Foucault, M. (2006), *Die Geburt der Biopolitik. Vorlesung am Collège de France 1978–79* (Frankfurt a. M.: Suhrkamp).

Kasumba, A. (2015), 'Opportunistic youth', *Daily Monitor*, 3 April, p. 12.

Ntarangwi, M. (2009), *East African Hip Hop: Youth Culture and Globalisation* (Urbana, IL: University of Illinois Press).

Ojok, D. and Kabassa, B. (2016), 'The crossover: Exploring the party identification paradox in Uganda's multiparty politics', *Journal on Perspectives of African Democracy and Development*, 1(1), pp. 41–54.

Oyango-Obbo, C. (2015), 'Why Ugandans think we are headed in the right direction: The case for a rethink', *Daily Monitor*, 25 March.

Vorhölter, J. (2014), *Youth at the Crossroads: Discourses on Socio-cultural Change in Post-war Northern Uganda* (Göttingen: Göttingen University Press).

Weber, M. (1961), 'Types of rationality', in T. Parsons (ed.), *Theories of Society: Foundations of Modern Sociological Theory* (New York, NY: Free Press of Glencoe), pp. 1063–65.

18
Neoliberal times: leisure and work among young men in rural eastern Uganda

Ben Jones

In eastern Uganda, there is a generation of young men who are educated and who also farm. This was not meant to be the case. The popular expectation was that education would be a way out of farming and into salaried employment, a view also promoted by the Ugandan government. But this sort of work is few and far between, instead what was found was an iteration of the 'jobless growth' that is a feature of contemporary Uganda. Instead the more usual form of work for young men is as motorcycle taximen, as petty traders or day labourers, and also as farmers, working the plots of land they had inherited. When I talked to young men in the trading centre of Atine Atirir, farming was not something they liked to talk about; instead they preferred to talk about 'leisure time', a phrase that was new to me. 'Leisure time' meant passing time in the company of other, mostly educated young men, playing ludo or cards, waiting for the next premiership football game to be screened. They described themselves as unemployed, but were working. Some affected the urban 'style' of hip hop stars and footballers that could be seen on their mobile phones, others dressed like would-be officer workers, others dressed more like an older generation. These young men also went to burials, attended church and many had young families. They were neither of the town nor entirely of the village, they were educated but did not belong to the salaried economy. 'Leisure time' and the continued but often difficult relationship farming forms the focus of the chapter.

My discussion of 'leisure time' adds to a body of scholarship pointing to the contradictions and variations in what could be termed 'actually existing neoliberalism' (Collier 2012: 192, Kingfisher and Maskovsky 2008, Ferguson 2015). This means looking at the ways in which people adapt and make sense of what is involved in being unemployed while farming; in living with the gap between desired work and work that was available; in affecting urban styles while going to a grass-thatched church or attending a burial. As the Introduction to this volume points out, approaches to the study of neoliberalism in Africa, and elsewhere, are increasingly recognising the uneven nature of policies that promote market-based reforms, or the inconsistencies in neoliberalism as a broader ideological project (Kipnis 2008: 280, Ferguson 2010). This means making sense of policies and discourses and the way they play into ongoing social, cultural and economic formations (Kipnis 2008: 280, Ferguson 2010, Hilgers 2013). My interest in leisure time in eastern Uganda is in how it rubbed up against older obligations and relationships (cf. Bayart 1996).

There is already a growing literature on the relationship between neoliberalism, youth and unemployment in Africa (Masquelier 2013, Sommers 2012, Mains 2007, Wiegratz 2016) and while there is not always perfect agreement in these accounts of what is meant by 'neoliberalism', there is a shared concern with looking at the non-structural, open-ended ways in which state policies and global discourses trickle down (cf. Kingfisher and Maskovsky 2008, Ferguson 2010), and noting that there are too many Western biases in the examples given (Parnell and Robinson 2011, Kipnis 2007). Analyses of unemployed, educated youth in several African urban centres report a situation where youths feel they should be productive and able to progress, and where broader cultural shifts encourage the desire for certain sorts of jobs and lifestyles. There is a sense of time passing, where the inability to secure an urban, employed future makes the present more difficult. The puzzle of education and unemployment produces new cultural formations – tea-drinking groups of *jeunes diplômés* in Niger; groups of idlers in Addis Ababa. In such instances 'neoliberal capitalism has acted as a vise that has closed off any opportunity for a growing population' to achieve their aspirations (Mains 2007: 664). It is a literature that emphasises a set of frustrations produced by neoliberalism and finds its echo in the 'uncertainty and ambivalence' discussed in Vorhölter's chapter on 'youth entrepreneurs' in Gulu (this volume).

I take a slightly different line, pointing both to the frustrations produced by the lack of work, but also to the ways farming, 'leisure time' and the rural economy also offered some space for variation. I am interested in the way relationships – between generations, between men and women, husbands and wives, fathers and children – continue to develop alongside the emerging culture of 'leisure time'. I make two related points. First, the discourse around 'leisure' helped young men feel they were associated with the lives of those who were 'urban' or more 'developed'. Young men talked about the lifestyles of non-governmental organisation (NGO) workers, the lives of Premier League footballers, the new large houses being built by successful people from the area, all of whom were felt to have their own 'leisure time'. This was a different way of passing time than had been the case for previous generations, which was shaped by the agricultural calendar. Second, young men continued to be part of a rural economy, where farming and family obligations were part of their lives. These men were poor, a step down from the urban, educated youths more typically the focus of research on education and youth (cf. Jeffrey 2010). Many of the young men I spoke to had moved back into working either the plots of land their parents owned, of land they had already inherited, and spoke of the relationships and obligations that characterised life in the area as well as their 'leisure time'. It is, perhaps, the mixture of frustration and variation that best captures the experiences of young men with which I was able to spend time. To put a face to these observations, I start with a description of two young men: David and Robert.[1]

'Leisure time': two young men playing ludo

I met David and Robert in the trading centre of Atine Atirir, in the northern part of the Teso region of eastern Uganda.[2] The trading centre lies parallel to the newly tarmacked road between Soroti and Lira. Both David and Robert are ludo players. I met them on a weekday morning when many others were busy in the gardens (I visited the area during the growing season). David and Robert were with a group of friends and were sat in front of one of the verandas that flanked the main road. They were under a grass-thatched shade. A reasonable crowd had gathered, and by the time I arrived there were twelve men either watching or playing the game. At first I was surprised by the openness of the space in which ludo was played (I knew that the activity invited criticism). The game was played for small sums of money. Robert was nominated to speak with me. He would rather have continued watching the ludo game that was going on. Robert was selected, it seemed, because he was felt to be more educated than some, and also younger and so less able to refuse. David came and spoke of his own accord.

The ludo board – the usual board divided into four coloured quadrants – was reinforced by a high-sided wooden frame. This allowed for fairly violent throws of the dice. The game is played with more style, wit and performance than might be expected. Different players have a certain way with the dice, and the game commands a degree of attention, not only among the players, but also with the wider audience. The board is divided into four quadrants – red, blue, green, yellow. Each quarter is named after a Premier League football team – Arsenal, Chelsea, Manchester United, Liverpool in that order (Arsenal is the most popular) (cf. Vokes 2010). Robert and David were not involved in a game when I arrived, and so I asked them to sit inside the shop. It had a few items for sale – tea, some sweets, biscuits. It was poorer than many of the other shops I had seen. In place of the shelves that I was used to seeing in better provisioned stores, there was a roughly hewn table on which a few items were placed, while a number of other goods hung from lines of string above. (The owner of the shop received a small fee for letting the ludo game go ahead.)

At the time of the interview Robert was still at home, with his parents. He was not married. He told me that before getting married he wanted to find a proper job, by which he meant salaried employment. He was helping his parents on the farm, and said that he was also trying to find sponsorship for further studies. He turned up in his farming overalls. Robert had left Katine Secondary School after completing his A-levels three years ago. When asked about what he wanted to study, I was told 'Mass Communication and Journalism'. This seemed to relate to the after effects of a development project that had been running in the area, which had been funded by Barclays Bank and *The Guardian* newspaper and run by an NGO (www. guardian.co.uk/katine). The NGO had set up a 'community resource centre' where people could go and use the internet to find friends and, hopefully, a sponsor for future studies. One of Robert's Facebook friends lived in Canada. When asked about what he discussed with this friend, he said 'we exchange views on life here, and life there'. Robert said that he could spend about six hours a week online, though he worried that he would have to find another way of connecting with people once the NGO stopped its work the following month. When I suggested that he might end up as a farmer, he said that this would be 'wasting' his education. The money used to play ludo was mostly from day labouring, or from his parents. Spending time in the trading centre – among peers, of the same gender – was also the closest thing he had to the social experience of being at school.

David ran a barbering 'salon' in the trading centre. He had a pair of electric clippers and worked from a small grass-thatched shade, and cut hair for 500 shillings. On a good day he told me he could cut the hair of about twenty or so customers and make about 10,000 shillings (about four dollars). His business was started with the help of his brother, also a barber. David had only recently started joining the men who played cards, a slight slip in the eyes of some of his peers; card playing, unlike ludo, was strongly associated with drinking alcohol (Ludo was played by young men who attended the local Baptist church; Baptists are teetotal and, as a rule, try to avoid situations where alcohol is consumed). David had a family that he was bringing up in the village. He had married and had a wife and two children, he had still to complete the payment of the bride price owed to his wife's family (a common situation). David and his wife farmed three plots of land (*amisirin*) next to his home. David told me that he preferred his work in the trading centre as there were more opportunities. He was also a member of a Village Savings and Loan Association – a form of microcredit organised around a self-selected group of villagers – also a product of the NGO's work in the area. Members received loans that were valued against the assets – typically livestock – they had. David had been educated up to O-level. He wore a baseball cap and an Arsenal shirt.

In watching the ludo game play out, I was reminded that this has become a feature of life in trading centres across the Teso region. It was a change from what I had observed in such places a decade earlier. I was also struck by the fact that Robert and David had a relationship, in one way or another, to farming (even though they both told me they preferred to stay in the trading centre or town). Robert, younger and with slightly more education, helped his parents in the garden, while also hoping to go for further studies. David, older and with less education, had been helped by his brother into working as a barber; while his commitments as a husband and father meant that farming had become more of a fixed part of his future. Both puzzled over what to do. The presence of a Facebook friend, the Arsenal T-shirt, the Village Savings and Loans Association, the degree in Mass Communication showed the different ways in which signifiers of the neoliberal economy made its presence felt in the area, in ways that, as we shall see, were not always consistent or perfectly aligned with one another.

'Actually existing neoliberalism' in eastern Uganda

Robert and David live in the Teso region of eastern Uganda. As with the rest of Uganda, and much of sub-Saharan Africa there has been a rush for education in the past decade. Alongside free government primary schools, there have been fee-paying primary and secondary schools, and various universities and colleges that have sprung up in

Kampala and a number of provincial towns; the expansion of higher education in particular has been one of the main avenues for wealthy Ugandans to invest and profit setting up private business. In the sub-county of Katine, all of the parishes had their own primary school, some of them 'mango tree' schools that have few school buildings; others, 'community schools' where there may be a few government paid teachers, alongside teachers whose salary is paid for by the parents; there are also government schools where the entire roster of teachers are on the Ministry of Education payroll and where the buildings are the responsibility of the District Education Office in Soroti. Katine Primary School and Katine Secondary School, both down the road from the trading centre, are examples of this sort of 'government' schooling. There are also fee-paying private primary and secondary schools such as the one end of the trading centre of Atine Atirir.

In Atine Atirir the message coming from above is that education leads to upward mobility. This rubs up against a reality where jobs are few and far between; the youth unemployment rate in Uganda as a whole – defined as those without work but available for work – is 78 per cent, with the situation in the countryside particularly acute (GoU 2015: 4). It was difficult for those in Atine Atirir who did not have connections to get salaried employment (the few employed younger people in the sub-county already had an older family member in paid employment). Furthermore the decreasing value of high school certificates, diplomas and degrees – proportionate to the increasing number of graduates – has created a gap between what is the most probable future for young men such as Robert and David, and their aspirations, neoliberal iterations of 'diploma disease' (Dore 1976) or 'diploma inflation' (Bourdieu 1984: 142–43). In the previous genera-tion a primary school leaver's certificate was enough to become a parish chief, while a secondary school leaver's certificate was enough to become sub-county chief. Today you need a university degree to be a sub-county chief.

Bourdieu writes of a 'broken trajectory' to describe the situ-ation where education failed to lead to the sort of jobs that were expected. It should be said that this sense of a trajectory was less pronounced in rural Teso than elsewhere in Uganda. The incor-poration of the region into the colonial system in the first half of the twentieth century focused on a shift to a small-holder economy where households were expected to grow cotton for onward sale, and where much of the middle work of buying and selling was managed by Asian traders (Vincent 1982). Education was a rare thing, and salaried jobs were limited to the few individuals who joined the local government system, the army or the police. In contrast to some of the sites in sub-Saharan Africa where wages and salaries have been common – migrant labour settlements, plantation farming – salaried work has always been rare in Teso. The decline of cotton in the post-colonial period did little to shift the economy away from a mixture of farming, petty trading and casual labour.

One significant change in the past decade or so has been the growing number of NGOs working in the area. The fact that Robert had Facebook friends and David had joined a microcredit scheme was the result of an NGO working in the sub-county. While the sector as a whole offers few opportunities in terms of long-term salaried employment, it is important for the ideologies and objects it puts in front of people. As with other development initiatives the project that Robert was a part of emphasised what Manzo has characterised as a 'neoliberal conception of community development' (2012: 552). There was an emphasis on 'good governance', 'entrepreneurship', 'rights-based' approaches and 'idioms of individualism and choice' (Ellison 2009, Englund 2006), and a language that framed images of successful development around the skills and capacities of the individual.

But perhaps the most obvious changes in rural Teso have been around new cultural formations. The desire for Facebook friends, of long conversations about Arsenal's prospects in the premiership, of 'leisure time' belong to what can be thought of as a 'commodification of culture', signifying a shift in 'the cultural knowledge and self-making of individuals' (Comaroff and Comaroff 2009: 83). Video halls have sprung up across the region, giving people access to satellite television, while there is a growing number of commercial radio stations, many of which contain a large quantity of religious programming. Indeed the ludo board and leisure time are not entirely separate from the language that has developed around new forms of Christianity. The advent of growing numbers of people professing a 'born again' identity sits alongside a growing concern with notions of self-management and personal development. In what follows, I suggest that new cultural objects – television, bill-board advertising, the popularity of the English Premier League, the growing availability of Nollywood films, telenovelas, porn films, 'born again' churches – help to produce urban styles alongside rural forms of employment.

'We are passing our leisure time'

In making sense of unemployment in Atine Atirir, young men spoke of the importance of 'leisure' and 'leisure time'. This language was new to me. While older generations understood the importance of the distinction between work and rest, this was framed in a different language, one where the agricultural seasons – the dry season being a time for relaxation – played a role. Older men and women also spoke of the celebrations that accompanied marriages and other public occasions, and the sociality that accompanied farm work. Perhaps the most obvious form of rest, one that has its origins in the colonial period, came on Sunday, when people attended church. This gave the seven-day week its structure, with the other six days given over to work, what Vincent termed an 'ideology for the capitalist economy' of the early colonial period in Teso (1982: 136). The word 'leisure' meant something different and new and had a different sort of temporality. And I will try to explain what I understood young men to mean by the term.

The first point was that leisure formed part of a nexus with employed work. When young men spoke of 'leisure' and 'leisure time', it was because 'leisure' was also a thing enjoyed by those who had salaried employment. It was a way of associating yourself with work, even if you did not have a job. Those who were rich or successful showed their success through leisure with a sort of conspicuous consumption: driving the best four-wheel drives, building a villa-style bungalow, moving from one place to another. Leisure was worth holding onto, I was told, because it gave the sense – however remote – that one day you might become a worker. This also explains why some of the high school students around the ludo board also spoke of 'leisure time' as something they cultivated. While older people may regard those engaging in 'leisure time' as 'idlers', for younger people it also meant participating in a cultural formation that signalled, paradoxically perhaps, the possibility of work:

> Ludo we just play for passing time. Yes, some old men criticise us for wasting time. They say we are just idle here. But they don't know that we are passing our leisure time.

Robert went on to describe the way older people did not fully understand the world of the young. The absence of 'leisure' in the older generation was because they were 'not educated', he felt. (A secondary school education was rare among those over thirty.) For this older generation, sociality was mostly experienced through farming, visiting neighbours and the home.

'Leisure time' implied new practices of consumption and modes of belonging (Weiss 2009, Introduction). To be passing 'leisure time' implied certain pursuits that had an 'urban' style – cards, ludo, watching football, listening to new types of music. In thinking about the question of passing time there is also a point about new practices of consumption (Goldstein 2012). Video halls and premiership matches were something new to Atine Atirir, as were Arsenal T-shirts, and baseball caps. In a similar way to the elaborate tea-drinking ceremonies Masquelier documents, the joblessness of young men in rural Teso produces a 'neoliberalised economy' of leisure (Wiegratz and Cesnulyte 2016: 10). Ludo games took half an hour to play and several hours could pass with the same group of men around the ludo board. There was also the English Premier League, which had become the focus of the weekend for many young men, and had made Saturday rather than Sunday the most important day in their week. Weekday nights were also shaped by the timings of football fixtures.

The most popular football team, Arsenal, had an underdog status. They were not particularly good at winning trophies. Arsenal was also popular because it had a record of promoting black, often African, players. Vokes makes a similar point in explaining Arsenal's popularity in a sub-county in south-western Uganda (Vokes 2010: 10). When watching Arsenal play in one of the video halls in the trading centre, there were obvious signs of consumption, not least in the adverts for brands that had a continent-wide audience – Rolex, Vodafone, Heineken. There was also the possibility of seeing your team lose as well as win, and of young men succeeding without necessarily conforming to the rules. At one of the screenings I attended in the trading centre – a match involving Liverpool – the focus for much of the time was on Luis Suarez, who had been benched for biting the ear of a fellow player in a previous match. He was 'flash' in his style, someone who did not necessarily submit to others. For some of the younger men his independence and lack of respect for the rules of the game resonated.

Here the best parallel, perhaps, is Weiss's work among barbers and their clients in Arusha, Tanzania. Weiss suggests that consumerism and self-fashioning offer examples of what he terms the neoliberal 'production of value' (2009: 17).[3] He points to the ambivalence surrounding the sorts of consumptive practices that are emerging in Arusha and looks at the appeal of a musical form – hip hop – that celebrates consumerism and also contains within it space for opposition and criticism. Weiss suggests that hip hop is popular precisely because it allows for a 'productive engagement' with people's sense of visible (dis)connection to other parts of the world. Young men identified with hip hop stars not just because they were young and successful, but also because they talked about alienation and outsider-ness. Something similar could be observed among younger men in Atine Atirir, particularly those who had only just left school. A footballer like Suarez was popular with some of the men because he did not always play by the rules of an older generation, because he liked to show off his wealth and because he was young and free to make his own choices (he was sat on the sidelines with his wife Sofia Balbi).

At the same it is important not to overstate the degree to which the men around the ludo board were singular in their attitudes or opinions. Many of the young men I spoke to emphasised responsibilities and obligations, and were critical of a player like Suarez. This was particularly true for those who were a few years out of school and were moving into family life. They had less regard for an ill-disciplined player. I was also told about the difficulties many young men faced in dealing with an older generation that needed care, and younger siblings who needed help with school fees. What was particularly striking, given the emphasis in the wider literature on the 'stuckness' of African youth, was the way many of these young men had taken on the markers of adulthood: marriage, children, farming, a home (Cole 2005, Comaroff and Comaroff 2006). They found ways of becoming men while still having 'leisure time'.

'We do our garden work and then we come to play'

In the above it is clear that young men in Atine Atirir aspired to something like an 'urban culture'. And yet their lives continued to be lived in ways that bound them to farming (and by implication to relationships and obligations far removed from the idea of the educated, self-sufficient individual). Farming typically meant working the small amount of land that they had inherited, or helping out parents with their land. Robert, the high school student hoped to do a degree in Mass Communication, he also helped his parents in their gardens. David, who worked as a barber, continued to do farmwork, and he and his wife used the three gardens he had inherited from his father to feed and support the family. What emerged in conversation with young men was a developing relationship with family, and participation in farming, day labouring and other sorts of work that had little to do with their education. It was a connection they sometimes disdained and often tried to downplay when they sat around the ludo board, but which continued to be a means of making a living. (When I first asked Robert whether he helped his parents, he demurred, despite the overalls he was wearing, and others had to prompt him to tell me that he had been digging in his parents' garden in the morning.)

It should be said that this demurral was in spite of a fairly concerted effort by the Ugandan state (and the NGO sector) to promote farming as an economic activity and as something that was tied to an idea of progress. Much of the 'livelihoods' work done by NGOs around Atine Atirir pushed farming as a way out of poverty. A recent project led by Farm Africa, for example, selected a number of 'model farmers' giving them cash crops and fertilisers and training aimed at turning them into 'micro-entrepreneurs'. Farm Africa had, with the support of another NGO, also built a large community co-operative next to the sub-county headquarters for the purposes of helping farmers market their products. The young men I spoke to did not buy this idea of 'marketing, seeing economic success more as a result of corruption and connections. In other words, the 'cultural formation' that developed around the neoliberal economy was not a straightforward translation of government or NGO discourse. Instead the changing relationship to farming was shaped more by the sense that wealth and success lay in the towns and the capital city, and that farming did not appear to belong to the future. A view reinforced by advertising, television, the expanding lifestyle sections of national newspapers, the English Premier League.

In choosing the somewhat different cases of Robert and David it is possible to see variation in the relationship to education, joblessness and farming. Robert, one of the younger men in the group, still claimed the status of a student who was jobless while helping his parents in their gardens. At the moment he was keen to be seen as an 'educated youth' and in pursuit of further education. As he got older his relationship to his status as educated would change, with the most likely scenario one of marriage and a mixture of day labouring, farm work or petty trading. It was difficult for men in their late twenties to still consider themselves 'youths'. David, who was older, was further down the road to making a living, which no longer connected to his past as a student. He was no longer someone who was both 'jobless' (in the sense that he was hoping for future paid employment), but who had also graduated into being a man. He was a barber, who had to pay off the rest of his bride price and who also managed the land he and his wife farmed.

What further complicates the picture, is the way this sort of 'actually existing neoliberalism' sits at a right angle to scholarship that emphasises neoliberalism as a 'responsibilising discourse' that places blame, or a lack of success, on the individual (Rose 1999, Kingfisher and Maskovsky 2008). In Atine Atirir there was much less sense that individuals were being blamed for their joblessness, and this may also have made it easier for young men to make some sort of accommodation with the problem of joblessness. When I asked a local businessman about whether there was a problem with these young men, I was told:

> they [idlers] are there. But there is a lack of jobs and these are men who cannot manage the life of a farmer. Even those without jobs go to the garden for 2,500 (less than a dollar) for labouring.

Explanations about joblessness almost always focused on the structural absence of work (rather than the 'failure' of young men to find jobs). The businessman quoted above knew that it was difficult for young men with an education to get a job, and it was hard for them to go back to farming. He sympathised with the pattern of labouring, waiting and passing time. Most of the discussions around unemployment in Atine Atirir had a sociological rather than a pathological quality. Older men who had achieved some success in farming or in business told me that unemployment came about mostly because of a lack of paid employment. And while it was understood that many would in the end have to find their way back to farming, it was reasonable to expect the transition to be slow and difficult, a mixture of frustration and accommodation.

Conclusion

The Ugandan government, as well as many of its international backers, makes a fairly instrumental and straightforward set of links between schooling and jobs. It bears little reality for educated youth living in the country. For Ugandans it remains difficult for those without connections to get salaried employment (Wiegratz 2016). The majority of those who have gone through the education system continue to live in rural areas, continue to be part of the rural economy, and lack salaried work. Many young people have also been exposed to the world in new ways, through smartphones and video halls, through moving between the village and the town, through going to school (Weiss 2009). They find themselves stuck between the government's claims of a skills and jobs revolution and the absence of the sort of work that would make sense of their years of formal education and their aspirations (Appadurai 1996). This is what we might think of as 'actually existing neoliberalism' the sort of experience of 'reordering' outlined in the Introduction to this volume.

In this chapter I have looked at a rural setting and the concept of 'leisure time' to set alongside the urban bias of much of the literature on neoliberalism, unemployment and youth in Africa and elsewhere. In the above I have suggested the complexity and ambiguity of the situation. New forms of consumption celebrated success while also provoking frustration and criticism. Football matches existed alongside burials and church, 'leisure time' with farm work, education with joblessness, while worries among older villagers sat alongside a degree of understanding and sympathy for younger men. In this way it was possible to detect the often incremental and uneven ways in which the wider political economy is made sense of. It is possible to regard the rural youth of Teso discussed here as slightly different in their outlook from the 'youth entrepreneurs' of a large town discussed in the chapter by Vorhölter (this volume). While there is an emphasis on frustration, uncertainty and ambivalence in both accounts, what may be different here was the way the rural setting may also have produced more space and variation.

Robert, two years out of school, helped his parents in their garden; David, slightly older, was a married man who did barbering and farm work. Robert continued to emphasise the fact that he was a 'student' hoping to return to education, while David was more clearly committed to a life in the 'jobless' rural economy, farming in the village and doing petty business in the trading centre. As such, the case of young men playing ludo in Atine Atirir suggests the importance of seeing neoliberalism not only as a broad structural shift to which people have to respond, but also as a situation that is particular and not always consistent.

In offering this account of 'actually existing neoliberalism' I would also like to point out that these young men were not the 'floating youth' that haunts urban studies, nor were they the young men 'forever in a state of becoming' described in accounts of Africa's cities (Porter *et al.* 2010: 786). Rather they sometimes went to burials and attended church, got married and worked in the fields; their good behaviour was commented on, as were their slips and transgressions.

Notes

1 I am aware that the chapter focuses on young men to the exclusion of young women, and am working on research that looks at the way education and joblessness affects the lives of younger women in the region.

2 I have worked in the Teso region since 2001. My initial period of work in the region took place over an eighteen month period (Jones 2009). I have since tried to the visit the region every year for a period of one to two months. It is partly the changes between the 'then' of 2001 and the 'now' of the time of publication that have shaped my response to the neoliberal focus

of the book. Data for the chapter was collected in the sub-parish of Katine on three separate visits, in 2015, 2016 and 2017.

3 Other studies place neoliberalism more in the background, as a context against which to make sense of new objects and practices. Vokes (2010) takes the example of the popularity of the English Premier League in Buganda to make an argument about connection and disconnection, while Manzo (2012) looks at the role football plays in community development projects to contrast post-colonial and neoliberal models of development.

References

Appadurai, A. (1996), *Modernity at Large: Cultural Dimensions of Globalisation* (Minneapolis, MN: University of Minnesota Press).

Bayart, J.-F. (1996), 'L'historicité de l'Etat importé', in J.-F. Bayart (ed.), *La greffe de l'Etat* (Paris: Fayard), pp. 11–39.

Bourdieu, P. (1984), *Distinction: A Social Critique of the Judgment of Taste* (Cambridge, MA: Harvard University Press).

Cole, J. (2005), 'The Jaombilo of Tamatave (Madagascar), 1992–2004: Reflections on youth and globalization', *Journal of Social History*, 38(4), pp. 891–914.

Collier, S. (2012), 'Neoliberalism as big leviathan, or ...? A response to Wacquant and Hilgers', *Social Anthropology*, 20(2), pp. 186–95.

Comaroff, J. and Comaroff, J. (2006), 'Reflections on youth, from the past to the postcolony',

in M. S. Fisher and G. Downey (eds), *Frontiers of Capital: Ethnographic Reflections on the New Economy* (Durham, NC: Duke University Press), pp. 267–281.

Comaroff, J. and Comaroff, J. (2009), *Ethnicity, Inc.* (Chicago, IL: University of Chicago Press).

Dore, R. (1976), *The Diploma Disease: Education, Qualification, and Development* (London: George Allen and Unwin).

Ellison, J. (2009), 'Governmentality and the family: Neoliberal choices and emergent kin relations in southern Ethiopia', *American Anthropologist*, 111(1), pp. 81–92.

Englund, H. (2006), *Prisoners of Freedom* (Berkeley, CA: University of California Press).

Ferguson, J. (2010), 'The uses of neoliberalism', *Antipode*, 41(1), pp. 166–84.

Ferguson, J. (2015), *Give a Man a Fish: Reflections on the New Politics of Distribution* (Durham, NC: Duke University Press).

Goldstein, D. M. (2012), 'Decolonising "actually existing neoliberalism"', *Social Anthropology*, 20(3), pp. 304–09.

Government of Uganda (GoU). (2015), Second National Development Plan (NDPII) 2015/16–2019/20, Available at: http://npa.ug/wp-content/uploads/NDPII-Final.pdf [accessed 11 January 2018].

Hilgers, M. (2013), 'Embodying neoliberalism: Thoughts and responses to critics', *Social Anthropology*, 21(1), pp. 75–89.

Jeffrey, C. (2010), 'Timepass: Youth, class, and time among unemployed young men in India', *American Ethnologist*, 37(3), pp. 465–81.

Jones, B. (2009), *Beyond the State in Rural Uganda* (Edinburgh: Edinburgh University Press for the International African Institute).

Kingfisher, C. and Maskovsky, J. (2008), 'Introduction: "The limits of neoliberalism"', *Critique of Anthropology*, 28(2), pp. 115–26.

Kipnis, A. (2007), 'Neoliberalism reified: Sushi discourse and tropes of neoliberalism in the People's Republic of China', *Journal of the Royal Anthropological Institute*, 13(2), pp. 383–400.

Kipnis, A. (2008), 'Audit cultures: Neoliberal governmentality, socialist legacy, or technologies of governing?', *American Ethnologist*, 35(2), pp. 275–89.

Mains, D. (2007), 'Neoliberal times: Progress, boredom, and shame among young men in urban Ethiopia', *American Ethnologist*, 34(4), pp. 659–73.

Manzo, K. (2012), 'Development through football in Africa: Neoliberal and postcolonial models of community development', *Geoforum*, 43(3), pp. 551–60.

Masquelier, A. (2013), 'Teatime: Boredom and the temporalities of young men in Niger', *Africa*, 83(3), pp. 470–91.

Parnell, S. and Robinson, J. (2012), '(Re)theorizing cities from the global South: Looking beyond neoliberalism', *Urban Geography*, 33(4), pp. 593–617.

Porter, G. K. *et al.* (2010), 'Moving young lives: Mobility, immobility and inter-generational tensions in urban Africa', *Geoforum*, 41(5), pp. 796–804.

Rose, N. (1999), *Powers of Freedom: Reframing Political Thought* (Cambridge: Cambridge University Press).

Sommers, M. (2012), *Stuck: Rwandan Youth and the Struggle for Adulthood* (Athens, GA: University of Georgia Press).

Vincent, J. (1982), *Teso in Transformation: The Political Economy of Peasant and Class in Eastern Africa* (Berkeley, CA: University of California Press).

Vokes, R. (2010), 'Arsenal in Bugamba: The rise of English Premier League football in Uganda', *Anthropology Today*, 26(3), pp. 10–15.

Weiss, B. (2009), *Street Dreams and Hip Hop Barbershops: Global Fantasy in Urban Tanzania* (Bloomington, IN: Indiana University Press).

Wiegratz, J. (2016), *Neoliberal Moral Economy: Capitalism, Socio-cultural Change and Fraud in Uganda* (London: Rowman & Littlefield).

Wiegratz, J. and Cesnulyte, E. (2016), 'Money talks: Moral economies of earning a living in neoliberal East Africa', *New Political Economy*, 21(1), pp. 1–25.

19
The transformation of national performance arts in neoliberal Uganda

David G. Pier

As of this writing, Uganda's National Cultural Centre (UNCC), popularly known as the National Theatre, is threatened with demolishment, to be replaced by a high-rise multiplex for mixed commercial, cultural and governmental occupancy. Artists and arts enthusiasts have been protesting online under the hashtag #SaveUNCC. They do not buy the developer's assurances that the proposed mega-facility, described by one newspaper as a 'shopping mall', will equal and improve upon the old 1959 Centre as an accessible public space for the arts. For other Ugandans, however, this redevelopment of UNCC is both inevitable and desirable: they feel no particular fondness for a late-colonial-era arts edifice which has been steadily deteriorating. UNCC sits on a prime plot in the middle of downtown Kampala, a city which since the mid-1990s has experienced explosive growth and commercialisation. To supporters of the redevelopment, it seems only natural that UNCC's planners would yield to the imperatives of this growth, trusting market-savvy developers to build something up-to-date and bigger that will serve both the public arts and the commercial sector.

The planned redevelopment of the UNCC is emblematic of general trends in the Ugandan 'national' arts during the neoliberal era. The idea that productive partnerships should be sought between the government and the private sector in most matters of development, including the development of national arts, has been heavily promoted, to the extent that for some it has become a kind of common sense. Uganda has seen the rise of what this book's Introduction terms the 'market/corporate state', both as a structural reality and as an object of ideological elaboration. Even in rural villages, people expect branded multinational corporations to exercise influence over their lives, alongside the state. The government, at every level, encourages these expectations of corporate–state synergy, with local officials taking the stage at branded events put on by telecom, beverage and cosmetic companies. Politics are being branded and brands politicised in unprecedented ways. It is an open secret that President Museveni himself owns large stakes in a number of multi-national corporations operating in Uganda – most famously the telecom giant MTN, which shares the brilliant yellow colour of his National Resistance Movement party (NRM). Pop musicians, for example the regionally popular Jose Chameleone, have made their allegiances to both the government and the MTN brand known by featuring both in their songs and/or stage apparel. Ordinary voters buy yellow MTN phone cards and wear yellow MTN T-shirts to signify their support for the ruling party.

Some are open to the idea of privatised development in large part because state-stewarded development seems to have failed so abjectly. Public buildings fall apart from neglect; public highways are left unfinished. Citizens harbour few illusions about corporate motivations, but in the end, they ask, can corporations do any worse for the people than a series of corrupt and self-serving regimes have done, from colonial rule onward? Actually, it is often neoliberalism's processes of privatisation themselves that bring about deteriorations of public goods. The case of UNCC illustrates this well. In recent years, while neglecting to update the Centre's infrastructure and technology, the government has increasingly been renting out spaces in the facility for private functions, notably 'wedding meetings', where families and friends gather to raise money for their nuptial festivities. Artists who arrive at the Centre ready to rehearse have found their spaces already occupied by rent-paying revellers. This regular renting-out of spaces to private interests, justified by the government as a means of keeping a struggling institution afloat, itself contributes to the growing popular sense that the Centre is too small, too crowded and inadequate for the needs of a growing nation. In a vicious circle, privatisation itself does much to generate the dilapidated conditions that are then used to justify calls for further, more radical privatisation.

'National arts' was a potent idea in Africa's independence era; every new African state strove to have its own national theatre and national museum, for this was seen as one way of establishing a state's legitimacy on an international stage, while stirring up patriotic sentiments and promoting unity among culturally diverse citizens. Now, Ugandan national arts institutions, and African national arts more broadly, are being so transformed by the processes of neoliberalisation that the 'national' category itself may be becoming blurry and unstable in the public imagination. What remains of the 'national' in national art, when art projects under this banner increasingly have little or nothing to do with the nation-state, but are instead initiated by multinational commercial interests for commercial ends?

In this chapter, I explore neoliberalism's effects on Ugandan national arts by focusing on two case studies. The first of these is the Senator National Cultural Extravaganza, a traditional dance competition for amateur artists, sponsored by a multinational brewing company, East Africa Breweries, Ltd. (EABL). The second was a contemporary dance troupe, housed at UNCC, known as Uganda National Contemporary Ballet (UNCB). The latter was not a commercialised arts project, but rather high-concept dance initiative run by an artist from France, Valérie Miquel, with sponsorship from European aid institutions. I include UNCB in order to expand upon the point that neoliberalisation is not simply a synonym for commercialisation or privatisation. As the Introduction to this volume argues, neoliberalisation is more broadly a process of the making of capitalist market societies grounded in certain kinds of market-adjusted subjectivities, which must themselves be systematically produced. Citizens are being encultured to imagine themselves, and their societies, in market-compatible metaphors. In this project of cultural transformation, non- and even anti-commercial projects have important roles to play, alongside commercial ones. In this volume, Bompani, Jones and Vorhölter each discuss processes of neoliberal subjectification in the areas of evangelical worship, 'leisure time' and arts-based 'identity entrepreneurship', respectively. Here, I will considering how neoliberal subjectivity, in its different aspects, was engendered in both the Senator Extravaganza – a corporate project which required its non-corporate agents to think like marketers – and UNCB, an activist, experimental arts project which did not ask its participants to imagine themselves in capitalist roles (quite the opposite), but did encourage them to experience themselves as radically autonomous, liquid, nomadic individuals, in a way that, I argue, is at least compatible with neoliberalism's entrepreneurial ideal.

Commercial appropriation of national arts

The Senator National Cultural Extravaganza was a traditional dance competition, staged annually from 2005 to 2013, which doubled as a participatory marketing campaign for a brand of beer. I made the Extravaganza the focus of my ethnography, *Ugandan Music in the Marketing Era* (Pier 2015). Vorhölter (this volume) also writes about 'Senator' as a competition Acholi youth dancers had trained for in hopes of winning money. At Extravaganza events, which took place in small towns across the country, dancers, instrumentalists and singers were expected to perform in their local ethnic-traditional styles, wearing their local traditional costumes. One of the perform-ance pieces required of each group was an original composition in praise of Senator Extra Lager, a cheap, strong brew specially devised by EABL to entice low-income rural drinkers. In East Africa, indus-trial brewers have long sought to open up markets for their bottled beers in rural markets, where residents have tenaciously stuck to their own homemade brews for their cheapness, wholesomeness and association with traditional beer-sharing gatherings (Willis 2002). EABL correctly predicted that amateur performers in villages would compose, sing and dance advertisements about Senator beer for little or no payment, given a grand-prize incentive on the one hand (about $3,000 to the country's top group), and a patriotic incentive on the other – proudly representing their ethno-regional heritages on a national stage. The resulting festival was a curious melding of commercialism and nationalism, with, for example, local politicians showing up at events to praise the beer along with performing groups, as though 'Senator' were a government official, rather than a brand. An entrepreneurial spirit of competition was cultivated throughout, with audience members in addition to performers involved as partic-ipants in side-show contests, such as bicycle races and beer chugging battles.

Apart from its participatory marketing component, the Extrava-ganza much resembled the Uganda National Schools Competition, the country's longest running and most important national arts training ground. It has been mainly in the Schools competition that post-colonial generations have rediscovered and reinvented an array of indigenous traditional dances, each carefully indexed to a partic-ular ethnic group. In the early decades of independence, the Schools Competition, originally a missionary school affair, was embraced by the state as a means of inspiring a positive sense of multi-ethnic nationhood in young people and their audiences. If Uganda's diverse ethnic groups could compete energetically and equitably in the dance arena, each holding on to its own cultural identity, then surely a multi-ethnic Uganda could thrive off-stage as well, under the new government's guiding supervision.

The two men who designed the Senator Extravaganza and oversaw its rollout on the ground, Godfrey Alibatya and Akram Kintu, were not direct employees of EABL, but rather college trained experts on traditional music (at their request, I do not use Kintu and Alibatya's real names). Both had grown up competing in the Schools Competition and saw the Extravaganza first and foremost as an opportunity to extend that uplifting national arts celebration to a broader population of performers and audiences. Talented adults rather than schoolchildren would have an opportunity to perform, and events would be staged in rural villages where ordinary peasants could appreciate them. Alibatya and Kintu saw the present-day Schools Competition as a sadly deteriorated institution, starved of government funding and corrupted by bureaucracy. In the early years of the Extravaganza, they were enthusiastic about the prospects of reinventing the Schools Competition with commercial, rather than government, support. The corporate sponsor, they believed, would give them free rein to conduct the Extravaganza any way they saw fit, so long as they could consistently meet sales expectations. At least initially, both men seemed buoyed by an entrepreneurial spirit, feeling the financial and political power of one of East Africa's most powerful companies at their backs. The beer marketing component of the project, while distasteful to both men, seemed like a tolerable trade-off given the national arts revival they hoped to kindle around the countryside.

Alas, this quest to rebuild national arts with corporate rather than government sponsorship did not go smoothly. EABL had made it clear early on that its level of long-term commitment to the Extravaganza was low: if Alibatya and Kintu could not show substantial and consistent beer sales improvements, the whole event would be scrapped. Reimbursements for expenses incurred were often grudgingly late, and the two organisers often found themselves having to spend from their own bank accounts. Finally, in 2013, the corporation pulled the plug on the event, citing inadequate profits. In an interview, Alibatya told me that his view of EABL and corporate sponsors generally had darkened: while corporations, steeped in corporate-responsibility boosterism, claim to care about more than the bottom line, this often proves in the end to be little more than a false front for base profiteering. Alibatya and Kintu have remained dedicated to the ideals of national arts, but they are today less sanguine about the prospects of building national arts through commercial sponsorship. The irony is that, having witnessed the Senator Extravaganza's five-year run from the sidelines, the Ugandan government today may be even less likely to renew its own efforts at national arts development. Why pay for a nationalist celebration of multicultural dance traditions from government coffers, when a moneyed corporation like EABL has shown willingness to run the same kind of event for free? As in UNCC's redevelopment, the usual response to failures of privatisation is more privatisation.

As for the village performers who devoted their time, organising energy and meagre resources to the Extravaganza, the cancellation of the annual competition came as no great surprise. Rural Ugandans have grown accustomed to fly-by-night operations in their midst, whether these are run by corporations, the government, missionaries, candidates seeking votes or development non-governmental organisations (NGOs). One never knows who will arrive next requesting celebratory and 'mobilising' songs and dances in local languages, and so performers endeavour to project an image of ready availability and flexibility. Group leaders, in neoliberalism's prescribed entrepreneurial mode, constantly worry aloud how best to 'promote' themselves to as yet unknown potential sponsors. While these Ugandans live in places that may seem remote from the metropole, they are in fact strongly aware of, and attempting to engage with, a global attention economy. (Who with deep pockets is paying attention to rural Uganda/Africa, and how do we capture some of that attention before it flits away?) The Senator Extravaganza, with its participatory marketing element, reinforced the growing sense among these Ugandans that brands are powerful agents in the world, and that ethnic arts heritages, once harnessed to the nation-state, might now profitably be hitched to commercial brands. This popular, strategic assimilation of the idea of branding in Uganda is pursued further in my book (Pier 2015), and by Vorhölter in this volume.

The promotion of neoliberal subjectivity in foreign-sponsored 'contemporary' arts

The Senator Extravaganza exemplifies the commercial penetration of national heritage arts which is a signature trend of the neoliberal era. Neoliberalisation is not limited, however, to the commercialisation of public goods. On a more profound level, it entails the production of subjects who will experience marketisation as natural, inevitable and even progressive. Such neoliberal subjectivity is composed of entrepreneurial dispositions: e.g. an understanding of freedom in terms of individual autonomy and limitless choice, an orientation toward self-help and self-promotion, a penchant for competition and an appetite for fluidity and risk. The sociologist Zygmunt Bauman used the term 'liquidity' to encapsulate this way of being in the world, which we are all increasingly expected to manifest (Bauman 1998, 2012).

According to Bauman, Euro-modernity has been defined since its beginnings by a liquefying logic, according to which all that is solid in economic, political and social life must eventually be 'melted' for the sake of capital's relentless progress. What remains after this melting of social institutions are free-floating, nomadic individuals, who are able to surf along with global capitalism's currents, or else wind up swirling in its waste-filled eddies. Globally, our contemporary cultures tend to encourage us to become ever more liquid in our ways and values, so that we might continue to psychologically endure, and lend support to, an increasingly liquefying capitalism.

The cultivation of liquid, neoliberal subjectivity occurs in many milieus, some of which are removed from, and even ideologically opposed to, the worlds of consumer and corporate capitalist activity. Here, I focus on how this liquid subjectivity, key to neoliberalism's entrepreneurial ideal, was promoted in the embodied practices of a contemporary dance troupe, Uganda National Contemporary Ballet – a troupe which would have never tolerated invasive commercial branding of its performances, and indeed sometimes performed dances that were explicitly opposed to commercial culture. My intent is not to dismiss UNCB's critique of consumer capitalism (a critique notably absent from Senator Extravaganza performances), but rather to highlight the irony that a project critical of neoliberal culture may in fact share in the fundamental premises of that culture, so that, in the final analysis, it may wind up reinforcing as much as undermining it.

UNCB, when I first encountered it in 2011, was exemplary of a certain kind of European-managed, politically liberal 'arts for development' project which has proliferated in Uganda in recent decades. Some of the most significant recent transformations in Uganda's art world have been wrought not by commercial corporations like EABL, but by not-for-profit arts initiatives conducted by foreign-led NGOs. In global development circles, a prevailing idea has been that cultural interventions may be more efficient than merely economic ones in achieving sustainable change. If a target community can only be nudged in the right direction culturally – if it can, as the nostrum goes, be 'taught to fish' – that community will work to advance its own development from the bottom up, eliminating the need for more expensive top-down projects (Swidler and Watkins 2009). Global development institutions are especially supportive of cultural interventions that target people's experience of self, encouraging them to understand themselves more as autonomous, expressive, rights-bearing, entrepreneurial individuals and communities.

This trend in global development strategy has been in some ways a boon for artists, African and European/American alike, in that they have been able to market their ability to engage participants at the profound level of artistic self-experience. European and American sponsors have been especially encouraging of arts that exude grassroots resistance and uplift. For example, hip hop arts, with their compelling backstory of youthful, entrepreneurial, up-from-the-streets resistance in the Bronx, have received considerable international donor support in recent years (Shipley 2013). If, in the colonial era, European missionaries were most concerned to encourage 'civilising' arts in Africa – e.g. the disciplined choir singing of churches and school assemblies – today's arts interventions tend to promote more individualistic, rebellious, youth-oriented practices like breakdancing, rapping and filmmaking – for it is hoped that in these activities young Africans will cultivate more entrepreneurial subjectivities.

Despite the words 'national' and 'ballet' in its name, UNCB was nothing like the state-sponsored 'national ballets' of Africa's independence era, with their patriotic revues of folkloric dance, music and drama. It was, rather, a project of 'contemporary dance', an international genre of experimental modernist/postmodernist character. The troupe was directed by Valérie Miquel, a white dancer and choreographer from France. Miquel took credit for all the choreography and danced in prominent roles alongside the Ugandan members of the troupe. In UNCB's dancing, fragments of modern dance, classical ballet, hip hop, Indian classical dance and Ugandan traditional dance were blended in a playful postmodernist collage, with modernist formal principles like 'line' lending aesthetic coherence. Thematically, the dancing, when not highly abstract, was pointedly political, focusing on liberal, human rights topics, as evident in the titles of productions: e.g. *Memories of Child Soldiers*, *Cry for Women's Dignity* and *STOP: The Rape Is a Violation of Human Rights*.

In an earlier, more fiercely nationalist era, objections would likely have been raised to UNCB's self-description as a 'Uganda National' project, given a white artist's prominent position at the head of a black troupe. Today, however, the institutional space of Ugandan national arts has been so thoroughly occupied by international collaborative projects that such a European-led 'national' project does not seem so out of place. Today, UNCC hosts dozens of foreign NGOs who oversee arts workshops and festivals. Many of these projects are quite brief in duration: European experts in a particular art fly in, engage for two or three days with aspiring young Ugandan artists who have been assembled for the occasion, and fly out again. The Centre has become a much more globally oriented space, where artistically inclined Kampala youth come to make foreign connections, learn the latest global artistic and cultural styles, and practise representing themselves and their cultures to foreign audiences. This is an exciting venue for many young artists, but one no longer so dedicated to the production of specifically national spirit. Its creative energies tend to be projected outward, toward a global market, rather than inward toward the assembled peoples of the nation. It is increasingly an institution that celebrates global movement and entrepreneurial fluidity, rather than self-sufficient nationhood.

Miquel first came to Uganda in 2007, having won grants from Alliance Française and Goethe-Institut to conduct a dance ethnography project on child soldiers. She travelled to the north of the country to interview young men who had been drafted as children into Joseph Kony's Lord's Resistance Army, then used these interviews as material for a contemporary dance piece, *Memories of Child Soldiers*, which premiered at Kampala's Ndere Centre in that same year (a video of excerpts from UNCB's 2012 revival of *Memories of Child Soldiers* is available on YouTube). This production shares with Miquel's broader choreographic oeuvre a strong focus on elemental, extreme emotions – often at the expense of historical specifics. It begins with half-naked dancers on a dark stage, writhing in agony over a spooky electronic soundtrack. Projected on a backdrop is a digital video piece by French artist Cyril Ducottet, pulsing with abstract, neuron-like shapes which morph into tortured human figures. There follows a sequence of fight scenes, at the culmination of which Miquel is thrown to the ground and raped by male assailants – her infant child (a doll) beaten to death by one of the soldiers. As a traumatic aftershock, there is a surreal montage of hysterical child's play, with the adult dancers jumping rope, playing ball and snuggling up to oversized stuffed animals, while a voice in the soundtrack repeatedly intones 'Our childhood is destroyed'. The piece ends on a hopeful note, with a scene of mystical redemption: the dancers, now dressed in red togas, sit *zazen* style, hands raised in a meditative *mudra* as electro yoga-music drones over the speakers.

Memories is a spectacle of raw, interior psychological trauma that could really be about any war-torn place. Only rarely does a signifier of Uganda appear on stage, and there is no attempt to grapple with the historical complexities of the long war in the north. The production's uplifting ending, correspondingly, seems to be about redemption purely from within – a kind of yogic transcendence of the world's evils. This emphasis on self-awareness and self-trans-formation, and eliding of historical specifics in favour of universal psychological/spiritual phenomena, is not uncommon in African Contemporary Dance as a globalised genre, as will be discussed in the next section.

African Contemporary Dance as a global interventionist genre

African Contemporary Dance arose as a 'global arts circuit' in the 1990s (Kringelbach 2013: 147). This was a decade of globalist enthu-siasm: one of 'world beat' music, as well as, in the museum arts, a globalist 'biennial culture' – both of which were turned especially toward Africa (O'Neill 2012). Significantly, the 1990s also saw a 'body boom', as Americans and Europeans, spurred by the likes of Jane Fonda, rediscovered the idea of self-transformation through fitness and dance; in European cities, African dance workshops, led by African dancers, became popular options for those seeking to get in shape while immersing themselves in exotic cultures (Sieveking 2008). As it turned out, the notion that Europeans might empower themselves through participation in multicultural kinetic arts was easily inverted, so that people of the Global South, rather than Euro-peans, could be figured as the primary beneficiaries of cross-cultural dance empowerment. State institutions like the Institut Français, which had been sponsoring African dancers to come to teach work-shops in Europe, began to sponsor African contemporary dance projects in Africa, under the banner of African aid and development.

   Ayoko Mensah, an outspoken critic of the global African Contemporary Dance phenomenon, has questioned the motives of European state-sponsored events like 1995's seminal 'Rencontres de Création Chorégraphique Africaine' in Luanda, which, she notes, was conveniently staged on the eve of France's signing an economic agreement with oil-rich Angola (Mensah 2005: 167). In Mensah's view, European interests shaped the early development of African Contemporary Dance to such a degree that the genre amounted to little more than 'corps noirs, regards blancs' – black bodies performing for the white gaze, with little regard for the tastes and political concerns of ordinary Africans. Ten years later, Mensah's critique seems too stark, accounting too little for the agencies of African dancers and choreographers (Sieveking 2014). Yet Mensah's basic point remains salient: African contemporary dance has served in many instances as a tool for African outreach that serves Western diplomatic interests, while satisfying Western liberal cosmopolitan desires for artistic/activist engagement with Africans on comfortable moral and aesthetic grounds. African artists' ability to define African Contemporary Dance on their own terms, independent of Western institutional support, has been limited by their lack of independent resources – a problem compounded by the withdrawal of African states from arts sponsorship roles. For the great majority of aspiring African contemporary dancers, entering into the global arts circuit means depending at least to some degree on the stewardship of European institutions and their on-the-ground representatives like Miquel.

Artists and critics tend to resist any attempt to define contemporary dance as a fixed style or genre. If there is a single principle that runs through the movement, it is one of proud eclecticism: artists should feel free to create whatever they want, borrowing omnivorously from dance cultures from all over the world, 'high' cultures as well as 'low'. A common contemporary dance technique is to set culturally distant styles of movement in unresolved juxtaposition in order to challenge viewers' assumptions about what each bodily expression signifies and what kinds of movement combinations may be culturally appropriate. Indeed, such eclecticism may be felt as an imperative of the genre: if one wishes to be classified as a 'contemporary' dancer, one should take care that one's dancing does not become too associated with any single tradition, any single place or time.

According to dance scholar Hélène Neveu Kringelbach, individualistic 'self-fashioning' has been a characteristic agenda of the global African Contemporary Dance movement (Kringelbach 2013: 26). Participants in dance workshops are taught various techniques for going inside themselves, there to find their most authentic, untapped self-expressions. This emphasis on the cultivation of the rebellious, interior self was already present in the 'modern' dance developed in the early twentieth century by the likes of Isadora Duncan and Martha Graham (Foulkes 2002). As I have documented elsewhere, modern dance was implemented in some Ugandan schools as an art for cultivating independent, 'modern' selfhood in African students (Pier 2016). What distinguishes today's contemporary dance from earlier, similarly individualistic, modern dance is its even more avid embrace of disorienting liquidity. In its liquidity, contemporary dance can be used to symbolically destabilise rigid systems of power/

knowledge. This critical, deconstructive capacity of the genre is much celebrated by its advocates. On the other hand, contemporary dance may be accused of aligning with neoliberal ideology, in that it commonly confronts the injustices of the world with spectacles of entrepreneurial fluidity, slippage and unfettered artistic choice. David Harvey has suggested that any dominant mode of production tends to give rise, dialectically, to 'a mode of opposition as a mirror image to itself' (Harvey 2016). In its exultant liquidity, contemporary dance, while politically left-leaning, may unwittingly be mirroring and reinforcing the neoliberal worldview.

Subjectivities of nomadism and immobility

In the contemporary art world, a celebrated archetype parallel to that of the entrepreneur in capitalism is that of the creative nomad, who slips with apparent ease from culture to culture, tradition to artistic tradition, without becoming beholden to any single one. In our first interview, at a coffee shop near the National Theatre, UNCB's leader Miquel described herself as a 'chameleon' – someone innately gifted at blending into diverse cultures, who had become even more adept at self-transformation through her world travel experiences. Her biography, as she recounted it to me, was one of progressive distancing from her Parisian home culture. Starting out as a young girl in a classical ballet and modern dance, she quickly developed an interest in foreign dance traditions, travelling eventually to India and then North Africa, where she lived for six months with a group of Tuaregs. She described wearing the traditional Tuareg veil as a transformative experience. When, at the end of her sojourn, she took the veil off, she felt 'exposed' in ways that proved to her that she had absorbed Tuareg culture on a deep, embodied level.

This experience of 'becoming nomad' (Kaplan 1996), inspired in Miquel a new sense of her own character and artistic calling in the world. From here on, she would use dance not only to explore new cultural territories on her own, but also to assist others in freeing themselves from their own ingrained cultural habits and prejudices. In this regard, she told me that she found her Ugandan dance collaborators unprofitably stuck in some of their cultural ways and beliefs – e.g. their (supposedly) conservative attitudes about sex, religion and food. She considered it part of her mission to help them unstick themselves culturally, in and outside of dance practice. Along these lines, she wrote on her website,

When I arrive to a place I come with an open mind, ready
to share my knowledge and also to learn about the others ...
I use my knowledge that I've got through all my travels and
experiences to help people to become confident with themselves,
in harmony with their body and ready to live their life fully.

Because Miquel considered herself essentially a chameleon, unbound
by any fixed identity, she claimed to feel no misgivings about being a
white European leading an all-black troupe. Certainly, she acknowledged, her race was a complicating factor, but she believed that it
is in the self-reinventing artist's power to transcend such identity-
based tensions. Indeed, her acquired nomadic ability to live beyond
such matters enhanced her sense of her rightful authority over the
group. The cultural openness she had acquired through her travels
was, in her view, something she could and should impart to others.

If Miquel presented herself as a cultural chameleon and enlight-
ened global traveller, the Ugandans in the group – in 2011, four men
and one woman – were correspondingly keen to be globally mobile,
flexible artists. They were already versed in a variety of dance styles,
from hip hop, to Latin dance, to modern dance, which enabled them
to take part in other global-circuit opportunities that touched down
in Kampala. In short, the Ugandan dancers in Miquel's troupe were
nomadic by artistic inclination and personal ambition. Yet economic
and political circumstances rendered their lives far less mobile than
Miquel's. At the time I met them, they were living typical lives of
youth scraping by in Kampala: holding down odd jobs and running
small entrepreneurial ventures, maintaining their social independence and long-shot prospects for international travel – perhaps at
the cost of more secure careers and closer proximity to their families.

In his writing on liquid modernity, Bauman posits a hardening
global class division between those who have the means to freely
travel and experience liberation in their mobility (Bauman dubs this
class 'tourists'), and those who are either stuck in place, or forced
into mobility against their will by the liquefying and destructive
effects of capital ('vagabonds') (Bauman 1998: 92). Increasingly,
people around the world experience mobility as an existential neces-
sity; the rewards of international movement and the pitfalls of stasis
are everywhere on display. Yet, in reality, only the world's wealthiest
few are able to enter into the global nomadic lifestyle in its empowered, rather than involuntary, mode. This class division, between
the exuberantly mobile and the desperately immobile, manifested
tensely in UNCB as a project, as it does in many western African

projects that proclaim a spirit of equitable collaboration. Miquel's ambition was to help the Ugandan dancers free themselves through self-searching, eclectic artistic practice, yet there were structural barriers to these Ugandan youth achieving genuine mobility and freedom which no amount of expressive dancing, on its own, could overcome.

Miquel told me that it was imperative for her to find foreign touring opportunities for the group, but these were not always forthcoming, causing simmering discontent to sometimes boil over. Rehearsals, which entailed vigorous, improvised, physical contact among the dancers, sometimes became rough and tumble, with the men using their larger physiques to intimidate Miquel, or, in one seeming accident I saw, send her sprawling. Later, I learned that there had been other damaging political problems in the group, with one of the men eventually having to be dismissed for insubordinate behaviour, another fired for drinking too much. Fiona Mirembe, the other woman in the group besides Miquel, one day vanished without warning. As it turned out, she had left abruptly for the United Arab Emirates, lured by a promise of lucrative foreign work. Finally, in 2017, Miquel herself left Uganda, to direct a new dance project in Ghana, Dance Institute Ghana (DIG), again sponsored by Alliance Française. Leadership of UNCB has passed to one of the Ugandan dancers, Patrick Khalifa. It remains to be seen how the internal dynamics of the group, as well as its career prospects, will change now that it is an all-Ugandan project under Khalifa's direction.

Conclusion: national arts and neoliberalism

In Uganda today, the field of national arts is being rapidly transformed by commercial penetrations on the one hand and foreign-led arts activism projects on the other. This two-pronged transformation is evident, first of all, at the UNCC, a venerable national arts facility slated to be demolished and replaced with a commercial complex – which has, in any event, been increasingly rented out to private parties, as well as to global NGO-sponsored arts projects like the UNCB. The commercialisation of national arts is further exemplified in the Senator National Cultural Extravaganza, a participatory dance event in which local artists were asked to voluntarily devote their creative powers and heritage resources to building a beer brand, as they once devoted them to building the nation. Beyond corporate projects like the Extravaganza, interventionist 'contemporary' art projects like UNCB, are in their own way helping to advance neoliberalism in Uganda – namely by promoting the kind of mobile, flexible, autonomous, entrepreneurial subjectivity on which a neoliberal system culturally depends. This European sponsored and directed arts project, which sought to empower Ugandan youth at the level of self-awareness and self-expression, advocated liquid artistic subjectivity as a means to freedom, while doing nothing to address the underlying economic and political constraints that keep youth from becoming as truly mobile and flexible as they would like to be. Whatever its merits artistically, UNCB did not strike me as being a 'national' project in anything but name. That is to say, it did not seem to be dedicated to the cultural articulation of something so solid as a nation-state, which might provide shelter and collective autonomy to Ugandans amid global capitalism's relentless liquefying processes. In the independence era of the mid-twentieth century, this was the promise of national arts in Uganda and throughout Africa: to lend cultural support to self-sufficient nation-states wherein African communities and individuals might develop their own distinctive modernities. Today, it is increasingly unclear what the signifier 'national' might mean in Ugandan arts, if indeed it continues to designate any distinctive institutional space at all, set apart and protected from neoliberalism's cultural pressures.

References

Bauman, Z. (1998), *Globalization: The Human Consequences* (London: Polity).

Bauman, Z. (2012), *Liquid Modernity*. 2nd edition (Hoboken, NJ: Wiley).

Foulkes, J. (2002), *Modern Bodies: Dance and American Modernism from Martha Graham to Alvin Ailey* (Chapel Hill, NC: University of North Carolina Press).

Harvey, D. (2016), 'Neoliberalism as a political project: David Harvey on what neoliberalism actually is – and why the concept matters', *Jacobin*, 23 July.

Kaplan, C. (1996), *Questions of Travel: Postmodern Discourses of Displacement* (Durham, NC: Duke University Press).

Kringelbach, H. (2013), *Dance Circles: Movement, Morality, and Self-Fashioning in Urban Senegal* (New York, NY: Berghahn).

Mensah, A. (2005), 'Corps noirs, regards blancs: retour sur la danse africaine contemporaine', *Africultures*, 62, pp. 163–71.

O'Neill, P. (2012), *The Culture of Curating and the Curating of Culture(s)* (Cambridge, MA: MIT Press).

Pier, D. G. (2015), *Ugandan Music in the Marketing Era: The Branded Arena* (New York, NY: Palgrave).

Pier, D. G. (2016), 'Dance, discipline, and the modern self at a Ugandan Catholic boarding school', *African Studies Review*, 15(3), pp. 33–59.

Shipley, J. (2013), *Living the Hiplife: Celebrity and Entrepreneurship in Ghanaian Popular Music* (Chicago, IL: University of Chicago Press).

Sieveking, N. (2008), *Abheben und Geerdet Sein: Afrikanisch Tanzen als transkultureller Erfahrungsraum* (Münster: LIT Verlag).

Sieveking, N. (2014), '"Create your space": Locating contemporary dance in Ouagadougou', *Africa,* 84(1), pp. 55–77.

Swidler, A. and Watkins, S. (2009), '"Teach a man to fish": The doctrine of sustainability and its effects on three strata of Malawian society', *World Development,* 37(7), pp. 1182–96.

Willis, J. (2002), *Potent Brews: A Social History of Alcohol in East Africa, 1850–1999* (Columbus, OH: Ohio University Press).

Conclusion: neoliberalism institutionalised

Jörg Wiegratz, Giuliano Martiniello and Elisa Greco

> If economy grows, costs go down, private investors are attracted
> and the future becomes easy to handle. (Museveni on his Twitter
> account, 10 May 2017)

This collection has sought to contribute to debates about the character and trajectory of change in contemporary Uganda. To do this,
it has questioned mainstream narratives of a highly successful (and
socially beneficial) post-1986 transformation, and contrasted these
with empirical evidence of a prolonged and multifaceted situation of crisis generated by a particular version of severe capitalist
restructuring, or neoliberal reforms. This analytical approach has,
to date, occupied little space in the context of neoliberal academia.
We thereby also sought to challenge the decades-long ideational and
discursive hegemony of powerful international and national reform
designers, implementers and supporters. This hegemony – or cognitive intervention and restriction – has produced and defended a
severe ideological and analytical containment and impoverishment
concerning key societal themes that have long demanded a response
in the form of analytical 'missiles' (Harrison 2011). We thus critique
and challenge what Ngugi Wa Thiong'o calls, with reference to the
European colonialism in Africa, mental domination – a domination
that is so characteristic of neoliberal social order across the contemporary 'free world': 'Economic and political control can never be
complete or effective without mental control' (Wa Thiong'o 1986: 16).
As thinkers from Luxemburg to Orwell noted, contesting the 'truth'
of the ruling classes, pronouncing what is going on and offering alternatives to establishment accounts of 'reality' (and thereby 'history'),
is a crucial political act. The fact that this politico-cognitive activity
is necessary more than ever is confirmed, amongst others, by recent
utterances that are made by powerful and influential representatives of the global governance and aid architecture. The Labour
Day 2018 speech of the UN Resident Coordinator and UNDP
Resident Representative in Uganda, Rosa Malango, is exemplary
in that regard. As the speech, titled 'Revitalize Local Government
System to Build Public Spirit for Service', outlines: 'Uganda is widely

recognized for producing a wide range of excellent policies on social, economic and development issues' (Malango 2018). Against this background, this collection has initiated a hermeneutic debate on political, economic, social and cultural change by contesting the existing dominant set of data, interpretations, languages and policy demands. We know that analysis by itself can be sterile if it does not engage with existing social and political movements, especially in the formulation of alternatives and in supporting the ongoing processes that show potential for socially progressive change. At the same time, we maintain that critical analysis is a necessary and important step in the struggle against the status quo. That said, this collection has shed light on neoliberalism as a project, process and ideology. Contributions from different disciplines show how neoliberalism in Uganda (and elsewhere) is creating a fully fledged market society, which operates above all in the interest of capital by conflating it with public interest. We now take stock of the chapters' findings to distil our contribution to a better understanding of the neoliberal restructuring of Uganda. Below we offer ten analytical points that emerged from the chapters.

First, neoliberal restructuring emerges indeed as an all-encompassing process. Such reforms have altered state–society, state–economy and society–economy relations. Neoliberalisation is a hetero-directed process, one that diffuses from multiple poles of power, discourse, interest and wealth. As such it is not simply exogenous to, or imposed on Uganda, it is rather articulated with, and metabolised within, society and politics, at many interconnected levels.

Second, neoliberalisation was a joint exercise of power by way of an alliance of resourceful foreign and domestic actors, and across various power dimensions. The power alliance – with members including amongst others, donors, international organisations (IOs), large firms and government – rolled out its agenda of reform in various ways over vulnerable populations. They put in place the power architecture of 'disciplinary neoliberalism' (Gill 1995), which is a particular 'concrete form of structural and behavioural power' (*ibid.*: 411) that includes the structural power of capital and the ability to produce institutionalised and bureaucratised forms of discipline in state and economy (*ibid.*: 411–12). Neoliberalisation allowed foreign economic and political actors to penetrate, influence, control and drain the Ugandan economy at an arguably unprecedented level in the country's post-colonial history. The structure of international development aid as an industry has also fostered high aid dependency within the country, with its multiple repercussions.

The reforms favoured a small, restricted number of disproportionately powerful players, particularly foreign capital (like a few
multinationals and international banks); the local comprador class;
and some local businesses, each of which has thrived in the new set
up. The local capitalist class allied with foreign actors to advance the
agenda of capital vis-à-vis other classes. Numerous members of the
state elite played, in many ways, the classical role of the comprador
class. Domestic elites often helped advance, rather than stand against
interests of foreign economic actors. There was regularly a merging
of interests and agendas of powerful national and international
actors. Other than the early reform period dispute over the state's
defence budget size, there has hardly been a major publically known
incident where government has stood strong against major economic
policy diktat from Western capitals (Wiegratz 2014) – showing how
these power complexes, framed as partnership relations, legitimate
and (re-)produce neoliberal restructuring and existing asymmetries
of power.

Third, as in other societies where neoliberal thinking and interests
are pervasive, economic growth has become the centre of gravity
of political activity and the key indicator of political success, at the
expense of other societal considerations including social justice,
emancipation, equality, political and civic freedoms and human
rights. Debates about economic transformation and development
in Uganda have been profoundly influenced, if not dominated, by
World Bank reports and neoclassical economic analyses (WB 2011,
2012, 2013). These analyses have often placed emphasis on notions
of market efficiency, utility maximisation, efficient division of labour,
perfect competition, economic equilibrium and methodological individualism. This has contributed to the construction of economics as
the only truly scientific discipline regulated by its own laws, those of
the interested calculation and of the unlimited competition for profit
(Fine 2000). From this approach, there is the danger of 'economics
imperialism' foreclosing the analytical agenda (and thus limiting
knowledge production) at the expense of approaches based on the
political economy of capitalism, while simultaneously reducing
economic and social analyses to issues such as market imperfections
and respective non-market responses (*ibid.*). In this way, the maximisation of private profits imposed itself as the dominant principle that
informed policy making. In a recent tweet following a meeting with
EU diplomats, Museveni wrote: 'it's okay to talk of human and other
rights but growth of the economy should be the first right to empha-
size'. Such a quote is reminiscent of a famous statement made by

one of the pioneers of liberalism, Friedrich von Hayek: 'Personally I prefer a liberal dictator to democratic government lacking liberalism' (El Mercurio 1981).

The last thirty years of Ugandan 'politics' cannot be explained as something that emerges primarily and ultimately from Museveni as a politician and as a 'case'. Internalist characterisations of the drivers of social, political and economic transformation have contributed to an analytical concealing of the inter-linkages between local, national and international power structures and patterns of capital accumulation. As shown in Part I of the book, part of Museveni's hegemony has been reinforced by 'foreign' influences and interests that fuelled the neoliberal project, co-existing with endogenous social and power structures.

Notably, top officials have 'advised' journalists that extensive ('exaggerated', 'sensationalist') media coverage of corruption, fraud and insecurity, and general problems can endanger Uganda's economic development, for example the country's global economic reputation (thus investment flows) and sector-specific business interests, especially in sectors like tourism and extractives. A recent example of this discourse is captured in an opening statement during a press conference by Finance Minister Matia Kasaija admonishing the press not to report inconvenient truths on government's actions and decisions:

> I have said it before, let me repeat it: This is your country …
> When you are writing a story, ask yourself: the story that I am
> going to be putting out, is it going to help build Uganda, or it
> will destroy Uganda? That's what you call responsible journalism.
> Bear that in mind. Is it going to bring peace in the country, or
> it will bring anarchy? … So, please be very careful when you are
> putting up a story that [it] does not destroy the long-time effort
> that we have been making to make your country governable, to
> make your country secure, to make your country stable. (NTVU
> 2018a)

The political rhetoric deployed against some of the most potent criticisms of neoliberal orthodoxy and reality is that of 'economic sabotage' and 'anti-development'. In this political climate, the National Resistance Movement (NRM) and the establishment have repeatedly verbally targeted what stands in the way of neoliberal types of investment, development, distribution and discourse (see also Beresford *et al.* 2018). The latest example of this particular phenomenon of neoliberal order in Uganda is the 'Cuban doctors' case; i.e. Museveni's response to critics of the government's move to import about 200 medical doctors from Cuba as a reaction to what he called the 'blackmail' from 'selfish' Ugandan doctors who in late 2017 had been on strike demanding better pay and working conditions (Daily Monitor 2018d). In his speech at the 2018 May Labour Day celebrations that were themed: 'Promoting Public Spirit in Public Sector' he said:

> I wanted to bring Cuban doctors because our doctors behaved very badly, and unprofessionally. They tried to incite doctors to abandon patients so that patients die. ... When we were under that blackmail, I said, no, I cannot be blackmailed, if necessary, I will import doctors to bring discipline to this crooked behaviour of people who say they are doctors; when in fact, they behave as if they are not doctors ... A doctor who goes on a strike is not a doctor; he is an enemy of our people and we shall treat him as such. In fact ... I wanted to go back to the bush but some people [restrained me]. (NTVU 2018b)

The statement – and the policy more widely – caused widespread public debate.

Fourth, we argued that Uganda is a striking example of authoritarian neoliberalism, in which coercive state practices and administrative and judicial state apparatuses contain oppositional forces limiting the challenge to neoliberal policies (Bruff 2014, Tansel 2017). Sector restructuring through privatisations and liberalisations was often executed in a rushed and uncompromising way, with ample use of authoritarianism and state violence. Part II of the book provides evidence of often little concern for environmental and economic sustainability in policy making, and the magnitude of the harmful repercussions of restructuring for large parts of the population. In this context, the state capitalised on foreign donors and investors, allied with particular domestic societal groups and established its hegemony by promoting the image of a government led by a benevolent, well-meaning, trustworthy power, and generally moralised the neoliberal project. A number of powerful actors from the realm of religion and culture were not threats but part and parcel of the political and economic establishment.

International financial institutions (IFIs) and other foreign actors of the international development sector directly and indirectly enabled the build-up of powerful and oppressive security apparatus, and more generally the state's coercive and violent practices of power, over many years. There are various ways in which these actors are implicated, directly and indirectly, in the growth of corruption, authoritarianism and militarisation, and a more explicit turn towards crony and rentier capitalism (Standing 2016). The oppression of sections of the population by the state (aka the state's hard-handedness) is thus in-fact an oppression of the state-donors-capital bloc. In Gramscian terms, an *historical bloc* refers to a particular 'congruence of material interests, institutions and ideologies, or broadly, an alliance of different class forces politically organized around a set of hegemonic ideas that give strategic direction and coherence to its constitutive elements' (Gill 2002: 58). In the case of Uganda the formation of this power bloc developed through a series of national and transnational political networks and discourses which converged around a certain vision and form of organisation of society. This bloc also put in place and advanced the particular neoliberal capitalist form of structural violence. Violence has been an intrinsic component of the neoliberal project, rather than its antithesis. Like other neoliberal societies, violence escalation has taken multidimensional forms (military, disciplinary, economic, political, cultural, verbal); state policies (especially those that hit the poor) have unleashed systemic violence and corresponding widespread and cruel social harm (Cooper and Whyte 2017).[1] Territorial militarisation and securitisation is one of these forms of neoliberal violence. The militarisation of whole villages and districts to curb dissent and protest – for instance, against large-scale land acquisitions and related displacing dynamics – has been a constant feature of post-1986 Uganda (Martiniello 2015, Greco 2015). The emerging oil and mining sectors are also driving this agenda further. The then Minister of National Security General Henry Tumukunde, talking about the new oil-related security situation, stressed the need to fund security services and to recruit and train specialist security staff – something that 'will require a completely different budget':

> If you have oil and gas coming to your country, you've got 40,000 foreigners; you've got people like these ones operating in the midst of nowhere, for example in western Uganda; they borrow very sensitive money; their business depends on for example stock exchange readings. Don't you want to imagine this is a new scenario that requires special attention [i.e. a much higher security budget]? (NBSU 2017)

In March 2018, the new Inspector General of Police, Martin Okoth Ochola, declared the merger of the Directorate of Oil and Gas with the Directorate of Counter Terrorism, announcing that the new unit will be headed by an FBI-trained officer (NBSU 2018b).

Fifth, there exist notable similarities and continuities between the neoliberal and colonial development projects, especially with regard to access and control to key natural resources and the accelerating extractive logic of capitalism. Part III of the book shows that Uganda is undergoing a deep structural transformation, not so much into the much coveted 'middle-income country' that populates the imaginary of many, but rather into an extractive and authoritarian enclave where foreign interests are tackling land, water, oil, forestry and conservation areas as sinks for resource extraction. A colonial matrix of dispossession and domination persists in the neoliberal period through structures of power that link state-corporate actors, comprador bourgeois classes and racialised social groups and classes within states reproducing neo-colonial structures of inequality and projects of subjugation through development projects, market violence, land theft, looting of natural resources, exploitation and cultural assault (Kapoor 2017). The question of land concessions is a case in point. To stimulate the settlement of Europeans and the extra-version of the colonial economy towards metropolitan exigencies, the colonial government in the 1920s offered huge land concessions for large-scale sugar plantations to European companies and Indian family firms, such as Metha and Madhvani (Ahluwalia 1995, Hundle's chapter), which have since become today's sugar giants. Currently, the government is in many ways mirroring this approach by allocating land inhabited and cultivated by farmers to foreign and national agribusiness companies. The legitimation discourse, which in the colonial period was anchored in the *terra nullius* principle, is today revamped as land considered non-utilised or underutilised (or in any case strategic for investment) as the basis for being taken over by the government for development purposes (Martiniello 2017).

There are also crucial discontinuities between colonial and neoliberal restructuring, not least in terms of the degree of legitimation and consensus enjoyed by the neoliberal modernisation project. While (late) colonial domination faced substantial opposition and nationalist agitations, major aspects of the neoliberal project have gained significant social legitimacy among some social constituencies in Uganda. Economic achievements such as GDP growth, the upgrading of the road network, the building of new homes, hotels, shopping arcades and office blocks, the opening of new schools, universities and hospitals, access to cheap mobile communication technologies and a wide range of media outlets and products and global communication platforms, or the spread of markets and market infrastructure – that are, however, distributed in an uneven manner across classes, gender, ethnicities and geography – are discursively (and instrumentally) mobilised to strengthen national pride, making neoliberalism appear desired, especially among the middle classes, civil servants and professions, amongst others. In other words, by the late 2010s neoliberalism has, for various reasons, gained significant acceptance, i.e. a notable taken-for-granted, common sense status (also Wiegratz 2016).

Another important point to make in this context: one major portrayal of neoliberal political economy suggests that this complex only works because of and to the benefit of the 1 per cent, and that its regressive outcomes such as social inequalities and ecological destructiveness, are prevalently due to the power and wealth of these elites (i.e. 'greed' of the powerful). Yet this take on actually existing neoliberalism is analytically and politically misleading as it discounts the fact that neoliberalism is not only maintained by the often-blamed and much talked about ruling class; in Ugandan discourse: the 'clique' around Museveni, tycoons, godfathers, crony capitalists, top officials (including from the military) and so on. Instead, we argue that there is a plethora of non-elite actors in many sectors of the economy that shape, benefit from and reproduce, i.e. are entangled in the neoliberal complex of power and capital. From sugarcane and fisheries, to charcoal and illegal ivory trade, there are social groups such as intermediaries, landowners, brokers, transporters, councillors, local chiefs etc., who take advantage of economic opportunities linked to the operation of the neoliberal political economy to the detriment of communities and environments. This is evidenced in numerous studies and news reports (latest example include Branch and Martiniello 2018, Titeca 2018). The constant expansion of commodity frontiers (Moore 2015) and the overall extractivist tendencies which are intrinsic to the neoliberal project (Veltmeyer and Petras 2014) have in other words increasingly become socially legitimate, i.e. are perceived by respective actors as the only avenues to keep profits and incomes flowing. This in part explains why neoliberalism has over time become hegemonic and pervasive from local to national level, and why it has been so effective at keeping alternative modes of organising society, economy and polity at bay.

Next, despite so much material and immaterial, political, economic and cultural investments in Uganda by imperialist countries and

Western donors in the last three decades, the list of sustained successes is quite limited, while its fractures are very widespread. The health sector is a good example of this, as shown in Ssali's chapter in this collection; by revealing that it is precisely the (restructuring-advancing) 'investment' and interference of foreign actors that are repeatedly crisis-producing and/or -accelerating. Further, after years of civil war, in 1986 economic standards were very low, thereby taking 1986 as a threshold to measure reform success is misleading; any reform would have produced some sort of improvement on some aspects, while making comparisons with pre-1986 Uganda is not a very strong test and argument for neoliberalism either.

Finally, the advancements under neoliberalism produce ambivalence for many Ugandans. For the large majority of families, investing in their children's education entails indebtedness and uncertainty, while political connections appear the only way into a good job. Similarly, the economic opportunities of city life come with marginalisation, loneliness, violence, and crime; enclaves of wealth creation sit alongside mass poverty; the promise of food abundance through corporate agri-food and large-scale plantations stands alongside the return of famines and food scarcity for millions.

Sixth, neoliberalisation has advanced inequalities between classes and exacerbated social injustice. Many neoliberal interventions had a pro-powerful – rather than a pro-poor character. Systemic elite bias and elite capture in development projects turned these into tools to advance the process of class formation, consolidating the power of dominant classes. Neoliberalism increased the power of a range of domestic actors, especially but not only elite actors. Major foreign economic actors benefited in significant ways. The presence of foreign capital was backed by various ideological devices, including 'foreigners as investors' and 'business interest equals public interest' ideologies. Museveni's rhetoric has been consistent and insistent over the years on the role of foreign investors in his vision for the country. He proudly argued that 'Uganda has liberalised more than China, the only thing we haven't sold is State House, however China has attracted more foreign direct investments' (Independent 2008). In a recent case raised by residents of Kiryandongo over alleged displacements caused by foreign investors, the president reportedly apologised to investors for the inconveniences Ugandans have caused them (Daily Monitor 2018e).

Inequality has been aggravated through both market and non-market mechanisms. Extractivism and land enclosures have intensified landlessness, redistributing land from the poor to the rich. Land enclosures increased not only through direct coercion, but also through foreclosure and distress land sales, brought about by increased small producers' indebtedness. Increased cost of living, alongside constantly rising electricity and food prices, as well as school and medical fees – and compounded by generalised high inflation – have recurrently pushed families to sell their land. Increased cost of living, coupled with a deep financialisation of everyday life, including facilitating access to business loans, has further entrenched land dispossession. In the case of bankruptcies, defaults or failure to repay loans, banks have ended up legally taking over land from the debtor. Notably, the investigations of the current commission of inquiry into land matters, headed by Justice Catherine Bamugemereire, has produced ample evidence of the collusion between state and private actors in often violent and illegal land dispossessions, corruption and fraud across state levels, and the role of rackets and organised crime in this process.

Symptomatic of neoliberal Uganda is furthermore an acceleration of 'jobless' economic growth, whereby much of the investments take place in the extractive and financial sectors, with little or no linkages to local economies, and with wealth captured by a plethora of actors with little societal redistribution. As such, the making of the new market society has gone hand in hand with increasing resource inequalities, as uneven access to natural resources paved the way for capital accumulation in the hands of few. Stanbic Bank – the biggest bank in the country, commanding a 20 per cent market share and controlling more than 50 per cent of industry assets – is (according to public information) largely owned by foreigners, and so are other key services like telecommunications. A recent report documented – in an arguably rather conservative estimation – that the top 10 per cent own 35 per cent of the economy, while the poorest 20 per cent own only 6 per cent of the economy (Nuwagaba and Muhumuza 2017). The escalation of inequality and class divisions is inherently linked to neoliberal restructuring.

Seventh, neoliberal policies have produced socially regressive effects for the most vulnerable parts of the population. The financial demands and pressures on the subaltern classes to just survive and recover from ill-health, for example, are extraordinary. Health and education reforms resulted in a social crisis for significant sections of the poor, threatening their life chances and advancing inequality and class divisions. Further, the multiple and interacting crises produced by neoliberal restructuring are often addressed by more neoliberal reform which bring rather little advancement – the bank interest rate case is a prime example in this regard. At the time of writing these conclusions, the Ugandan debate revolves around deteriorating public finance, tax revenue shortfalls, escalating external and domestic public debt and related interest payments, and declining per capita state expenditure. The EAC heads-of-state summit in Kampala is in the news, announcing that 'Museveni calls for private investors in health' (New Vision 2018). National television channels cover themes like a major foreign bank sponsoring a school competition that is said to empower students to become job creators; a major foreign telecom company running free 'health camps' in northern Uganda in the name of 'giving back' to communities; teachers demanding best-teacher-awards competitions; microfinance being extended to refugees; the president supporting the policy demands of sugar barons for restricted competition for peasants' sugar cane; and experts talking about the advantages of the public–private partnership model. These themes are complemented by government's announcements on further promotion of large-scale investment projects, the entry of Uganda within the new African Continental Free Trade Area and the promotion of domestic Free Trade Zones – supported by tax incentives overseen by the new Uganda Free Zones Authority – and of industrial parks.

In contrast with the announcements of grand plans for investment, the news on social issues are alarming, as well as revealing regarding the evolution of Uganda's market society. For example, in the context of severe blood shortage across the country, patients in a public hospital in Kamuli were advised to 'seek outside support', for a price of UGX 50,000 (NBSU 2018a). Police staff have been facing a severe cash crisis, with reportedly only 5 per cent of units countrywide funded, the consequence being that police intervention can often only occur if the citizens involved can fund it (Observer 2018). The picture is one of a country where basic services, from blood transfusions to police interventions, are for sale. Commodification in a context of generalised poverty means that everything – from election votes to health certificates, from school exam scripts to university marks and degrees, to killings on the street – are commodities (e.g. Daily Monitor 2015, 2016, 2017c, 2017f, 2017g, 2018a, 2018c, Saturday Monitor 2017, Maserejje 2018, Muguzi 2015). Media reports about such developments are like a running commentary on the state of the market society project. The Ugandan media has for years now offered remarkably insightful and critical reporting and discussions about 'Issues on the ground: real people, real issues' (as one of the various relevant TV formats is called).

The version of neoliberalism observed in Uganda is in key aspects arguably more extreme, crass and unequal than some places elsewhere – a neoliberalism with Ugandan characteristics. Neoliberal reason has become increasingly embedded in Ugandan society and it is by now a habit of thought, a cognitive frame that shapes the way many people see themselves, others and the social world, and consequently the ways in which they act in that context (Peck 2010, Mirowski 2013, Duroy 2016). As Duroy notes, 'the issue is ... that individuals act as if everything is an economic transaction, leading to a type of hyper-focused individualism which crowds-out pro-social behavior' (2016: 606).

Given the above, we do not see a 'post-neoliberal' project or era being advanced in Uganda. The hegemonic regime is based on a neoliberal state project, where state action in key issue areas has very limited responsibility towards its citizens, especially when it comes to public service provision. 'Solutions' are regularly postponed into the future – often just 'buying time' – and thereby sidelining actually facing up to, and addressing, the problem (Streeck 2006). Corporate and other non-state actors feed on the crisis of public provision. Given the negative societal track record of various reforms in both economic and social sectors, the dominant narrative on the success of reforms is an expression of the ideological power of the donors (IFIs, IOs, bilateral donors, etc.) and their allies in the domestic establishment.

Eighth, neoliberal discourses – from good governance to empowerment – provided a positive, sanitising spin to a brutal exercise of power and restructuring that has locked in a capitalist social order and its societal hierarchy based on increased inequality and a permanent social crisis. Neoliberal ideology provided a message of win–win, progressive change, hope and optimism, a 'human' face, a technical, natural flavour to a process that produced substantial regressions and crises. This resulted in the depoliticisation and sterilisation of debates about development and change. Donor-led development narratives and ideologies systematically concealed the class interests behind the neoliberal reforms. Some chapters in this collection evidenced that there are classes, both in Uganda and abroad, which are actually gaining from the poverty and vulnerability of a significant section of Ugandans.

The gap between neoliberal rhetoric and reality looms large, for instance, in the debate on economic empowerment and free and fair competition. Key sectors of the economy – telecommunication, banking, electricity – underwent massive centralisation and increasing monopolistic and oligopolistic control by foreign capital, specifically European and South African capital – in Ugandan common parlance, the 'Whites'; and Indian capital – the 'Asians'. Prices were thus, yet again, a function of corporate power and of political connections. For years, there have been public outcries and debates about these sectors that are controlled by a few foreign firms, especially given the very high prices (against wanting service quality), epitomised by the case of the telecommunication sector, where the 'abuse' of market dominance led to severe overpricing (MacMillan Keck and Acacia Economics 2017); here, there were issues concerning product and service quality, fees transparency and billing practices, amongst others. Narratives of liberalisation, free markets, empowerment and competition among free individuals thus tended to conceal the substantial concentration of wealth, monopolistic tendencies and resulting profit levels, and the coercive and conflictive character of the neoliberal economy. Reform programmes that promised a better-governed, efficient, orderly, clean, accountable, humane, pro-people polity and economy, i.e. a harmonious social order (Harrison 2005), thereby engendered a society shaped (and scarred) by heightened violence, criminality, opaqueness, conflict and social harm.

Ninth, the process of neoliberalising Uganda has occurred in continuity with key aspects of the colonial project, substantially contested on the ground by those who have mostly suffered its nefarious social, political and ecological implications. Protests have taken different forms and contributed to shaping important alliances among diverse social constituents which carved up a new political space by challenging the implementation of neoliberal development projects. As we write these conclusions, a myriad of social struggles is taking place around key areas of societal transformation, including renewed civil society and social movements' mobilisations around the protection of access to and reproduction of indigenous seeds currently challenged by the Biosafety Act, which parliament passed a few months ago. In Busoga, plantation workers organised strikes at sugar plants and estates against deteriorating working conditions and looming salaries. In the Amuru district in Acholi, there is sustained, open resistance against large-scale sugar plantations. Throughout Uganda, farmers repeatedly rejected the distribution of free 'fake' – sub-standard or expired – seeds by the state's extension services which have become increasingly militarised under the UPDF-managed Operation Wealth Creation. In the northern regions, there is significant underground resistance to maintain access to land and commons against enclosures driven by conservation and protected areas. Youth groups often protest against high unemployment; workers protest against low and/or delayed pay and difficult working conditions in general; communities criticise deficient road conditions and the related corruption in state projects; journalists complain about state mistreatment, including recurring intimidations, threats, abductions and disappearances. Social media has become a protest platform which the state constantly strives to restrict in order to control dissent and criticism of state action. We note, amongst others, the case of Makerere University academic and activist Stella Nyanzi, who was imprisoned on charges of 'cyber harassment' and 'offensive communication' for criticising the NRM. In particular, she was charged on the basis of her criticism of the Education Minister and First Lady, Janet Museveni, and President Museveni, for their failure to deliver on Museveni's 2016 presidential election promise to provide free sanitary pads for school girls (e.g. Daily Monitor 2017d).

In Kampala and Entebbe, but also other areas of the country, people often critique police and army officials' involvement in extortion and theft cases, or inadequate state responses to the most recent violent crime waves that nowadays also include (fatal) kidnaps for ransom; while annual crime reports have reportedly not been published for three years (Daily Monitor 2018b, Saturday Monitor 2018, Daily Monitor 2017a, 2017b, 2017e). University and college students protest about high fees, fraud and mismanagement. This permanent mobilisation has emerged as a social response to the neoliberal restructuring of Uganda. It at times has helped opposition parties to win seats, and forced the state to respond by alternating its iron hand – political violence – to its soft hand – consent seeking.

Tenth, the material presented in this book analysed Uganda as a case of neoliberalism-in-practice (Harrison 2010). All the parts have analysed how an actually existing neoliberal market society operates with all its crises and contradictions. The exclusion, inequality, violence, precarity and crises that large sections of the subaltern face are thus not caused by a 'malfunctioning' market, or a 'deviated' capitalist trajectory. Rather the opposite is true: it is precisely the functioning of neoliberal restructuring and institutions that causes widespread social, political and economic crises. To frame the dynamics, problems and challenges ahead predominantly in terms of remaining bottlenecks, infrastructure, catch up, poverty reduction, democratisation, effective states and inclusive development, political settlement, resilience, policy implementation etc. – as much of the mainstream often does – is, mildly put, analytically inadequate and politically reckless. Hardly any of this, it seems to us, captures the operation of the system in its entirety; hardly any of these frames are currently (sufficiently) interested or able to offer an account of the evolving *capitalist* social order in all its complexity, tension and socially regressive, unsustainable and harmful character. The largest part of African studies, development studies and economics – the dominant academic streams that inform analysis and policy on the continent – are currently ill prepared for this analytical undertaking, while the glocal establishment that restructures and rules Uganda is unlikely to self-correct their reading of the country's dynamics. Of course, Gramsci's advice regarding keeping a pessimism–optimism balance remains vital at this juncture all the same.

We are herewith signalling in strong terms that the Ugandan situation is in no way particular to the country, but is part and parcel of institutionalised crass capitalism globally. The reading that we propose in our collection suggests that there is no way out of these crises unless the key pillars of neoliberal order are questioned, and inroads towards a significant de-neoliberalisation of the country, especially of its political economy, are made (Wiegratz 2016). We do not see this removal of the neoliberal cage happening in the near future, as the neoliberal restructuring is now well embedded in the Ugandan 'instituted neoliberalism' (McMichael 2017: 336), also understood as 'a new institutional architecture for managing capitalist social relations' (Cahill and Konings 2017: 19). This institutionalised character of neoliberalism applies to the regional and the global levels too, where it produces a wide array of 'material and epistemic demands' (McMichael 2017: 336) that will push for further restructuring.

To conclude, mainstream narratives claiming that more private sector development will produce a future that is, as Museveni put it, 'easy to handle', are a fallacy. Current in-crisis countries, such as Mexico, once celebrated success stories of neoliberal restructuring, are by now telling cases of its regressive outcomes. Uganda, as other neoliberalised countries in Africa and elsewhere, could go down a similar path, breeding a future of permanent social crisis.

Uganda is a prime example of neoliberal restructuring in Africa, where the neoliberal project does not seem to have been significantly challenged so far. The key processes and practices underpinning social transformations in the country are not unique to Uganda. Several African countries have in many ways undertaken similar paths of political, social, economic and cultural transformation.

Yet the spectacular transformations that have occurred in the country in the last thirty years reveal the potential trajectories of transformation upon which other African countries could embark in the near future (or that are already underway). The prevalence of extractive and enclave economies, the hegemony of the (before mentioned) state-donors-capital block, and the expanding marketisation of society, represent the common denominator for many African countries. The analyses of social, political, economic, ecological and cultural change advanced in this book offer possible exploratory frames and entry-points in the study of the operation of political complexes and capitalist transformations across 'neoliberal Africa' (Harrison 2010).

The concept of neoliberalism thus remains analytically useful for the foreseeable future. We are at best in late neoliberalism, or if one takes the longer view, perhaps only even in the early stages of a market society era. The future will tell. Beyond Uganda, we hope to counter the argument concerning the demise of the explanatory concept of neoliberalism. Instead, we argue for a better, deeper understanding of neoliberal transformation and society in Africa (and elsewhere). The study of neoliberalism on the continent would benefit from a comparative approach, which would identify similarities and differences in the capitalist social order across African countries. For example, our book showed that the comprador class was highly decisive in Uganda's transition to a market society. Do we see this in other countries? If to a lesser degree, why is that so?

For all these reasons, it is all the more important to reopen the field of critique of the political economy of Uganda and to encourage the flourishing of an epistemic community of scholars who envision bringing truly progressive change and a liberating future for the majority of Ugandans. Questioning the current dominant ideology and its hegemonic power (and the corresponding mix of policies and programmes) is a key element of this endeavour. We hope the book will intervene in the Ugandan (and African) public debate and stimulate an alternative vision for a just, progressive future.

Note

1 The handling by the Ugandan state of the political dynamics around the Arua election in August 2018 – including the treatment of the 'Arua33' (which resulted in, amongst others, the arrest and physical abuse of popular 'ghetto' musician and recently elected MP Robert Kyagulanyi, *aka* Bobi Wine) and the emergent 'people power' movement more widely – has

provided further insights into the operations of the current power complex. This modality of response regarding political challenges to and criticisms of the political-economic *status quo* is a regular feature of authoritarian neoliberalism in Uganda and worldwide.

References

Ahluwalia, D. P. S. (1995), *Plantations and the Politics of Sugar in Uganda* (Kampala: Fountain).

Beresford, A., Berry, M. and Mann, L. (2018), 'Liberation movements and stalled democratic transitions: Reproducing power in Rwanda and South Africa through productive liminality', *Democratization*. Available at: https://doi.org/10.1080/13510347.2018.1461209.

Branch, A. and Martiniello, G. (2018), 'Charcoal power: The political violence of non-fossil fuels', *Geoforum* (forthcoming).

Bruff, I. (2014), 'The rise of authoritarian neoliberalism', *Rethinking Marxism*, 26(1), pp. 113–29.

Cahill, D. and Konings, M. (2017), *Neoliberalism* (Cambridge: Polity).

Cooper, V. and Whyte, D. (eds) (2017), *The Violence of Austerity* (London: Pluto).

Daily Monitor. (2015), 'Politicians, voters shun campaign against vote buying', 28 October.

Daily Monitor. (2016), 'Government revokes Busoga University licence over fake degrees', 21 December.

Daily Monitor. (2017a), 'Gangs fuelling crime in Mbale – new report', 7 February.

Daily Monitor. (2017b), 'Hitmen invade Teso, kill and torture with impunity', 17 March.

Daily Monitor. (2017c), 'Makerere probes forged admission to university', 17 March.

Daily Monitor. (2017d), 'Dr Nyanzi arrested over offensive communication', 8 April.

Daily Monitor. (2017e), 'Women murders: Another body found in the bush', 19 September.

Daily Monitor. (2017f), 'UNEB confirms O-level exams leak, sets hotline for reporting malpractices', 26 October.

Daily Monitor. (2017g), 'Exam leaks: UNEB must clean up its house', 27 October.

Daily Monitor. (2018a), '49 charged over UCE exam leak', 7 February.

Daily Monitor. (2018b), 'Editorial: Police should get back to basics of policing', 28 February.

Daily Monitor. (2018c), '8 police officers commit crime every month', 27 January.

Daily Monitor. (2018d), 'Striking doctors enemies of the state, says Museveni', 2 May.

Daily Monitor. (2018e), 'Museveni silences MP on complaints over investors', 13 April.

Duroy, Q. (2016), 'Thinking like a trader: The impact of neoliberal doctrine on habits of thought', *Journal of Economic Issues*, 50(2), pp. 603–10.

El Mercurio. (1981), Interview with Friedrich von Hayek, 12 April.

Fine, B. (2000), 'The imperialism of economics and the new development economics as Kuhnian paradigm shift?', *World Development*, 30(12), pp. 2057–70.

Gill, S. (1995), 'Globalisation, market civilisation, and disciplinary neoliberalism', *Millennium*, 24(3), pp. 399–423.

Gill, S. (2002), *Power and Resistance in the New World Order* (Houndmills: Palgrave Macmillan).

Greco, E. (2015), 'Local politics of land and the restructuring of rice farming areas: A comparative study of Tanzania and Uganda', LCSV Working Paper No. 12.

Harrison, G. (2005), 'Economic faith, social project, and a misreading of African society: The travails of neoliberalism in Africa', Third World Quarterly, 26(8), pp. 1303–20.

Harrison, G. (2010), Neoliberal Africa: The Impact of Global Social Engineering (London: Zed).

Harrison, G. (2011), 'Poverty reduction and the chronically rich', Review of African Political Economy, 38(127), pp. 1–6.

Independent. (2008), 'Quotes', Independent, 31, 31 October.

Kapoor, D. (2017), Against Colonization and Rural Dispossession: Local Resistance in South and East Asia, the Pacific and Africa (London: Zed).

MacMillan Keck Attorneys & Solicitors and Acacia Economics. (2017), Draft non-confidential summary of final report, public consultation document, Support to the Uganda Communications Commission on USSD and SMS services, Kampala.

Malango, R. (2018), 'Revitalize local government system to build public spirit for service', The Observer, 6 May.

Martiniello, G. (2015), 'Social struggles in Uganda's Acholiland: Understanding responses and resistance to Amuru Sugar Works', Journal of Peasant Studies, 42(3–4), pp. 653–69.

Martiniello, G. (2017), 'Agrarian politics and land struggles in Northern Uganda', Community Development Journal, Special Issue on Social Movements, 52(3), pp. 405–20.

Maserejie, J. (2018), 'Is exam malpractice the new cancer in our education system?', The Observer, 26 February.

McMichael, P. (2017), 'The shared humanity of global development: Bio-politics and the SDGs', Globalizations, 14(3), pp. 335–36.

Mirowski, P. (2013), Never Let a Serious Crisis Go to Waste: How Neoliberalism Survived the Financial Meltdown (New York, NY: Verso).

Moore, J. (2015), Capitalism and the Web of Life: Ecology and the Accumulation of Capital (London and New York, NY: Verso).

Muguzi, H. (2015), 'The political economy of elections in Uganda: Vote buying and selling', National Conference on Religion Rights and Peace, Makerere University, 14–15 October.

NBS Uganda. (2017), 'Gen. Tumukunde on security budget', 4 May, Available at: www.youtube.com/watch?v=6FmoXFBNpyM.

NBS Uganda. (2018a), 'Blood shortage in Kamuli: Patients parting with 50,000 shillings', 25 February.

NBS Uganda. (2018b), 'IGP Ochola shakes up police force', 20 March.

New Vision. (2018), 'Museveni calls for private investors in health', 23 February.

NTV Uganda. (2018a), 'Government refutes claims that it borrowed 700 Bn to pay salaries of civil servants', 20 February.

NTV Uganda. (2018b), 'President Museveni says he ordered the importation of Cuban Doctors', 1 May.

Nuwagaba, A. and Muhumuza, F. (2017), Who Is Growing? (Kampala: Oxfam).

Observer. (2018), 'Police runs out of cash, only 5% units funded countrywide', 27 February.

Peck, J. (2010), Constructions of Neoliberal Reason (New York, NY: Oxford University Press).

Saturday Monitor. (2017), 'How Mak staff forge exam marks', 18 March.

Saturday Monitor. (2018), 'Panic as new wave of kidnaps hits Kampala', 24 February.

Standing, G. (2016), The Corruption of Capitalism: Why Rentiers Thrive and *Work Does Not Pay* (London: Biteback).

Streeck, W. (2014), *Buying Time: The Delayed Crisis of Democratic Capitalism* (London: Verso).

Tansel, C. B. (ed.) (2017), *States of Discipline: Authoritarian Neoliberalism and the Contested Reproduction of Capitalist Order* (London: RLI).

Titeca, Kristof (2018), 'Illegal ivory trade as transnational organized crime? An empirical study into ivory traders in Uganda', *British Journal of Criminology*, Online first, Available at: https://academic.oup.com/bjc/advance-article-abstract/doi/10.1093/bjc/azy009/4967883?redirectedFrom=fulltext.

Veltmeyer, H. and Petras, J. (2014), *The New Extractivism: A Post-neoliberal Development Model or Imperialism of the Twenty-First Century* (London: Zed).

Wa Thiong'o, N. (1986), *Decolonising the Mind: The Politics of Language in African Literature* (London: James Currey).

Wiegratz, J. (2014), 'Rejecting the West on policy: Uganda, neoliberalism and the Anti-Homosexuality Bill', *African Arguments*, 30 April.

Wiegratz, J. (2016), *Neoliberal Moral Economy: Capitalism, Socio-cultural Change and Fraud in Uganda* (London: RLI).

World Bank. (2011), *Rising Global Interest in Farmland: Can It Yield Sustainable and Equitable Benefits?* (Washington, DC: World Bank).

World Bank. (2012), *Uganda: Promoting Inclusive Growth* (Washington, DC: World Bank).

World Bank. (2013), *Uganda Economic Update. Jobs: Key to Prosperity* (Washington, DC: World Bank).

Index